John Frain

THE CROSS *and the* THIRD REICH

Catholic Resistance in the Nazi Era

FAMILY PUBLICATIONS

ISBN 9781871217957

Cover Images: *Top* Entrance to Auschwitz camp, courtesy of P Lefebvre
Bottom Pius XII blessing © 1955 Fox Photos / Hulton Archive / Getty Images

published by

Family Publications
Denis Riches House, 66 Sandford Lane
Kennington, Oxford OX1 5RP

www.familypublications.co.uk

Printed in Lithuania
through s | s | media ltd

CONTENTS

Foreword

At the end of this remarkable book, John Frain tells us that he is neither an historian nor a theologian – just a layman who wants to describe truthfully and honestly the role played by the Catholic Church in Nazi Germany. He has no need to be modest or apologetic, for this is a significant contribution to the understanding of that fateful era and the reaction of Christians to Hitler's murderous ideology.

Disturbed by the repetition of claims of Catholic collaboration and indifference, Dr Frain decided to revisit the sources, test the arguments, and examine the charges. He does so in carefully authenticated detail, painstakingly assembling the facts, bringing back to life extraordinary men and women.

This account of what happened in Germany some seventy years ago is given contemporary edge and is enriched by his personal accounts of visits he made to the concentration camps and by his talks with survivors of the era.

What emerges is a rich text of great scholarship, both refuting baseless and headline-grabbing caricatures, while reminding us of the great bravery and faith of those who did stand in Hitler's way. He rightly reminds us that all human beings err, and does not gloss over institutional failings and errors of judgment – such as the role of Austria's Archbishop, Theodor Innitzer (or the Vatican's immediate rebuke). He also faithfully examines the narrow range of options open to individual laymen, pastors, bishops and the papacy, and the ease with which retrospective decisions based on hindsight, and which cost nothing, can be made. This is a labour of love and a labour of truth.

Although those who hate the Church may find its scholarship inconvenient, any fair-minded person who believes that we should never appease secular ideologies when they threaten humanity will learn from these accounts and, indeed, be inspired by them.

History is a great teacher and the wise man will have regard to the past if he wishes to predict what will occur in the future.

History has a habit of repeating itself – 'Never again' too often happens all over again. This book holds many clues for those who are interested in averting such calamities in the future.

How we reacted to the great tyrannies of the twentieth century can be instructive in shaping our response to the continuing genocides and crimes against humanity that erupt, from Cambodia to Rwanda, from the Balkans to Burma, from the Congo to Darfur, from the Middle East to the Caucasus.

As I read the accounts of the torture and misery inflicted on those who opposed Nazism, my own mind travelled back to a visit I made in 2004 to the genocide sites of Rwanda. One site, Murambi, had been a technical college where men, women and children took refuge. Fifty thousand people were murdered there.

Murambi is now a memorial. Some of the mass graves have been excavated. The classrooms are filled with human remains. In some cases the corpses have been preserved and retain tufts of hair and recognisable features. Now in the classrooms lie thousands of white skeletons, sometimes frozen in the positions in which they fell. It is as if a man-made Pompeii had swept over the hill and through the buildings. Some still clutch their rosaries. Some of the women were clearly pregnant. Skulls bear the marks of the machetes used to hack them down.

It is because of places like Murambi that we need constantly to remind ourselves of the importance of taking a stand. 'Never again' must not be allowed to occur, casually, all over again.

While I have been reading John Frain's text, Pope Benedict XVI has been making his pilgrimage to Jerusalem and to the Holy Land. Just as history can repeat itself in new outrages of genocide, so can attempts to re-write history and to traduce reputation and character. During Pope Benedict's visit we heard echoes of the false charge laid against Pius XII that he was 'Hitler's Pope' and the repetition of the lie that Catholics seek to deny the Holocaust.

Pope Benedict's visit to Yad Vashem, the Jewish memorial to the six million Jews who died in the Holocaust, was bound to be a profoundly sensitive and poignant moment, because of the Pope's own German origins and because, like other young Germans, his name was included in the membership of the Hitler Youth. In his autobiography, the then-Cardinal Ratzinger speaks of his brief and enforced membership. He never played any part in its activities, being opposed to Nazism all his life, and is horrified by the crimes committed by his countrymen. At Yad Vashem he said: 'May the names of the victims never perish! May their suffering never be denied, belittled or forgotten! And may all people of goodwill be vigilant in rooting out from the heart of man anything that could lead to tragedies such as this.'

Pope Benedict's insistence that the despicable denial of the Holocaust – such as that enunciated by Richard Williamson (a formerly excommunicated follower of Marcel Lefebvre, who gave him Episcopal rank) – can have no place in the Catholic Church may disappoint those who want to caricature the Catholic Church as a cat's cradle of anti-semitism, but it is utterly consistent with the stand taken by the men and women whose lives are described in this book.

Anti-semitism is not merely an historical phenomenon. In one recent year official figures reveal 547 anti-semitic attacks in Britain (the second-worst figure on record). There is only one place of religious worship in Britain where believers are advised not to linger outside after services: the synagogue. Even in places like leafy Surrey there have been reports of swastikas being daubed on vehicles, pavements and signposts.

All forms of hatred against people – whether on the basis of their race, religion, sexuality or outlook – are an unqualified and unmitigated evil. For those of us who call ourselves European, the Holocaust means that anti-semitism holds a unique and special horror. It is a horror that had its origins in 2000 years of hatred directed at the Jewish people. Blood libel and caricature have mutated into new forms of hatred, sometimes masquerading on the internet under the guise of free speech, sometimes originating as part of virulent ideologies from heads of state.

The Iranian President, Mahmoud Ahmadinejad has famously denied the Holocaust, has described the Jewish people as 'filthy bacteria', and said he would like to use a nuclear capability to wipe Israel off the map:

'Anybody who recognizes Israel will burn in the fire of the Islamic nation's fury . . . Israel is a rotten, dried tree that will be annihilated in one storm . . . They have invented a myth that Jews were massacred and place this above God, religions and the prophets. The Zionists avail themselves of the fairy tale of the Holocaust as blackmail and justification for killing children and women and making innocent people homeless.'

Jewish people often try to put a brave face on all of this and make light of such systematic hatred – like the rabbi who quipped that a telegram was sent by a relative to his family: 'Start worrying; details to follow.'

Well, we know precisely what details have invariably followed.

We also know that anti-semitism never stops with the Jews – its tentacles extend and embrace every other form of intolerance too. In this dangerous world it is more vital than ever that we understand one another's stories and stand alongside each other – a sentiment brilliantly expressed in *The Home We Build Together* by our British Chief Rabbi, Dr Sir Jonathan Sacks.

So much for the contemporary reasons to worry, but when the industrial killing at Auschwitz and the other death camps was being orchestrated how did the international institutions, including the Catholic Church, react?

Dr Frain carefully documents the Church's repeated denunciation of anti-semitism and Nazism from 1928 onwards. In that year the Vatican issued a 'binding condemnation' of 'that hate which is now called anti-semitism'.

He also details the year by year condemnations issued by the German bishops: beginning in 1929 with Bishop Johannes Gföllner of Linz warning against 'the false prophets' of Nazism and telling the Catholic faithful: 'Close your ears and do not join their associations, close your doors and do not let their newspapers into your homes, close your hands and do not support their endeavours in elections.'

In 1930 the Bishop of Mainz declared Nazism and Catholicism to be *irreconcilable*; in 1933 the bishops of Cologne, Upper Rhine and Paderborn said they would deny the sacraments to anyone involved in parties hostile to Christianity; and the bishops of Bavaria condemned Nazi racism and their eugenic ideology with its scorn for the sanctity of life of the unborn and its belief in euthanasia.

Even before the Second World War began the Reich had begun the elimination of what it called 'useless eaters', people possessing 'life unworthy of life' – which the Vatican condemned in 1933 as a government degenerating into cattle breeding laboratories and in 1940 as 'contrary to both the natural and the divine positive law.' Also, in pursuit of its racial theories, 400,000 victims had been compulsorily sterilised before the end of the Third Reich.

In 1937 Pope Pius XI condemned events in Germany stating: 'Seldom has there been a persecution so heavy, so terrifying, so grievous and lamentable in its far-reaching effects. It is a persecution that spares neither force, nor oppression, nor threats, nor even subterfuge of intrigue and the fabrication of false facts.' In 1938 he said that no Christian could be anti-semitic because 'spiritually, we are all Semites'.

Above all others, the story of Bishop von Galen, the Lion of Münster, is one of immense courage and bravery – with Martin Bormann demanding his execution – and Dr Frain is right to record the details of von Galen's heroic stand. Bishop von Galen described the National Socialists as 'the hammer', and 'we are the anvil', and 'the anvil is harder than the hammer.' He resolutely lived up to his family motto: *Nec laudibus nec timore*: Neither men's praise nor fear of men shall move me.

In many ways, *The Cross and the Third Reich* is at its very best when it animates us with the spirit of those who gave their lives speaking for truth. Here are the stories of Erich Klausener, the General Secretary of Germany's *Catholic Action*, who was shot dead; Adalbert Probst, Director of the Catholic Youth Sports Association, also murdered; Fritz Gerlich, a Catholic journalist murdered at Dachau (known as 'the priests' camp' because 2,670 priests from around 20 countries were held there: 600 died at Dachau and another 325 during 'transport of invalids').

We are reminded of the arrest of Catholic politicians, the suppression of Catholic political activity, the confiscation of Church property and the suppression of over 200 Catholic publications.

Some stories – those of Blessed Titus Brandsma, St Maximilian Kolbe, and St Edith Stein are quite well known. Others such as Fr Jacques

Bunel, Blessed Marcel Callo, Fr Alfred Delp SJ, Blessed Nikolaus Gross (a miner and Catholic trades unionist), Blessed Franz Jägerstätter, the Austrian farmer beheaded by the Nazis, Blessed Restituta Kafka, guillotined on Bormann's orders, Blessed Karl Leisner, Blessed Bernhard Lichtenberg (declared 'Righteous Among the Nations' at Yad Vashem), Blessed Rupert Mayer SJ, Fr Max Metzger, Fr Franz Reinisch – are less well known.

Dr Frain is also right to recall the role of the Protestant members of the 'Confessing Church', particularly Dietrich Bonhoeffer, Karl Barth and Martin Niemöller; and the Catholic and Protestant members of the *White Rose* student resistance movement led by Hans and Sophie Scholl.

In 1931 there were around 21,000 Catholic priests in Germany and over 8,000 of them, one third, clashed with the Reich and several hundred were eliminated by the Reich.

Fr Maximilian Kolbe, who gave up his life for another prisoner at Auschwitz, said 'No-one in the world can change truth, and beyond the hecatombs of the extermination camps, of what use are the victories on the battlefield if we are defeated in our innermost personal selves': words that sum up the spirit of all men and women cited by John Frain, who rightly asks 'how can any of these facts ever be made to sound like complicity?'

Page after page of this book refutes the libel that German bishops were docile or indifferent when confronted with Nazism.

Perhaps the greatest calumny of all concerns the role of Pope Pius XII. Dr Frain describes the 'cottage industry' of detractors and their failure to examine the facts objectively. He cites Rabbi David Dalin, who describes such books as 'bestsellers made out of bad history'.

Rabbi Dalin says that 'the truth about Pius XII must be restored. This hijacking of the Holocaust must be repudiated.' Dalin cites Pinchas Lapide, an historian and Israeli consul, who said that Pius XII 'was instrumental in saving at least 700,000, but probably as many as 860,000 Jews from certain death at Nazi hands.' In the context of the 6 million who perished he contrasts this record with the abject failure of others to save the Jews.

In his forensic analysis of the facts Dr Frain details what the Nazis themselves said about Pius – 'he has always been hostile to National

Socialism'; 'Pacelli was the live spirit which stood behind all the anti-German activities of Rome's policy.' The Nazis described Pius as 'Jew-loving'.

Most telling of all are the recorded comments of the Jews who were contemporaries of Pius XII. After the War he was thanked by survivors of the Holocaust and tributes included one from Israel's first President, Chaim Weizmann, and Isaac Herzog, Chief Rabbi of Israel. Rome's Chief Rabbi, Israel Zolli, became a Catholic and took the Pope's name as a tribute to him.

At the time of his death, in 1958, Golda Meir said 'When fearful martyrdom came to our people in the decade of Nazi terror, the voice of the Pope was raised for the victims.' The *Jewish Chronicle* recorded: 'Confronted by the monstrous cruelties of Nazism, Fascism and Communism, he repeatedly proclaimed the virtues of humanity and compassion . . . many hundreds of fugitive Jews found sanctuary in the Vatican when hunted by the Nazis. Such actions will always be remembered.'

There is no doubt that the recent attempts to rewrite this history have placed a barrier between closer Catholic-Jewish relations. This is something which has motivated a New York Jew, Gary Krupp, to found the *Pave the Way* organisation. He says that a proper understanding of the history of this period, and the role of Pius XII, is crucial because 'Pius XII, in just one day, hid 7,000 Jews from the Nazis.' Krupp says he 'grew up hating Pius'. Having carefully researched the facts Krupp has come to the conclusion that 'he was the greatest hero of World War Two. We can prove it. We have something on our side – documented proof – where the revisionists haven't a scrap of paper to support their theories.'

One of the most telling refutations of Vatican indifference to the rise of Nazism and the appalling events of the Holocaust came from Albert Einstein, who had escaped Nazi Germany. In 1940 he said: 'Only the Church stood squarely across the path of Hitler's campaign for suppressing the truth . . . I am forced thus to confess that what I once despised I now praise unreservedly.'

Those who read this excellent book may not be able to bring themselves to Einstein's conclusion – and perhaps we should all be wary of extolling or praising anything unreservedly – but John Frain has surely done us a great service in reminding us of the truth of something else: that the world is dangerous place, not only because of the people who are evil, but because of the people who don't do anything about it.

This book is a chance both to celebrate the memory of those who *did* do something about it, and to be challenged in our own lives and our own times to face up to the evils that confront us.

David Alton

(Lord Alton of Liverpool is Professor of Citizenship at Liverpool John Moores University)

PREFACE

War stirs opposing feelings within us. On the one hand we are repelled by its slaughter and its capacity to arouse the worst instincts. On the other hand it provides opportunities to see human nature at its best, to observe how heroic, how compassionate, those engaged in war can often be.

Like countless others before it, this book is about the worst war in history – Hitler's war. When it began I was nine years old and sixteen when it ended. I was terrified when the bombs fell, and I wept at the death or capture of relatives and friends. In all the sixty-odd years since it ended thoughts about it have been part of my daily diet. During the war I was an Army cadet and immediately after it I served in the RAF. So, until recently, my preoccupations with the Nazi era have been decidedly military.

In the last few years, however, for reasons I explain in Chapter One, I have extended my reverence and awe to include certain men and women who, in spite of the terrors and moral ambiguities of that time, stood by their Christian faith, though often their lives were forfeit as a result. Telling their story has enabled me to draw, in truth and justice, upon the role played by the Church to which they belonged. A key objective in writing the book has been fuelled by my desire to emphasise the record of the Catholic Church during the war, a record which has been deliberately distorted by its detractors. I hope that what I have written will, in some small way, witness to what the Church really did in those years when many other institutions concerned themselves only with the ethics of survival.

I owe a debt to a number of people for their encouragement and support. Father David Morland OSB, Sister Walthera Brands OP, and Colin Mason, Managing Director of Family Publications, immediately come to mind, and Colin, incidentally, transpired to be a superb editor. The sustained interest of Isabel Ferguson, Margaret Fowler, Eveline Paulson, John Davies, Therese de Rouffignac, Colin Lee, Winefride Wang, Dr Catherine Kerr and Brian and Debbie Murphy certainly helped the project towards its completion. Library and archival support has been readily and efficiently provided by Joan and Alan Bond of Britain's National Catholic Library; Kevin Roach of the William Brown Library, Liverpool; René Kruis of the Dutch Institute for War Documentation, Amsterdam; the staff of the Wannsee Conference Centre in Berlin and Father Gerald O'Mahoney SJ, of Loyola Hall, Liverpool. Important background information on the major Nazi concentration camps was supplied by Dr J P J Frain and on individuals and institutions in occupied Europe by Ruth Frain. I am also greatly indebted to the many authors on whose work I have drawn (please see the Bibliography). Finally, Sybil Williams prepared the work for publication with patience and consummate skill.

This book could never do justice to the story it seeks to tell, but merely to have been encouraged to tell it is more than sufficient reward for the effort it involved.

Dr John Frain
Liverpool, June 2009

Chapter One

AN IDEA EMERGES

We approached the gate of the concentration camp. It was a day in late August and though not yet mid-morning, it was already hot. The summer of 2004 seemed determined to make a memorable exit.

Could this really be Mauthausen which, with its satellite camps, was once a byword for human cruelty? Certainly the entrance gate easily evoked brutality but to the right of it, rather disconcertingly, was a not unpleasant building of glass and steel. We learned later that this was the recently-built information centre.

We halted. Immediately in front was where the grim roadway must have been. Thousands had trudged along it en-route to their extermination. Then another 'surprising' note: the right flank of the road had been offset by a pleasant paved area.

Yet two aspects of the scene confirmed that we had, in fact, arrived at our place of pilgrimage. First, over to the far left, and unfenced even now, was the rim of the vast, notorious stone quarry, where so many of Hitler's victims had, quite literally, been worked to death. Second, and looking to our right again, the paved area was littered with blocks of stone. Then, a possible explanation evolved: Jewish people invariably place small stones on the memorials to Holocaust victims. Perhaps, here in Mauthausen, they had descended to the quarry and, as a mark of reverence, returned with these heavy lumps of granite.

In Mauthausen's record of deaths ('Totenbuch') there are 40,000 entries. They include the names of Jews from Austria, Holland, Italy and Hungary. Members of the Resistance from France, Belgium and Holland also perished here along with many others. These 'others' had included Father Johann Gruber, an Austrian priest and Father Jacques Bunel, a French Carmelite. Before their own deaths in Gusen I, a satellite camp, both men, in their witness for Christ, had saved the lives of many of their fellow prisoners. Their selfless dedication had illumined this darkest place with God's love and compassion.

I am not a courageous man but looking again at the lumps of stone I felt impelled to leave some mark of respect for the slaughtered. I told my son and daughter-in-law that I would descend to the quarry for a stone to place on the paving. They seemed unsure and even my grandchildren were concerned. My 'advanced middle age' was not mentioned but I sensed it was an issue. Nonetheless, the four of them followed me . . . across to the rim of the quarry and down the notorious 186 steps to the quarry floor. At the bottom we gaped at the vast granite amphitheatre towering over us.

After some preliminary failures I managed to dislodge a one foot cube of stone from the quarry walls. I set off for the steps, gritting my teeth at the weight of it. When I had climbed forty or fifty steps the strain began to tell. The sun was a torment. Concentrating on what the victims must have endured helped me to struggle on.

The ascent was a peril because the burden of the stone was making my climb jerky. There was marked variation in the treads and risers of the steps so I was never sure of my footing. It made me more unstable. I realised how much more dangerous the steps had been for the poor souls forced to climb them in wind, rain and snow . . . and when there was only ice for a footing. If I stumbled now, my family close behind were there to save me. When a prisoner stumbled there had been only the lash and the jackboot to urge him on. Also, unless he collapsed on the way, he would have to make this tortuous journey several times each day, from sunrise to sunset. Today, before my one ascent, I had been fortified with a full English breakfast in Vienna. The prisoner's daily dole was a litre of 'soup' and a scrap or two of bread – a diet to ensure that unless he died of overwork beforehand, he would surely die of starvation.

Halfway up the steps I became painfully breathless. I was sure I could go no further but when I thought again of what the camp's victims had endured it made me resolute. Eventually I reached the rim of the quarry and tottered towards that paved area which now seemed so far away. When I set down my stone the agony in my arms and legs was indescribable. What had these exertions achieved? In physical terms, very little, for compared to what the prisoners had endured my own 'ordeal' had been a pitifully slight business. Mentally, however, I had achieved much, for now I had learned more about the nature of what went on in the camps than I could ever have gleaned from the avalanche of books on Hitler and the Third Reich.

I thought again of 'Papa' Gruber and Père Jacques, priests who, for love of God and neighbour, had been called to martyrdom here. Then the names of other martyrs of that time came to mind – Titus Brandsma, Restituta Kafka, Alfred Delp, Franz Jägerstätter. I wondered how many people, Catholics even, knew of the nature of their sacrifice. This was when I decided to investigate the extent of Catholic resistance to the Nazi regime and to set out my findings in a book. Luckily I found that Family Publications, a leading Catholic publisher, shared my enthusiasm for the idea.

Of course, I already knew a great deal about such well-known martyrs of the period as Maximilian Kolbe and Edith Stein. And although their stories were already well publicized I was keen to feature them in my own book, for such was the nature of their heroic virtue it would stand any amount of repetition. But which other Catholics had opposed Hitler and, affirming their faith, had perished for it? A few months' research soon provided a list of people, each one of which provided a ringing endorsement of Tertullian's dictum that 'the blood of martyrs is the seed of the Church.' My list was lengthy and I could have added to it without difficulty.

Through this preliminary screening survey I realised more fully how the relentless persecution of individuals was part of a broader picture, in that Hitler's objective was to expunge the Catholic faith from European culture and replace it with a creed of his own. This should not have surprised me for Christianity, a religion of love, could hardly co-exist with Nazism, a religion of hate. At all events this suggested that the book might widen its reach, recording persecution at two levels: that of individual Catholics and that of the Catholic Church as an organization.

The sacrificial significance of the individuals who died would enrich any book on the era – the task for its writer would be to tell their stories in a way worthy of them. How the Catholic Church responded to Nazi persecution required further thought. Some historians have taken the view that the Papacy and the hierarchy used their authority to repudiate Nazi policies and they have said so clearly. Other historians have claimed that the Church should have challenged and resisted the regime more actively, particularly regarding its treatment of the Jews.

With a little effort it is possible to quarry enough material to refute completely this gross calumny. Michael Burleigh, eminent historian, is interesting here: 'Making use of the Holocaust as the biggest moral club to use against the Church, simply because one does not like its policies on abortion, contraception, homosexual priests or the Middle East, is as obscene as any attempt to exploit the deaths of six million European Jews for political purposes.'[1] Sir Martin Gilbert, official biographer of Sir Winston Churchill and one of Britain's foremost historians, has paid due tribute to the efforts of the Catholic Church in defence of Europe's Jews, drawing attention, among other things, to the alarm created among the Nazis by Pope Pius XII's 1942 Christmas Message; the Church's sheltering of Jews and its protests against deportation; and the rescue efforts, for example of the Church's representative in Budapest.[2]

As to the Jews, there has been criticism of Pope Pius XII sustained enough to be seen as an attempt to dishonour his memory. Ironically, in the immediate post-World War II period, his record was accorded a respect, from both Jew and non-Jew, verging on adulation. Yet, since the 1963 appearance of Hochhuth's play *The Deputy*, denigration of Pius has become a way of life for some writers. In turn, there have been other voices to oppose the revisionists, pointing out that they present little or no evidence for their opinions.

So, what is the truth? And if the Church was not trenchant enough for some, how difficult were decisions to resist when confronted with the immoral contours of Nazism in all its power? Seeking an answer had a powerful intuitive appeal to me and while I determined that my researches would be as dispassionate as possible, what I discovered

---

1. M Burleigh, *Sacred Causes*. London, 2006, p. 282.
2. M Gilbert, *The Righteous – The Unsung Heroes of the Holocaust*. London, 2002, pp. 11, 434, 466 amongst others.

in the end had both spiritual and inspirational value. If it is not too grandiose an aspiration, I hope that others will find such benefits in the book.

There is another point: this work sets out to record, as truthfully as possible, the responses of the Catholic Church itself, and of individual Catholics, at a time of continuous persecution. It is not a treatise on the political history of the period for that has been written many times over. Nevertheless, before we can understand what influenced the Church and its faithful to act as they did, it is important to say something on why and how Hitler acceded to power in an intellectually gifted nation with a strong Christian tradition.

Accordingly, Chapter Two provides an outline of the economic, psychological and social forces which created the fallow situation in which National Socialism could germinate. It also seeks to describe how certain factors such as the 'Kulturkampf' experience, the 'Weltpolitik' and the 'Lebensraum' traditions combined with the 'Völkisch' concept so as to provide within the German psyche an in-built acceptability for neo-pagan Nazism.

Taken together, Chapters Three, Four and Five provide a chronological survey (1933-45) of the Catholic Church's attempt to maintain its role of bringing souls to God, at a time of Nazi hegemony. It reviews the hopes, disillusion, dilemmas and occasional despair which accompanied this process. In order to clarify the quality of the Church's resistance these chapters draw on original documents (i.e. encyclicals, sermons, diocesan reports etc.) from the period. Chapter Six provides portraits of eighteen individual Christians who, in their witness for Christ, became instruments of His truth, His mercy and His compassion.

Chapter Seven provides profiles of the two Popes who served the servants of God in the Nazi era – Pius XI and Pius XII. The evidence adduced here will explain why, in the immediate aftermath of the terror, the Papacy was held in world-wide esteem. It may, for the nay-sayers, provide sufficient facts to move them from cocksure ignorance to thoughtful uncertainty. Chapter Eight provides some reflections on the facts set out in the book and the conclusions an unbiased reader may reasonably draw from them.

Reflecting my own background and faith, the tenor and tone of the book is almost exclusively Catholic but I have tried to draw attention to some aspects of Protestant resistance which merit our reverence. Perhaps this will encourage some other writer to give this the wider treatment it deserves.

Chapter Two

THE PATH TO PERIL

It was Monday 30 January 1933. From twilight to midnight Berlin was jubilant as tens of thousands of Nazi storm troopers marched by torchlight. From the Tiergarten they came, through the Brandenberg Gate then down the Wilhelmstrasse. Their jackboots beat out the undertones as bands played the old tunes of glory and the new Horst Wessel song.

At noon, before Field Marshal von Hindenburg, President of the Republic, Adolf Hitler had taken the oath as the new Chancellor of the German Reich. Now, a little way down the Wilhelmstrasse at an open window of the Chancellery, he repeatedly returned the Nazi salute to his marchers. So, the Third Reich had been born and the former Austrian tramp, in an ecstatic utterance, had vowed it would last for a thousand years.

Twelve years and four months later Germany, along with much of Europe, lay in ruins. The rubble of what had once been its major cities was still smoking. Transport and communications were largely destroyed. The apparatus of government, national and local, was in chaos. A starving population saw its problems magnified by the millions of refugees fleeing from a Soviet army intent on revenge.

Three million of Germany's armed forces had perished. One million were prisoners of the Russians. Only a handful of these would ever come home. And the general population now understood fully the meaning of 'total war', for a half million civilians had been killed in air raids.

Germany lay in ruins because of her defeat in the Second World War, 1939-1945. It was a war instigated by Hitler and his lieutenants.

It must be regarded as perhaps the most cataclysmic event in human history. It had raged over Europe, Africa, Asia, the Atlantic, the Mediterranean, the Pacific and many other parts of the world. Even in a century of unparalleled bloodletting its savagery was unique, for it destroyed over 50 million people and left millions more physically or mentally scarred. In Europe Nazi hegemony at its zenith extended from the Urals to the Atlantic shore and from the North Cape to the Mediterranean. Before the world managed to rid itself of this regime much of Europe's cultural heritage had been obliterated, its political systems effaced and the very basis of its civilisation undermined. Before it had run its course National Socialism earned for itself such synonyms as 'repression', 'arbitrary arrest', 'torture', 'forced labour', 'starvation', 'blood purge', 'concentration camp' and 'Holocaust'. This last refers to the slaughter of six million Jewish men, women and children, usually by highly geared, highly mechanised procedures.

This book's purpose is to provide examples of Christian witness in the Nazi era at both the institutional and the individual level. So the political history of those times is not our main concern – and there are countless volumes on the history of Nazism for those in need of wider introductory reading. Nevertheless, to better understand the nature and quality of the Christian response it seems important to provide some description of the context which shaped it. Inevitably, the first question is – why did one of the most intellectually gifted and industrious nations in the world become subjugated to an indolent, argumentative, autocratic, tedious habitué of a Viennese doss-house? Below are some of the elements from a tangled skein of factors and circumstances.

Defeat in the Great War had left Germany shocked, humiliated and bitterly resentful. Many believed that the nation had not lost the war but had been 'stabbed in the back' – a legend Hitler quickly turned to his advantage. Defeat was bad enough, but worse was to follow; for in the Summer of 1919 the terms of the Versailles peace treaty were made known. Germany had played no part in the peace conference. This, in itself, generated a feeling of betrayal. Moreover, the treaty's terms were handed down in the form of a diktat – no discussion was possible. Finally, Germany was given a mere 14 days (subsequently increased to 21) to agree the terms, otherwise hostilities would be resumed.

Germany's then government, the Weimar Assembly, had awaited the outcome of Versailles with some trust, for it had cast off the Hohenzollern rule which had led the nation during the War and had established a democracy. It was appalled when the German delegation returned with the terms:

- Alsace-Lorraine was to be ceded to France;
- the Rhineland was to be demilitarised and occupied by the Allies;
- West Prussia and Posen were to be ceded to Poland – which would divide East Prussia from the rest of Germany by what would become known as the Polish corridor;
- Danzig, formerly German, was to become an international city;
- all the nation's overseas colonies were to be surrendered;
- the country was to be stripped of its warships and aircraft and its Army was to be limited to 100,000; Germany was also to be prevented from re-arming; and
- the nation was to pay reparations to the Allies – an immediate sum of five billion US dollars with more undisclosed amounts to follow.

As a result of these provisions Germany lost 25,000 square miles (13%) of territory and approximately six and a half million subjects of whom 50% were German speaking. She was also to lose vast amounts of her most valuable raw materials, e.g. 75% of her iron ore, 68% of her zinc ore and 26% of her coal.[1] The loss of Alsace would mean the loss of her textile industries and her entire potash production.

There were two other outcomes of Versailles that generated much anger: (1) the veto by the Allies of the union of Germany and German-speaking Austria; and (2) the requirement that Germany must admit responsibility for all loss and damage sustained by the Allies 'as a consequence of the war imposed on them by the aggression of Germany and her allies'. (Clause 231)

It was this 'War Guilt' Clause which united Germans of every political persuasion in their bitterness. Its fundamental objective was to legitimise the financial reparations to compensate France and

---

1. W Carr, *A History of Germany, 1815-1990*, 4th edn. London, 1991, p. 261.

Belgium, particularly for their losses due to more than four years of German occupation. It was stipulated that financial reparations were to be paid in gold and two million tons of Germany's merchant shipping; 5,000 railway engines, 136,000 coaches and 24 million tons of coal were also seized.

This necessarily brief outline of the Treaty will perhaps clarify the belief that the seeds of the Second World War were sown at Versailles. In the aftermath of Versailles, turmoil and strife became the daily lot of the German nation. Within an economy near to total collapse, a crushed and hungry population struggled to exist. Brought to the point of signing the Treaty, Chancellor Philipp Scheidemann resigned, feeling he could not sign a document inflicting such vengeful terms on the Fatherland. The Socialist Gustav Bauer stepped into his role. The Weimar Government sustained a great blow to its prestige as a result of its submission to the Treaty. From this time the German people had little confidence in it and its continuation was threatened. A 'crisis of democracy' had arisen. This was not confined to Germany, of course, for dictatorships emerged in Italy, Spain, Portugal and Yugoslavia. Now, ominously, a fallow situation was being prepared for the arrival of the Nazis.

The once sedate streets of German cities became the scene of violent clashes between Communists, inspired by the Russian Revolution of 1917, and the Freikorps, which the government looked to in answer to the street fighting and assaults on its police. The Freikorps was a right-wing association of army veterans, nationalists, university students and the unemployed and it fell to its task with enthusiasm, shooting first and asking questions afterwards, as in the instance when it shot thirty sailors peacefully queuing for their pay. In just a few days the Freikorps killed 1,000 people in their determination to ensure Germany would not succumb to 'Red revolution'. It should be noted that its members deemed both Social Democrats and Jews as being the 'traitors' responsible for Germany's plight.

At this point we will break with our narrative to relate some incidents, which are intriguing, certainly relevant, but perhaps not widely known.

On 13 May 1917 Monsignor Eugenio Pacelli had been ordained a bishop and sent to Munich as Archbishop and Papal Nuncio. He was to come face to face with Communist aggression. By April 1919, Communists had taken over the government of Bavaria and declared the region a separate Communist state. When all other diplomats in Munich fled to Berlin Nuncio Pacelli chose to remain.

What were described as 'fanatics and maniacs' machine-gunned the Nunciature. On another occasion they broke into the premises and threatened the Nuncio at gunpoint. They also attempted to take away his official car but his chauffeur had disabled the transmission. Undeterred, they returned to tow away the vehicle. These political thugs had completely overridden the diplomatic immunity of the Nunciature.

The Archbishop confronted his attackers and told them he was in Bavaria in the service of peace and in the name of God. The insurgents then withdrew without harming him. Subsequently, as Secretary of State at the Vatican and then Pope Pius XII (1939-1958), he was to gain a reputation as a 'man of peace'. It was an earned distinction. The Munich incidents also portray him as a man of courage. Beyond that, however, they serve to demonstrate his fidelity to Christ's teaching on forgiveness, for when the Republican German government regained control of Munich they began to hunt down the Communists. To discover who his assailants were, government representatives visited the Nunciature. Pacelli was always 'unavailable', for he sought neither revenge against nor victimisation of those who had endangered his life.

At about this time, Achille Ratti, distinguished scholar and Vatican librarian was consecrated titular Archbishop of Lepanto and sent by Pope Benedict XV as Nuncio to Poland. It seemed a surprising appointment because Ratti had been a librarian for virtually the whole of his working life and though a gifted linguist, he had no knowledge of Slav languages. He found Poland in ferment for the country was now free from Tsarist rule, the Catholic Church itself was in the process of reconstruction, and, following the Bolshevik Revolution, it seemed quite possible that the whole of Eastern Europe would be subjugated by Russia.

In August 1920 Bolshevik troops laid siege to the Nunciature in Warsaw. Like his colleague in Munich, Archbishop Ratti refused to flee. So when he termed Communism the worst enemy Christian Europe had ever faced, like Eugenio Pacelli he spoke from close personal knowledge of it. It is reported that the Warsaw incident shaped much of his policy to Communism when Nuncio Ratti became Pope.[2]

We should bear both incidents in mind when seeking explanation for why the Catholic Church was at least prepared to negotiate with right-wing dictatorships. More of this later; at this point we return to our narrative.

In 1920 the Freikorps was prominently involved in an attempt by Wolfgang Kapp, a right-wing journalist, to seize Berlin and establish a right-wing government. This 'Kapp Putsch' did not succeed, primarily because it failed to secure the support of Germany's leading generals. Yet it did give early warning of the gathering strength of German nationalism. It also had a sombre side effect for it brought the Swastika symbol into the national consciousness. Later this near pagan emblem would be appropriated by the Nazis and become the notorious logotype, hated and feared wherever its shadow fell.

It was from within the widespread tumult that the National Socialist German Workers' Party (NSDAP or 'Nazi' party) emerged. By that time Adolf Hitler had become a minor official of Munich's local government. He had been told to investigate the NSDAP and assess its threat to civil order. Ominously, he discovered its programme so much in phase with his own extremist ideas he decided to join it. In its programme of 1920, the key 'demands' of the NSDAP were: the unity of all Germans in a Greater Germany based on the right of self-determination; the revocation of the Versailles treaty; the acquisition of land and territories to feed the German people and settle its surplus population ('Lebensraum' – see below); the restriction of state citizenship to those of German blood; and Jews to be excluded from membership of the 'Volk' (see below also).

It is germane to an understanding of the political and social context in which Christian organisations had to operate for us to consider some of the terms in the NSDAP programme above. Firstly, in post-1918 Germany the idea of *external threat* was useful for political programmes, and such a threat seemed feasible to claim. Imperialistic ideological traditions were extremely well developed in Germany. During the Weimar period they became more convincing and more

2. E Duffy, *Saints and Sinners, a History of the Popes*, 3rd edn. Yale, 2006, p. 335.

widely accepted than ever.

Second, the *Weltpolitik* tradition indicated that Germany's economic and social future was threatened if she could not regain her place in international politics and insist on her rightful role in the economic development of the world. The threat emanated from interest groups in other industrial countries seeking to take advantage of Germany's weakened state by prohibiting her from economic expansion.

The *Lebensraum* tradition identified a threat, which would hem in the German people territorially, preventing them from acquiring the space necessary to protect their national culture and the source of their strength.

The concept of *Volk* cannot simply be translated as 'nation'. It is grounded on the idea of an organic Volk based on purity of blood and race so as to form a national community (*Volksgemeinschaft*). The community transcended every individual within it. It produced a true 'national' socialism, as anti-liberal as it was anti-capitalist and anti-bourgeois. At the same time it bound each individual to the service of that community through subordination to leaders of notable ability, wisdom and substance.

In this overview we can discern the core ideology of the Nazi party. These aspects of German culture provide some reason why, though all Germans did not welcome the Nazis, there nestled in the national psyche a form of in-built acceptability for their ideology. In a substantial historical work on the period[3] the völkisch variant of nationalism, with its extreme nationalism, racial anti-Semitism and mystical notions of a uniquely German social order, is described. It began to be popularised initially through the racist works ofTheodor Fritsch and Houston Stewart Chamberlain and in innumerable schools and youth organisations. German culture was to be venerated for its undoubted superiority over the forces which threatened it, particularly Slavic and Jewish forces. Thus was provided the seed-bed for Hitler's notions of the struggle for survival (Social Darwinism), racial purity, expansion eastwards and the Führer cult of charismatic leadership, based on his own belief in his historical mission to save Germany. The succeeding events in his rise to power are now briefly summarised.

---

3. I Kershaw, *Hitler, 1889-1936, Vol I: Hubris*. London, 1998, p. 135.

The Munich Putsch of 1923 was an attempt to seize power by Hitler and General Ludendorff, the leading Nazi in the German military. It was intended as a preliminary to a march on Berlin (after the manner of the march on Rome by Italian dictator Mussolini). The so-called 'putsch' failed because such press-ganged supporters as Gustav Ritter von Kahr, leader of the Bavarian conservatives, General Lossow, the region's Reichswehr commander, and Seisser, the state police chief, withdrew their support late in the day. In fact it was the Bavarian police who killed 16 of the Nazi marchers and scattered the rest. Subsequently Hitler was tried for treason and sentenced to five years' imprisonment.

The political failure became propaganda victory for it passed into Nazi folklore as 'Martyrs Day', commemorated annually. A mere five years imprisonment for the crime of 'high treason' may seem ludicrous enough (Ludendorff was actually acquitted) but Hitler's 'fortress incarceration' at Landsberg lasted less than a year. In that time he received no fewer than 500 visitors who came to his cell bearing flowers, presents, letters and telegrams. More importantly, he dictated to fellow conspirator, Rudolf Hess, *Mein Kampf* (My Struggle).

The style of this book is uniquely bad, being by turns slovenly, illogical, pretentious – a hotchpotch of extraordinary allegations, none of which the author attempts to prove. Ralph Manheim, one of its many translators down the years, says of the book: 'Often there is no visible connection between one paragraph and the next. The logic is purely psychological: Hitler is fighting his persecutors, magnifying his person, creating a dreamworld in which he can be an important figure.'[4] In his introduction to the Manheim translation (Pimlico 1992 edition), Donald Cameron Watt, Stevenson Professor of International History in the University of London, adds: 'It is lengthy, dull, bombastic, repetitious and extremely badly written. As a historical picture of Hitler's life up to the time he wrote it, it is also quite unreliable. Most of its statements of fact and the entire tenor of the argument in the autobiographical passages are demonstrably untrue.'[5] In spite of all this, the publishers of this 1992 edition handily summarise why we should engage with this turgid tome for in their cover notes they declare: '*Mein Kampf* is an evil book, but it remains necessary reading for those

4. R Manheim (trans.), A Hitler *Mein Kampf*. London, 2006, reprint, p. vii.
5. D Cameron Watt, ibid., Introduction, p. xi.

who seek to understand the Holocaust, for students of totalitarian psychology and for all who care to safeguard democracy.'[6]

So *Mein Kampf* is an important source document for scholars of Nazi history, containing, as it does, clear indications of Hitler's war aims and a thundering résumé of his visceral hatred of the Jews. On this latter point consider the following quote from page 53 of Manheim (2006 reprint). Hitler is describing his early days in Vienna, when he first began to notice the Jews as an ethnic group. He reflects: 'Was there any form of filth or profligacy, particularly in cultural life, without at least one Jew involved in it? If you cut even cautiously into such an abscess, you found, like a maggot in a rotting body, often dazzled by the sudden light – a kike.'[7] Immediately preceding his suicide, Hitler dictated his Last Will and Testament to Gertrude Junge, one of his secretaries. These two documents survive and demonstrate that this man, destroyed by absolute power, had learned precisely nothing, for he claimed that it was untrue that he or anyone else in Germany wanted war in 1939 – it was wanted and provoked exclusively 'by those international statesmen who either were of Jewish origin or worked for Jewish interests'; he also claimed that the 'sole responsibility' not only for the millions of deaths suffered on the battlefields and in the bombed cities but also for his own massacre of the Jews – rested on the Jews. Between the appearance of *Mein Kampf* and the dictation of his 'Political Testament', as he put it, he had been responsible for the deaths of six million Jews yet here, at the end of his life, it is plain that his hatred of the Jews had not been appeased.

When Hitler came to power the book became a best-seller, for not to buy it was virtually a treasonable act. Its content makes clear his view that racial conflict was the mainspring of history and that the Jews were the sworn enemy of the German race. Under the direction of the Nazi movement, the sacred mission was to break their international power and eliminate them entirely. The Weimar judiciary's resolution and quality of judgement met with the obloquy it deserved when, in deciding to be lenient with Hitler and his co-conspirators, it found that they had been 'led in their action by a pure patriotic spirit and a most noble will.'[8] The

---

6. Pimlico (Publisher), ibid., cover note.
7. A Hitler, op. cit.
8. R J Evans, *The Coming of the Third Reich*. London, 2003, p. 196.

judgement was condemned even by right-wing politicians. At this point Hitler decided that the ballot box and the street fight were now to be the instruments of his ascendancy.

After Hitler's arrest and imprisonment the Nazi party and the 'Brownshirts' (its 'Storm Division' of paramilitary thugs) were now illegal organisations. However, Hitler was not without important friends. The most significant of these was Franz Gürtner, Bavarian Minister of Justice, who found the Nazi brand of nationalism most appealing. By 1925, thanks to Gurtner, the ban on the NSDAP had been lifted. Hitler was now free to refound it and his first move was to invite his former followers back to the fold, provided they unconditionally acknowledged his leadership. Then began his machinations to move his most serious rivals to virtual anonymity.

The remainder of the 1920s were not particularly fruitful for the Nazis. Their Reichstag elections performance saw a May 1924 return of 6.6% (32 seats) fall to 3.0% (14 seats) by the following December. By the election of May 1928, their proportion was practically off the scale (2.6% – 12 seats only). In effect there was an inverse relationship between the state of the German economy and the success of the Nazis. The current economic recovery had reduced the popularity of extremism.

After the grave inflation of 1924 there had been a decided upturn in the country's fortunes – industrial production increased, unemployment fell and more reasonable repayment terms on reparations had been negotiated. Then things changed drastically, for when the Wall Street Stock Exchange collapsed in October 1929 the world moved into severe recession.

Like other European nations, Germany had become so dependent on American investment it could not escape the consequences of 'the Crash'. The United States began to call in its loans and ultimately there were failures within the German banking system. A rapid fall in the demand for manufactured goods resulted in higher unemployment. Shopkeepers and other small traders went out of business. An alarming loss of confidence now ensued for the dire situation of 1918 seemed to have returned. The sensitivity of the Nazis' popularity to economic indicators was again demonstrated by the Reichstag election of 1930 in which they improved their performance to 18.3% (107 seats). At this time one German commentator was sanguine even so: 'If the sun shines once more on the German economy, Hitler's votes will melt away like snow.'

In July 1932, the resounding result of 37% gave them 230 Reichstag seats. Collateral to an upturn in the economic situation, their support had fallen to 33.1% by November 1932 (196 seats). Even so, the Nazi party was now a substantial power in the land. It appealed to all classes, but particularly the lower-middle classes who had felt most at the mercy of economic events. By the beginning of 1933 over 6 million Germans were unemployed – one in three of the working population. Some observers believe this an underestimation and suggest that widespread short-time working meant half the families in Germany were affected by the slump. Fear of financial catastrophe brought the nation close to panic. The already unpopular Weimar Republic seemed to have little idea how to take grip of the situation.

By now the Nazis, despite the loss of 34 seats in the 1932 election, were the country's largest single party. Their leader was perceived by many to be the strong man suited to the hour. His appeal was being reinforced by his powerful oratory and skilled use of propaganda. Traditional support for the party had come from the lower middle class, some Protestant voters and the small town and rural voters of northern and eastern Germany. But the party had now broadened its appeal to some of the educated middle class and the professional voters. It had achieved this by continual emphasis on 'the Communist threat', 'the Jewish menace', and so on: unemployment, the 'iniquitous' Versailles treaty and the necessity to take resurgent violence on the streets under firm control.

Despite deep personal misgivings, President Hindenburg invited the 'Austrian corporal' to take up the Chancellorship. The conservative politicians around the President calculated they could best neutralise Hitler by bringing him into office. Before long, events were to demonstrate what wishful thinkers they were. The man himself was overjoyed – not only had he attained power, he could boast of how he had done so by legitimate means. As for the nation, it had taken its first step along the pathway to disaster.

The aftermath of these events was grievously to affect millions of people, none more so than the Jews of Europe. The Christian groups were also relentlessly persecuted and in this volume we shall look at some of the evidence for that, as well as consider how Christians, at the institutional and individual level, responded to it.

Looking first at the 'institutional' question, some historians have taken the view that there were some members of the hierarchies who undoubtedly used their authority to repudiate Nazi policies. Having said that, they go on to claim that, as formal institutions, neither the Catholic Church nor the Protestant denominations actively challenged or resisted the Nazi regime and particularly with respect to its treatment of the Jews. All writers appear to accept there were many Christians willing to die for the love of their Saviour and the tenets of their faith. In this book we shall venerate a number of these martyrs and examine, dispassionately, whether criticism of the Catholic and Lutheran Churches at the institutional level is well founded.

As a 6-year-old boy, Adolf Hitler, a baptised Austrian Catholic, attended classes at the Benedictine monastery at Lambach, in the vicinity of Linz. There he sang in the choir, served as an acolyte and, on his own telling, became so overawed by the solemn splendour of the liturgy and the church festivals he dreamed one day of ordination – though predictably the disputes with his tutors were frequent.

In his speeches en route to power he made frequent references to 'God' and 'Providence'. In 1922, in Munich's Bürgerbräukeller, to counter a statement by Count Lerchenfeld, minister president of Bavaria that he, himself, 'as a human being and a Christian' could not be anti-Semitic, Hitler declared: 'My Christian feeling points me to my Lord and Saviour as a fighter.'

To prolonged applause he went on: 'It points me towards the man who once lonely and surrounded by only a few followers, recognised these Jews and called for battle against them and who, as true God, was not only the greatest as a *sufferer* but also the greatest as a *warrior*.' So we see him as being perfectly willing to subvert the message of Christianity if it served his broader purpose of eliminating Jews. It has been suggested that by 1919, as a thirty-year-old ex-soldier, any trace of Catholic thoughts and feelings had disappeared and what replaced it was a Völkisch religion grounded in his hatred of the Jews. Thus, when in *Mein Kampf* he writes of 'acting in accordance with the will of the almighty Creator', he continues: 'by defending myself against the Jews I am fighting for the work of the Lord.'

Although in his heart and mind he had abandoned Christian beliefs he continued to invoke God's name in support of his actions and declared himself a defender of the Christian faith. Later we shall see some examples of his root-and-branch mendacity There is an additional point here – while he despised its priests, referring to them among other hate-filled descriptions as 'black bugs', he admired the Catholic Church's implacable hostility to pagan forces and the 'blind faith' of its adherents. He felt that if the 'fanatically religious' ingredient of Catholic belief could be won over to his own political strategy it would prove of inestimable value.

No doubt this is why, at the beginning of the Nazi era, his dealings with both the Catholic and Evangelical Confessions comprised a mixture of reassurance on the one hand and stealthily increasing repression on the other. They were told their autonomy was perfectly secure while all aspects of their life and work were being systematically undermined.

As part of his political design Hitler invited the Vatican to conclude a 'concordat' with his regime. A concordat is 'an agreement binding in international law between Church and State, especially between the Pope as head of the Roman Catholic Church and a head of State.'[9] The Vatican had, as a fundamental part of its apostolic mission, concluded forty of these in the 1920s. It is important to look at the 1933 Concordat with Germany in some depth for its purpose, from the Church's standpoint, has been widely misunderstood and in some cases misrepresented. We shall do this in Chapter Three. For now, it is worth repeating that the initiative for the concordat came from Germany.[10] It should also be emphasised that 'concordats were not signs of special papal favour, but a means of defining relationships with what might be called problem (or rogue) states through solemn legal documents.'[11] From Hitler's standpoint the value of the concordat to the international image of his regime inevitably carried weight with him though, as we shall see, he had no intention of being bound by its terms.

---

9. A Kee, in *Christianity – The Complete Guide*. London, 2005, p. 954.
10. See *Mit brennender Sorge*. Vatican, 1937, para. 3.
11. M Burleigh, *Sacred Causes*. London, 2006, p. 161.

Allegedly, the Catholic and Lutheran Churches were phlegmatic at best, and positively welcoming at worst, to Hitler's ascendancy. Probing the truth of the claim means taking a deeper look at the world in which he came to power. The threat posed to Christianity by Communism in that troubled age must be the first consideration. Pope Pius XI had spoken of a 'terrible triangle' concerning the anticlerical atrocities which had taken place in Russia, Mexico and Spain.

With regard to Russia, Michael Burleigh, respected historian, summarises the persecution in a single impressive paragraph.[12] He explains that on the eve of the Bolshevik coup d'état the Orthodox Church claimed a hundred million adherents, two hundred thousand priests and monks, seventy five thousand churches and chapels, over eleven hundred monasteries, thirty seven thousand primary schools, fifty seven seminaries and four university level academies, not to speak of thousands of hospitals, old people's homes and orphanages. Within a few years that Church's institutional structures had been swept away and the churches were destroyed, vandalised or put to secular use. Many of the clergy were imprisoned or shot, while with grim irony the first of the regime's concentration camps was opened in a monastery in the Arctic region.

Burleigh goes on to describe the Bolshevik combination of repression and ridicule which did irreparable damage to the Orthodox Church as an institution including show trials, shootings, degrading of the Church's legal personality, nationalisation of its land and properties, confiscation of its valuables and the opening of coffins containing venerated bodies. The godlessness of the Communists was spotlighted by the blowing up of the Cathedral of Christ the Saviour, the plan being to use the site for the construction of the world's tallest building, which would accommodate a Palace of Soviets and would be surmounted by a massive statue of Lenin.[13]

As for revolutionary Mexico it was the Queretaro Constitution of 1917 which locked Church and State into a seeming death struggle. Its various Articles secularised education, banned religious orders, restricted worship to within the churches and laid down obstacles to

12. Ibid., p. 40.
13. R Service, *A History of Twentieth Century Russia*. London, 1997, p. 204.

the Church's ownership of property. Beyond these, however, Article 130 cut particularly deeply, for it forbade the clergy from wearing clerical garb, removed their voting power and banned them from criticising government officials and using Catholic publications to make political comments.

In the time of President Alvaro Obregon, these provisions were only patchily enforced, but things took a different turn when he was succeeded by Plutarco Elias Calles who hated the priesthood so intently he became apoplectic at the very mention of its name. Virtually as he came into office 73 convents, 92 churches and 129 religious colleges were forced to close. Crosses were removed from graves and, under the supervision of the regime's young 'Red Shirts', one thousand women were encouraged to burn statues of the saints.

There followed a Catholic rebellion against Calles in a number of Mexican states. This resulted in a three year rampage of atrocious reprisals extending from murder on the one hand (ninety priests were executed solely by virtue of their office) to petty spite on the other – the place-name Vera Cruz ('True Cross') was contracted to Veracruz; the wearing of crucifixes was banned; and in one state even the traditional farewell ('Adios') was banned since it referred to God.[14]

With the Law for Reforming the Penal Code, 1926, anti-religious malice intensified, for now priests were fined 500 pesos for wearing clerical garb and criticisms of the government earned them five years in jail. So these are just some details from a catalogue of crime so hateful that in *Acerba Animi*, 1932, his second encyclical dealing with Mexico, Pius XI compared the ferocious anti-clericalism in some of its federal states with the persecution 'raging within the unhappy borders of Russia.'

By May 1931, while the NSDAP in Germany was steadily progressing to power, in nearby Spain approximately 100 Church properties in Madrid and other cities were being sacked and burned, again as a result of left-wing anti-clericalism. With the utmost cynicism the government of the day did nothing to control the mobs declaring 'all the convents in Madrid are not worth the life of one

---

14. M Burleigh, op. cit., p. 125.

republican',[15] and it found time to order that all religious symbols must be removed from schoolrooms.

In the very next month the pattern of persecution intensified with the election of a left-Republican and Socialist coalition. The elements familiar to the equation were in place – the Church's banishment from education, the restriction of its property rights and investments, and the repression of the religious, taking the form on this occasion of the dissolution of the Jesuits (in the country of St Ignatius Loyola). The public celebration of religion was now subject to the approval of State authorities and both civil marriage and divorce were legalised. There followed in 1933 a law which nationalised all Church property and, breathtakingly, taxed the clergy for its subsequent use. Parties who may have donated the property in the first place had no say in the matter.

Pope Pius XI's encyclical, *Dilectissima Nobis* (June 1933) was a fierce condemnation of what had happened. Spain's recent laws were a product of 'a hatred against the Lord and His Christ nourished by groups subversive to any religious and social order, as alas we have seen in Mexico and Russia.' Republican Spain had now brought up the third side to the 'terrible triangle'. Its objective, primarily, was the eradication of religion.

It is a matter of record, of course, that worse was to follow, for the bloodletting of the Spanish Civil War was to claim 750,000 victims. Within this total, in the Republican-held areas, nearly seven thousand clerics were murdered. According to one source, these comprised more than 4,000 diocesan priests, thirteen bishops, 2,365 male regulars and 283 nuns. Staggeringly, the majority of these deaths took place between July and December 1936. If we wish to understand the atmosphere engendered within Germany by these happenings, since they played a part in the acceptability of the Nazis as the men of order, it might be helpful to consider one or two other examples of happenings in Spain at that time:

- In the Catalan provinces of Lerida and Tortosa 66 per cent of diocesan clergy were murdered. The massacre was as high as 88 per cent in Barcelona.

---

15. J M Sanchez, *The Spanish Civil War as a Religious Tragedy*. Notre Dame, 1987, p. 9.

- In some coastal districts pious Spaniards were forced to bring their objects of worship to the shore where children had great fun defacing religious statues before they were heaped onto bonfires.
- A photograph which was widely distributed showed a column of Republican militia detailed to shoot at the statue of the Sacred Heart of Jesus which surmounted the Cerro de los Angeles on the outskirts of Madrid. Subsequently, the statue was blown up.
- A correspondent of the *Daily Telegraph* described joining a crowd outside a convent near the British Consulate. Inside he found a long wall lined with opened coffins. These contained the bones and rotting bodies of nuns. At the same time more bodies were being exhumed from the convent cemetery. For a peseta a long stick could be hired with which to beat these poor, shrivelled remains while subjecting them to the most foul obscenities. The correspondent reports that the stench and the horror drove him out of the convent.

Though the Pope and his Secretary of State had already had close, personal encounters with communism in action, as Hitler was coming to power, these were the revelations now reaching the German bishops. For his part, the Führer had written in *Mein Kampf*: 'The first requirement is the elimination of the Marxist poison from our national body. . . . It (is) the very first task of a truly national government to seek and find the forces which [are] resolved to declare a war of annihilation on Marxism.'

There are numerous examples in Hitler's speeches of his loathing for Communism and the Communists and one of the most vivid of the third-party comments on this hatred comes from the first chief of the Gestapo, Rudolf Diels. He reports that while standing with Hitler, Göring, Goebbels and other Nazi leaders before Berlin's burning Reichstag building on the night of 27-28 February 1933, Hitler with a face that was 'flaming red'

> . . . shouted uncontrollably, as I had never seen him do before, as if he was going to burst: "There will be no mercy now. Anyone who stands in our way will be cut down. The German people will not tolerate leniency. Every Communist official will be shot where he is found. The Communist deputies must be hanged this very night. Everybody in

> league with Communists must be arrested. There will no longer be any leniency for Social Democrats either."[16]

News of the effects of Communism was also filtering out of Russia. Along with the rest of the world, Germans learned that, resulting from the collective farming campaigns of the Bolsheviks in the main grain growing regions, there had been a new famine. Not only did it result in the deaths of three to four million people, it left the Russians with constant threat of starvation due to the depletion of seed grain.

Perhaps it is not impossible to see then why many patriotic Germans were coming to perceive National Socialism and its leader as the best prospect of protecting the community from the 'Red menace'. Hitler was seemingly the 'strong man' who would restore order. After all had he not fought the Communists in the streets and continually denounced them in his speeches?

Here we should remember that, though servants of God first, the bishops were also patriotic Germans. They were concerned with the threat of Communism to the Christian faith and ultimately its threat to the Fatherland, which was after all inextricably bound up with the pastoral care of their flocks. A 'wait and see' attitude to his accession, at the least, therefore seemed justified.

Next, any consideration of the factors conducive to this 'wait and see' attitude must take account of the *Kulturkampf* ('Struggle over Culture'), a campaign carried out by Imperial Chancellor von Bismarck and other Protestant rulers against the Catholics. The 'new Germany' was a Germany united from 1871 under the headship of Prussia. It excluded Austria, whom most of Germany's Catholics had supported in the German Civil War of 1866. So the major change of the nineteenth century was the passing of German leadership from Austria, the historical and Catholic power, to Prussia, the foremost of the Protestant states. In the old Confederation, 52% of the population was Catholic and 48% Protestant. Now the Catholics had become a minority of 37% in a Protestant state under a Protestant emperor. Because of their past affiliations, they were treated as suspect. This affirmed the post-Reformation mind-set, in Germany, England and other countries, that the Catholics were really an alien element under the sway of Rome – a calumny that persisted despite the demonstrable loyalty of the Catholics to their nations.

---

16. E A Johnson, *The Nazi Terror*. London, 2000, pp. 161-2.

Nevertheless, Bismarck saw the Catholics, located mostly and handily in discrete geographical areas – Bavaria, the Rhineland and occupied Poland – as a threat to the unity of the new Germany. Consequently from 1871 until 1880 he mounted an aggressive campaign to exclude Catholics from public life and labelled it *Kulturkampf.* Principally, though not entirely, the persecution was confined to Prussia. Firstly, Bismarck expelled the Jesuits prior to the expulsion of other religious orders. Then education, including the training of clergy, was brought under state control. Imprisonment was the lot of any bishop or cleric who resisted. There is a view that Bismarck's attitude may have been influenced by the First Vatican Council, 1870, which affirmed the doctrine of papal infallibility. The Council re-stated the ancient belief that when the Pope spoke *ex cathedra* (i.e. as Shepherd and Teacher) and defined a doctrine concerning faith or morals to be held by the whole Church, he was incapable of error. This has nothing to do with the Pope's ability to sin, in which he is as human as all humankind, nor suggests that he is automatically correct when speaking on any matter. Nevertheless, the alarm bells rang loudly in Protestant and Liberal circles and gave rise to the misconception that Catholics in Germany were alien, owing their temporal as well as their spiritual loyalty to the foreign potentate in the Vatican.

The atmosphere of suspicion and mistrust, the growing power of Protestant Prussia and mounting liberal hostility, drove Catholics further on to the defensive and, accordingly, Catholic members of the Prussian lower house formed their own national party, the Centre. It was unique in that it drew support from all social strata: aristocratic, middle class, working class. It had become by 1871 the second largest party in the Reichstag, with 58 seats, and was pledged to defend the Church, support confessional schools and oppose civil marriage. It resisted extensions of imperial power and favoured decentralisation and greater autonomy for the states.

Since the 1830s the Church had always had a watchful eye on the excesses of *laissez-faire* capitalism, maintaining a keen commitment to social reform. (Ultimately this resulted in Pope Leo XIII's Encylical of May 1891; titled *Rerum Novarum* it became popularly known as the 'Workers' Charter'.) The Centre Party's activities on this social dimension may have persuaded Bismarck that 'an ephemeral anti-

Prussian political alignment in the Reichstag was in reality a Vatican-inspired conspiracy of malcontents bent on destroying the Empire he had so painfully created.'[17]

The Catholic Church has always shown remarkable resilience in the face of persecution and secular meddling. Predictably the bishops instructed their flocks to resist Bismark's measures. Thus, by 1876 he was beginning to realise that the *Kulturkampf* had merely succeeded in deepening Germany's religious divides and was hardly likely to succeed anyway. So most of the *Kulturampf*'s activity was being quietly abandoned within a mere ten years of its inception, but it did sow doubt in the national psyche as to where Catholic loyalties lay. Within the Catholic psyche, doubtless including the attitudes of the bishops, it fostered a determination to demonstrate that a Catholic was as German as any German.

So, this glimpse into contextual matters may shed some light on why the Church seemed willing in some instances to await events as the Nazis came to power. Yet from such considerations as the threat of Communism and the effects of the *Kulturkampf* no inference can truthfully be drawn that the Catholic Church, faced with Hitler's accession, was at best weak and vacillating and at worst welcoming to, and supportive of, Nazi ideology. Such an inference defames the memory of noble, courageous individuals and in this volume we hope to adduce enough evidence to show that resistance not concurrence was the Church's standpoint. We make a start on this below.

As early as 1 October 1921 the Bavarian newspaper, the *Bayerische Kurier* reported a warning from Nuncio Pacelli: 'The Bavarian people are peace loving. But just as they were seduced during the revolution by alien elements – above all Russians – into the extremes of Bolshevism, so now other non-Bavarian elements of entirely opposite persuasion have likewise thought to make Bavaria their base of operation.'[18]

This was the precursor of many other warnings from him. In their biography of Pope Pius XII, Tolansky and Scott explain that of 44 public speeches he made in Germany between 1917 and 1929 at least forty contained attacks on National Socialism or Hitler's doctrines.[19]

---

17. W Carr, op. cit., p. 126.
18. E Tolansky and H Scott, *Pius XII*. London, 2003, p. 23.
19. Ibid., p. 23.

He was not alone in his condemnations, for between 1920 and 1927 the German bishops warned their flocks that National Socialism was totalitarian, racist, pagan and anti-Christian.

Five days after the Munich putsch of 1923 Pacelli reported to Vatican Secretary of State Gasparri that its supporters had made Munich's Cardinal Michael Faulhaber the scapegoat for its failure, savagely condemning him. The Nuncio wrote: 'The attacks were specially focused on this learned and zealous Cardinal Archbishop who, in a sermon he gave in the Cathedral on the 4th of this month, and in a letter to the Chancellor of the Reich published by the Wolff Agency on the 7th had denounced the persecution of the Jews.' On this issue of actions against the Jews, Burleigh comments: 'One might add that the head of the Franciscan seminary in Munich Erhard Schlund had written a critique of the Nazi Party programme, in which he specifically denounced its unchristian anti-semitism.'[20] He also reports on the student demonstrations against Faulhaber where they denounced the Pope, the Archbishop, the clergy and Minister President von Kahr, a Protestant, but nonetheless perceived by one of the agitators as an honorary Jesuit.

Pacelli linked Catholics and Jews as victims of Nazi persecution when he reported to Secretary of State Gasparri on a 'vulgar and brutal' press campaign waged against them by Nazi supporters. He added that 'Nationalism is perhaps the most dangerous heresy of our times.'[21]

In 1928, six years into the papacy of Pius XI, the Holy Office issued a 'binding condemnation' of 'that hate which is now called anti-Semitism', and Britain's then representative to the Holy See, Sir Ivone Kirkpatrick, referred to the 'pungent terms' in which Pius expressed his views on Hitler's persecution of the Jews.[22]

Let us now turn to a number of extracts from the speeches of German and Austrian Catholic bishops. They completely contradict the picture of a non-interventionist stance which has gained credence in the recent past. It should be emphasised they are but a small selection from a list which could be featured here. They clearly provide a picture of disgust and condemnation.

---

20. M Burleigh, op. cit., p. 169.
21. Ibid., p. 169.
22. Sir I Kirkpatrick, *The Inner Circle, Memoirs*. London, 1959, p. 47.

'Close your ears and do not join their associations, close your doors and do not let their newspapers into your homes, close your hands and do not support their endeavours in elections.' (Bishop Johannes Gföllner of Linz, 1929, warning the faithful against the 'false prophets' of Nazism.)[23]

'The Christian moral law is founded on love of our neighbour. National Socialist writers do not accept this commandment in the sense taught by Christ; they preach too much respect for the Germanic race and too little respect for foreign races. For many of them what begins as mere lack of respect, ends up as full blown hatred of foreign races, which is unChristian and unCatholic. Moreover the Christian moral law is universal and valid for all times and races; so there is a gross error in requiring that the Christian faith be suited to the moral sentiments of the Germanic race.' (Bishop of Mainz, 1930 in his declaration that Nazism and Catholicism were simply irreconcilable.)[24]

'We deplore everything which detracts from the good reputation of our nation and Fatherland, and which presents, both to the minds of our own people and to those of neighbouring nations, the appearance of cruelty and injustice: this is true of the practice, unfortunately increasing, of removing loyal citizens and men of industry and merit from the positions they have hitherto occupied.' (From a manifesto signed by the Bishops of the Ecclesiastical Province of the Upper Rhine and their Metropolitan, Archbishop Conrad Gröber, in Freiburg-im-Breisgau, April 1933.)[25]

And here are four extracts from a document issued by the Bavarian bishops to their flocks and calling for national co-operation but nonetheless expressing misgivings in spite of the Führer's assurances.

'Just as harmonious co-operation between Church and State is necessary and beneficial, so disastrous effects follow, as history teaches us, when the State abuses its power in order to interfere with the life of the Church, when the Church and State are fused together, or when the Church is degraded to the status of a servant of the State.'

'We hope that the Reich Government does not approve of the efforts and proceedings of those who on principle apply a different legal standard, or seek to employ the word "uniformity" (*Gleichschaltung*) in a manner which is in conflict with the assurances given by the

23. M Burleigh, op. cit., p. 170.
24. Ibid., p. 170.
25. Reported in *The Persecution of the Catholic Church in the Third Reich: Facts and Documents*. London, 1940, p. 13.

> Chancellor of the Reich.'
>
> 'The rights and duties of parents with regard to the spiritual, religious and moral training of their children ought not to be impeded or even pared down and curtailed by measures taken by educational authorities or the State ... On no account can we ever agree to universal (i.e. undenominational) schools of whatever form.'
>
> 'We are no advocates of a form of criticism which combats and discounts all State authority, which conceives it to be its task to agitate and to undermine, which stirs up the nation and seduces it, and indeed makes its living out of agitation and unrest. But there is no reason why such abuses should lead to a complete suppression of free opinion and free expression, especially in the daily press.' (Issued in May 1933.)[26]

It was at this time that bishops in the provinces of Cologne, Upper Rhine and Paderborn cautioned clergy against becoming involved with the Nazis and as proof of their resolve threatened any leader of a party hostile to Christianity with denial of the sacraments. In Bavaria, Catholic bishops excluded Nazi formations from attending funerals or services while carrying banners or in uniform. At this time they also condemned the Nazis' racism and their eugenic ideology with its scorn for the sanctity of the unborn.[27]

An event of those times, perhaps little known, is that on Sunday, 29 January, just one day before the Nazis came to power, one hundred thousand workers made for the centre of Berlin. Crowding into the Lustgarten they demonstrated against the prospect of Hitler as Chancellor. Bearing in mind a general strike had saved the Republic at the time of the Kapp putsch in 1920, a leader of this 1933 demonstration tried to contact General von Hammerstein to propose joint action by organised labour and the Army should Hitler become head of government.

Though the move came to nothing it provides more evidence that not all Germans wanted Hitler to succeed and this was certainly true of the Catholics, for in the 1930 elections when the Nazi share of the vote leapt from 2.6% to 18.3%, in such Catholic-dominated regions as Cologne-Aachen, Koblenz-Trier and lower Bavaria their

---

26. Ibid., p. 14.
27. M Burleigh, op. cit., pp. 170–1.

share averaged only 14%. In the July 1932 election when the National Socialists doubled their vote (18.3% to 37.4%), in Rhineland and lower Bavaria where Catholics predominated, they obtained the lowest segment of support (19.9%).

While it is true that, in general, the Nazis found themselves more popular with Protestant than with Catholic voters, we must bear in mind the latter were obviously attracted to the Centre Party, with its Catholic ideology. There was no religiously-based party for Protestant voters, many of whom voted for the Social Democrats. The appeal of the NSDAP was stronger among Protestants with right-wing or nationalist leanings.

We shall be looking at the implication for Protestants of the Nazification of Germany in the next chapter. In the meantime, below are two interesting vignettes from within a Protestant family.[28]

On the evening of 30 January 1933, a few hours after Hitler's accession, Rudiger Schleicher, brother-in-law to Dietrich Bonhoeffer, later to be murdered by the Nazis, came home and said: 'This means war!' His view was shared by the rest of the family, even at this early stage. Later when friends probed Dietrich about the seemingly exaggerated pessimism of Rudiger's opinion, he replied that while the estimated time of the event might have to be revised there could be no doubt about it coming.

Karl Bonhoeffer, father of Dietrich, was from 1912 until his death in 1948, Berlin's leading psychiatrist and neurologist. Towards the end of his life, recalling the events of 1933, he said this: 'From the start the Victory of National Socialism and Hitler's appointment as Reich Chancellor was in our view a misfortune – the whole family agreed on this. In my own case, I disliked and mistrusted Hitler because of his demagogic propaganda methods, his telegram of condolences after the Potempa murder, his habit of driving about the country carrying a riding crop, his choice of colleagues – with whose qualities, incidentally, we in Berlin were better acquainted than people elsewhere – and finally because of what I heard from professional colleagues about his psychopathic symptoms.'[29]

---

28. E Bethge, *Dietrich Bonhoeffer*. London, 1970, p. 191.
29. Ibid., pp. 191-2.

The 1933 German election

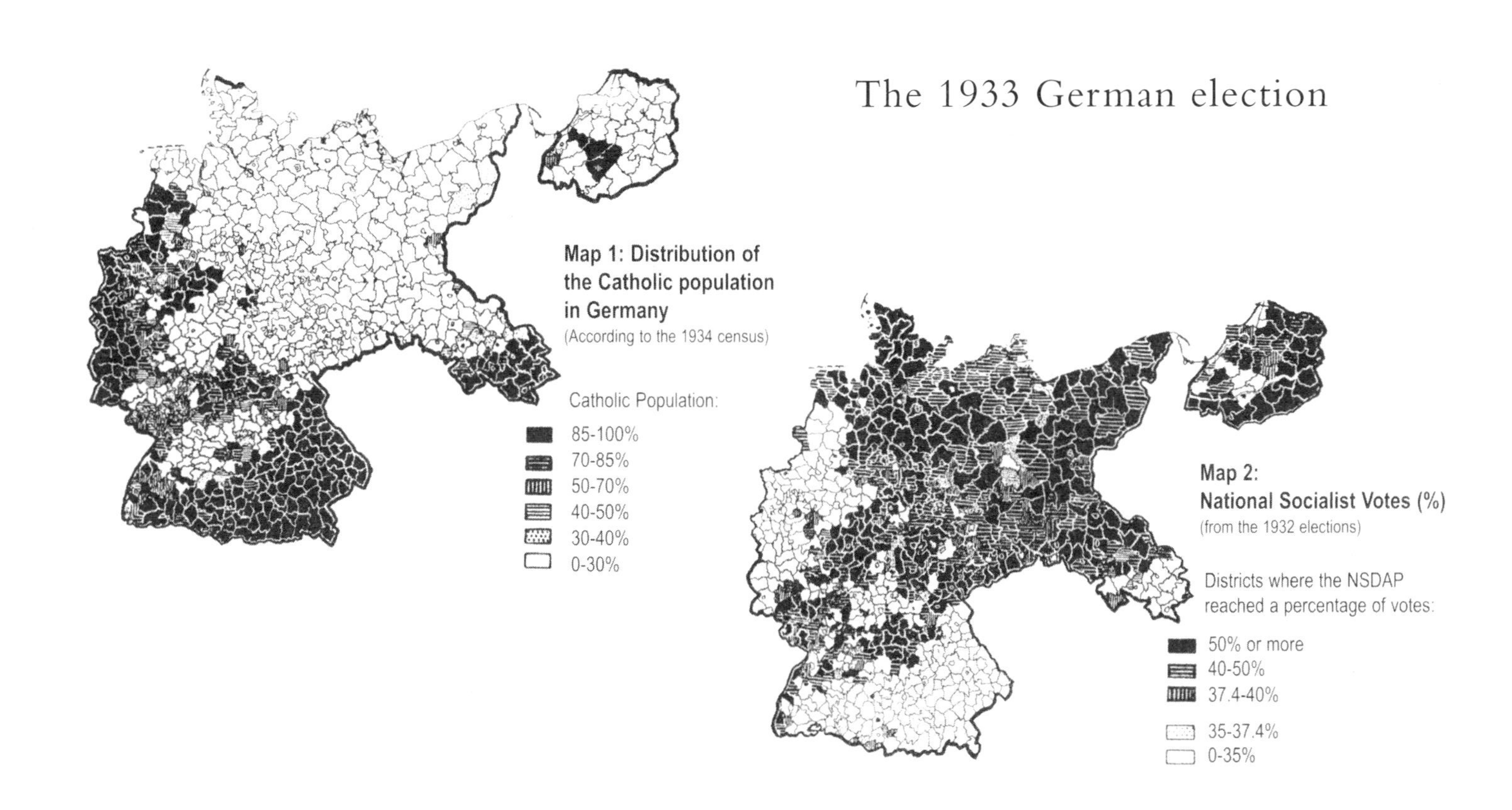

At 3 am on the morning of 31 January 1933, when the storm troopers' torchlit river had run its course, Joseph Goebbels, Hitler's propaganda chief, confided to his diary: 'It is almost like a dream . . . a fairytale. . . . The new Reich has been born. Fourteen years of work have been crowned with victory. The German revolution has begun!'[30]

It was to be a revolution unbelievable in scale and unimaginable in its horror. Among its victims were to be thousands of Christian faithful.

30. W L Shirer, *The Rise and Fall of the Third Reich*, Vol. I. London, Folio Ed., 2004, p. 5.

Chapter Three

THE EARLY YEARS:

'Co-ordination', Conflict, the Concordat

In the Nazi era, even language was corrupted. It was the golden age of euphemism: 'extermination' became 'resettlement', 'holocaust' became 'racial purification', and 'nazification' became 'co-ordination'. We used to refer to 'the covering of sin with smooth names'; in Hitler's Germany, the process was stretched to its limits in order to mollify doubters and protesters.

'Co-ordination' or *Gleichschaltung* (literally 'putting into the same gear') signified the process of bringing all aspects of German life – economic, military, political, artistic, social and religious – under National Socialist control. In this chapter we shall examine how the Nazi State attempted to rule the Catholic and Evangelical Churches and the nature of the Christian response.

Circumstances could not have been more propitious for Hitler to establish his dictatorship. Kershaw has described how *Gleichschaltung* was, in the main, achieved not only voluntarily but with alacrity.[1] He considers the Christian bodies to be exceptions to this, however. This should be emphasised, for, by 1933, adulation of the new Chancellor was becoming firmly rooted: everything from the planting of trees, honorary membership of towns and cities, to the production of poems were merely the first signs of an extraordinary personality cult.

The commercially impelled production of commemorative pictures, badges, busts, penknives, figures etc. became such a tasteless

---

1. I Kershaw, *Hitler, 1889-1936*. Hubris. London, 1998, p. 435.

torrent that propaganda chief Goebbels intervened as early as May 1933 to prevent the future use of Hitler's image on such artefacts.[2] More soberly, the *Deutsche Algemeine Zeitung* reflected, on 30 January 1934, the anniversary of the accession: 'There is no doubt at all about it: that Hitler as a personality enjoys a unique trust, that during this year in the nation's consciousness (and in foreign opinion) he has grown into a confident leader and that this immediate trust must be unshakeable for the sake of the nation.' So any reflection on what the German bishops did or didn't do at this time must take account of the prevailing atmosphere which was inimical to any criticism of this new leader.

Self-satisfied, Hitler could reflect that he had achieved office by legitimate means, that he had worked within the constitution and had even attracted the conservative establishment and the army to his cause. He was, however, a sworn enemy of democracy which was the antithesis of his personal concept of power – a power for himself which was total, for he was the 'strong man' whose historic mission it was to save Germany. While he abhorred parliamentarianism, his failure in the Munich putsch had been sobering enough for him to confide to colleagues that: 'We shall have to hold our noses and enter the Reichstag against the Catholic and Marxist deputies.'[3] The cunning of the regime was unconsciously affirmed by his then deputy, Rudolf Hess, who confided to a party member in a written reply that parliamentary participation should be seen as a strategy to subvert the parliamentary process itself. 'Participation' did not entail 'co-operation' but the fiercest opposition, obstruction and constant criticism so as to render parliamentarianism an absurdity.

Now the question was – how could Hitler's present position be transformed into the dictatorship of a one-party State? At first it seemed his approach would be the same tactical rich mixture for, having persuaded von Papen, Deputy Chancellor in the Coalition Cabinet, to appoint Hermann Göring as Prussian Minister of the Interior, Göring then immediately used his powers to enrol the Brownshirts as auxiliary policemen.

As was their way, they rampaged through towns and cities wrecking

---

2. R Steinberg, *Nazi-Kitsch*. Darmstadt, 1975.
3. I Kershaw, op. cit., p. 228.

trade union offices, breaking up Social Democrat meetings and assaulting opponents, particularly Communists. Adroitly, for the Reichstag election was due on 5 March, Hitler distanced himself from the turmoil even though the old NSDAP stamp of skilful use of propaganda coupled with intimidation of opponents was enjoying full employment. Suddenly, on 27 February, fate gave the Nazis a wonderful opportunity, for Marinus van der Lubbe set fire to the Reichstag building.

This 24-year-old arsonist had acted alone in protest at the bitter burdens being imposed on the working classes by capitalism. He had been immediately arrested, had confessed to the deed and had explained the nature of his protest. The police arresting the youth were convinced both of his story and the claim he was acting alone, but when Göring then Hitler arrived, the notion of a 'Communist plot' seemed too fitting and timely to ignore. When Hitler had become Chancellor in January he had declared that 'Germany must not and will not sink into Communist anarchy'. Now Göring bellowed: 'Not a moment must be lost!' because, as Hitler was yelling to von Papen: 'This is a God-given signal, Herr Vice-Chancellor! If this fire, as I believe, is the work of the Communists, then we must crush out this murderous pest with an iron fist!'[4]

No later than the following morning, Wilhelm Frick, Reich Minister of the Interior, had produced the draft of a decree for 'the Protection of People and State'. It ratified the use of emergency measures in the whole of the Reich, was discussed at a meeting of Cabinet and obtained the assent of President Paul von Hindenburg. At a stroke, civil liberties and the right of habeus corpus were suspended. Freedom of speech, of association and of the press were rendered inoperative. Hitler was now able to have the offices of the Communist Party raided and its representatives arrested. As a political force in Germany, Communism was now powerless.

The way to dictatorship had opened wide. When von Papen had persuaded Hindenburg to appoint Hitler into the Cabinet on 30 January he had gleefully confided to others: 'Now we have him where we can control him.' It may be that he was already regretting his words – and worse was to come.

---

4. Ibid., p. 458.

Joseph Goebbels set himself skilfully to the task of capitalising on the fire as part of his propaganda drive for the election of the NSDAP to the Reichstag. Making effective use of the new media (radio and cinema) he rhapsodised on the prospects of a strong Nazi government led by Hitler as the only way to save the nation from 'Red' revolution. He was assisted in this by Göring and his SA Brownshirts who so terrorised the other political parties their campaigns were stifled. The result was an increase in the Nazi share of the vote from 33% to 44%, swelling its numbers of Reichstag seats from 196 to 288.

In *Mein Kampf*, Hitler had set out his belief in dictatorship as the ideal political structure: 'in the smallest as in the greatest problems, one person must have absolute authority and bear all responsibility.' Buoyed up by the election result, he now set about obtaining dictatorial power. Again he would do so by legal means.

On 23 March 1933, the newly elected Reichstag members met in Berlin's Kroll Opera House to debate the establishment of his Enabling Act. With grandiose euphemism this was called the 'Law for Removing the Distress of the People and the Reich'. If passed it would effectively end democracy and see Hitler installed as Germany's Overlord.

The atmosphere was tense. Outside the building were chanting Nazi storm troopers. As the voting took place, more of them lined the aisles and hallways. It was an exercise in the most grotesque intimidation. By now the Nazis had successfully inculcated the belief that the Communists had fired the Reichstag building as a prelude to their widespread uprising. In his speech to the assembly Hitler pledged to use restraint when taking the necessary steps to safeguard the peace and security of the nation. He also pledged to end unemployment and enter into peaceful negotiations with France, Great Britain and the Soviet Union. Clearly, however, none of this could happen without the Enabling Act.

For any constitutional amendment to be valid, two thirds of the deputies had to be present and the passage of the Bill had to attract two thirds of the votes of those present. As eighty one Communists had been arrested by the provisions of the Reichstag fire decree, they were already excluded. Now, however, the Nazis feared that if 120 Socialists stayed away from the voting and persuaded another 15 deputies to do likewise, the Act would surely fail for lack of an adequate majority. Prompted by Hitler, Göring breathtakingly changed the rules of procedure in that all deputies were to be counted as present unless excused and the (Nazi) President of the Reichstag (Göring) would decide whether they were excused or not.

Hitler made another move: Ludwig Kaas, a Catholic priest and Chairman of the Catholic Centre Party, was approached to support the Act in exchange for the Nazis' promise to help it achieve civil recognition of Catholics and Catholicism and the institution of quotas and protection for Catholic civil servants and schools. The Centre Party had also asked for the maintenance of Constitutional protection for civil liberties – for the repeal of the Emergency Powers and a return to Constitutional rule. When the voting began Kaas was assured that the guarantees he had negotiated were being typed up. Subsequently, he received no written confirmation of any kind. Hitler's talk of civil war and a resort to force had worked for, though opinion among the Centre Party deputies was still divided, Kaas had countered that 'the Fatherland is in the greatest danger. We dare not fail.' Eventually, as Kershaw reports, 'with the greatest reservations and evincing their feelings of responsibility for the nation, other leading figures such as Heinrich Brüning (the former Chancellor), Joseph Ersing (one of the party's most prominent trade unionists) and the rest of Zentrum deputies supported him.'[5]

Only Otto Wells, leader of the Social Democrats, spoke against Hitler. Quietly he said: 'We German Social Democrats pledge ourselves solemnly in this historic hour to the principles of humanity and justice, of freedom and socialism. No enabling act can give you the power to destroy ideas which are eternal and indestructible.' Hitler was furious. Jumping to his feet he bawled: 'You are no longer needed! . . . the star of Germany will rise and yours will sink! Your death knell has sounded.'

The result of the voting was declared: 441 votes for the Act and only 94 (the Social Democrats) against it. The Nazis rose, clapping, stamping and shouting, then singing their anthem, the Horst Wessel song.

5. Ibid., pp. 467-8.

The Reichstag had voted itself out of existence as a democratic body. From now on it would be no more than a stage setting for the Dictator's pronouncements. On 14 July, the government introduced a law banning all political parties other than the Nazi party. The Enabling Act was set to expire in 1937 but, anxious to maintain the charade of 'legality', Hitler had the puppet Reichstag extend the Act twice. Now 'co-ordination' of all Germany's institutions, including the Christian bodies, could commence. The construction of the concentration camps was arranged. Darkness was descending.

When the process of Nazification was completed, the Catholic and Evangelical Churches seem to have survived the process to a greater extent than Germany's other major institutions. There were at least two underlying causes for this: (i) the Nazis were largely taken up with eliminating other types of opponent; (ii) they had no long-range strategy for the role of the Churches anyway. In this sphere at least, Hitler was unsure of himself.

Article 24 of the NSDAP Programme, published in 1920, reads as follows: 'We insist upon freedom for all religious confessions in the State provided they do not endanger its existence or offend the German race's sense of decency and morality. The Party as such stands for a positive Christianity, without binding itself denominationally to a particular confession. It fights against the Jewish-materialistic spirit at home and abroad and believes that any lasting recovery of our people must be based on the spiritual principle: the welfare of the community comes before that of the individual.'[6]

In 1926 Hitler had declared the Party Programme unalterable but, in fact, it became steadily out of phase with the real intentions of the NSDAP. However, the reference in the Programme to 'positive Christianity' proved of great tactical value in convincing both the Catholic and Protestant congregations that they could support National Socialism without compromising their religious convictions.

When the Nazis came to power two thirds of the German people could be described as 'Protestants'. Unlike the Catholic Church, however, Protestantism in Germany was no monolithic entity. Quite the reverse, for the structures of German Protestantism at the time present such a bewildering array of theological possibilities as to

---

6. A Rhodes, *The Vatican in the Age of the Dictators, 1922-45*. London, 1973.

make analysis of them somewhat difficult. For example, the Protestant faith was known officially as 'Evangelical' – though British Anglicans would have been misled if they thought that the Evangelical Church of Germany reflected what they understood as 'Evangelical'.

The German Evangelical Church was divided into three Confessions – Lutheran, Reformed and United. In Prussia, Lutheranism and Calvinism had been brought together into a Union of Protestant Churches. Beyond this there were 28 'Land Churches' (*Landeskirchen*) – geographically determined in phase with the States and Princedoms existing before Germany was united. The Landeskirchen were highly protective of their independence not least for reasons of doctrinal belief. If we add to them other denominations such as Methodists, Adventists and Jehovah's Witnesses the list becomes bewilderingly long, and difficult to unthread. In this book, therefore, all these faith possibilities will be subsumed under the title 'Protestant'. In doing this we shall, even so, lose very little in considering the impact of Nazism on the Christian denominations.

To begin, we shall review the case of the Protestant organisations. In this case, it is important to find some meaning for the vague term 'Positive Christianity'. One writer, in 1939, felt that by 'positive', the Nazis meant practical Christianity. They were not concerned with church-going and dogmatic theology. Their aim was to destroy atheistic Communism and weld together a broken nation in a fellowship of mutual service thus making the good of the community prevail over the selfishness of the individual – sentiments well in accord with Christian belief. However, Nazi fundamental concepts of Race, Blood and Soil from a Christian standpoint were negative, not positive. Their anti-Semitism, their idealization of the 'Nordic' race and of military virtue were certainly not rooted in Christianity but inimical to it.

Based on what we now know of the real Nazi attitude to the Christian faith it is clear that 'Positive Christianity' was really racism thinly disguised by theological terminology. For Hitler the 'Aryan' man was 'the highest image of the Lord . . . the founder of all higher humanity . . .'[7] For the Nazis it was clear that God had sanctified the 'Aryan' way of life. What was really immoral was racial 'Mongrelisation'.

---

7. M Burleigh, *Sacred Causes*. London, 2006, p. 107.

Legislation was obviously necessary to prevent more racial pollution, not least by Jews.

Since Communism was their declared arch-enemy the Nazis considered themselves, if no more than nominally, on the side of Christianity. And there were important political considerations here: for one thing it would be counter-productive to alienate that large majority of the population declaring itself to be Christian. In addition, if they could harness the enthusiasms of religious believers to their own cause it would undoubtedly be fortified. It was true that the Catholic Church's early judgement of them was unfavourable and though they declared themselves to be neutral between denominations they had great hopes that the Protestants would be more amenable. Perhaps, in time, there might well be an attitude-shift among the Catholics.

The Nazis were willing to welcome any form of Christianity if it refrained from politics per se and accepted the politics of National Socialism. In the event, Hitler adopted two seemingly opposite stances in his approach to the Churches. On the one hand he promised earnestly that under his regime they would maintain their autonomy. On the other, he set about dismantling, where he could not assimilate, their activities and structures. At the onset, because it attempted to combine Christianity and National Socialism, what did receive his approval was the 'German Christians' movement.

The 'Positive German Christians', as they called themselves were, within the faith movements, the most complicitous with Nazi objectives. They despised the atheistic Communists and the 'foreign spirited' (Catholic) Centre Party. The only true advocates of the German race were the National Socialists. Obviously the Jews, as well as those Jewish aspects of Christianity – particularly the Old Testament and the 'rabbi' Paul – which were alien, were also polluters of 'pure Christianity'.

In the German Evangelical Church elections of 1932, the German Christians gained a majority. The extracts below, taken from the 'Platform of the German Christians',[8] indicate the overwhelming political motivation of this 'Faith Movement':

---

8. J F Harrington, *A Cloud of Witnesses. Readings in the History of Western Christianity*. Boston, 2001, pp. 468-70.

> 'We are fighting for the union of the 29 churches embraced by the "German Evangelical Church Federation" in one evangelical National Church and we march to the call . . .' (ex Article 2)
>
> 'We want a living People's Church (Volkskirche) which is the expression of all the religious powers of our nation (Volk).' (ex Article 3)
>
> 'We take our stand on the platform of positive Christianity. We affirm an affirmative style of Christian faith as appropriate to the German spirit of Luther and heroic piety.' (ex Article 4)
>
> 'The church has not yet marshaled [*sic*] for decisive battle against the God-hating Marxism and the foreign-spirited Center [*sic*] party. In the fateful battle for German freedom and future, the church has shown itself too weak in its leadership. . . . . We want our church to fight in the forefront in the decisive struggle for the existence or extinction of our nation. She dare not stand aside or indeed shy away from the fighters for freedom.' (ex Article 5)
>
> 'The way into the kingdom of God leads through battle, cross and sacrifice, not through false peace.' (ex Article 6)
>
> 'We see in race, national character and nation orders of life given and entrusted to us by God, to maintain which is a law of God for us. Therefore racial mixing is to be opposed. On the basis of experience, the German foreign missions have for a long time called to the German nation: "Keep yourself racially pure" and tell us that faith in Christ doesn't disturb race but rather deepens and sanctifies it.' (Article 7)
>
> 'We know something of Christian duty and love towards the helpless, but we demand also the protection of the nation from the incapable and the inferior.' (ex Article 8)
>
> 'In the mission to [convert] the Jews we see a grave danger to our national character. It is the entry way for foreign blood into our national body . . . Marriage between Germans and Jews is especially to be forbidden.'(ex Article 9)
>
> 'We want an Evangelical Church with roots in the national character, and we repudiate the spirit of a Christian cosmopolitanism.' (ex Article 10)

Among the German Christians, who longed for a new German religion under a new Reich Bishop, the NSDAP was well visible. Even before Hitler's accession a number of the NSDAP's Evangelical supporters had come together demanding that the three Confessions of the Evangelical Church – Lutheran, Reformed and United – the Prussian Union of the Protestant Churches and the 28 Landeskirchen be reorganised into one Reichskirche (Reich Church). During their meeting of 3-4 April 1933 these Nazis demanded an immediate Gleichschaltung of all the Protestant Churches. While they were willing for the Landeskirchen to be autonomous in matters of creed and liturgy, they were adamant that the overall administration of these churches was to be transferred to the national government. So here we see the thin end of the wedge, for with their freedom thus compromised, a fallow situation for complete Nazification would be created.

Yet, it is very important to note that there were Protestant forces ready to fight for the unadulterated Christian message. Alarmed by the machinations of the German Christians, a group of German pastors issued a collective statement on the 'Dangers and Disruption of Public Life'. Issued before Hitler's accession (11 January 1933) it became known as the 'Altona Confession'. According to Helmreich,[9] a noted author on the German Churches of that era, it was a well-formulated declaration in the best tradition of German theological scholarship. Esteemed theologian Karl Barth and his circle influenced its composition and it maintained that no particular form of State was best. It continued: 'We are called to be obedient to the government. If it should happen that the government acted contrary to the "best interests of the state", then each person must decide when the moment has come when one must obey God more than man. . . . All that we have stated here is derived from the message of the cross and from God.'

The statement presaged the formation of the 'Pastors' Emergency League' and the 'Confessing Church' which were implacably opposed to the moves of the German Christians. Before we look at these it is important to say just a little more on how the general political situation was developing.

In the Spring of 1933, Hitler had 3 broad aims: i) to seize and retain control of the German government – and he had accomplished this by the Enabling Act, which vested unlimited power in the Chancellor,

---

9. E C Helmreich, *The German Churches under Hitler – Background, Struggle and Epilogue*. Detroit, 1979, p. 128.

initially for 6 months. The period was automatically extended by a supine Reichstag so that Germany retained a dictatorship until Hitler's death in 1945; ii) to mobilise the German people for war and conquest; and iii) to eliminate the Jews.

The first signs of the aim to create a pathological Judeophobia were not long in coming. On 9 March, in Berlin, Magdeburg and the Rhineland, Nazi storm troopers blocked the entrances to Jewish businesses and department stores. Potential customers were confronted by these SA (*Sturmabteilung*) thugs and warned not to buy goods from 'the racial enemies of the German people'. Leaflets were distributed and SA bands marched or drove through predominantly Jewish districts with the same message.

There now began a more widespread and intensive persecution of the Jews. On 7 April 1933, Reich Minister of the Interior, Wilhelm Frick, promulgated the government's 'Law for the restoration of the civil service.' Its most trenchant provision was that 'Officials of non-Aryan origin are to be retired.' Within a few days, Frick had defined non-Aryan: 'Anyone is considered non-Aryan who is descended from non-Aryan and, in particular, Jewish parents or grandparents. It suffices for one parent or grandparent to be non-Aryan.'

Aryans were perceived by Nazi ideology as having been specially chosen by God to accomplish a redemption mission on earth;[10] they were the sublime essence of the human race. The Jew, on the other hand, was everything that was unholy: materialistic, anarchic, individualistic and a pernicious threat to a nation's culture. Whereas the Aryan, in the image of God was idealistic, altruistic, other-directed and creative, the Jew, in the words of Joseph Goebbels, was 'indeed the Antichrist of world history.' And the Aryans were perpetually threatened by dilution of their virtue if they mixed with other races. They had to be constantly alert to safeguard Aryan blood as pure and undefiled. The destructive influences of the Jews were the greatest danger.

The then Nazi perception of the Christian bodies was of institutions only half-Aryan. The Old Testament and the 'rabbi Paul' were responsible for this. Thus it was clear that only the National Socialists had the

---

10. M Burleigh, op. cit., p. 107.

faultless interpretation of Christ's message. 'True Christianity' could only be achieved under their stewardship. As early as 1921, Hitler had said: 'I can imagine Christ as nothing other than blond and with blue eyes, the Devil, however, only with a Jewish grimace.'[11]

Now more legislation appeared to remove Jews from public institutions: the universities were not to employ them as teachers nor were they to be appointed to the judiciary. They must be prevented from practising law and serving the insurance industry as physicians. Within schools of all types their teaching numbers must not exceed 15%. Even Jews who had served in the First World War or the Freikorps would not have escaped these punitive provisions but for the intervention of Hindenburg. Soon he would die, of course, then no-one could protect them.

In furtherance of the NSDAP's ideology the Positive German Christians met in April 1933 to demand an immediate Gleichschaltung of all Evangelical Churches, with the overall administration of the Evangelical Church to be put into the hands of the government. Naturally, if implemented, such a move would have compromised spiritual autonomy. At this April meeting, they also called for the election of a Reich Bishop and the establishment of a national synod. Following a stormy meeting in September, the German Christians succeeded in getting Ludwig Müller, Hitler's friend and adviser on Protestant affairs, elected as the new Reich Bishop.

Much has been written of the willingness, even the enthusiasm, of Protestant pastors and congregations at this stage in German history to embrace National Socialism. They have been depicted as at best too irresolute and pliable, easy victims of totalitarian wiles, and at worst as infected with Nazi ideology as any storm trooper. Obviously there were thousands of National Socialists within the Evangelical Church but that is not the full story – the attempts of a minority to impose their creed and objectives on the majority met with courageous opposition.

Matters came to a head when, in the September meeting of the Prussian general synod, in which the German Christians held a two-thirds majority, the 'Aryan Paragraph' was introduced and adopted. This now meant that Aryan origin was a decisive criterion for clerical

11. Ibid., p. 108.

office. To understand how so many apparently upright people were willing for the Nazi motto of 'One Volk, one Reich, one Führer!' to be expanded to include 'one Church', it is necessary, in a manner of speaking, to mention a situational factor. During the Weimar Republic, the Evangelical Church had lost the government support to which it had been historically accustomed. The dilution of its strong links with both the State and the people had led to a type of identity crisis. At worst it seemed that the concept of the Evangelical Church's survival as a free institution was in some danger.

Now Hitler had appeared, promising them a strong Church, fully supported by the State and guardian of the moral principles of his new, pure Germany. Many had already seen Hitler's ideas as fully acceptable; now there was this added attraction. Hermann Grüner, spokesman for the German Christians accordingly declared: 'The time is fulfilled for the German people in Hitler. It is because of Hitler that Christ has become effective among us. National Socialism is positive Christianity in action.'[12]

However, although his view was endorsed by many Protestant leaders, Pastor Martin Niemöller, of the Church of Jesus Christ at Dahlem, the fashionable suburb of Berlin, could not concur. In the First World War, Niemöller, one of Germany's most successful U-boat captains had been awarded the Iron Cross, First Class. No-one could doubt, therefore, his loyalty to Germany and after the War he had become politically active. He had joined the Freikorps and, at the beginning, had found the Nazi views on race and nationality perfectly acceptable. Nevertheless, he was to become a notable figure in the opposition to Hitler. A fuller profile of Niemöller is provided in Chapter Six ('Heroic Virtue').

The decision to appoint Ludwig Müller as Reich Bishop had led to Pastor Niemöller's disenchantment but it was really intensified by the application of the Aryan Paragraph to the clergy. So there now arose an underground movement called the 'Pastors' Emergency League', with Niemöller as its leader. By November 1933 it had about sixty members. Though its pastors objected not to anti-Semitism as such but to the State's appropriation of the right to dismiss pastors on racial

---

12. B Alex, *Dietrich Bonhoeffer*. Copenhagen, 1996, pp. 20-21.

grounds, it quickly came to Hitler's notice: at a meeting in January 1934, Niemöller was warned by Hitler himself to 'leave concern for the Third Reich to me and look after the Church.'[13]

His warning went unheeded and the Emergency League became the Confessing Church. By then it comprised a network of over 5,000, possibly 7,000, pastors. They affirmed that the church of Christ was neither an extension of a secular authority nor of a political ideology. Rather than hate and divisiveness as propagated by the German Christians, its primary concern was to radiate charity and unity.

Six months after the formation of the Pastors' Emergency League, Niemöller organised a conference at the Ruhr village of Barmen. Attended by 140 delegates from Protestant churches throughout Germany, from it emanated the Barmen Declaration, 1934. Perhaps the best method of conveying the substance of the Declaration is to set out a list of its 'repudiations'; [14]

1. We repudiate the false teaching that the church can and must recognise yet other happenings and powers, images and truths as divine revelation alongside this one Word of God as a source of her preaching.
2. We repudiate the false teaching that there are areas in our life in which we belong not to Jesus Christ but another lord.
3. We repudiate the false teaching that the church can turn over the form of her message and ordinances at will or according to some dominant ideological and political convictions.
4. We repudiate the false teaching that the church can and may, apart from this ministry, set up special leaders (Führer) equipped with powers to rule.
5. We repudiate the false teaching that the state can and should expand beyond its special responsibility to become the single and total order of human life, and also thereby fulfil the commission of the church.
6. We repudiate the false teaching that the church can and should expand beyond its special responsibility to take on the characteristics, functions and dignities of the state, and thereby become itself an

---

13. P Matheson, *The Third Reich And The Christian Churches*. Edinburgh, p. 43; also in M Burleigh, op. cit., pp. 206-7.
14. J F Harrington, op. cit., pp. 471-2.

organ of the state.

7. We repudiate the false teaching that the church, in human self-esteem can put the word or work of the Lord in the service of some wishes, purposes and plans or other, chosen according to desire.

Niemöller's key colleague in the establishment of the Confessing Church was Dietrich Bonhoeffer. He was a young theologian and a pastor of significant promise who was also keenly interested in the ecumenical movement. As we shall see in Chapter Six Bonhoeffer's induction into resistance through the Confessing Church led him to more direct action to subvert the regime. Shortly before the end of the war he was to pay for this with his life at Flossenbürg concentration camp, so his signature to the Barmen Declaration did more than jeopardise his entire career; it led ultimately to his death. Another important point to bring out in introducing Bonhoeffer is that he was also involved in the most direct way in attempting to save Jews.

After the Declaration, its signatories and their countrywide supporters were systematically persecuted by the Nazis. By 1939, the Nazis had succeeded in ridding themselves of these dissenters, for the Confessing Church was dissolved. By then the majority of its pastors were either imprisoned or drafted into the Army. Even so, although its active opposition within Germany was effectively at an end, some of its members continued their fight though in exile. Some 700 of its members were arrested. Its theological mentor, Karl Barth, professor of theology at Bonn University, who had opposed Nazism tirelessly had, in 1935, to flee to a life of exile in Basle, Switzerland.

It is hoped that this outline will help to counter the misconceptions about Germany's Protestants in the Nazi era. While it is true that many of its adherents, pastors and congregations entered its churches wearing demi-pagan uniforms and bearing NSDAP banners, there were others who opposed Nazism root and branch and paid for this with imprisonment and sometimes death.

We now turn to the relationship between the Catholic Church and the State at the time of Hitler's accession. At the end of Chapter Two we saw examples of the hostility towards the regime expressed by both the Vatican and the German bishops. So it may seem astounding that a Concordat with the new German government was signed by the Holy See on 20 July 1933 and ratified on 10 September. Possibly the word 'Concordat' generates misunderstanding in this context, carrying as it does undertones of amity, when it was really grounded in the suspicion and mistrust that each party to the agreement harboured for the other.

For a most useful explanation on this point we can turn to an esteemed Catholic writer of the period, Monsignor Ronald Knox. In his 1940 pamphlet he explained that the Concordat 'was interpreted in the world at large as expressing a measure of agreement between the ecclesiastical and the civil authorities which never in fact existed.'[15] He drew attention to the popular misconception that a concordat reflects the especially friendly terms subsisting between 'Rome' and the country concerned whereas the opposite is the case – if a country was on 'ideally good terms' with Rome a concordat would be superfluous. The existence of the document implies that to some degree or other, the parties are distrustful of each other's intentions. It is an attempt to set out rules in a difficult situation by binding each party, on paper at least, to 'a minimum of good behaviour'. Ronald Knox then adds: 'Nothing could be more absurd than to represent the transaction as if it meant that the New Germany and the Vatican were working hand in glove.'

Klaus Scholder, Protestant historian, produced a significant two-volume history on *The Churches and the Third Reich* (1977, 1985). In volume two he suggests that Hitler's support for the German Christians, in the summer of 1933, as well as a uniform Protestant Reich Church, was to provide a counterbalance to the Catholicism 'which he feared.'[16] And it is not difficult to perceive some of the mainsprings of that fear. Firstly, the Catholic Church was powerful, well organised and exercised significant international influence. Secondly, one third of the people in the German homeland were Catholic and since, no doubt, he already had the annexation of Catholic Austria on his agenda, the Catholics would become once more the majority confession in his new Greater German Reich. Obviously there would

15. R Knox, *Nazi and Nazarene*. Macmillan War Pamphlets No. 5. London, 1940, pp. 9ff.
16. K Scholder, *The Churches and the Third Reich*, Vol II 1934. London, 1988, p. 10.

be a heavy price to pay for their alienation.

In his first volume, Scholder also points out that between 1930 and 1933 the opposition to Hitler by Catholics faithful to the Church ranked, not least for Hitler himself, as one of the most constant factors in German domestic politics.[17] In this regard it is worth adding the comments of the historian Burleigh who draws attention to the fact that there was no Catholic equivalent to the Nazi-Protestant German Christian movement which had nearly six hundred thousand members and in whose creed anti-semitism played a crucial part.[18] He adds that the Catholic intelligentsia emerge favourably from any comparison with their Protestant counterparts. An analysis of Robert A Kreig's work on *Catholic Theologians in Nazi Germany* provides numerous examples of opponents of the regime and few supporters[19] (as an aside here: Kreig relates that when the Gestapo destroyed Catholic printing presses, Catholics demonstrated their ecclesial loyalty by participating in religious ceremonies – in Aachen alone, eight hundred thousand people took part in a pilgrimage) whereas Robert P Ericksen's study *Theologians under Hitler* discloses the support for Nazism among those of the Lutheran confession.[20] In Chapter Six we shall return to Catholic theologians of the period when we examine the life of Max Metzger who was executed by the Nazis in 1944.

From Hitler's standpoint we can summarise the attraction of the Concordat as follows: it might mitigate the existing opposition from Catholics within Germany; by removing clerics from its leadership it might fatally weaken the Centre Party (for under the terms of the Concordat the Church would play no further part in German politics); trade agreements had been concluded with Russia in May 1933 and Britain, France and Italy were about to enter into a Four Power Pact with Germany – so this international recognition, already well in hand, would be enhanced by the Concordat; and, if the negotiations collapsed, he could always point to the Concordat as the brain-child of his Deputy Chancellor, von Papen.

---

17. Ibid., Vol. One 1918-1934. London, 1987, p. 146.
18. M Burleigh, op. cit., p. 176.
19. R A Kreig, *Catholic Theologians in Nazi Germany*. New York and London, 2004, p. 155.
20. R P Ericksen, *Theologians under Hitler*. New Haven, 1985.

This last point has an added importance in this volume for it seems never to have entered into the public consciousness that the initiative for the Concordat stemmed from the Nazi government and not the Catholic Church.

A number of historians have attacked the Catholic Church firstly for allegedly persuading the Centre Party to vote for the Enabling Act and then, supposedly, pressuring the Party to dissolve itself once the Church had, through the Concordat, secured its own interests. Thankfully, as Burleigh points out,[21] we have to be indebted to the scholarship of Rudolf Morsey and Konrad Repgen for the truth of the matter, which is that no 'deals' of this nature were ever done. What their research demonstrates, moreover, is that when the Vatican responded to von Papen's offer of a concordat there was no intention either to desert the Centre Party or to agree to curtail all clerical participation in politics. We shall return to this point later in this chapter. Another aside worth the mention is Giovanni Sale's finding that at precisely this point in time the Vatican, not for the first or last time, took the opportunity of condemning the persecution of the Jews.[22]

Writing in 1980, O'Carroll believed that the Concordat with Nazi Germany was the most controversial event in Cardinal Pacelli's years as Secretary of State.[23] Then he added that the debate had never had much reference to fact. He doubted whether even the most trenchant critics had any idea of the context or even the content of the treaty. Let us briefly consider both of these factors.

Concordats were hardly new to the Church's diplomatic schema. The first concordat, granted by Urban II to Roger of Sicily, was concluded at Worms in 1122. According to the compiler of the textual collection, the number concluded up to 1954 was 148. Prior to the advent of the Nazis, concordats had been negotiated with Bavaria (1925), Prussia (1929) and Baden (1932). Now a new government had appeared which had taken total control of the whole country. So these regional agreements and, indeed, the Weimar Constitution itself, were due for examination anyway.

Critics of the Catholic Church have said that it abandoned the

---

21. M Burleigh, op. cit., p. 172.
22. G Sale, *Hitler, la Santa Sede e gli Ebrei*. Milan, 2003, p. 107
23. M O'Carroll CSSp, *Pius XII – Greatness Dishonoured*. Dublin, 1980, p. 36.

Centre Party for the illusion of protection by legal guarantee. This is another charge which will not withstand scrutiny. Ludwig Kaas, a close friend of Eugenio Pacelli and a member of the Reichstag, had been the leader of the Centre Party since 1928. He was also one of Europe's last priest politicians. As Nuncio, the then Archbishop Pacelli had been largely credited with the successful negotiations for the concordat with Protestant Prussia (1929). In turn, he said: 'The Concordat which has been concluded will remain as a perpetual monument raised to the glory of the Centre Party'. In 1933 it was Kaas who ensured that 72 Centre deputies voted for the Enabling Act. It has been suggested that his action was compounded of fear of what the Nazis might do on the one hand and vague assurances concerning religion on the other.[24] But was Kaas as naive and pliable as all that? Earlier, as Archbishop Pacelli had affirmed, Kaas had been highly visible in the concordat negotiations with Prussia – not merely a Protestant power but *the* Protestant power. And Prussia had been led to accept negotiated consensus with the heirs of the Counter-Reformation. Given their past record it may at least be reasonable to suggest that both Kaas and former Nuncio Pacelli might have believed they could repeat their success with Prussia when negotiating with the national government.

And were Hitler's assurances concerning religion as vague as all that? Here was a leader, at the peak of his popularity, pontificating in a major speech about 'the political and moral cleansing of our national life' and rhapsodising about his government's objective of 'creating and securing the conditions for a really deep and inner religious life.' He believed Christianity to be 'the unshakeable foundation of the moral and ethical life of our people.' Of course, with all the acuity that hindsight provides some would claim that Hitler should have been seen for what he was.

As we shall see shortly, Eugenio Pacelli, by now Vatican Secretary of State, was not without his doubts. As for the German bishops, while there were some more ready to trust Hitler than others, they were as a collective hardly indifferent judges of men and their motivations. What they did say at this stage is that they were sufficiently impressed by his proclamations to hope that their previous general warnings and

24. On this issue see M Burleigh, op. cit., p. 172.

prohibitions need no longer be considered necessary but they would *not* revoke their previous judgements on certain religious and ethical errors.[25] If they had been hoodwinked, of course, they would hardly have been alone in this at the time.

Some observers refer to the Catholic Church in the period of the demise of the Centre Party as being reprehensible and the use of such terms as 'abandonment' and 'shoddy deal' suggests their objective is to keep their prejudices warm rather than to serve scholarship. Moreover they refuse to acknowledge that in the move to the one-party state (NSDAP), *all* other political parties disappeared. In February 1933 the Communists were driven into hiding. On 22 June the Social Democrats disappeared. A few days later, the conservative-nationalist DNVP was gone. The first week of July saw the death of the Bavarian Catholic Party and the right-wing DVP. So it is simply unrealistic to suggest that the Centre Party could have remained in being. Ironically, had it done so then the description of the Concordat as a 'shoddy deal' would have been more accurate.

Nor is it the case that the Vatican was an accomplice to the departure of the Centre Party. In the early days of July the Centre Party abolished itself and thanks to the researches of Konrad Repgen it is now clear that the first that Secretary of State Pacelli knew of this was when he read of it in the newspapers. It is also clear that he disapproved of the development. A moment's thought will make plain that he would scarcely have wished for its decease, important element as it might have been in future negotiations with the German government.

Now we must consider why the Catholic Church responded positively to the offer of a concordat. The overriding responsibility of the Pope and the Church is to bring souls to God. As father and protector of the faithful the Pope must constantly strive for a situation where, grounded in the laws of God and the Church, they are able to worship peacefully in accordance with their consciences. But protecting the faithful means more than providing priests and places of worship. It entails the provision of schools, youth groups, medical care, newspapers, trade unions, monasteries, convents, social facilities and all other aspects of Catholic culture. This was certainly the case in the Germany of the time where Catholic worship and culture

25. Ibid., see p. 172 on this also.

were imperilled and where the need for a concordat to provide a permanent, legal and hence defensible basis for Church-State relations was clearly evident.

There were at least grounds for hoping that agreement could be reached with a regime which apparently shared the Papacy's antagonism towards Communism, materialism and the degenerate aspects of Weimar culture. Even so, Repgen's researches disclose that within the Vatican there were different shades of opinion on the possible response to von Papen's initiative. Repgen draws on a report by Robert Leiber SJ to the Austrian ambassador to the Vatican. Leiber makes clear the Austrian government's concern about the prospect of a concordat with a country which was energetically undermining its (i.e. Austria's) stability. He also outlines how one group in the Vatican was decidedly against any agreement which might provide prestige for a regime hostile to Catholicism. German Catholics might well be demoralised by such negotiations.

Another group believed that though Nazi ideology was repellent, the Vatican had a duty to protect Catholicism by whatever legal safeguards it could negotiate. A third group felt that though the Church should in no way approve of Nazism it should adopt a pragmatic stance and negotiate as many benefits as possible. The Vatican felt that if the Nazis infringed the terms of the agreement, as it expected, then it could formally revoke the agreement which could then only harm the prestige of the regime.

As mentioned earlier, the three existing German concordats appeared to be superseded so to do nothing was not an option. From Berlin, Nuncio Orsenigo had reported that some aspects of Nazi ideology were already appealing to Catholic youth which might go the way of its Protestant peers. He also drew attention to a more general threat – if a Protestant Reich Church under a single Reich bishop took shape and resulted in a consolidated mass of forty million Protestants then the Catholics would become a powerless minority. Would this raise the spectre of another Kulturkampf? The dilemma of the Holy See at this time was described by Pope Pius XI speaking in 1937:

> When, in 1933, we consented, Venerable Brethren, to open negotiations for a Concordat, which the Reich government proposed ... we were prompted by the desire, as it behoved us, to secure for Germany the

> freedom of the Church's beneficent mission, and the salvation of souls in her care. . . . Hence, *despite many and grave misgivings* [This writer's emphasis], we then decided not to withhold our consent, for we wished to spare the faithful in Germany, as far as was humanly possible, the trials and difficulties they would have had to face . . . had the negotiations fallen through.[26]

Secretary of State Pacelli similarly showed he was under no illusion about the other party to the Concordat negotiations. When Sir Ivone Kirkpatrick expressed the hope that Hitler might now be less hungry for power, Pacelli replied: 'I am afraid not, we shall see that with every year power will make him more extreme and difficult to deal with.'

The idea projected by critical historians and journalists of a Vatican conscious only of its own interests and wheedling away to have these agreed in writing simply does not accord with the facts. Cardinal Michael Faulhaber of Munich (about whom the more one learns the more one likes) expressed the caution and concern of German bishops having to deal with the Nazis when he said: 'With the Concordat we are hanged, without the Concordat we are hanged, drawn and quartered.'

We come finally to the actual provisions of the Concordat. An examination of the document itself makes the purpose of the negotiations abundantly clear. Had the Church's critics examined it, their barbs would never have been slung for it dispenses entirely with the notion that National Socialism was in some way favoured by the Church. Set out below is a summary of each of the agreement's 34 Articles. In most cases these have been reduced to a single sentence but a scrutiny of the document itself will affirm that each Article's intent has been faithfully recorded.

Article:

1. The German Reich guarantees freedom of the profession and public practice of the Catholic religion.

2. The Concordats concluded with Bavaria, Prussia and Baden remain in force and the rights and privileges recognised therein are secured

---

26. *Mit brennender Sorge*. Encyclical given at the Vatican on Passion Sunday, 14 March, 1937. Vatican City, para. 3.

unchanged within the territories of the States concerned.

3. In order to foster good relations between the Holy See and the German Reich, an Apostolic Nuncio will reside in the capital of the German Reich and an Ambassador of the German Reich at the Holy See, as heretofore.

4. In its relations and correspondence with the bishops, clergy and other members of the Catholic Church in Germany, the Holy See enjoys full freedom.

5. In the exercise of their spiritual activities the clergy enjoy the protection of the State in the same way as State officials.

6. Clerics and Religious are freed from any obligation to undertake official duties and such obligations as, according to the provision of Canon Law, are incompatible with the clerical or religious state.

7. The acceptance of an appointment or office in the State, or in any publicly constituted corporation dependent on the State, requires, in the case of clergy, the *nihil obstat* of the Diocesan Ordinary of the individual concerned, as well as that of the Ordinary of the place in which the publicly constituted corporation is situated.

8. The official income of the clergy is immune from distraint to the same extent as is the official salary of officials of the Reich and State.

9. The clergy may not be required by judicial or other officials to give information concerning matters which have been entrusted to them while exercising the care of souls, and which therefore come within the obligation of pastoral secrecy.

10. The wearing of clerical dress or of a religious habit on the part of lay folk, or of clerics and religious who have been forbidden to wear them by a final and valid injunction made by the competent ecclesiastical authority and officially communicated to the State authority, is liable to the same penalty on the part of the State as the misuse of military uniform.

11. The present organisation and demarcation of dioceses of the Catholic Church in the German Reich remains in force.

12. Without prejudice to the provisions of Article 11, ecclesiastical offices may be freely constituted and changed, unless the expenditure of State funds is involved.

13. Catholic parishes, parish and diocesan societies, Episcopal sees,

bishoprics and chapters, religious Orders and Congregations, as well as institutions, foundations and property which are under the administration of ecclesiastical authority shall retain or acquire respectively legal competence in the civil domain according to the general prescriptions of civil law.

14. As a matter of principle the Church retains the right to appoint freely to all Church offices and benefices without the co-operation of the State or of civil communities, in so far as other provisions have not been made in previous Concordats mentioned in Article 2. . . . Furthermore, there is accord on the following points:

1. Catholic clerics who hold an ecclesiastical office in Germany or who exercise pastoral or educational functions must:
   a. Be German citizens.
   b. Have matriculated from a German secondary school.
   c. Have studied philosophy and theology for at least three years at a German State University, a German ecclesiastical college or a papal college in Rome.

15. Religious Orders and Congregations are not subject to any special restrictions on the part of the State, either as regards their foundation, the erection of their various establishments, their number, selection of members, pastoral activity, education, care of the sick and charitable work, or as regards the management of their affairs or the administration of their property.

16. Before bishops take possession of their dioceses they are to take an oath of fealty either to the Reich Representative of the State concerned, or to the President of the Reich.

17. The property and other rights of public corporations, institutions, foundations and associations of the Catholic Church regarding their vested interests, are guaranteed according to the common law of the land.

18. Should it become necessary to abrogate the performance of obligations undertaken by the State towards the Church, whether based on law, agreement or special charter, the Holy See and the Reich will elaborate in amicable agreement the principles according to which the abrogation is to be carried out. Legitimate traditional rights are to be considered as titles in law.

19. Catholic Theological Faculties in State Universities are to be maintained.

20. Where other agreements do not exist, the Church has the right to establish theological and philosophical colleges for the training of its clergy, which institutions are to be wholly dependent on the ecclesiastical authorities if no State subsidies are sought.

21. Catholic religious instruction in elementary, senior, secondary and vocational schools constitutes a regular portion of the curriculum, and is to be taught in accordance with the principles of the Catholic Church.

22. With regard to the appointment of Catholic religious instructors, agreement will be arrived at as a result of mutual consultations on the part of the Bishop and the Government of the State concerned.

23. The retention of Catholic denominational schools and the establishment of new ones is guaranteed.

24. In all Catholic elementary schools only such teachers are to be employed as are members of the Catholic Church, and who guarantee to fulfil the special requirements of a Catholic school.

25. Religious Orders and Congregations are entitled to establish and conduct private schools, subject to the general laws and ordinances governing education.

26. With certain reservations . . . the ecclesiastical marriage ceremony should precede the civil ceremony.

27. The Church will accord provision to the German army for the spiritual guidance of its Catholic officers, personnel and other officials, as well as for the families of the same.

28. In hospitals, prisons and similar public institutions the Church is to retain the right of visitation and of holding divine service, subject to the rules of the said institutions.

29. Catholic members of a non-German minority living within the Reich, in matters concerning the use of their mother tongue in church services etc. to be accorded no less favourable treatment than individuals of German origin and speech living in foreign states.

30. On Sundays and Holy Days, special prayers, conforming to the liturgy, will be offered during the principal Mass for the welfare of the German Reich and its people in all episcopal, parish and conventual churches and chapels of the German Reich.

31. Those Catholic organisations and societies which pursue exclusively charitable, cultural or religious ends and, as such, are placed under the ecclesiastical authorities, will be protected in their institutions and activities.

32. . . .The Holy See will prescribe regulations for the exclusion of clergy and members of religious Orders from membership of political parties, and from engaging in work on their behalf (in view of the guarantee provided in this Concordat to safeguard the rights and privileges of the Roman Catholic Church).

33. All matters relating to clerical persons or ecclesiastical affairs . . . will be regulated for the ecclesiastical sphere according to current Canon Law.

34. This Concordat shall be ratified as soon as possible. It will be in force from the date of exchange of certificates of ratification.

The originals were signed in the Vatican City on 20 July 1933 by Eugenio, Cardinal Pacelli and Franz von Papen as plenipotentiaries. Ratification took place on 10 September 1933.

By the time the 'co-ordination' process had been carried through, all the major institutions of the German nation had been brought under Nazi control – the armed forces, the judiciary, the universities, the trade unions and a very large part of the Evangelical Church. Even the nation's industry and commerce had learned to dance to Hitler's tune. Yet here in outline, the contents of the Concordat make plainly visible the struggle of the Catholic Church to maintain its independence in spiritual and pastoral matters. What a pity the Church has been maligned rather than respected for this. There is, of course, the matter of the oath of fealty (Article 16) which we will address in the following chapter.

Chapter Four

THE CATHOLIC CHURCH AND HITLER'S GERMANY

1934-39: Persecution Intensifies

Critics of the Catholic Church and its Concordat with the Nazis have pointed particularly to Article 16. This required its bishops, before taking possession of their dioceses, to take an oath of fealty to the State concerned or the President of the Reich. For a commonsense assessment of this Article we can again turn to Ronald Knox. He points out that in agreeing to this, Pope Pius obviously did not intend 'anything more than a recognition of the German government as the constituted government of the country.'[1] Catholic bishops might thus swear loyalty to it much the same as Anglican bishops swear loyalty to the monarch. They do not intend, by doing so, to accept every step, without protest, the government might make.

Article 32 of the Concordat requires the Church to restrain its clergy from party political activities. This, too, has been pressed into service by the Church's opponents. Here Knox, writing in 1940 asks whether this means that bishops and clergy would be bound to silence in the face of encouragement by the State of a pagan philosophy; of scurrilous attacks on religious in Party newspapers; and against invasion of the rights guaranteed by the Concordat. He declares that 'no reasonable political theory would admit such a conclusion.'[2] In

---

1. R Knox, *Nazi and Nazarene*. Macmillan War Pamphlets, No. 5. London, 1940, pp. 12-13.
2. Ibid., p. 13.

fact, since Article 32 states that the Church's undertaking to avoid politics is made because of the Concordat's guarantee to safeguard the rights and privileges of the Roman Catholic Church,[3] then the opposite conclusion is the reasonable one. Of course, Knox adds, it is unfortunate that the Nazi government construes all criticism of it and its measures as 'political activity'. So everything must be accepted in silence. Thus it becomes clear that the parties to the agreement are not using terms in the same sense. Here the Nazis are at fault for coining a new language to promote their ideology.

When the Concordat was concluded. Cardinal Pacelli confided to Sir Ivone Kirkpatrick, a Catholic official at the British Embassy in Rome, that the choice had been between a treaty promising greater concessions than anything hitherto and the virtual elimination of the Church in Germany. In conversation with French diplomat François Charles-Roux, the Cardinal added that without the Concordat the Church would have had no basis for protest against the regime's actions. He demonstrated he had no illusions about the Nazis when he said finally to Kirkpatrick: 'They will scarcely break all the Articles at the same time.'

It was not long before the Nazi government showed its complete lack of integrity. At the very same Cabinet meeting which approved the Concordat, it introduced the Law for the Prevention of Hereditarily Diseased Progeny. This provided for eugenic sterilisation policies. These were completely contradictory to fundamental Catholic belief as set out, only three years earlier, in the encyclical *Casti Connubii*. The encyclical had been devised as a result of the alarming spread of eugenic sterilisation in a number of US States. The Nazi law extended to manic depressives, cripples, epileptics, and those with hereditary forms of blindness. Decisions to sterilise were to be made locally and appeals could be lodged only with special 'eugenic courts'.[4] Appalling enough in itself, this legislation would prove to be the precursor of the euthanasia programme and the establishment of its T4 and KdF agencies which would become fully operational in the war years in furtherance of Hitler's wish to eliminate all 'useless eaters'. As we shall

---

3. Burns Oates, *The Persecution of the Catholic Church in the Third Reich*. London, 1940, Appendix 1, p. 521.
4. M O'Carroll CSSp, *Pius XII – Greatness Dishonoured*. Dublin, 1980, p. 39.

see in Chapters Five and Six the name of Bishop von Galen will always be venerated for his courageous and implacable hostility to this outrage. As Burleigh points out, even *before* the Second World War this law resulted in 350,000 people being eugenically sterilised and at a time when the hereditary nature of their conditions was not scientifically proven.[5] As early as 1933 *L'Osservatore Romano* had inveighed against governments degenerating into cattle breeding laboratories. Burleigh also draws attention to the fact that when two Catholic academics publicly supported the sterilisation law, Secretary of State Pacelli instituted canonical proceedings against them, and suspended them from teaching seminarians.

The Catholic bishops, through their representatives Berning and Gröber, secured agreement from the Minister of the Interior that they could continue to make their views on sterilisation known. They also obtained an exemption for Catholic doctors to prevent them being legally compelled to initiate sterilisations. Nurses from religious Orders and Catholic clinical sisters were forbidden by the Church to take any part whatsoever in sterilisations. Much to the annoyance of the regime, Catholic diocesan newspapers ensured that the programme stayed within public view through their routine publication of the Catholic standpoint and the judgements of the Hereditary Health Courts.[6]

The duplicitous nature of Hitler's approach to the Concordat was revealed by the Nazi press itself, which declared that the agreement could be seen as a victory for the Nazis and evidence of the Holy See's capitulation to Germany. Pope Pius XI spoke of his anxiety for the future to a great pilgrimage of German youth: 'We are by temperament and by choice optimist – the future is in the hands of God; We must then hope, but our hope cannot hide the danger from us.' There now began to spread the ideology that 'purity of blood' must be affirmed as the basis for German racial superiority. Nothing was of any real good to German humanity that was not itself wholly German. From this concept, the Nazis distilled the justification for the purge of all inhabitants of 'mixed' blood, the sterilisation law

5. M Burleigh, *Sacred Causes*. London, 2006, pp. 179-80.
6. Ibid., p.180

itself, and open advocacy of the restoration of German paganism as the national religion. The attempt to 'Germanise' Protestantism and widespread attacks on the Hebrew elements of Christianity were important ingredients in the brew.[7]

These developments drew the Pope in his Christmas Allocution of December 1934 to speak of the folly of recent attempts to make Law and Justice depend on particular types of national or racist law. Christian Law was a superhuman creation but what the world could now behold was the new paganism being developed. At this point attacks on the Catholic Church began in earnest. Catholic trades unions were absorbed into Nazi unions. On all manner of pretexts, there were instances of Catholic priests being arrested and maltreated. An attempt was made on the life of the Archbishop of Munich, Catholic societies were broken up, magazines suppressed and Catholic Action was declared to be incompatible with National Socialism. Catholics came under great pressure to surrender their schools and, in Bavaria, the Catholic training colleges were suppressed.

We have already seen that, in Catholic circles at least, there had been longstanding misgivings about the Nazi movement. Now disquiet in the general population became apparent. For Hitler, the 'honeymoon' period appeared to be over. People began to ask themselves whether this was the leader they had hoped for. Obviously, the moves against religion were worrying enough but equal dangers to the new government's acceptability were now coming from the movement itself particularly because of the antics and excesses of the SA 'Brownshirts'. Many Germans were horrified at their violence, drunkenness and homosexual behaviour. It seemed that in endorsing a leader who had promised to bring order out of the post-Versailles chaos they had imported into their lives an organisation equally menacing and frightful.

Forewarned by Goebbels, Göring and other Party leaders, Hitler began to realise the futility of dealing with 'external' opposition without dealing with the miscreants within his own ranks. He had been furious, for example, when Franz von Papen, the Catholic Deputy Chancellor and Germany's signatory to the Concordat, had,

7. P Hughes, *Pius XI*. London, 1937, p. 299.

in June 1934, given a public speech at Marburg University which criticised Nazi methods and called for a return to freedom. Papen had inveighed against the attacks on free speech and condemned the implementation of *Gleichschaltung*.

But the Führer's worst anger was reserved for Ernst Röhm, leader of the SA. An old comrade since the birth of the NSDAP it has been said that he, more than anyone, was responsible for Hitler's rise to power. Yet he had never felt subservient to Hitler and, when in his cups, was given to saying so. Moreover, the men he led were not happy. Jobless ex-soldiers in the main, they had pinned their hopes on a just reward for their efforts. Now they were feeling overlooked and in danger of being replaced in the pecking order by the 'March Violets' who had scrambled for places in the Party in 1933 when it was clear which way the wind was blowing. So they pined for a 'second revolution' in which the old power groups – aristocrats, landowners, industrialists and liberal bourgeoisie, would be swept away and the SA would claim its inheritance.

These hopes were hardly fanciful. Röhm's organisation, 70,000 strong in 1931, had by then grown to over 4,000,000. So the German Army, limited by the Versailles Treaty to 100,000 was dwarfed by the SA and when Röhm claimed that it was the true army of the new Nazi Germany, there was panic among the generals. There had been international protests about the brutal behaviour of the SA, which was more than Hitler wanted, and now it seemed that a putsch by Röhm's organisation was perfectly possible. So, aided and abetted by his henchmen – Göring, Himmler, Heydrich, Lutze, Blomberg and others – Hitler had lists prepared of those who should be eliminated in order to protect the regime. Ironically, the compilation included Röhm's own data on SA officers due for promotion.[8] At dawn on 30 June 1934, Hitler flew to Munich to supervise personally what became known as 'Die Nacht der langen Messer' ('Night of the Long Knives'). After 48 hours of bloodletting, all the leaders of the SA, including Röhm himself, had been murdered.

Röhm had formed an alliance with Gregor Strasser, another notable from the early days of the Party and one who claimed its ideological leadership. The pair had been anxious for the second revolution in

8. J Taylor and W Shaw, *Dictionary of The Third Reich*. London, 1997, p. 240.

which ultimate power would be seized for the workers – they were determined that the 'socialism' of 'National Socialism' would mean what it denoted. Strasser, like Röhm, was liquidated but whereas Röhm was shot, after refusing to commit suicide, Strasser's death was more protracted. With the support of the Army and of industrialists such as Krupp and Thyssen, Hitler had carried out an operation latterly regarded as the single most important element in his consolidation of personal power. Subsequently, on Hindenburg's death in the summer of that year, Hitler stepped into his role, with the titles of Führer and Reich Chancellor, adroitly suggesting that the title 'Reichpresident' should die with Hindenburg.

He had promised to rearm the Army and within its expansion pride of place was given to the SS (*Schutzstaffel*), which had carried out the 'Röhm Purge'. Originally the bodyguard of Hitler, the SS was transformed into a state within a state with Heinrich Himmler at its head and Reinhard Heydrich as his deputy. Within its organisation structure were the Waffen SS, which at its zenith numbered 40 divisions and almost 1 million men, the Secret State Police (or 'Gestapo') and the Totenkopfverbände (Death's head units) concentration camp guards. In July 1934, the SS was formerly separated from the SA and it went on to become the core agency for sanctioned murder in Germany and Occupied Europe.

From this point on, democracy was fully and finally dead. All Germany's soldiers were required to take a personal oath of unconditional obedience not to the State but to Hitler himself. Many ordinary Germans had been sickened by the excesses of the SA and approved of the action Hitler had taken. Those with eyes to see, however, realised their country was now in the grip of a dictator. His 'blood purge' was also a time of disposing of certain leading lay Catholics who had emerged as influential opponents of Nazism. These included Erich Klausener, the general secretary of Catholic Action, who was shot dead on the orders of Heydrich for his part in the drafting of von Papen's Marburg speech. Adalbert Probst, director of the Catholic Youth Sports Association, was also murdered. Fritz Gerlich, a convert to Catholicism and a journalist who had published repeated attacks on the Nazis was, sometime during the Night of the Long Knives, taken to Dachau from Stadelheim Prison and likewise liquidated. The purge was not only to attend to the SA situation, it was an opportunity to settle old scores. The Bishop of Berlin protested against the Nazi claims that Erich Klausener had committed suicide. He interred his ashes with formal religious ceremony and ordered that Klausener's obituary be read out at every church in the diocese. Anxious to defend Klausener, he wrote letters of protest to Hitler. These proved fruitless.[9]

Alfred Rosenberg, designated as the Party's philosopher and educational adviser to the Führer, had set out the new gospel of race and blood and the duty of the individual's total subjection to the state in his book *Myth of the Twentieth Century*. Like many others, Hitler had no great opinion of it, dismissing it as 'stuff nobody can understand'.[10] It is worth noting here, however, that it was placed on the Vatican's Index of prohibited books and a detailed statement on the errors it contained was promulgated. On Whit Sunday 1934, Pope Pius canonised the German Franciscan, Conrad of Parzham, and spoke of the situation in Germany. He indicated that in contrast to the great German then being honoured, ideas and practices that were not Christian, nor even human, were becoming established together with an exaltation of race which could only produce a monstrous pride, the very antithesis of the Christian spirit, and even of the spirit of humanity itself.[11]

Many examples give an indication of how persecution of the Church was developing during this period. Members of the Catholic youth groups were harassed by the Nazis to prevent them displaying their emblems and pennants; in February 1936 leaders of the Catholic Young Men's Association were charged with treasonable involvement with Communists; Catholic newspapers and journals were either closed or changed beyond recognition; diocesan newspapers were curtailed 'because of paper shortages'. By 1935, none of the four hundred Catholic daily newspapers still existed, and between January 1934 and October 1939 the number of Catholic weeklies and periodicals fell from 435 to 124 either through suppression or withdrawal of newsprint (which was in abundant supply for Nazi publications).

In addition, the Nazi press frequently insulted Catholics and their

9. M Burleigh, op. cit. London, 2006, p. 177.
10. Ibid., p. 96.
11. P Hughes, op. cit., p. 300.

organisations. It was claimed that Secretary of State Pacelli was in league with the Bolsheviks. The SS media carried similar attacks on the Pope, calling him among other things, the 'Chief Rabbi of all Christians'. In spite of the guarantees of the Concordat with respect to freedom of religious education, the Nazis attacked church schools because they were 'disruptive of national unity'. The jobs of parents working for national and local government were threatened so as to force them to vote for the transfer of Catholic schools to the non-denominational 'community' sector. Continuous efforts were made to laicise religious instruction and to reduce the time devoted to the subject. The flow of qualified instructors was curtailed due to the closure of all religious teacher training colleges. The regime set about reallocating teaching posts in theology to such growing fields as 'racial science'. Finally, Nazi racial dogma was subtly insinuated into a wide range of educational subjects. Burleigh reports, for example, that the Nazification of mathematics would be furthered by asking children to calculate how many houses could be built for 'healthy national comrades' if the 'unhealthy' provision of 'luxury' lunatic asylums were terminated.[12] He also draws attention to the fact that between September 1933 and March 1937 Secretary of State Pacelli signed over 70 protests against Nazi violations of the Concordat.

The Persecution of the Catholic Church in The Third Reich, published in 1940 by Burns Oates is no polemic. It is a translation from the German of 'Facts and Documents' which provide exhaustive and orderly presentation of what the Church and its faithful had to endure. The picture of how the Church's hierarchy reacted to this oppression has often been painted, by secular historians especially, in unattractive colours. By letting the facts speak for themselves the publishers succeed in rebutting the accusations that all Catholics in authority, from the Vatican down, were dilatory, compliant even, in the face of this oppression. If we consider just a small selection from what the German bishops had to say at that time it becomes clear how inaccurate and unjust such charges are. The extracts below are taken from the book:[13]

---

12. M Burleigh, op. cit. p. 183.
13. Burns Oates: op. cit., pp. 15-35.

i) In the summer of 1934, at a pilgrimage to Dietrichswalde, Bishop Kaller of Ermland declared with sorrow that 'in the last year or two' movements and currents of opinion had appeared and strengthened which were directed against the fundamental truths of the Catholic Church and aimed at setting up a new religion – a German national church founded on the myth of blood and race.

ii) In 1934 also, at the celebration of the feast of Christ the King in the Stadthalle of Koblenz, Bishop Bornewasser of Trier pointed out that Germany's Catholics were acutely aware of the tremendous dangers that threatened the life of the Faith and the existence of the Church from the neo-pagan movement in Germany. He pointed out that the dangers to Catholic Youth were above all else a cause for anxiety, referring to a statement made in Berlin on the 5 of November that 'Rosenberg's way is the way for German Youth'.

iii) In his Lenten Pastoral of 1935 Cardinal Schulte of Cologne praised the faithful for their inflexible determination by reason of which the continual outrages against their most sacred feelings and beliefs were being used by them as an opportunity of publicly demonstrating their uncompromising Catholic loyalty.

iv) Also in 1935, when the new Bishop of Berlin, Count von Preysing, was taking leave of the Episcopal Theological and Philosophical College of Eichstätt, he declared there could be no possible doubt that Christians were engaged in a hard fight. The new religion of blood had declared war; its battle cries ranged from a cold rejection of Christian doctrine to an exacerbation full of hate.

v) That same year the combined Pastoral of the bishops assembled at Fulda was awaited 'with eager suspense'. On the 20 August it appeared and in it the German bishops demonstrated their watchful care but growing anxiety. The number of enemies of the Christian Faith and the Catholic Church had become legion. It was no longer a question of attacking individual dogmas or beliefs as in former religious conflicts; now the whole essence and basis of Christianity must be overthrown. In carrying out their war of annihilation they (i.e. the opponents) were agreed it was principally against Rome and the Roman Catholic Faith that their attacks must be directed.

vi) 1936 was the year when the assault intensified. In early January the assembled bishops at Fulda once more referred to the dangers that menaced the faithful and in spite of everything the struggle did not appear to be dying down but rather it raged with growing intensity around the souls of the German people.

vii) On 9th February Bishop von Galen of Münster made a famous speech at Xanten. Forcefully he drew attention to how Holy Church, the Pope, the bishops, priests and religious, and the loyal children of the Church were insulted, reviled and derided publicly and with impunity. Priests and laymen had been attacked and insulted in the press and at public meetings, had been driven out of their jobs and professions and imprisoned and ill-treated without any judicial sentence. There were fresh graves in German soil in which were lying the ashes of those whom Catholic people regarded as martyrs for the Faith since their lives had given witness to their most dutiful and loyal devotion to God and to the Fatherland, to the nation and the Church, while the dark secrecy which surrounded their deaths was most carefully preserved.

viii) On 29th September 1936, Bishop Michael Rackl, in a sermon preached at Buchsheim, was nothing if not outspoken. He believed that the agitation against the Catholic Church often assumed a form which went 'far beyond that to which we are accustomed in Russia.'

ix) Towards the end of 1936 in a sermon in Regensburg Cathedral, Bishop Buchberger declared that a violent attack was raging, especially against the Catholic Church. To be a Catholic and to live in a Catholic fashion was for many the equivalent of being un-German. And this after the World War, in which none fulfilled their duty to the Fatherland more loyally than the Catholics.

x) In 1937, the great assault on all Catholic positions was carried still further. It caused Archbishop Gröber of Freiburg to point out, with the greatest grief and deepest concern, in his New Year Pastoral, that in the last few months it had been apparent, even more clearly, that the enmity towards the Church and towards Christianity in general had greatly increased both in its extension and in the intensity of its hatred.

xi) At this same time, Bishop Kaller of Ermland in his Pastoral was no less forthright. He lamented the fact that never before had the German Fatherland been the arena for a struggle against the existence of Christian heritage so bitter as that which was raging: '. . . Yes, we are at war and no Concordat, no solemn profession of the Führer, is able to offer protection against the fanaticism of the enemies of Christ.'

xii) In July 1937, Cardinal Faulhaber, in a sermon in Munich occasioned by the arrest of Father Rupert Mayer SJ, was relentless in his exposure of the ultimate aims of the war against the Church. The fight had broken out in a form hitherto unknown, especially in press articles and caricatures directed against the truths of faith and morality, against the Church, Pope, bishops, priests and faithful . . . and 'not merely by journals long known as opponents of Christianity; no, Party organs with the very widest circulation, directed and recommended by those in leading positions, are in the forefront of the battle, which is being carried on with all available weapons, even with poisoned weapons – with insult, scorn, mockery, falsehood and misrepresentation.'

xiii) During a pilgrimage to Weingarten on 10 October 1937 Bishop Sproll of Rottenburg spoke with such effect that, due to the bursts of applause, he continually had to beg for silence. Having spoken of the Papal Encyclical on the Holy Rosary, which had been confiscated in Germany because it dared to criticise National Socialism, he exposed without mercy the methods of the regime in the struggle for Catholic education producing documentary evidence that the solemn undertaking with regard to teachers of religion had been violated and he urged that, in consequence, the National Socialist press should no longer receive credence. As he gave, from the pulpit, one example after another of misrepresentation of facts and outlined the tactics of the 'Immorality' trials (discussed later in this chapter) he thundered, time and again: 'That is a lie'.

xiv) In February 1938, Cardinal Faulhaber of Munich delivered a moving sermon in which he also pointed out that as a spoliation manoeuvre the State subsidy for priests would be curtailed in 1939 or even completely withdrawn. Notwithstanding this, he reported that young men were continually offering themselves for the priesthood and the same applied to young women wishing to become nuns.

xv) The Lenten Pastorals of 1938 protested, with one accord, against the religious persecution. After a visit to the Pope, Bishop Albert Stohr of Mainz issued a Pastoral (April 1938) in which he declared that, following the promulgation of *Mit brennender Sorge* (see later pages of this chapter), Catholics had hoped for some improvement. Instead, things had worsened – a regular flood of calumnies, insults and derision had surged forth against the Church. From that time on the Church's position had worsened from week to week and day to day, while the anxiety of the bishops grew ever deeper. The freedom of religious instruction, which had been guaranteed, was disregarded. The printing of the encyclical itself was treated as a crime against the State.

xvi) In the context of the persecution, the combined Pastoral letter of the bishops, issued at Fulda on 19 August 1938, was regarded as the most important document of the year. Considerations of space will not permit publication of the full text here, or even part of it, but it is important to quote at least one sentence verbatim: 'When with incomprehensible arrogance it is even demanded of a German bishop that he should leave his diocese, and when, after his return in the ordinary course of his duty, he is continually harassed by commotions, tumults and deeds of violence directed against him, without any official action being taken to protect him, then the Catholic population can scarcely rid themselves of the fear that at no distant date we bishops in general will be handed over in a similar manner to the rabble deliberately incited for the purpose.' So here we have it – the bishops knew full well that their opposition might well result in their own grievous injury or even death . . . but the records show that, from this time on, their protests continued unabated.

xvii) In his Lenten Pastoral of 1939 Bishop Stohr of Mainz was defiant. He declared that: 'We will not allow ourselves to be robbed of this faith, or of the heritage which enshrines it for us, by anything at all. Nothing shall rob us of it, not even the siren-songs of the new prophets, not even the hint that it might perhaps be of advantage to us if we ceased to belong to the Church.' Bishop Stohr also emphasised the paramount importance of the family at that time. His comments ran completely counter to Nazi ideology of course, for, through indoctrination in the 'community' schools and the Hitler Youth, children were encouraged to spy upon and even denounce their parents for any single infraction of the reverence due to the Führer and his regime. A good example of the damage done to family love and loyalty was the case of the young woman who denounced her parents to the Gestapo when they objected to her intention to marry a member of the SS.

In these previous pages, we have 17 examples to refute the charge that the German bishops were docile when confronted with Nazi oppression. These emphasise that the hierarchy's protest was not confined to one or two voices but was a general struggle for the Catholic Church in which the bishops spoke up resolutely for the Faith and for their flocks. Once again it is worth pointing out that these examples are a mere selection. A whole volume would be required to set out the sea of protest from the Catholic bishops about what was then happening in Germany. And the names of many other bishops would be included in it. So it is difficult to understand why the bishops are criticised for their 'inertia', particularly by historians who have no direct personal knowledge of the era or its horrors.

We will now turn to an outline of the efforts made by the Pope and his Secretary of State to counter the neo-paganism arising in a country for which they had much love and esteem. The single most significant example of their resolve was the Papal Encyclical *Mit brennender Sorge* ('With Burning Anxiety'), which emerged from the Vatican on Passion Sunday, 4 March 1937. The remainder of this chapter will deal with its development, its scope and content, and the reaction of the Nazis following its promulgation.

In the autumn of 1936, because of continued violations of the Concordat, the Fulda Conference of German bishops sought a collective interview with Hitler. After a month's delay they were told that such a meeting was out of the question. However, on 4 November, to see whether some agreement was possible, Hitler agreed to give Cardinal Faulhaber a private audience at the Obersalzberg, his retreat above the village of Berchtesgaden in South Germany. 'Audience' was the appropriate word for the meeting, since Hitler did most of the talking. He declared he was most disappointed with the Church's hostility to Nazism and its response to Nazi racial policies, dismissing any attacks on the Church as 'small and risible bagatelles'. Despite the Cardinal's attempts to intervene, the interview transpired to be no more than one-way traffic.

At the Fulda plenary conference on 12-13 January 1937 the bishops considered the fruitless outcome of the meeting, censured the government for its violations of the Concordat and decided to send a deputation to Rome to discuss their concerns with Secretary of State Pacelli. They were starkly frank with him, explaining that the Church in Germany was engaged in a life-and-death struggle, its adversaries bent on its destruction. Cardinal Pacelli handed Cardinal Faulhaber some notes he had already made on the situation and asked him to develop these into a draft document, which would form the basis of a Papal encyclical. It was also decided to publish the encyclical in German for, apart from the technical difficulty of rendering certain German terms in Latin, it was felt that an encyclical in the vernacular would increase its impact. Faulhaber spent three nights on a draft which condemned the Nazi ideology of race and state. Cardinal Pacelli then developed the draft into 'an extremely trenchant but subtle condemnation of National Socialism.'[14] The Secretary of State also amended Faulhaber's title of 'With Great Anxiety' to 'With Burning Anxiety'.

The encyclical begins by explaining how, from the summer of 1933, the Vatican had resumed negotiations for the Concordat 'in spite of many serious misgivings'. Below are a number of extracts from a translation of the original encyclical. These will serve to demonstrate

14. M Burleigh, op. cit., p. 190.

why, in the words of one historian: 'The German encyclical is an immensely astute critique of everything that Nazism stood for.'[15]

§4 ... now on the horizon of Germany there is to be seen not the rainbow of peace but the threatening storm clouds of destructive religious wars.

§5 We have done all we could to defend the sanctity of the solemn pledges, the inviolability of obligations freely entered into against theories and practices which, if officially approved, must destroy all confidence and render intrinsically worthless every future pledge.

§5 We shall not cease to oppose an attitude of mind which seeks with open or secret violence to stifle a chartered right.

§8 Whoever transposes Race or People, the State or Constitution or the executive or other fundamental elements of human society (which in the natural order of things have an essential and honourable place), from the scale of earthly values and makes them the ultimate norm of all things, even of religious values, and deifies them with an idolatrous cult, perverts and falsifies the divinely created and appointed order of things. Such a man is far from true belief in God and from a conception of life in conformity to it.

§11 Only superficial minds can fall into the error of speaking of a national God, of a national religion, and of making a mad attempt to imprison within the frontiers of a single people, within the pedigree of one single race, God, the creator of the world ...

§15f Only blindness and self-will can close men's eyes to the treasure of instruction for salvation hidden in the Old Testament. He who wishes to see Bible history and the wisdom of the Old Testament banished from church and school blasphemes the word of God.

§21 In your territories Venerable Brethren, voices are raised in an ever louder chorus, urging men to leave the Church, and preachers arise who from their official position try to create the impression that such a departure from the Church and the consequent

15. Ibid.

infidelity to Christ the King is a particularly convincing and meritorious proof of their loyalty to the present regime. By disguised and by open methods of coercion, by intimidation, by holding out prospects of economic, professional, civil or other kinds of advantages, the loyalty of Catholics to their faith, and especially of certain classes of Catholic officials, is subjected to a violence which is as unlawful as it is inhuman . . . the only way of salvation for the believer lies in heroic fortitude.

§23 Whoever does not wish to be a Christian ought at least to renounce the desire to enrich the vocabulary of his unbelief with the heritage of Christian ideas.

§27 The Church of Christ, which in all ages up to those which are nearest to us counts more heroic confessors and martyrs than any other moral society, certainly does not need to receive instruction from such quarters about heroic sentiment and action. By foolishly representing Christian humility as a self-degradation and an unheroic attitude, the repulsive pride of these imitators only makes itself an object for ridicule.

§29 The number of such fools who presume to separate morality from religion has to-day become legion. They do not perceive, or they do not wish to perceive, that by banishing confessional (i.e. clear and definite) teaching from instruction and education, by preventing its co-operation in the formation of social and public life, they are treading the paths of moral impoverishment and decadence.

§29 To hand over moral teaching to subjective and temporary human opinions instead of anchoring it to the holy will of the everlasting God and to His commandments means opening wide the doors to the forces of destruction.

§33 [To Youth] By a thousand tongues today there is preached in your ears a gospel which has not been revealed by the Heavenly Father: a thousand pens write in the service of a sham Christianity which is not the Christianity of Christ. The printing press and the radio flood you daily with productions, the contents of which are hostile to faith and to Church, and unscrupulously and irreverently attack what, for you, must be sacred and holy . . . We know well how many an unknown soldier of Christ is to be found in your ranks, who, with broken heart, but with head erect, bears his lot and finds comfort solely in the thought that he suffers reproach for the name of Jesus (Acts 5:41).

§39 We address a particularly heartfelt greeting to Catholic parents. Their rights and their duties in their education of the children God has given them are at the present moment at a crucial point in a struggle than which none graver could scarcely be imagined. The Church of Christ cannot wait to begin to mourn and weep until her altars have been despoiled and sacrilegious hands have destroyed the houses of God in smoke and fire. When the attempt is made to desecrate the tabernacle of a child's soul, sanctified by baptism, by an antichristian education, when from this living temple of God the flame of belief is cast out and in its place is put the false light of a substitute for faith which has nothing in common with zeal for the Cross, then the spiritual profanation of the temple is at hand, and it is the duty of every believer to separate clearly his responsibility from that of the other side, and to keep his conscience clear from any sinful collaboration in such unhallowed destruction.

§42 Just as in other times of the Church, this time too will be the harbinger of new progress and inner purification, when determination to profess the faith and readiness to endure sacrifices on the part of Christ's faithful is strong enough to oppose to the physical force of the oppressors of the Church an invincibility of interior faith, the inexhaustibility of hope anchored in eternity, and the compelling omnipotence of active charity.

§43 He who searches the hearts and the reins (Psalm 7:10) is Our witness that we have no more heartfelt wish than the restoration of true peace between Church and State in Germany. But if through no fault of ours there is not to be peace, the Church of God will defend her rights and her liberties in the name of the Almighty whose arm even today is not shortened.[16]

---

16. All the quotations from the Papal encyclical *Mit brennender Sorge* are set out in full as Appendix II in the Burns Oates 1940 volume *Persecution of the Catholic Church In The Third Reich*.

In addition to its vehement protest against the, by now, clear persecution of the Church, and its affirmation of Christian teaching, the encyclical skilfully destroyed the spurious claims of Nazi ideology. It also set out, in the clearest fashion, the Church's philosophy of law and of the State. In this regard, because its philosophy was consistent, the Catholic Church had a very great advantage over the Protestant confessions in its opposition to the creed of the National Socialists. It is reported, for example, that Rosenberg regarded the Dominicans, who are the Thomists *par excellence*, as his most dangerous enemies.[17]

The blow struck by the encyclical was maximised by the steps taken for its distribution and promulgation. The Vatican recognised that if even a glimmer of its contents became known *Mit brennender Sorge* would never have got beyond Germany's frontier posts. Accordingly, not only was it published in German, it was printed in Germany. Clandestinely it was sent out to hundreds of towns and villages, printed there, then distributed to the dioceses. Moreover, those responsible for its physical delivery took no chances. Rather than entrust the supplies of it to public transport or the mail it was distributed throughout Germany by motor cyclists. Cathedrals and churches received it on Saturday night and the early hours of Sunday morning, for reading on Sunday from the first Masses. It received even further impetus, for the bishops themselves read it from the pulpits, wherever possible.

All of this was a body blow to Hitler and his followers. It was, at the same time, a great strengthening of the resolve of ordinary Catholics – the Vatican had noted their plight and did not intend to remain silent. Moreover, as German diplomats informed Berlin, the encyclical was given a good reception beyond Germany. In Hungary, for example, not a single newspaper supported the Nazi regime, stating that it was responsible for the conflict with the Vatican. From Switzerland came the news that the attitude of Swiss Catholics towards Germany was decided by the Vatican statement. For them, the encyclical was addressed not merely to German Catholics but to the entire Catholic world. At a Catholic meeting in Belgium the view was expressed that the Church was less in danger from Communism, which at least

17. N Micklem, *National Socialism and the Roman Catholic Church*. London, 1939, p. 173.

attacked it openly, than from the secret, creeping poison of National Socialism. In Chile, the encyclical had been most effective 'in turning the people against Germany'. On Christmas Eve 1937, the German Ambassador in Washington reported that because of its anti-Catholic campaign, Germany was losing support in the United States and its Catholic population (then 25 million) stood 'united and determined behind their Church.'[18]

As we have noted, *Mit brennender Sorge* was described as 'an immensely astute critique of everything that Nazism stood for'.[19] No wonder the secret state police moved immediately. Not a word of the encyclical was allowed to appear in the newspapers. Diocesan offices were raided and every copy of the encyclical confiscated. All the presses which had printed it were closed and sealed. Bishops' diocesan magazines were proscribed. Paper supplies for church pamphlets and secretarial work were severely restricted. Notwithstanding the provisions of the Concordat, State grants to theology students and needy priests were reduced. Some measures were plainly petty e.g. the prohibition of Catholic flags at religious ceremonies, towns and villages with religious names (Mariendorf, Gottesberg etc.) being given more secularly acceptable titles.

Hitler was furious but his first move was symbolic – on a visit to Rome and contrary to the demands of protocol, he pointedly refused to make a formal call at the Vatican. His next move was intended to do more damage and the Catholic clergy were the targets of his venom. He issued instructions that they were not to be made martyrs but declared: 'I shall open such a campaign of propaganda against them, in press, radio and cinema, that they won't know what's hit them.'[20] A two-pronged attack was then launched consisting of prosecutions for (i) currency offences and (ii) immoral behaviour.

With regard to the currency charges, a little background detail is necessary perhaps. To safeguard the regime's popularity its propaganda had made grandiose claims about the nation's economic recovery and the ending of its unemployment. But from 1934 Germany's balance

---

18. A Rhodes, *The Vatican in the Age of the Dictators 1922-45*. London, 1973, p. 206.
19. M Burleigh, op. cit., p. 190.
20. A Rhodes, op. cit., p. 207

of payments had gone into deficit. Between January and September of that year its gold and foreign exchange reserves had fallen by more than a half. On 14th June, the Reichsbank had to impose a six-month stop on the repayment of all long and medium-term foreign debts.[21] The stability of the currency was a *sine qua non* in discouraging inflation. So it was therefore necessary for the government to keep a tight control of the economy (especially if that economy had to support military expansion en route to war). And an important facet of economic control was control on the amount of currency finding its way abroad.

This was reasonable enough for Germany but the Catholic Church was not exclusively German – it was world-wide. In its ordinary day-to-day activities, not least in support of its overseas missions, it had to have recourse to moving currency about. Moreover, when from 1935 Germany began to bring clerics to trial for alleged currency offences, it was merely following the fashion of all twentieth-century dictatorships. And so the trials began. On 15 May 1935, Sister Catherine Weidendorfer, at Moabit (Berlin), was found guilty of having illegally exported capital to Belgium. She was sentenced to five years imprisonment. On the 29 May, Franciscan Otto Goertler was convicted of a similar offence and received a ten-year sentence. These cases were seized upon by the Nazi press to vilify both the Church in Germany and the Vatican. *Völkischer Beobachter* talked of 'the systematic robbing of the nation by criminals wearing soutanes,' while *Das Schwarze Korps* featured a caricature of the Pope in front of a huge sack of gold.[22]

There followed a wave of arrests and trials and there can be no question but that in some cases the defendants were aware of acting contrary to the Currency Laws, for which they were openly condemned by the ecclesiastical authorities. Yet this could not excuse the blatant sensationalism with which the accounts of these trials were reported nor the large, slanderous headlines which accompanied them: e.g. 'Brazen Blasphemy', 'Pious Tricksters go to Prison', 'Millions skilfully smuggled from Convents'. Members of Religious Orders were held to be devoid of all national loyalty, considering

---

21. R J Evans, *The Third Reich In Power*. London, 2005, p. 355.
22. A Rhodes, op. cit., p. 198.

nothing but their own financial gain. And although their Superiors had explicitly condemned this type of offence, the Church as a whole was denounced. Reports of court proceedings devoted much space to speeches for the prosecution. Speeches for the defence were either exceedingly brief or not reported at all. While much was made of a condemnation, nothing was published about an appeal or an acquittal. At the same time, where members of the National Socialist Party were found guilty of embezzlement, little or nothing was reported.

In many instances, Catholic nuns were depicted by State attorneys as traitors to the community. Word pictures were woven of Jewish capital being used to further the designs of the Catholic Church. Although the trials were held before special courts, designed to give speedy verdicts, many accused, including invalids, were detained awaiting trial for a month or more. During the hearings, little care was taken for the physical needs of the accused. Despite a doctor's testimony that a Canon Heisig of Lauban was in a state of complete nervous collapse and could not be held responsible for his words or actions, the Canon was sentenced to three and a half years' imprisonment. His solicitor's request for an acquittal was ignored and no extenuating circumstances were taken into account.

Solicitors for the defence often complained that they were not allowed sufficient time to prepare cases or to discuss complicated details with their clients. The intricacies of the currency regulations themselves were not taken into account. One lawyer, Reichling of Münster, defending the Hiltrup Fathers, said he had known experienced colleagues, even judges and State attorneys, who had failed to master the theoretical basis of the Currency Law and had thus made errors. Here it must be emphasised that even where the Religious accused had 'profited' from their 'crimes', that profit had been completely devoted to charitable objectives. As the Burns Oates *Compilation of Facts and Documents* tellingly comments concerning these defendants: 'Both before and after their Currency transactions they lived in poverty.'[23] In fact, in one case – that of a missionary of the Sacred Heart at Hiltrup, where both he and the Superior of his Order were labelled 'swindlers' by the State Attorney – he had been

23. Burns Oates, op. cit., p. 297.

acting in Germany's interests through a scheme intended to benefit German nationals in the South Seas.

In these cases, ethical and psychological factors were never served as a reason for leniency. An important example here is of a case involving the Sisters of Mercy. Throughout the trial their ignorance of the world and simplicity in money matters was plainly evident. While they could administer the affairs of charitable causes adequately enough they had no skills in business methods and book-keeping. They had no idea of the effect of their transactions on the stability of the national currency and little practical grasp of the scope and function of the Currency Laws. The Church had to be able to send monies abroad for the upkeep of its institutions and activities. The Nazis made use of this fact to discredit the Church as their own riposte against *Mit brennender Sorge* and the protests being made in many other ways.

Let us now turn to that other stick which they used to beat the Church, the immorality trials. The so-called 'trials' had begun in 1935. After the promulgation of *Mit brennender Sorge* Hitler intensified his intention to 'crush [the Catholic Church] like a toad'[24] by stepping up these trials. His strategy, however, was not to make martyrs of his Catholic opponents but to stamp them as 'stupid criminals'. The 'immorality' approach was to accuse clergy and religious of homosexual crimes, sexual misconduct with minors and other crimes of a sexual nature. Three conclusions emerge from an examination of the details of a number of these cases: because of the tendentious nature of the Nazi controlled press reports, it was impossible for the German public to learn the whole truth behind the overwhelming majority of these cases; in no sense was the purpose of these cases to improve moral standards and conduct but rather maliciously to attack the honour of the Church and irreparably damage her good name, and as a corollary, it would then be easier to lever Germany's young out of Catholic schools and youth associations and into the secular schools and Hitlerjugend where inculcation of Nazi ideology was now well under way.

At this time, a torrent of newspaper headlines confronted German readers, with examples such as: 'Catholic student of Theology exposed

---

24. R Royal, *The Catholic Martyrs of the Twenieth Century*. New York, 2000, p. 133

as Sexual Criminal' (from *Der Alemanne*, a Party newspaper in Baden); 'From Incest to Ordination' (from *Schwarze Korps*, an infamous Nazi publication); 'An Ill-Chosen Christian Worker – Three Years' Imprisonment for the Founder of a Catholic Youth League' (from leading Nazi publication *Völkischer Beobachter*). Dr Joseph Goebbels, Nazi Propaganda Minister, in his speech of 28 May 1937, which was relayed by all German wireless stations, declared that: 'A vast number of Catholic clerics have been tried for sexual crimes . . . It is not a matter of regrettable individual lapses, but of a general corruption of morals such as the history of civilisation has scarcely ever known . . . We cannot allow thousands upon thousands of priests and brothers of religious Orders to escape scot-free . . .'[25]

If we consider the actual facts behind the above headlines we get a clear impression of what Goebbels' tirade was worth: the 'Catholic Student of Theology' had been, in reality, a student in one of the lower classes of the secondary school at Sassbach. After a short probationary stay he was dismissed for unsatisfactory work and conduct. With regard to the 'incest case', the *Schwarze Korps* had gone on to say that the Roman Church had 'sheltered the sins of one of its members.' This led the diocesan authorities of Freiburg-im-Breisgau to issue the following declaration to be read from all pulpits: 'The daily papers have recently published accounts of a trial held *in camera* of a young man who had committed serious sexual offences with members of his own family. This nineteen-year-old youth was not a youth leader of all Catholic Youth Associations in Baden, as has been repeatedly stated, and his connection with such organisations was limited to work lasting roughly six months, some two years ago, with the diocesan leaders of the Catholic Youth League. Since April last he has attended the Upper Fifth Class of a private secondary school in Baden. We wish to state with the greatest possible emphasis that the deeply offensive insinuation of continued official, ecclesiastical patronage being given to this young man's education contains no grain of truth. The ecclesiastical authorities knew nothing of the unhappy youth's crimes until his imprisonment was announced.'[26]

---

25. Burns Oates, op. cit., p. 305.
26. Ibid., p. 300.

The third headline related to a forty-four year-old Munich man, Karl Krieger, who had appeared before the Munich court to answer a charge of criminal assault upon a minor. Krieger was the founder of a Catholic Youth League, he submitted, because of a personal interest in Christian social work. In fact, this 'Christian worker' was not a priest and the 'Catholic Youth League' he founded was not a Catholic Youth organisation, though Krieger may well have disguised it with some such name. Neither Kreiger nor his League was known to ecclesiastical authorities.

During the period of the slanderous media campaign German diplomats abroad were supplied with plenty of extracts culled from it. Yet the results were hardly what Goebbels could have hoped for. The bemused Consul in Caracas complained that he received nothing but cases of homosexuality. He felt moved to write: 'Owing to the unpleasant incidents at the court of Wilhelm II, not to mention the more recent sexual habits of Röhm and his friends, homosexuality has come to be known in Colombia as "the German vice" – and these cases against German priests only add to this unfortunate impression. Could we not therefore have a few *heterosexual* incidents?' Author Anthony Rhodes points out that his request was soon gratified by a number of photographs showing priests in compromising attitudes with half-naked women (the method being, according to the Catholic newspaper, *Der Deutsche Weg*, to entice a priest on some pretext into a private house, where a naked woman would suddenly throw herself on his neck while a flashlight photograph was taken).[27]

More evidence of foreign cynicism was provided by the 14 June 1937 issue of the Vienna *Reichspost* in which the following appeared: 'Certain North German papers published an account of dreadful immoralities practised in a monastery at Biberach. A little later it was clearly established that no monastery exists at Biberach and that nobody living there knew anything detrimental to the character of any members of religious Orders. In the neighbourhood of Biberach three or four priests reside and manage a Retreat House and they stand very high in the esteem of their neighbours.'[28]

In his speech Goebbels had referred to the involvement of 'thousands

---

27. A Rhodes, op. cit., p. 209.
28. Burns Oates, op. cit., pp. 303-4

and thousands' of priests and brothers. One tactic of the Nazis was to delay bringing many cases to trial. These would then suddenly be released into the judicial process so as to give the impression of a wave of vice. Even more serious, the nature of 'immoral crimes' was manipulated so as to include infractions of the law that had nothing to do with sexuality. In its 14 December 1937 issue, the Lucerne paper *Vaterland* dealt with this neatly. An article reported a statement by Hans Kerrl, Nazi Minister for Ecclesiastical Affairs, that there had been some 7,000 convictions of Catholic clergy since 1933. A summary of the article reads as follows:

> The Minister so juggled with his figures, quietly including cases of libel, "abuse of the pulpit", offences against the Flag Law (i.e. not flying of the Swastika on stated occasions) and so on, that he over-reached himself in his efforts to show that the *Sittlichkeitsprozesse* represented a perpetual practice of vice on the part of the priesthood as a whole. It is obvious, for example, that "abuse of the pulpit" must occur more frequently amongst priests than amongst other members of the community! Similarly the figures given of 7,000 cases involving 16,000 members of religious Orders for men was only arrived at by adding into the sexual offences many other infringements of the law on the part of nuns and secular priests. Anything to give an imposing total! One can only conclude that such figures are a striking testimony to the good repute rather than the depravity of the German clergy; for such juggling with figures is surely a sign of a deplorably weak case![29]

Not only was there a weak case, the Nazis were clumsy and inconsistent with their data. At Fulda on 14 December 1937, Herr Kerrl had spoken of '7,000 convictions'. At Hagen, Westphalia, just two weeks earlier, he had given the following figures for the 'Immorality trials': Persons condemned – Priests 45, Brothers and Nuns 176, Employees etc. 21. Total 242. Cases still in progress – Priests 93, Brothers and Nuns 744, Employees 118. Total 955. Cases withdrawn or convictions not obtained – Priests 29, Brothers 127, Employees 31. Total 187. In fact the accurate figures for immorality could then only be obtained if non-sexual offences such as those against the Flag Law, 'abuse of the pulpit', 'consorting with communists' etc., were subtracted from these figures. Examples of gross exaggeration are legion – in the Summer

29. Ibid., p. 306.

and Autumn of 1936, District Leader Streicher declared that 100 trials for sexual offences involving the clergy of Baden were then in progress. Archbishop Gröber of Freiburg intervened – the total was at most five or six and it was by no means sure the cases would end in convictions. The extent to which the Nazis falsified their statistics is made plain when it is realised that members of religious Orders nursing the severely incapacitated and handling their genitals to assist their bodily functions, were accused of 'immorality'.

The ecclesiastical authorities refused to remain silent in the face of these accusations. Through the only channel now left open to them, the pulpit, the Catholic bishops made the following declaration:

> We have asked all German bishops to send in exact statistics of priests and members of Congregations who have become involved in "immorality" trials. Of the Congregations, representing some 100,000 men and women, exact figures are not yet forthcoming. With reference to priests, however, we can state that of the 21,461 priests in Germany, 49 have been involved in these trials. Of these, 21 have been convicted, 28 still await sentence. Of 4,174 priests belonging to religious Orders, 9 have been charged, 1 convicted; the rest are still on trial. Out of a total, therefore, of 25,634 priests, 58 cases have arisen, accounting for 1 priest in every 500.[30]

During this widespread campaign of vilification, when the appeals mechanism was either distorted or suppressed, immorality in the Nazi ranks was concealed. However, in May 1939, a Dr Wick, described as a 'well-known Swiss Deputy' produced an article for Lucerne's *Vaterland* which indicated that post-1933 juvenile crime in Germany had risen at an alarming rate. He demonstrated that the education given in the Hitler Youth, with its watertight organisation and independence from the influences of school, home and Church had led to 'grave moral delinquency'. He incorporated statistics from the official 'Statistical Year Book of the German State'. These cast an alarming spotlight on the corruption of German youth, as can be seen below.

> Number of juveniles convicted of immoral practices
> 1932 – 619; 1933 – 612; 1934 – 779; 1935 – 1,058; 1936 – 1,465; 1937 – 2,374.

30. Ibid.

> Criminal assault on children
> 1934 – 478; 1937 – 1,065.
>
> Unnatural vice
> 1934 – 121; 1937 – 973.
>
> Homicide and abortion among girls
> 1935 – 57; 1937 – 158; 1938 (1st half only) – 109.
>
> Manslaughter
> 1934 – 18; 1935 – 42; 1936 – 65; 1937 – 70; 1938 (1st half only) – 45.
>
> Damage to property
> No. of condemnations among children period 1934-37 – 25% increase.
>
> Theft
> 1934 – 6,947 children condemned; 1937 – 12,475 children condemned.

Dr Wick's article continues:

> One must not omit to consider the fact that the "honour of the Party" causes many things to be passed over and hushed up nowadays, while much that would formerly have been called moral degeneration now passes as racial *Weltanschauung*. Parents complain with such rapidly increasing bitterness of the moral degradation of their children that we may rightly entertain doubts about the moral outlook for a "noble" Aryan race in Germany.[31]

Perhaps the last word to be said in this outline of the 'immorality' trials, concerning the integrity of the process, is that in September 1944, when the Allied armies were on the move towards the German homeland, all documents concerning the trials were destroyed by order of the SS.[32]

Before concluding this chapter it is important to consider two events which occurred in 1938. The first of these was the Anschluss and the second was Kristallnacht. The Anschluss was the Nazi take-over of Austria. The German invasion began at dawn on the 12 March with agents of the Gestapo and the SD (the Nazi Party's own intelligence and security body) following the troops. Hitler elevated his grabbing of the country to some quasi-mystical event with himself as its ministering spirit. He was participating as the instrument of the

---

31. Burns Oates, op. cit., pp. 317-8.
32. A Rhodes, op. cit., p. 209.

country's destiny. In reality the arrests began; in Vienna alone they were to total 76,000 and Dr Schuschnigg, the Catholic Chancellor, was sent to Dachau concentration camp. As the Nazi terror got under way, an Austrian camp was established at Mauthausen where, it is reported, 35,000 victims of the Anschluss lost their lives.

What is pertinent to the subject-matter of this book is the 'issue' of Theodor Innitzer, Catholic Cardinal Archbishop of Vienna. As the Anschluss proceeded he arranged for cathedral bells to be rung and churches to be festooned with swastikas. He also delivered a joint letter from the Catholic bishops of Austria praising the take-over and thanking God that because of Nazi intervention the danger of godless Bolshevism would be fended off. Not that the seeming euphoria was restricted to Innitzer. It is rarely reported that the leading spokesman for Austria's Protestant minority was also effusive. Hitler had come as the deliverer of all Austria's Germans. 'God bless your progress through this German land, your Heimat!', he cried.[33] The Social Democrat leader and former Chancellor, Karl Renner, added his endorsement. Hitler insisted on a post-Anschluss plebiscite to give his action an aura of response to felt-need. And surely enough, 99% of the country's voters declared in favour of 'the reunification of Austria with the German Reich'. No doubt the glittering promise of Germany's economic recovery and fear of Bolshevism, as well as pan-German sentiment, played their part in the result. So it is somewhat misguided to cast Innitzer as the solitary villain of the piece.

Ironically, the Innitzer issue came to show the Vatican in a wholly positive light for what is often omitted from the generality of post-war writing is the action immediately taken in Rome to counter the Cardinal's pro-Nazi behaviour. There follows a summary of what actually happened.

Following the takeover, the SA squads lost no time in demonstrating who now controlled the country. Among their first actions was the house arrest of Monsignor Sigismund Waitz, Archbishop of Salzburg. The first intimation he had of their intention was the stones which came crashing through the windows of his residence. The central seat and some of the branches of the Catholic Action Association

---

33. C M Cianfarra, *The War and the Vatican*. London, 1945, pp. 116-7. See also M Burleigh, op. cit., p. 149.

were forcibly closed – in spite of the fact that its operations had been guaranteed by concordat. Five priests of the Archdiocese of Salzburg were imprisoned including Canon Seinwender who was physically assaulted. The SA also took possession of the Kilpinghaus, a home for young Catholic skilled workers. Its priest, nuns and residents were ordered to leave.

The Convent of the Most Precious Blood was searched and money found there was seized. Organisations of Catholic women and Catholic young women in the Archdiocese were dissolved, as were women's organisations in the Diocese of Linz. In Salzburg also, the offices of the Catholic University were taken over and all practising Catholics holding senior posts there were dismissed. Overnight the Austrian Catholic Press became totally controlled by the Nazis and all its principal staff were either discharged or imprisoned. In the office of every Catholic newspaper and publishing house a Reich commissioner was installed. The Nazis forced their way into the house of Monsignor Ferdinand Pawlikowski, Bishop of Graz, seizing books and documents, which they destroyed. The Bishop was then imprisoned but subsequently set free. An apology came from Berlin with the explanation that he had been gaoled in order to protect him from 'threatened Communist aggression'.[34]

In this tense atmosphere Cardinal Innitzer was summoned to meet Hitler who voiced his hopes, in meaningful fashion, that the Austrian Catholic Church might be more supportive of National Socialism than was the Catholic Church in Germany. Innitzer affirmed that the Austrian Catholics would be loyal to the regime but he hoped that the terms of the concordat would be respected. Then Innitzer went further by appealing to Austria's Christians to support 'the greater German state', and its Führer, in the fight against the criminal madness of Bolshevism, by voting for the Anschluss in the Nazis' arranged plebiscite.[35]

This development is usually reported or at least alluded to sententiously by many historians. What is less frequently reported is the Vatican's fury with the Austrian Cardinal and the steps it took to remedy matters – for it now faced a situation where, internationally,

34. C M Cianfarra, op. cit., pp. 115-6.
35. M Burleigh op. cit., pp. 149-50.

it seemed that the Catholic Church approved of the Anschluss when, in fact, based on its experience in Germany of Hitler and his empty promises, it feared the destruction of the presence it had enjoyed for eight hundred years in an almost totally Catholic country.

Pius XI lost no time in instructing Cardinal Pacelli that the Austrian Cardinal must report to Rome immediately. At that time, Camille Cianfarra was the correspondent in Rome of the *New York Times*. In 1945 he published his account of what happened subsequently.[36] No representatives of either the Holy See or its Secretariat of State were at the station to meet Innitzer. He went straight to the Vatican for a discussion with Cardinal Pacelli. This went on far into the night. Innitzer was asked why he had instigated a massive turn-around on the Anschluss when only one month previously he had made public his support for the Schuschnigg regime. Innitzer said that at the private meeting with Hitler he had been given guarantees about the future of the Church. Similar assurances had come from Hermann Göring and Josef Bürkel (organiser of the Austrian plebiscite and later Reichskommissar). Cardinal Pacelli was dumbfounded, particularly since the incidents which had already occurred clearly indicated the Nazi intention to smash Catholicism in the Ostmark (Austria).

At eight o'clock the following morning the Secretary of State's report was handed to the Pope. Cianfarra describes the ensuing audience as 'dramatic' and Vatican circles subsequently affirmed that Pius XI was prepared to remove the Cardinal from the Vienna See on the ground that he had flouted the previous Papal warnings and condemnation of Nazism. Just twenty-four hours after his arrival Innitzer was made to sign, on his own behalf and also in the name of the whole Austrian Episcopate, a statement which was published in *L'Osservatore Romano* on 7 April. The statement emphasised that the Cardinal's previous declaration should not be understood as an approval of what was not compatible with God's law and the freedom and rights of the Catholic Church. Nor must it be interpreted as binding in conscience upon the faithful or exploited for propaganda purposes. Moreover, the Austrian bishops insisted that there be no changes in the terms of the Concordat without previous agreement; there be protection for Catholic schools, education and the formation of youth; propaganda

---

36. C M Cianfarra, op. cit., pp. 116-7.

contrary to the Church and the Catholic religion be forbidden; and there be freedom for Catholics to proclaim, defend and practise their Catholic faith and Christian principles.

Cianfarra concluded his comments on this matter: 'It was past noon when the medium-built, stoop-shouldered, white-haired prince of the Church descended the stairway which leads to the Courtyard of Saint Damasus, where I had been waiting for him. His meek, thin, tired face was flushed. He looked at no-one as he waited for his limousine. In those few seconds I approached him and asked if he could comment on the Austrian situation. "No, no, I have nothing to say", he replied.' There were still troubled times in store for Theodor Innitzer after his return to Vienna.

The second event, or rather series of events, used to exemplify the Catholic Church's supposed indolence and indifference to the fate of others is that of Kristallnacht (The Night of Broken Glass). This occurred in Germany on 10 November 1938, beginning in the early hours and continuing until nightfall. Sir Martin Gilbert, the well-known British historian, has described it as the 'prelude to destruction' of European Jewry.[37] He relates how, in the space of a few hours, SA stormtroopers, some in their Brownshirt uniforms, others in civilian clothes, set on fire and destroyed more than 1,000 synagogues. Wherever the flames appeared to threaten other buildings these vandals used their hammers and axes to smash the synagogues to rubble. Tearing through Jewish neighbourhoods the paramilitaries burned the furniture and books they had pillaged from synagogues and private residences. The pogrom raged throughout the whole of Germany, from Berlin to the smallest towns and villages. In the streets Jews were reviled, physically assaulted and forced to run for their lives. Tens of thousands of Jewish shops and homes were ransacked in an orgy of destruction and at the end of the violence 91 Jews were dead. A quarter of Jewish men still in Germany and between the ages of sixteen and sixty (30,000 at least) were arrested and sent to concentration camps. Gilbert reports that there they were tortured and brutalised and more than 1,000 of them died.[38]

---

37. M Gilbert, *Kristallnacht, Prelude to Destruction*. London, 2007, pp. 15-17.
38. Ibid., p. 15.

When he referred to this infamous destruction of life and property no-one was a more stalwart defender of the Catholic Church than Pinchas E Lapide, a Jew who, after the War, had in fact been the Israeli Consul in Milan and had subsequently spoken with many Jewish survivors of the Holocaust. His 1967 book, *Three Popes and the Jews*, is distinguished by its scholarship and the breadth of its treatment. He explains how, immediately after Kristallnacht and at the instigation of Pope Pius XI, Cardinal Van Roey, Primate of Belgium, condemned 'racism and its blood myth' and how, in a pastoral letter, Cardinal Verdier of Paris associated himself with the words of Van Roey. Cardinal Schuster of Milan also took open issue with 'the racial myth'. Lapide also relates that, prompted by the Pope, Cardinal Faulhaber of Munich spoke up against the wholesale desecration of the synagogues and, in a highly symbolic gesture, provided the transport for the Chief Rabbi of Munich to save the Torah Scrolls before the ransacking of his own synagogue.[39]

In Lapide's account we also discover that in December 1938 when Italian theatres and other public institutions began to bar entry to Jews such measures amounted to 'acts of unchristian persecution' according to *L'Osservatore Romano*, and 'under Pius' redoubtable influence' during the Winter of 1938-39 *Civilta Cattolica* twice objected to being named in the Fascist press as an ally in praise of anti-Semitism. In Germany, towards the end of 1938, Jews were barred from the streets on Nazi holidays and Göring issued directives for the establishment of ghettos for their confinement. This was when, according to Lapide, the Pope energised the St Raphael's Association to speed the emigration of 'non-Aryan Catholics' (i.e. Jewish converts) and he records that, in 1938 alone, 1,850 'ex-Jews and half-Jews' as well as 261 Jews married to Catholics, were thus assisted to leave Germany and Austria.[40] On 10 January 1939 Pius asked the cardinals of the USA and Canada to help Jewish scholars and professors forced to leave Germany to obtain posts in North American Universities.

Four days later the Pope asked each ambassador accredited to the Holy See to obtain as many visas as possible from their own country

39. P E Lapide, *The Last Three Popes And The Jews*. London and Toronto, 1967, p. 114.
40. Ibid., p. 115.

'for the victims of racial persecution in Germany and Italy.' In early February he received Chamberlain, the British Prime Minister, and Lord Halifax in private audience. *The Times* of London subsequently reported the Pope's forceful comments on the 'reactionary regimes, the duties of the democracies, the racial persecutions, and the urgent need to help the refugees.'[41] Forty eight hours later he summoned the German bishop Berning to Rome and charged him with the task of organising a major emigration and resettlement project in Sao Paulo. Despite rapidly failing health and constant pain he was deeply involved in more efforts and appeals when he died on 10 February.

These examples serve to demonstrate that criticism of the Church for its supposed indifference to the fate of the Jews is unjust. Despite its own problems with the National Socialists, the Catholic Church was concerned and was prepared to help – and this from the earliest portents of the Holocaust. As the book proceeds we shall see that from the onset, and at the institutional and the individual level, Catholics were not found wanting and many Jews were prepared to testify to this. Martin Gilbert, for example, draws attention to the efforts of the British Catholic Committee for Refugees following Kristallnacht,[42] and, as we shall see in Chapter Six, only two months after Hitler's accession the sustained struggle of Monsignor Bernhard Lichtenberg to protect Jewish people, their property and their livelihood got under way. It was a struggle which led to his death.

---

41. Ibid., p. 115.
42. M Gilbert, op. cit., pp. 186-9.

Chapter Five

CATACLYSM: 1939-45 AND THE FIGHT FOR THE FAITH

Pope Pius XI, the now sick, old warrior, had one more week to live. Speaking to the Secretary of the Curia, Monsignor Tardini, he said: 'He will make a fine Pope!' He was referring to his Cardinal Secretary of State, Eugenio Pacelli, and expressing his fervent hopes for the Papal succession. Then he explained to Tardini that he had sent Pacelli abroad so frequently because he was preparing him for the Papacy. Now he was adamant . . . no 'perhaps' or 'possibly' but 'he *will* make a fine Pope!'

Pius's wishes were fulfilled, for on 2 March 1939, after the third round of voting, and in the shortest conclave since 1623 (it lasted less than twenty four hours), the Vatican Secretary of State became His Holiness Pope Pius XII. No doubt he had chosen the name 'Pius' out of deference to his mentor, affirming at the same time his intention to continue his policies. In the profile of him, set out in Chapter Seven, we shall see why his election was so logical.

By now Europe, and subsequently the world, was on the brink of a war that would kill over fifty million people, lay waste vast elements of Europe's cultural heritage, and 'devastate its economy, deprave its politics, and devalue the moral basis of its civilization.'[1] Mindful of the terrors of war, some may have been somehow comforted to note that as Nuncio, the new Pope had spent a decade in Germany, was fluent in German and had frequently referred to the Germans with warmth and admiration.

---

1. J Keegan, *The Battle for History. Re-Fighting World War Two*. London, 1995. p. 9.

This has led some latter-day writers to assert that he was 'pro-German' or even 'pro-Nazi'. These are gross calumnies and the best evidence for the truth is provided by the Axis regimes themselves. Prior to the papal election there had been much diplomatic activity in support of this or that candidate. From this it was crystal clear that the Italian government was opposed to Eugenio Pacelli. The February 1939 issue of the Fascist *Relazioni Internazionali* warned that the new Pontiff would be well advised not to persist in Pius XI's habit of criticising and dissenting from the racial and religious policies of Italy and Germany. And, of course, Secretary of State Pacelli had been a loyal supporter of Pius XI's ideas and actions.[2]

Also, when Ambassador von Bergen of Germany addressed the College of Cardinals after the death of Pius XI, and speaking on behalf of the Diplomatic Corps, he indicated that the cardinals should choose a Pope who would support 'the new world' (i.e. of the Dictators) and not 'the old world' (of the Democracies). Reporting this, Anthony Rhodes points out that von Bergen had failed to consult his fellow diplomats on the content of his speech.[3] Moreover, the address was given in Italian (a language of the Dictators), rather than in French (the language of diplomacy), and was an implied criticism of Cardinal Pacelli's candidacy, a man for whom von Bergen had hitherto invariably expressed respect and admiration. These points led Rhodes to the conclusion that von Bergen had been instructed by Berlin on the stance to adopt.

Prior to the election itself, the Nazi press wasted no time on diplomatic niceties. Its antagonism to the prospect of Pacelli was symptomised by *Der Angriff*, whose foreboding against such a 'political Pope' led it to suggest he would 'lead a crusade against the totalitarian states.' By contrast, newspapers in the democracies welcomed the idea of his Papacy for, in addition to the plaudits of the British press, the *New York Times* forecast that he would 'uphold the claims of human personality and brotherhood against a sea of enemies.' France's *Le Populaire* was equally direct, headlining the election as a 'Set-back to Mussolini'.[4]

---

2. A Rhodes, *The Vatican in the Age of the Dictators, 1922-45*. London, 1973, p. 224.
3. Ibid., pp. 224-5.
4. Ibid., p. 225.

Pius XII was seized with the vital importance of preventing war and in May 1939 attempted to convene a conference at which the European countries likely to become belligerents (Britain, France, Germany, Italy and Poland) might meet to resolve their differences. His efforts went unrewarded and matters markedly worsened when, on 23 August, Germany and Russia signed a Non-aggression Pact thereby, in Hitler's mind, creating a good omen for his intended invasion of Poland. The threat of war had already increased when on 22 May Germany had concluded a formal alliance with Italy – and this despite the fact that earlier in the month Germany's foreign minister von Ribbentrop had assured the Papal Nuncio, Archbishop Cesare Orsenigo, that Germany was not interested in an alliance with Italy. At this point, the Pope decided to try to employ Mussolini as the conduit for his entreaties. The Pope was told that the ceding of Danzig must constitute the basis for any negotiations between Germany and Poland – and this, after all, would be but a small price to pay for peace. Monsignor Tardini advised that this would be playing right into Hitler's hands but Pius went along with the idea and informed Warsaw accordingly. It has been said that here Pius XII may well have committed the biggest blunder of his career.[5]

Pius still persisted in his efforts to avert war. On the evening of 24 August he broadcast on Vatican Radio an appeal to the world. He implored governments to lay down their arms and negotiate. Empires not based on peace were not blessed by God. He concluded with the phrases that will always be associated with him: 'Nothing is lost with peace. Everything can be lost by war.'[6] On 31 August he repeated his appeal for an international peace conference but it was all to no avail, for on the following day German troops seized the Polish Corridor (a ribbon of land between the Baltic Sea and landlocked Poland, which was established by the Treaty of Versailles). They then invaded Poland itself, a country with which, in 1934, Hitler had signed a ten-year non-aggression pact. On 3 September, in furtherance of their guarantees of Polish independence, Britain and France declared war on Germany. It was the first move in a six-year cycle of bloodletting and destruction on a scale that scarcely could have been imagined.

---

5. K D Lewis, *The Catholic Church in History*. New York, 2006, p. 161.
6. P Blet SJ, *Pius XII and the Second World War*. Leominster, 2005, p. 21.

Though the Pope's attempts to preserve peace had failed, Francis D'Arcy Osborne, British Envoy to the Vatican was moved to say of him: 'We are in a position to state that His Holiness, up to the last moment, has unceasingly tried to prevent hostilities, not only through the initiatives already known to the public, but also through more confidential steps.'[7] What we have seen, however, since the War is that whatever else he might have done, more than one ex-post-facto analyst, from the safety of the academic library, would have deemed it insufficient. Such criticism would not have been new to Pius for he had seen how Benedict XV had been denounced by both of the factions in World War I because of his partiality for 'the other side'. Mediation is a process with high risk and little reward. Also, if at that stage, Pius XII had abandoned the Vatican policy of inveighing against the generality of evil rather than its particular perpetrators, his impartiality would have been compromised and his role as mediator forfeit.

His ultimate responsibility for the safety and spiritual well-being of the thirty million Catholics in Germany weighed heavily on Pius. He was determined to make the utmost effort to preserve their religious and legal rights despite their having been regarded, since the days of the Kulturkampf, as second-class, somewhat suspect, citizens. Now he was also concerned about the Catholics in Austria and Poland. Though his enemies charged him with being 'political', he was, in essence, a man of peace and prayer. Ivone Kirkpatrick, sometime British Chargé d'Affaires at the Vatican, once commented that it did not require a long conversation with Cardinal Pacelli to realise that even in politics he believed in prayer and in the reality of divine intervention.[8] But his sanctity must not be taken for naivety. Referring to the German denunciation of the Treaty of Locarno he once remarked to D'Arcy Osborne: '... no signature of the present German government is worth the paper it is written on.' On the German remilitarisation of the Rhineland he said to the French Ambassador: 'If you had acted with 200,000 troops you would have done an immense service to the world.'[9]

It is possible to discern three major objectives underlying Pope Benedict's efforts to bring World War I to an end. These were: that

7. A Rhodes, op. cit., p. 233.
8. Extract from British Foreign Office document 371/17759, 20 March, 1933.
9. F Charles-Roux, *Huit Ans au Vatican*. (Reported in A Rhodes, op. cit., p. 223).

the Vatican act with absolute impartiality so as to secure an effective, credible role as peacemaker; that every possible effort must be made to alleviate the suffering due to the conflict; and that through encyclicals and calls to prayer it must be continuously emphasised that hostilities between nations are inevitably futile.

An analysis of Pius XII's actions yields a similar picture for the Papacy and World War II. Pius lost no time with the third objective for on 20 October 1939 he published his first encyclical *Summi Pontificatus*. In it he affirmed that: 'We left no stone unturned, no avenue unexplored, to prevent, in any way which our apostolic office or other means at our disposal made possible, a recourse to arms.' He also declared that: 'The blood of countless human beings, including many civilians, cries out in agony, a race as beloved by Us as the Polish, whose steadfast Faith in the service of Christian civilisation is written in ineffaceable letters in the Book of History, giving them the right to invoke the brotherly sympathy of the entire world.'[10]

Although Pius also denounced the deification of the State at the expense of the individual, the repudiation of treaty obligations and the resort to war as a method of solving problems, the Allies had hoped for an even stronger denunciation of the Nazis. This would have been well suited to the propaganda of Britain and France but if Pius was not to abandon his desired role as mediator it is difficult to see what more he could have done. Moreover, despite the theological language and the periphrasis typifying encyclical style, he must have made his meaning completely clear because Reinhard Heydrich, Head of German Security, immediately forbade the publication of the encyclical in Germany, adding that its effect would be to damage Germany's standing in the world.[11] This then is an outline of the Holy See's efforts as war began. Let us now turn to the early reaction of the German bishops.

When a nation goes to war, all of its people, including its bishops and clergy, are involved. Through no fault of their own, seven million of Germany's young men now faced death or wounds. As they marched away, countless thousands of the devout Christians among them would

10. A Rhodes, op. cit., p. 237.
11. Bundesarchiv, Koblenz, Reichskanzlei file R4311/15046, letter from Heydrich to Lammers, 10 November 1939.

have been fortified by their faith and looked for their pastors' blessing. How could this have been denied to them? Whether or not Catholic ecclesiastics regarded the war as unjust, or, at the least avoidable, this could not absolve them from their pastoral duties.

We have, from its earliest days, extensive evidence of the loathing very many bishops felt for Nazism. The 1920 declaration of future Bishop Clemens August von Galen that National Socialism included ideas 'which no Catholic could accept without denying his faith' and the five occasions between 1920 and 1927 when their bishops warned German Catholics against the Nazis are cases in point. In 1929 the Bishop of Mainz asserted that no Catholic could be a member of the National Socialists and in 1930 Cardinal Adolf Bertram of Breslau emphasised his opposition to their creed. The following year saw the Bavarian bishops denounce Nazism as heretical.[12]

So, at the onset of war, the dilemma for Catholic leaders was how to support their flocks in their country's cause without endorsing the actions of the Führer and his monstrous cohort. As noted earlier, many bishops and priests were patriotic Germans who had served with distinction in World War I. However, as Helmreich points out: 'Yet as the war ground on . . . and the basically un-Christian aims and practices of the Nazi regime became clearer, the Catholic leaders progressively came to make a distinction between fighting for fatherland, home and folk, and fighting for Hitler.' He then quotes from a 1941 speech by Bishop von Galen: 'Bravely we continue to fight against the foreign foe; against the enemy in our midst who tortures and strikes us we cannot fight with weapons. There is but one means available to us in this struggle: strong, obstinate and enduring perseverance.' Helmreich then concludes that 'strong, obstinate and enduring perseverance' had been the hallmark of church policy in the pre-war years 'and it continued during the war itself.'[13]

Throughout the War the sermons of the bishops and priests were carefully monitored by the Gestapo. One of its reports (12 November 1939) declared that the attitude of the Church had not changed. Another report summarised the 1939 New Year's Eve sermon of the

12. J D Holmes and B W Bickers, *A Short History of the Catholic Church*. London, 1992, p. 268.
13. R C Helmreich, *The German Churches under Hitler*. Detroit, 1979, p. 347.

Bishop of Eichstätt: Catholics had been summoned to do their duty and stand firm in the hard struggle Germany faced. In the interest of unity he (the Bishop) was willing to overlook all the hardships that had been inflicted on the Church and its priests. But the Gestapo official then reported that the Bishop would not go a step further and pray God to bless the work of the Führer for: 'They simply cannot bring themselves to do this.'[14]

Reverting to the Papacy, the period from late 1939 to early 1940 provides a clear example of the complexity of the issues Pius XII faced throughout the War. The Germans invaded Poland on 1 September 1939 and, according to Anthony Rhodes, the Nazis had good reasons for choosing Poland. The far east of this eastern country would provide secrecy and security for the proposed death camps.[15] Poland's Jewish population of 3 million was the largest in Europe. By the War's end all of these had been killed as well as 3 million Polish non-Jews. As a proportion of population (220 per thousand) this was a far greater loss than that borne by any other nation in World War II. One fifth of Poland's Catholic clergy were included in this massive slaughter.

The Primate of Poland, Cardinal August Hlond, had escaped to the West and from him the Vatican soon learned of the desperate situation of the Polish people. By the end of 1939, fifty thousand of them (including 7,000 Jews) had been killed. The country's reserve stocks of food and the means to produce it had been shipped to Germany so that 70% of the Polish population were facing starvation. In his Christmas address, the Pope spoke of 'a calculated act of aggression against a small, industrious and peaceful nation, on the pretext of a threat that was neither real nor intended, nor even possible . . .' He also denounced '. . . the unlawful use of destructive weapons against non-combatants and refugees, against old men and women and children; a disregard for the dignity, liberty and life of man, showing itself in actions which cry to heaven for vengeance.'[16]

Pius also instructed that the Primate's information be handed to Vatican Radio for transmission. The news was received throughout

---

14. Ibid., p. 347.
15. See Rhodes, op. cit., p. 341.
16. Pope Pius XII, 'The Pope's Five Peace Points'. Address to the Sacred College of Cardinals, Christmas Eve, 1939. See Burleigh, op. cit., pp. 223-4.

the world and reported in its press. One newspaper, the *Manchester Guardian* (which subsequently became *The Guardian*) reported on 24 January 1940 that 'Tortured Poland has found a powerful advocate in Rome.'[17] The Nazis, incensed, declared that the Pope's 'neutrality' was a mere sham. But even then, Casimir Papée, Poland's ebullient Ambassador to the Vatican was pressurising the Pope to be even more forthright for word was now arriving that the Polish situation was worsening rapidly. Then on 14 January 1940 the Pope received a letter from the Bishop of Danzig: the Gestapo were claiming that the Vatican broadcasts were behind increased resistance from the Poles. Because of this Catholic priests and teachers had been arrested and either shot, subjected to terrible torture leading to death, or deported to camps in the far eastern areas of the country. The Bishop of Danzig clearly wanted the broadcasts to cease. So the Vatican was now receiving conflicting advice from two sources, both Polish. Despite the exasperation of the Polish government-in-exile in London, and Casimir Papée, the broadcasts were terminated. The Jesuit superior who had to give the order for this was himself a Pole. He said that though he hated doing so, 'What else could one do?'

We have gathered some of the reasons why the Pope wished to be seen as neutral. So he was angry when British intelligence used the Vatican broadcasts to give the impression that the Vatican was now firmly on the side of the Allies. Nevertheless, he felt that peace at any price was infinitely preferable to the horror and devastation of war. Which is why he involved himself in a plot to overthrow Hitler – a fact which the post-war detractors of Pius seem reluctant to advertise.

During his time in Bavaria, Nuncio Pacelli had become friends with Dr Josef Müller, a lawyer and devout Catholic. Müller subsequently became a member of the German resistance to Hitler and used his frequent trips to Rome to pass on information to the Allies. He had in fact been arrested by the Nazis on several occasions, for they suspected him of disloyalty. It seems not to have hampered his activities. Through Müller's contacts with the Catholic priest Ludwig Kaas, by now in Rome as superintendent of St Peter's Basilica, and Robert Leiber, a German Jesuit and personal secretary to the Pope, Pius learned of the plot. A group of German generals, led by Ludwig Beck (who was

---

17. *Manchester Guardian* editorial, 24 January 1940. (See Rhodes, p. 238.)

also a friend from the Pope's days as nuncio), were planning a coup d'état, so as to prevent Hitler's projected invasion of France and the Low Countries. They intended to arrest Hitler and bring him to trial, ultimately replacing him by a democratic, conservative government. The generals would be anxious to negotiate peace at the earliest possible moment subject to 'reasonable, acceptable conditions'. In the meantime they wished the Allies to make no counter-move in the West until the coup d'état took place.

Learning of this, the Pope agreed to be the intermediary between the generals and the British Envoy to the Vatican, Francis D'Arcy Osborne. Pius felt his 'conscience would not have been easy' had he refused to do so. No doubt by this time he also realised the complete impossibility of Hitler sitting at a negotiating table with anyone and concluding terms that he (Hitler) intended to keep. It transpired that the British were indifferent to the proposal, Sir Robert Vansittart saying: 'I'm not a great believer in the German generals. There is always too much "jam tomorrow" about them. Their plan would provide the means for Germany to get away with the Hitler loot without any of the assurances we demand against ulterior aggression.'[18] D'Arcy Osborne was told to inform the Pope that the generals would be promised nothing until Hitler and his minions had been exterminated.

Although the plot came to nothing the link with Dr Müller proved most valuable to the Pope. Müller was also well-known to Admiral Wilhelm Canaris, Head of the Abwehr, the German military intelligence organisation. Despite his exalted status, Canaris was a resolute opponent of Hitler (he was subsequently hanged at Flossenbürg in the closing days of the War). Through Muller, he supplied the Pope with regular, high-quality information on the atrocities committed against Polish Catholics and Jews. As a result, on 23 December 1940, Pius issued his secret letter, *Opere et caritate*, to the bishops of Europe. It instructed them to help in every possible way any people persecuted by the Nazis because of their religion or race.

When in May 1940 Hitler invaded the Low Countries, the Pope sent telegrams of condolence to the King of the Belgians, the Queen of the Netherlands and the Grand Duchess of Luxemburg. Once again the Allies deemed the Pope's sentiments insufficient and Monsieur

---

18. A Rhodes, op. cit., p. 241.

Charles-Roux, France's Ambassador to the Vatican, told Monsignor Tardini, deputy Secretary of State, as much. Tardini replied that if he read the telegrams properly he would find in them all he desired. And once again the reaction of the totalitarians gives us the best clue as to the value of the Pope's action. While the Allies, looking for official condemnation of Germany, felt the Pope had been too restrained, Mussolini felt he had gone too far. On 25 August *Regime Fascista* declared preposterously: 'With these telegrams the Pope incites the Catholic King of the Belgians to cause the blood of his people to flow in order to help the Jews, the Freemasons and the bankers of the City of London.'[19]

In his audience with the Pope on 13 May, Italy's Ambassador to the Vatican, Signor Alfieri, had been more restrained but made it clear that the telegrams were 'a cause of serious displeasure' to Mussolini. Alfieri added, no doubt under orders, that because of the immense tension now evident in Fascist circles 'serious things' might happen. The Pope understood well enough what the threat conveyed. Showing once again his physical courage (Monsignor Montini noted that Pius was 'very tranquil and serene'), he replied that he was not all afraid of being seized by adversaries or committed to a concentration camp. Referring to the Munich incident of 1919 when he was confronted by Red revolutionaries, he added: 'We were not intimidated by pistols pointed at Us once and We will be even less frightened next time.'[20] By this stage too, in considering the tone and content of his responses to criminal actions by belligerent nations, he confided to Monsignor Montini: 'We would like to utter words of fire against such actions, and the only thing restraining Us from speaking is the fear of making the plight of the victims worse.'[21] By now, of course, there was ample evidence that his caution was justified.

His hatred for Nazism can be judged from his actions as well as his words. In March 1940 Dr Müller had informed his Vatican contacts of the date for Hitler's planned invasion of Western Europe. In secret, the Pope immediately passed on the information to the nuncios in

---

19. *Actes et Documents du Saint Siège*, Vol. 4, p. 34.
20. Ibid., Vol I, p. 313.
21. From notes of Mgr Montini of Pius XII's private comments, also reported in *Actes et Documents du Saint Siège*, Vol. I, p. 313.

Brussels and The Hague. In turn, they relayed it to London, Paris and the Low Countries. The advance news seems not to have availed the Allies very much for on 14 May the French were taken by surprise when German armour began hurtling through the Ardennes. A day later the Dutch Army surrendered and on the 17th the Germans entered Brussels. By the 20th Hitler's troops had reached the Channel, bisecting the Allied forces, and by the 27th the British began their evacuation from Dunkirk and other ports. On 14 June the Germans reached Paris and on the 22nd the French signed an armistice, at Compiègne, with a jubilant Hitler.

The Pope's sustained effort to deter Italy from entering the War had begun in 1939. By May 1940 he was being pressed by both Cardinal Suhard, Archbishop of Paris, and M. François-Poncet, French Ambassador to Italy, to try yet again to restrain Mussolini. The Pope, however, could only confirm that he had used up all his credit with the Dictator who no longer listened to him or read his letters. It came as no surprise to him perhaps that, on 10 June, Italy declared war on France and Great Britain. So now the Vatican City State had become a tiny independent enclave in a belligerent country. Perhaps not enough has been said of the effects of this on the Pope's already formidable anxieties. When, in the face of continued Papal intransigence, Mussolini had reached breaking point, it would have been a simple matter for him to have cut off the Vatican's water supply or prevent the entry of food and other necessities across its borders. Or, either the Italians or the Germans could, in a coup-de-main operation, have taken the Pope from the Vatican Hill to imprisonment or death. Neither would have had any compunction in doing so, therefore presumably only the possibility of overwhelming international response or the revolution of Europe's Catholics deterred them from doing so.

The Pope's worries were intensified because he now had to give shelter to more than one hundred Allied diplomats, their families and staff, who could not remain on Italian soil for this was now 'enemy territory'. Matters became even more complicated when, during 1942 and 1943, many South American Republics declared war on the Axis powers so His Holiness became host to even more diplomats – from Brazil, Peru, Bolivia, Venezuela, Colombia, Cuba, Ecuador and Uruguay. So it was not long before the smallest sovereign state in the world was being described contemptuously by Axis voices as 'a nest of spies'. Also, it seems not to have occurred to those lamenting the fact that the Pope did not take more 'direct action' that all he had to prevent the incursion of a German panzer division were one hundred Swiss Guards. It is noteworthy that all these tensions and pressures made little difference to Vatican Radio, for all its Jesuit operators continued to criticise the Nazi regime rigorously. This led Mr A W G Randall, in charge of Vatican Affairs at the British Foreign Office, to report on 21 July 1941 that: 'No other neutral power would have persisted so long in furnishing us with such useful material.'[22] Facts like these seem to elude many revisionist historians.

Perhaps not surprisingly France's political situation seemed to revivify its religious ardour, as was the case in Russia at this time. Anthony Rhodes reports that even Socialists and Free Thinkers invoked God's aid: 'In May 1940 when the German armies were crashing through the eastern defences, they came in a body solemnly to the Sacré Coeur to crave protection for the nation.'[23] (It reminds one of the dictum of Air Chief Marshal Sir Basil Embry, a practising Catholic with a magnificent World War II record, that 'there are no atheists in rubber dinghies'). Rhodes points out that most of France's population did recognise that 'in some strange way the Catholic Church is one of the pillars of French civilisation.' The defeat of 1940 made many Frenchmen who had been sceptical about religion turn to it again. Perhaps they conjectured that the country's defeat in 1940 was 'retribution for its sins of the 1920s and 1930s.' Even the well-known figure General Weygand believed that France had been beaten because for half a century religion had been expelled from her schools.

When France fell, Hitler agreed there would be an area in its south and south east which would be unoccupied by the Germans. It was to be governed from Vichy, in the north of this zone which thus came to be known as 'Vichy France'. At the head of its government was the eminent Philippe Pétain, Marshal of France and commander of its victorious armies in 1918. The French Church now hoped for better treatment under Pétain, a Catholic Head of State nurtured by Catholic

---

22. Minute by Mr A W G Randall on British Foreign Office document 371/30177.
23. A Rhodes, op. cit., pp. 311-313.

Conservative ideas. Before long he was deemed to be introducing 'a political and social programme which was clearly inspired by the twentieth century Papal encyclicals.'[24] The laws forbidding priests from teaching in schools were revoked and religious instruction was made compulsory in public schools. A number of property rights were guaranteed to monastic Orders and religious societies. Legislation was enacted against abortion and alcoholism, and divorce was made more difficult. Consequently, in the early days of 'Vichy' its churches were full and pilgrimages were regularly undertaken to Lourdes, Fatima and Notre Dame de Boulogne.

In spite of all this the Papacy was cautious about Pétain and marked time on opening negotiations for a concordat with 'Vichy'. At the onset, Cardinal Gerlier of Lyons had been an enthusiastic advocate of the Pétain regime but his ardour cooled after his visit to Rome in January 1941. It may well be that he was given instructions to be more conditional in his support. Moreover, as the war ground on and German pressure on Vichy increased, the prospects of any concordat evaporated. The Lyons diocese had emerged as a centre of resistance to the Germans and, according to the Nazi-controlled Paris press, Cardinal Gerlier was seen as the arch anti-collaborator. The cardinal is among the many unsung heroes of the Church in World War II. His growing intention to increase the Church's distance from the Vichy government became more apparent with the ascendancy of Pierre Laval who was to become Vichy's Premier. It might now be important to describe the action of Cardinal Gerlier and others of the Catholic hierarchy in that region.

In the occupied zone of France the Germans had banned Catholic youth organisations. Cardinal Gerlier had insisted that those in the 'Vichy' zone should be left in operation. For this he was personally congratulated by the Pope. Gerlier also denounced the deportation of the Jews and his message was read from all pulpits in his diocese. In spite of Laval's attempt to silence it, the message was also broadcast throughout France. When, on 10 September 1942, Laval stated his intention to 'cleanse France of its foreign Jewry' and ordered 20,000 of them to be deported for extinction in the East (10 September 1942) the Reich State Security (RSHA) reported that as a result of this a split

---

24. Extract from *Revue des Deux Mondes*, 15 September 1940.

was now evident between Church and State because Cardinal Gerlier had ordered Catholics to prevent the deportation of Jews, particularly children. At this time the RSHA noted the arrest of several Jesuits who had hidden hundreds of Jewish children and refused to give them up. Protests against Laval's measures had also appeared in a number of pastoral letters including, particularly, those of Archbishop Saliège of Toulouse. Up to that point, the Catholic Church had not dissociated itself from the State, as it had in the occupied zone where all the publications of Catholic Action had been suppressed, monasteries and convents had been entered and searched and Cardinal Suhard had been arrested and imprisoned for 'Judeo-Masonic activities'.

With the increasing power and perfidy of Laval the split between Church and State in the Vichy zone became clear. It was the French bishops of both zones who now protested about his actions:

> The mass arrest of the Jews last week and the ill-treatment to which they were subjected . . . has deeply shocked us. There were scenes of unspeakable horror when the deported parents were separated from their children. Our Christian conscience cries out in horror. In the name of humanity and Christian principles we demand the inalienable rights of all individuals. From the depths of our hearts we pray Catholics to express their sympathy for the immense injury to so many Jewish mothers and children. We implore you, M. le Maréchal [i.e. Pétain], to see that the laws of Justice and Right are not debased in this way.[25]

Archbishop Saliège arranged for an appeal to Christian ethics to be read from the pulpits of the Toulouse diocese. It insisted that the French had always respected the rights of the human being, whatever his race. His appeal ran:

> That men and women can be rounded up like a herd of cattle, that members of the same family can be separated from one another and transported to unknown destinations – to live through this horror, is that what is reserved for us today? In the concentration camps of None and Recebedon disgraceful scenes have taken place. Jews are men too! Jewesses are women too! They belong to the human race, they are our brothers and sisters. Let no Christian ever forget this!

Cardinal Gerlier was moved to confirm that the ways of Church and

---

25. Reported in A Rhodes, op. cit., pp. 316-317.

State had now parted in France. He was ready to lead the French people through 'the bitter days that lay ahead until the end of the war.' The Pope himself fully supported these statements. He told British diplomat Francis D'Arcy Osborne that he had instructed Monsignor Valeri, Nuncio to Vichy, that he too must protest against the persecution of the Jews in France. Further, the Nuncio was ordered to tell Pétain that the deportations were grossly in breach of the religious beliefs he (Pétain) had vouchsafed when he took office. The Pope then issued a formal protest to Pétain himself. He also suggested that all convents and monasteries should become refuges for Jews. So far as the French clergy were concerned, Nuncio Valeri was instructed to tell them that they must support the Pope's denunciations according to their Christian duty. Finally, in reporting these facts, author Anthony Rhodes adds a most important comment. He mentions the Pope also instructing Valeri that since the clergy in Germany *with the approval of the Vatican*, (my emphasis), were now in opposition to the 'pagan Nazi regime' in their country, it would be unthinkable for the French clergy to advise their flocks to collaborate with it.[26] Tragically, the ageing Pétain was no match for Laval and had, to all intents and purposes, relinquished control. Consequently nothing was done and the persecution continued. Historian Michael Burleigh states that though the people involved ran very grave risks, Catholic convents, monasteries and schools throughout France were deeply involved in hiding Jewish people throughout the occupation. He also draws attention to the efforts of Protestants in this regard and adds that 'predominantly Protestant villages in and around Le Chambon-sur-Lignon high on the Massif Central in south-central France managed to give sanctuary to five thousand Jews during the occupation.'[27] In Chapter Six of this work we shall return to the occupation of France when we look at a profile of Lucien Bunel ('Père Jacques') whose efforts to save Jewish children ultimately cost him his life.

By 1940, persecution of the Catholic clergy in Poland was well under way. Helmreich, for example, provides relevant data for the Archdiocese of Posen.[28] On 1 September 1939, it had a total of 828

---

26. See A Rhodes, op. cit., p. 317.
27. M Burleigh, op. cit., pp. 248-49.
28. E C Helmreich, op. cit., p. 357.

clergy. By 1 October 1941, only 51 of these were still spiritually active and 22 were now without permission to carry out their duties. 17 had died natural deaths, 57 were in hiding, 24 were outside the boundaries of 'Greater Germany', 451 were in concentration camps but still alive at that date and 120 had already been shot or had died there. It is reasonable to suppose that most of the discrepancy between the overall totals (828 and 742) is explained by deaths during transportation to the concentration camps. In 1939, 441 churches had been functioning. By 10 October 1941, only 45 were in use – the remainder had been closed or put to other uses. 83% of the 1,034 clergy who died in Dachau were Polish. Because of Hitler's intense hatred of the Poles, a staggering number of non-Jewish Poles, 3 million, were killed, as noted earlier, and the survivors endured barbarous persecution. Further, the Polish civilians sent to Germany for forced labour found the meagre allowances of food doled out to other labourers reduced in their case. This applied to Poles in the concentration camps, where their pains and torments were now intensified by virtual starvation. Polish clergy also suffered. Dutch, German and Norwegian clergy were used in Dachau for garden work but in 1942 Himmler ruled that Polish and Lithuanian priests must be used in work of all types. While the persecution fell, in the main, on the ordinary clergy, 9.78% of clerical inmates were higher clergy. In Dachau, Bishop Dr Michael Kozal of Poland, Bishop Gabriel Piquet of France and Bishop Dr Johannes Neuhäusler of Munich were held captive. Despite that in 1940 Nuncio Orsenigo and Bishop Wienken had negotiated some relief for clerical prisoners in concentration camps. It has also been said that, the Nazis were circumspect about imprisoning higher clergy for fear of producing martyrs, hence insurrection. Even so, abbots and other senior clergy were imprisoned: more evidence that, in the Nazi era, the Catholic Church was hardly compliant.

The deep-seated hatred of the Nazis for the Poles is exemplified by happenings in the Warthegau, a region of 46,000 square kilometres set up within the wreckage of the Polish state. Burleigh records grimly how the Nazis perceived the region as a blank slate for their ideology.[29] When war began it held about five million

29. M Burleigh, op. cit., p. 227.

ethnic Poles and 340,000 ethnic Germans. By 1944, the German element had been trebled. 'Dechristianisation' was also part of the programme. The region's Protestants were cut off from their associate organisations in the 'Old Reich'. The funding available via Church taxes to the Catholic Church, preponderantly the major Christian body, was stopped. Seminaries, monasteries and convents were closed, Church membership for children, schoolteachers and Nazi officials was forbidden, as was religious instruction in schools. The Polish and German communities were segregated, the 'German' churches bearing a 'Poles forbidden' notice.

In Germany itself, from July 1940, the elimination of 'useless eaters' recommenced. Initially, Lutheran pastors learned of a secret programme to eliminate these 'eugenic and economic burdens on the wartime national community,' who possessed 'life unworthy of life', Following the Lutheran Bishop Theophil Wurm of Württemberg, the Catholic bishops protested vehemently. Approaching government officials deemed free of the Nazi taint they denounced such policies as illegal and inimical to Christian belief; moreover, these policies could undermine the morale of the people and damage Germany in the world's eyes. Cardinal Bertram of Breslau remonstrated that ceasing to protect the lives of the innocent would lead to a steady widening of the expedient criteria for extermination (a current experience in the Britain since the enactment of its abortion laws). On 6 December 1940, euthanasia killings were denounced categorically by the Holy Office in Rome because they were 'contrary to both the natural and the divine positive law.' Within the protesting Catholic and Protestant German clergy, a highly visible figure was Bishop August Clemens Graf von Galen – the 'Lion of Münster'. A detailed profile of von Galen, elevated to Cardinal by Pius XII after the War, is to be found in Chapter Six.

In October 1939, Germany's Army High Command, in line with the Concordat, had directed that certain groups of Catholic clergy were exempt from military service. Principally these were bishops, parish priests and clergy in charge of a place of public worship. Other Catholic clergy could be called up for medical service only. Mobilisation for service with weapons would apply only to those theological students not yet instituted as sub-deacons. The policy differed sharply from that relating to Protestant clergy who were apparently called up for combat duty without demur. The Concordat had not been without success then, for it saved Catholic clergy from the moral dilemma of serving a regime hostile to the Church and often barbaric in countries it had invaded. There was an interesting development on 31 May 1941, for Hitler ordered that all Jesuit priests be immediately discharged from the armed services and not called up again. If he was fearful of the power of the Catholic Church, he reserved a special fear of the Jesuits.[30]

The German invasion of Russia in June 1941 found Stalin searching frantically for allies. This even extended to the Church for he told Father Stanislas Orlemanski, a Polish-American priest, that he wished to 'collaborate with the Pope against the coercion and persecution of the Catholic Church in Germany.' Stalin described himself to this priest as 'a champion of Freedom of Conscience and religion.'[31] This persuaded President Roosevelt that the approach was the thin end of a wedge ultimately leading to complete freedom of religion in the USSR. Noting that a number of churches had been reopened and permission granted for distribution of pastoral letters, some English Protestant clergymen were like-minded. The Vatican, however, was not so sanguine. Monsignor Tardini pointed out that the deep-dyed dogma of Communism emanated from Marx, Engels and Lenin, men determined to destroy religion.

To further the Communist creed, 24,000 churches and convents had either been destroyed or adapted for use as social clubs, cinemas or warehouses. In implementing the policy, thousands of priests had been murdered. According to Tardini, the word of Stalin was as valueless as those of the other dictators. Father J C Heenan (later to become Cardinal Archbishop of Westminster) had recently visited Russia and provided an important supplement: whereas in 1919 there had been 560 churches in Moscow to serve a population of 2 million there were now (1941) 22 churches for a population of 4 million. He concluded that those insisting there was no religious persecution in Russia were 'enemies of Christ's Church'.

Nazi conquests in Europe had led to the creation of new states.

---

30. E C Helmreich, op. cit., p. 354.
31. A Rhodes, op. cit., pp. 258-59.

These added to the increasing complexity of decision-making for the Vatican. The independent Slovak state, founded under German protection, was a case in point. The Catholic, and nationalist, Slovak People's Party, which subsequently became the Party of National Unity, was the ruling force. It controlled Slovakia in an uneasy relationship with the openly fascist Hlinka Guard. Matters became more complex for the Vatican when, in October 1939, Dr Jozef Tiso, Catholic priest and theologian, became the President. Pius XII regarded this as 'inexpedient'. Earlier he had told a group of German pilgrims that it was more than ever imperative for a priest to be wholly above political and national fervour. A priest's duties were: '. . . to console, to comfort, to help, to call to prayer and to penance, and himself to pray and do penance.'[32]

On 28 July 1940, Slovakia declared its intention to develop according to Nazi ideology, including 'Aryanisation'. Even worse, while consecrating a church Tiso declared the social doctrine of Christianity to be perfectly compatible with Nazism, bringing the Holy See to the brink of nullifying his clerical status. Tiso was popular with the Slovaks so Hitler left him in power but always under the gaze of Vojtech Tuka and Sano Mach, placemen operating as foreign and interior ministers respectively. It seems likely that, to retain office despite the machinations of the pair, Tiso agreed that Slovaks could fight the Russians and he also became involved in Slovakia's 'Final Solution'.

By September 1941, Tuka and Mach had introduced their 'Jewish Codex', which was far more punitive that Tiso's previous measures. As a result, Vatican Secretary of State Maglione protested that the 'Codex' contained 'various provisions directly opposed to Catholic principles.'[33] From early 1942 Jews began to be deported. The official word was that they were going to work camps near Lublin in Poland. The truth was they were being despatched to Auschwitz, Belzec, Majdanek or Sobibor and killed as they arrived. Of the 58,000 deported only 600 to 800 survived the War. The Catholic Church has been criticised for what happened in Slovakia at this time but history shows that, though the priest Tiso was seemingly out of control, the Vatican made

32. M Burleigh, op. cit., p. 259.
33. Ibid., p. 259.

exhaustive efforts to stop what was going on:

> 28 February, 1942 – Guiseppe Burzio, Papal chargé d'affaires in Bratislava sought out Vojtech Tuka. He was astounded that Tuka 'vehemently defended the legitimacy of the measures and dared to say (he who paraded himself as a Catholic) that there was nothing inhumane or anti-Christian with this.' Burzio insisted that deportation to the mercy of the Germans in Poland equated with certain death.
>
> 14 March, 1942 – Secretary of State Maglione summoned Karol Sidor, Slovak representative at the Holy See. He expressed his astonishment that 'a country inspired by Catholic principles will take such grave measures which will produce such harmful consequences for so many families.'
>
> 24 March, 1942 – Sidor was again summoned and told 'on the direct authority of Pius XII to take immediate action with his government to halt the deportations.'[34]
>
> April 1942 – The deportations having continued, Maglione again interviewed Sidor. Angrily, he dismissed the latter's claim that the Jews were being used within a 'labour conscription scheme'. He told Sidor that '. . . such actions were a disgrace, especially for a Catholic country.'
>
> End April 1942 – A pastoral letter from the Slovak bishops insisted unequivocally that: 'The Jews are also people and consequently should be treated in a humane fashion.'

Anyone doubtful of the effectiveness of the Vatican at this time should bear in mind that because of these interventions, deportations from Slovakia were halted between October 1942 and September 1944. Burleigh describes this as 'an unparalleled occurrence in the history of the Holocaust.'[35] He also reports that when the bishops learned that the deportations would be resumed they issued a pastoral letter which rejected the concept of 'collective guilt' (of the Jews) which the regime was using as justification; cited the Slovak Constitution's guarantee of liberty 'without regard to ethnic origin, nationality or religion'; and refused to accept any distinction between Jewish converts to Catholicism and other Jews, and invoked the Parable of the Good Samaritan.

---

34. L Rothkirchen, *The Vatican and the Jewish Problem in Slovakia*. Yad Vashem Studies 1967, 6, p. 39.
35. Citing L Rothkirchen, 'Czechoslovakia' in D S Wyman (ed.), *The World Reacts to the Holocaust*. Baltimore, 1996, p. 170.

In spite of the fact that Father Tiso was President of Slovakia, he had still continued as a parish priest. Accordingly, he was instructed to read this same pastoral letter from his own pulpit.

What remained of Royal Yugoslavia also proved a formidable challenge for the Church. Independent Croatia, a Catholic country, had been formed but it was subject to joint German and Italian occupation. Its own internal regime was controlled by the Ustashe, an organisation very closely identified with National Socialism and Italian Fascism. Ominously, its founding principles included such statements as, 'the Croatian nation belongs to Western culture and Western civilisation'. By the end of April 1941 it was issuing decrees designed to 'protect Aryan blood and the honour of the Croat people.'

The Primate of Croatia, Archbishop Aloysius Stepinac (later to become a Cardinal and be beatified), remained firmly loyal to the independent Croatian state, since freeing the Croats from Serbian Orthodox control ended the discrimination against Catholic Croats for government jobs. Nonetheless, by May 1943, he had made 34 separate interventions on behalf of Jews or Serbs against the wilder supporters of the State, principally the Ustashe. Ante Pavelic, founder of the Ustashe, had become Croatia's ruler ('Poglavnik'). His Ustashe fascists would be responsible for the mass murder of Serbs and Jews. In the beginning, however, the Croat Church welcomed the regime for it had prohibited abortion, contraceptives, freemasonry, pornography and even 'strong' language (to use our current euphemism). It had also assisted Catholic schools and seminaries and given financial aid to Catholic charities. But soon Mile Budak, education and culture minister, revealed the regime's true objectives when he warned that: 'For minorities such as the Serbs, Jews and Gypsies we have three million bullets.'

Breathtakingly, it was the Ustashe intention to deport or kill half the Serb population and forcibly convert the other half to Catholicism. From late April 1941, Aryanisation measures were also introduced against the country's Jews who were ordered henceforth to wear the Star of David. Archbishop Stepinac speedily protested. On 22 May he requested that the principles of human dignity be preserved and the order concerning the Star of David be revoked. He pointed out that the Holy See did not favour the laws now being enacted and diplomatic recognition could be withdrawn. He also requested that deportees receive medical care and be kept in touch with their families. Some aspects of the Church's continuing struggle against the activities of the Ustashe government include:

> 15 May 1941 – In order to avoid Ustashe murder squads, whole villages were desperately seeking to convert to Catholicism. The Archdiocese of Zagreb instructed its clergy to probe deeply into the motives of each would-be convert. Archbishop Stepinac warned against political incursion into policy areas rightfully belonging to the Church.
>
> August 1941 – Bishop Alojzije Mišić of Mostar informed Stepinac that newly converted Serbs were being seized and murdered. Each of the clergy was strictly forbidden to give absolution to any of these murderers.
>
> 17-20 November 1941 – The Archbishop convened a national Synod to discuss forced conversions. It condemned the Ustashe's claim to the right to convert people to Catholicism. The bishops insisted that the rights of the Orthodox Church be respected. In the case of persecution of the Jews, Stepinac intervened even more forcefully. Pavelic received a letter from the Synod, demanding he treat them in a humane manner.

Romania also became a member of 'the all-conquering German new order,'[36] and in September 1940 King Carol II had invited General Ion Antonescu to form a government. In Burleigh's words, the Romanian Fascists were rivalled only by the Nazis in their hatred of the Jews, and 'their fusion of political militancy with Orthodox mysticism' resulted in a 'truly lethal whole.' They went as far as to proclaim that 'God is a Fascist!' The country's Jewish population, three quarters of a million people, was the third largest in Europe. They were persecuted with an intensity revealed by the slaughter of 60,000 of them on 23-24 October 1941 by Romanian troops acting on the direct orders of Antonescu. This was the largest single massacre of Jews during the entire war. President Filderman of the Jewish community protested that Antonescu's measures meant only 'death, death, death without guilt, except the only guilt of being a Jew.'[37] Archbishop Andrea Cassulo, the papal nuncio, intervened effectively on behalf of the Jewish community and in early 1944 Chief Rabbi Safran of Romania

---

36. M Burleigh, op. cit., p. 270.
37. Ibid., p. 273.

and Grand Rabbi Herzog of Jerusalem wrote to Cassulo thanking him and the Pope for 'everything they had done for the Jews.'[38]

In Germany itself, on 6 July 1941, a Pastoral letter had been read from all Catholic pulpits. It was issued from Fulda and signed by five Catholic cardinals and five bishops. It protested against the closure of churches, schools, monasteries and convents. It spoke scathingly of a book (Rosenberg's *Myth of the Twentieth Century*) 'which asks us to choose between Christ and the German People'. The letter went on: 'With a flaming protest we refuse to make such a choice.' It also implored parents to educate their children in the faith so that the Christian home would become a small church of itself. We can perceive the value of the Church's resistance through the words of the Nazis yet again, for Reinhard Heydrich declared: 'The Fulda bishops' message constitutes a direct threat on the German State . . . Here we see what a bitter and irreconcilable enemy we have in the Catholic Church.'[39]

The Gestapo ignored the Church's protests and continued to seize its property. On the following Sunday, Bishop von Galen resolved to tell Catholic laity what was happening. He was typically hard-hitting. The confiscation of monasteries, for example, had nothing to do with wartime economies and now extended to South Germany, the Warthegau, Luxemburg, Lorraine and Westphalia. He also paid tribute to the courage of that 'noble German man', Martin Niemöller, Protestant pastor and enemy of the regime. He declared that justice was the foundation of a state but if it lost justice where would that state be? On the following Sunday he returned to the attack. There had been further confiscations including the provincial house in Hiltrup of the Missionaries of the Sacred Heart of Jesus. From there 161 men had gone to serve in the army, 53 as medical orderlies and 101 in the fighting services. Many of them had been decorated. They would return to find themselves homeless. And where was the chivalry in driving women from their homes? Of the regime he said: 'As long as they do not change, as long as they continue to rob the innocent, to drive them out of the land, to imprison them, so long as this continues,

38. Ibid., p. 275.
39. A.A. Pol III Inland, paks 44 and 45 Kirkliche Angelegenheiten pp. 0072 and 0073, letter from Heydrich, 7 October 1941.

I reject any community with them.' He compared his congregation to an anvil and implored them to 'become hard; remain firm; remain steadfast, as the anvil does under the stroke of the hammer.'[40]

The tone of his sermon on Sunday, 3 August, was if anything even more belligerent. After again mentioning the confiscations he turned to the euthanasia programme and fearlessly declared: 'If they start out by killing the insane, it can well be extended to the old, the infirm, the sick and seriously crippled soldiers. What do you do to a machine which no longer runs, to an old horse which is incurably lame, a cow which does not give milk? They now want to treat humans in the same way.'[41] The regime could not prevent copies of the von Galen sermons spreading throughout Germany and beyond, even to the Allied press. Among the alarmed was Germany's well-known aviator and war hero Colonel Werner Mölders. He immediately wrote to Marshal Göring, asking if the accusations were true. Nor did it rest there, for when Hitler was bestowing on him the diamond order of knighthood with oak-leaves and swords, Mölders asked the question again. Hitler and Göring had to lie – the government did not encourage euthanasia.

By now the Nazis felt something must be done about von Galen. Martin Bormann did not hesitate – the death penalty would be appropriate. Goebbels felt that: 'If we hang him we can regard the population of Münster and probably all Westphalia, as of no more use to us during the war. To postpone a measure, however, is not to renounce it. When the war is won . . .' Hitler himself was decidedly averse to making any Catholic martyrs. In Germany alone there were 30 million Catholics, many of whom were devout and serving in the armed forces. Goebbels' warning was well founded for when after his 'euthanasia' sermon von Galen was actually arrested, he had to be released immediately, so great was the public outcry. It is reported that 'the population of Münster carried him back in triumph.'[42]

On 30 July 1941, Hitler ordered that the seizure of church and monastic property must be stopped. On 24 August he issued instructions for the euthanasia programme to be halted. The influence of von Galen

---

40. E C Helmreich, op. cit., pp. 358-360.
41. Ibid., p. 360.
42. A Rhodes, op. cit., p. 296.

on the first of these decisions is clear. It would be overclaiming for his efforts to say they were the sole cause for the euthanasia decision, because there had been numerous requests from the public and from both Catholic and Protestant church leaders for the programme to be halted. Nevertheless it must be acknowledged that his powerful and sustained attacks manifestly contributed to the outcome. Which is no doubt why when Alfred Rosenberg's diaries were found in 1948 they contained the following cryptic entry: 'After the victorious conclusion of the war, Bishop von Galen to be shot.'

By a decree of 1 September 1941, all Jews were required to wear the Star of David. Cardinal Bertram advised his fellow bishops that 'rash measures that could hurt the feelings of the Jewish Catholics' should be avoided. Examples here would be the introduction of special Jewish benches, the separation of Jews from the main congregation when administering the sacraments, and the introduction of special services. He also suggested, should a reminder that Jewish Catholics be treated with love become necessary, a statement based on St Paul's warnings to the Romans and Galatians that among those believing in Christ there is neither Jew nor Greek, for all are one in Jesus Christ.[43]

The happenings of late 1941 provide two further examples of how decision-making by the Holy See had become so complex. Our first example relates to Europe. At this time Jewish leaders were well enough satisfied with the Pope's efforts on behalf of the Jews. On the other hand, the Poles wished him to say more about the Nazi atrocities in their country. In November, Archbishop Adam Sapieha of Cracow had pleaded that if the Pope spoke out the Poles would certainly gain heart. Actually, it had been due to earlier requests from their bishops that Pius had ordered Vatican Radio broadcasts on the Polish plight to cease. Accordingly, the Archbishop was told the Holy See now preferred to work through diplomatic channels. Even so, Pius sent a message to the Polish bishops only to discover the Archishop then suppressed it, because of the possibility of German reprisals against the clergy and laity.[44] The story is included here not as a criticism of Sapieha, who no doubt found the situation changing

43. E C Helmreich, op. cit., p. 361-62.
44. A Rhodes, op. cit., p. 288.

by the hour because of the unpredictability of Nazi savagery, but as a demonstration of Papal dilemma. Perhaps it was the capricious nature of the oppressors that subsequently led the Archbishop to write a letter to the Vatican on the appalling situation in the concentration camps, hand it to an Abbé Scavizzi, an almoner on an Italian hospital train, then change his mind and instruct the Abbé to destroy the letter. His fears were 'lest it fall into the hands of the Germans who will then shoot all the bishops and perhaps many others.'

The second example relates to Sunday 7 December 1941, when Japanese forces struck ruthlessly, and all within seven hours, at Malaya, Pearl Harbour (Hawaii), the Philippines and Hong Kong. On the following day, as a result of these attacks, the United States and Great Britain declared war on Japan. Three days later Germany, in her turn, declared war on the United States. The road to global war was now open. Pope Pius, ever the seeker after peace, was gravely concerned, for peace was now a pearl of even greater price. Matters worsened when, on 19 September 1942, he was visited by Myron Taylor, US special envoy to the Vatican who made clear the Allies' decision that diplomacy must now be abandoned. The Allies were interested only in total victory. From now on, any peace proposals would be considered as Axis inspired and deemed a blow to the Allied cause. Any future peace efforts of the Pope would be seen by the United States as the Vatican bestowing favour on Germany. The sequel to this development will emerge later in this chapter.

The year 1942 and the broader canvas of occupied Europe provide countless examples of how Nazi persecution of the Catholic Church intensified. Parallel examples of its defiance are readily to hand. Early in the year, invoking a Hitler decree of 29 May 1941, the Gestapo had seized the monastery of the Community of Benedictine Nuns of Perpetual Adoration in the Münster diocese. On 1 February, Bishop von Galen mounted his pulpit and thundered his response. Though he claimed a reputation for self-control, he admitted to having paced his study for ten minutes before he was able to consider the matter objectively. How could these sisters who spent their entire lives in prayer be considered enemies of the State? In any case, the monastery did not belong to the nuns; it had been a gift to the diocese from the King of Prussia in 1821. Thus it followed that he, the Bishop of

Münster, plus all the people of the diocese, were now enemies of the State and should be declared so. Hans Kerrl, Minister for Church Affairs, called for action against the bishop. Walter Tiessler, a key figure in the Ministry of Propaganda, proposed that he be hanged forthwith. Bormann supported this but Hitler, no doubt fearful of the consequences, still did not wish to make any direct move at that time. At a conference of the secret police it was decided, nonetheless, that the number of informers against the Church be increased.[45]

At this stage, Nuncio Orsenigo was pressing for the right to extend his jurisdiction to the territories annexed and occupied by Germany and for the provisions of the 1933 Concordat with Germany to be extended to them. This would have given the Church the right to protest against such specific violations as the elimination of confessional and private schools, the curtailment of subsidies and so on and would have provided the Vatican with freedom over the appointment of bishops and administrators about which the regime was usually difficult. The Nazis were in no mood to agree, however, complaining about the general attitude of the Catholic Church and 'its failure to understand the requirements of National Socialism.' On 10 June 1942, Hitler gave specific instructions that he did not want relations with the Catholic Church to be conducted uniformly for the whole (i.e. enlarged) Reich. The provisions of the Concordat were to be restricted to the 'Old' Reich. The Nuncio could continue to protest about the treatment of the Church in the occupied lands, and continue to advance his claims, but no attention would be paid to him.

By now, news of the treatment of the Jews was filtering out of Occupied Europe. It is interesting to note that on 8 July 1942, Britain's Cardinal Hinsley, Archbishop of Westminster, in a BBC broadcast, denounced the criminal behaviour of the Germans in Poland. Speaking of '700,000 Jews massacred since the beginning of the war,' he declared that: 'Their innocent blood cries out to the heavens for vengeance. And we have plenty of evidence, including copies of German documents describing the extermination.'

In July 1942 the deportations began of the Jews of Holland. These led to a formal protest from all the major Dutch Denominations, which devised a Joint Pastoral Letter. Here it is important to quote an

45. E C Helmreich, op. cit., pp. 360-61.

extract from it:

> The undersigned Dutch churches, already deeply disturbed by the measures against the Jews in the Netherlands, which exclude them from participation in the normal life of the people, have noted with horror the new measures by which men, women and children and entire families are being taken away to German Reich territory and subject territories. The suffering brought by this upon tens of thousands, the awareness that these measures conflict with the most profound moral consciousness of the Dutch people, and the infringement which these measures contain against everything that is our right and just duty in the sight of God, compel the churches to make the urgent request to you not to put these measures into effect.[46]

On 11 July this 'Announcement' was sent by telegram to the German Reich Commissioner in the Netherlands. Both Catholics and Protestants threatened to make their protest public if the deportations were not stopped. It is important to explain that there were a large number of baptised (i.e. converted) Jews in Holland – a greater percentage, in fact, than anywhere else in Europe. When the then Cardinal Pacelli had been negotiating the German Concordat he sought to have included a clause protecting baptised Jews. The Nazis would make no more than a verbal promise that they would be regarded as Christians. And up to the time of the Joint Pastoral Announcement they had not been troubled in Holland. Now, the German authorities promised that if the Churches would remain silent they would continue to make a special exception of the baptised. In face of this, according to Burleigh: 'While the Protestants tried to stop their pastors reading the message (i.e. from their pulpits), the Catholic hierarchy positively encouraged priests to do so.' Moreover, the Catholic Archbishop of Utrecht issued a Pastoral letter in which he drew attention to the 'sad destiny of the Jews and the plight of those deported for forced labour.' Concerning the Jews, he added: 'let us pray to God and for the intercession of Mary . . . that He may lend His strength to the people of Israel, so sorely tried in anguish and persecution.'

Nazi reaction was swift. In his book *Hitler's Holocaust*, Dr Guido Knopp appends this extract from the reaction of the German occupation authorities: 'Since the Catholic bishops – with no direct

---

46. G Knopp, *Hitler's Holocaust*. Stroud, 2001, p. 243.

interest in the matter – have interfered in it, all Catholics of the Jewish race will now be deported this very week. Any interventions are to be disregarded.'[47] The Germans delivered on their promise, for they arrested *all* the baptised Catholic Jews and sent them to the death camps. Among them was the philosopher-nun Edith Stein who was gassed with her sister on 9 or 10 August 1942. In 1998 she was canonised by Pope John Paul II as Saint Edith Stein, Teresa Benedicta of the Cross (see her Profile in Chapter Six). On the other hand, the Protestant Jews were not touched. These facts provide another example of the dilemmas faced by the Pope. Throughout the War, the parties to the conflict rushed to denounce their opponents. Whatever denunciations he issued were invariably 'not strong enough'. Yet whenever he spoke out strongly or authorised someone to take a firm line, the plight of the victims worsened.

There were other important developments in 1942. For example, in January, a decision was taken at the SS RSHA headquarters in Wannsee (Berlin) to eliminate all European Jews. By Spring and Summer it was being fully implemented. Even so, the Allies made no immediate response to this news. Burleigh reports that Stalin made only one passing reference to the Jews in all his public speeches during the War.[48] On 10 March, Nuncio Bernardini in Berne wrote on behalf of the Orthodox Jewish Agudas Israel, which had received no practical assistance from Jews in the US or Britain, urging the Pope to intervene in Slovakia. Burleigh also reports that although the US State Department received 'high grade intelligence' in August of what was happening it did nothing for four months until independent confirmation made a joint Allied condemnation unavoidable.[49]

More evidence is available to refute latter-day charges of Catholic indifference to the fate of the Jews. On 8 December, Britain's Cardinal Hinsley again spoke out. From the pulpit of Westminster Cathedral he declared: 'Poland has witnessed acts of such savage race hatred that it appears fiendishly planned to be turned into a vast cemetery of the Jewish population of Europe,' (on 30 June the BBC reported that

---

47. Ibid., p. 243.

48. Citing J K Roth and E Maxwell (eds), *Remembering for the Future. The Holocaust in an Age of Genocide*. Basingstoke, 2001, I, p. 355.

49. G M Riegner, in W Laqueur (ed.), *The Holocaust Encyclopedia*, New Haven, 2001, pp. 562-67; and in Burleigh, p. 253.

the Germans had already killed over a million Jews in all, of whom 700,000 had been in Poland). In July, Nuncio Orsenigo sent news from Berlin that he had been warned that 'the less he talked about the Jews, the better it would be.'[50] Notwithstanding this, the US Catholic bishops issued a statement, an extract from which reads: 'We feel a deep sense of revulsion against the cruel indignities heaped on Jews in conquered countries and upon defenceless people not of our faith... Deeply moved by the arrest and maltreatment of Jews, we cannot stifle the cry of conscience. In the name of humanity and Christian principles, our voice is raised.'

By this stage and throughout the rest of the Nazi occupation, Catholic convents, monasteries and schools were deeply involved in hiding Jewish people (see the profile of 'Père Jacques' Bunel, Chapter Six). On the 30 July, old and infirm though he was, Jules-Gérard Saliège, Archbishop of Toulouse, whose record of denouncing Nazism went back to 1933, said in his Pastoral letter: 'The Jews and the foreigners are real men and women. Everything is not permitted against them, against these men and women, against these fathers and mothers. They are part of the human species. They are our brothers, like so many others . . .' An even stronger condemnation emanated from Pierre Marie Théas, Bishop of Montauban and in September eight Jesuits were arrested in Lyons for refusing to identify the buildings where they were sheltering Jewish children. In the index of his book *The Righteous – The unsung heroes of the Holocaust*, Sir Martin Gilbert lists many Catholic individuals and institutions who gave sanctuary to Jewish people.

In the Spring of 1942, a Baron von Lersner had visited the Vatican in the hope of meeting certain high officials. He began making discreet soundings as to whether the Vatican would be prepared to act as mediator in any peace negotiations. Though he claimed to be speaking on his own behalf only, he felt the German generals believed that even a victory would not bring a proper peace. When Cardinal Secretary of State Maglione declared that a real persecution of Christianity was in progress in Germany, von Lersner completely agreed with this view. It has been argued that these 'personal peace proposals' coupled with President Roosevelt's 'Unconditional Surrender' declaration made clear

50. M Burleigh, op. cit., p. 254.

to the Vatican how the war was to end and it resulted in a yet more critical attitude being taken in Vatican policy towards Germany.[51]

In November 1942, Heydrich's RSHA reported that 'anti-German utterances by Italian priests during the Sunday sermons are becoming more frequent.' Typical of these was one in Albano San Alessandro. The priest regretted, he said, having to give up his church bells to make armaments, and then said, 'And what is worse, the order comes not from our own Italian government, but from the rulers of Luther's fatherland. In Italy to-day there are two Crosses,' he added, 'that of Christ the King, and the Hakenkreuz.'[52]

In September 1942, during the visit of Mr Myron Taylor, and at the instigation of President Roosevelt, His Holiness was informed that America and Great Britain had a close alliance with Soviet Russia with whom relations were excellent. Roosevelt's naivety about Stalin's intentions was disturbing – how could Christian countries have 'excellent relations' with an avowedly atheistic State? The Pope was incredulous and especially when Taylor pointed out that Communistic principles now extended to many parts of the globe and that people believed in them. News of Axis reverses was by now arriving and the thought of an enlarged Soviet Union in the post-war period only deepened the Pope's anxiety.

The protests of the German hierarchy did secure another success when in 1942 the German government was moving to enforce the dissolution of racially mixed marriages. Cardinal Bertram vehemently protested to the Ministers of Justice, the Interior, and Ecclesiastical Affairs. A large number of families were to be affected by such divorces, which were in any case contrary to Church doctrine. The Cardinal was supported by Bishop Wurm and other Protestant leaders. Also, importantly, hundreds of Aryan wives demonstrated in Berlin when their non-Aryan husbands were about to be transported 'to the East'. In the end, the compulsory divorce law was never promulgated.

The 1942 Christmas broadcast of Pope Pius XII is considered as perhaps the most important made by him during the entire War. In it, he is also considered to have been more forthright than ever before.

---

51. See Anthony Rhodes. op. cit., pp. 270-271.
52. In A.A. Akten Repetorium, *Italy at War,* p. 0026: and in Rhodes, pp. 299-300.

In a long address he spoke strongly of 'the hundreds of thousands who, through no fault of their own, and solely because of their nation or race, have been condemned to death or progressive extinction.' This reference to the Jews could hardly have been clearer and so it grieved the Pope to learn that the Western Allies still considered his condemnation not strong enough. In order to arrive at a balanced indication of the effectiveness of the broadcast we must turn to the Nazis again, for on 22 January 1943, Heydrich's RSHA was in no doubt about the damage the Pope had done to the Nazi cause. The following extract appears in RSHA documentation:

> In a manner never known before the Pope has repudiated the National Socialist New European Order ... his speech is one long attack on everything we stand for ... God, he says, regards all peoples and races as worthy of the same consideration. Here he is clearly speaking on behalf of the Jews ... he is virtually accusing the German people of injustice towards the Jews, and makes himself the mouthpiece of the Jewish war criminals.[53]

Rhodes notes that *L'Osservatore Romano* was still publishing interpretive articles on the Christmas broadcast in May 1943. He also points out that von Ribbentrop was worried enough about the Pope's message to instruct German Ambassador von Bergen that if the Vatican abandoned its traditional neutrality, Germany would not lack 'physical means of retaliation'. The Pope would be very clear about the meaning of these words – his possible kidnapping, murder or both. These possibilities were real enough as witness the arrest of Pope Pius VII in 1809 by Napoleon's troops. Ambassador von Bergen relayed Ribbentrop's message to Pius XII and, on 26 January 1943, reported that 'His Holiness remained quite silent.' Subsequently the Pope was to show, by both word and action, that such threats had no effect. In fact, at the end of the War, Sir Francis D'Arcy Osborne, Britain's Envoy to the Holy See, who came to know the Pope very well, remarked that with regard to the War the Pope 'without the slightest doubt ... would have been ready and glad to give his life to redeem humanity from its consequences. And this quite irrespective of nationality or faith.'[54] If nothing else, the Pope's efforts on behalf

---

53. In A.A. Abteilung Inland, pak 17, Vol. I, RSHA report, 22 January 1943; and in Rhodes, p. 273.
54. K D Lewis, op. cit., p. 165.

of the Jews of Rome (see Chapter Seven) shows D'Arcy Osborne's assessment to have been well founded.

It was in March 1943 that the deportation of Bulgaria's Jews began. Burleigh comments on the 'notable and honourable part' played by the Orthodox bishops of Plovdiv and Sofia to frustrate the Germans' intentions.[55] He also explains that 43 members of the parliamentary governing faction protested against the deportations. Further, he outlines the sterling work of Angelo Giuseppe Roncalli (subsequently Pope John XXIII) the then Apostolic Delegate to Istanbul. Monsignor Roncalli had a lengthy connection with Bulgaria as the Papal delegate to Sofia and he made repeated interventions on behalf of the Bulgarian and Slovakian Jews. He was also of great help to Jewish organisations by providing resourceful documentation for crossing Turkey en route to Palestine. There were multiple pressures on King Boris on behalf of the Jews with the result that he agreed that Sofia's 125,000 Jews be dispersed to the countryside where they would be safe from deportation to Poland and certain death.

Here it is necessary to make an important point concerning the nature of communication from the Vatican, this being, that although, for reasons outlined earlier, the Pope felt it necessary to couch all his public addresses in diplomatic language, in his private addresses to Heads of State he was certainly more forthright. For example, on 7 April 1943, in his message to the Slovak government, he made it perfectly plain that on its own account, as well as that of its almost wholly Catholic population, it should never proceed with the deportations of Jews. But now it seemed that the government would sanction the removal of the entire Slovakian Jewish population, including its women and children. He went on: 'The Holy See would fail in its Divine Mandate if it did not deplore these measures. Its pain was even more acute when these measures were carried out among a people of great Catholic traditions, and by a government declaring it was their follower and custodian.'[56] In June 1943, speaking to the College of Cardinals, he explained eloquently why every public statement he made put him in an alarming predicament: 'Every single word in Our statements addressed to the competent authorities and every one of

55. M Burleigh, op. cit., pp. 276-7.
56. A Rhodes, op. cit., p. 347.

Our public utterances, has to be weighed and pondered by Us with deep gravity, in the very interest of those who are suffering, so as not to render their position even more difficult and unbearable than before, be it unwittingly and unintentionally.'[57]

Notwithstanding these cautionary words, later that month he promulgated his encyclical *Mystici Corporis*. In it he condemned the 'legalised murder' of the deformed, the insane and the incurable – which was a violation of natural and divine law. He felt the attacks on Catholics for their faith as an offence against His own person. His hardening attitude towards the Nazis is revealed in a minute of the British Foreign Office in which he is reported as saying: 'If the Germans win, it will mean the greatest period of persecution that Christians have ever known.'[58]

It was at this time there was also some strain in the Vatican's relations with the Western Allies. The issue was whether Rome should, or should not, be regarded as an 'open city'. The Vatican pressed for it to be so, arguing that since it was the location for so many valuable shrines and art treasurers, it really belonged to the world and not to a single country. The Allies took a more instrumental view of things. Rome was, after all, the seat of an enemy government as well as a strategic centre for rail communications and the site of an airport. Moreover, if operations in southern Italy began it would be used by the Axis as a conduit for supplies to the war zone. And it greatly alarmed Vatican officials when a British air marshal stated that in its bombing campaign the RAF would not be influenced by 'sentimental considerations'.

Both Monsignor Tardini and Monsignor Montini discussed with the British Envoy the ghastly prospect of the centre of Christendom being under bombardment. They wanted to know precisely what was meant by 'sentimental considerations'. For once, they found D'Arcy Osborne immovable. The British clearly remembered Mussolini's gloating over the Italian contribution to the bombing of London in 1940. The Vatican had said nothing then about the bombing of Christian shrines in England. In the event, the Allies would not regard Rome as an 'open city' and bombed it in July and August 1943. In

57. M Burleigh, op. cit., pp. 252-3.
58. F.O. 371/33412, Sir S Hoare to Mr Eden, 28 October 1942.

the July attack, the main railway goods yard was destroyed and the nearby church of San Lorenzo was partially destroyed. Several hundred people were killed and, according to Rhodes, it was a tearful Pope who visited the devastation and offered his sympathy to the relatives of the victims.[59] This issue, and the situation of Italian clerics and missionaries left behind in Abyssinia and North Africa (and regarded as aliens by the victorious Allies there) were more burdens for a Pope already under almost intolerable strain.

There is hard evidence from the German diplomat Albert von Kessel (*Die Welt*, 6 April 1962), that between September 1943 and June 1944, Hitler almost certainly considered kidnapping the Pope and imprisoning him in the Wartberg in Upper Saxony.[60] The plan was that had Pius resisted, he would have been 'shot while trying to escape'. Albert von Kessel, in this context, gives due recognition to Ernst von Weizsäcker, Germany's new Ambassador at the Vatican. Since von Weizsäcker's adroit performance of his duties is perhaps not widely known some description may be helpful. Because he recognised full well the danger to the Pope, von Weizsäcker constantly tried to persuade him not to say anything to ignite Hitler's choleric temperament. On the other hand, by what von Kessel has called 'ingeniously phrased despatches', von Weizsäcker strove to establish in Hitler's mind the belief that the Pope was not too ill-disposed towards Germany and that Catholic gestures favouring the Jews had no significance and could therefore be ignored. Diplomat von Kessel also adds these telling comments:

> We knew that a violent protest by the Pope against the persecution of the Jews would have certainly put the Pope in great personal danger, and it would not have saved the life of a single Jew. Like a trapped beast, Hitler would have reacted to any provocation with extreme violence. Hitler, kept at bay by the Allies, and their Unconditional Surrender demand, was like a beast of prey pursued by hunters, capable of any hysterical excess or crime.[61]

It is easy to see, of course, how von Weizsäcker, proceeding from the

59. A Rhodes, op. cit., p. 277.
60. A von Kessel, 'Der Papst und die Juden', *Die Welt*, 6 April 1962: and in A Bullock, *Hitler: A Study In Tyranny*, p. 708.
61. A von Kessel quoted in A Rhodes, op. cit., p. 344.

best motives with his ostensibly duplicitous tactics, may well have done damage to the reputation of Pius in the eyes of history. In this regard, Burleigh points out this has undoubtedly been the case but at the time the stratagem succeeded in diverting the attentions of the Nazis away from the thousands of Jews hidden in Catholic churches and private houses in Rome. Burleigh concludes his observation: 'Such serpentine stratagems were as normal to those who had to negotiate these shoals at the time as they are alien to the academic moralists who deplore them with the luxury of hindsight.'[62]

On 10 July 1943, the Allies attacked Sicily and consolidated their landings there without difficulty. This put the Axis relationship under great pressure for, even before this, there was distrust between the German and Italian armed forces. Soon Hitler's fears were realised. On the night of 24-25 July the Fascist Grand Council met and subjected Mussolini to a torrent of criticism for his conduct of the War. On the following evening he was dismissed by King Victor Emmanuel and placed under arrest. A new non-Fascist government was formed, led by Marshal Pietro Badoglio. The Fascist party was then dissolved and its leaders dismissed. Hitler was astounded but quick to react. He sensed that Badoglio was duplicitous: he would make soothing noises but he was locked in underhand dealings with the Allies. So every available soldier had to be mustered to occupy and hold the Italian peninsula. Responding to his call, Hitler's lieutenants convened on the 26 July to discover that he had already prepared four plans: 1. *Eiche* ('Oak') for the rescue of Mussolini; 2. *Student*, for the occupation of Rome and the restoration of a Fascist government; 3. *Schwarz* ('Black') for the military occupation of Italy; and 4. *Achse* ('Axis') for the capture or destruction of the Italian fleet.[63]

On 10 September 1943 the Germans occupied Rome. The question immediately arose of what to do about the Vatican. When an aide of von Ribbentrop asked if the exits of the Vatican should be blocked, Hitler immediately retorted: 'I'll go right into the Vatican. Do you think the Vatican embarrasses me? We'll take that over right away. It's all the same to me. That rabble (the Diplomatic Corps) is in

---

62. M Burleigh, op. cit., p. 279.
63. A Bullock, *Hitler: A Study In Tyranny*. pp. 708-9.

there. We'll get that bunch of swine out of there. Later we can make apologies.'[64] According to distinguished historian Alan Bullock it was only after pressure from Ribbentrop and Goebbels that he agreed not to seize the Vatican, but for a number of days he continued to ponder the idea of an immediate coup against the Holy See. Any reader in doubt of Hitler's determination should examine the details of the Fosse Ardeatine massacre. When in 1944 a party of German soldiers were blown up by a bomb stealthily hidden in a Rome street, the Führer ordered all houses in the area to be flattened and every person living there, whether man, woman or child, to be shot. His order resulted in 350 deaths.

Hitler's self-control, always notoriously fragile, was now being clearly undermined by the war situation. Another incident at about this time clearly indicates his increasing frenzy. When Monsignor Orsenigo, Nuncio to Germany, raised the question of the Jews, Hitler jumped from his seat, crossed to a window and began to drum on its glass with his fingers. Despite having now to talk to Hitler's back, the Nuncio decided to continue with his entreaty. Suddenly, Hitler turned to Orsenigo, picked up a glass of water from a table and, in his anger, smashed it to the floor. Sardonically, Orsenigo reflected that 'confronted with this brand of diplomatic intercourse,' he could only consider his mission was over.[65]

In Germany itself, on 12 September, the Catholic bishops issued their Fulda Pastoral letter, *Ten Commandments as Laws of Life for Nations*. The bishops recognised, well enough, that the War was going badly and they gave words of encouragement to the faithful in the interests of 'internal unity'. Nevertheless, in no sense did these dilute their message. On the Fifth Commandment ('Thou shalt not kill') they made the following statement:

> Killing is bad in itself, even when it is done in the interests of the common welfare: against innocent and defenseless [*sic*] mentally ill and other sick; against incurable invalids and fatally injured, against those with inherited disabilities and children with serious birth defects, against

64. Ibid., p. 708.

65. Mgr Orsenigo to Professor Eduardo Senatra, reported in *Petrus-Blatt*, Berlin Diocesan newspaper, 7 April 1963 and quoted from the Documentation Catholique, 18 August 1962.

> innocent hostages and disarmed war and other prisoners; against people of alien race and descent. Even the government can and is permitted to punish with the death penalty only those who are truly death-deserving criminals.[66]

As Autumn progressed, the presence of German troops in Rome became all-pervading. Despite this, His Holiness instructed Italian bishops to open all convents and monasteries to Jewish refugees. Soon they could find sanctuary in a vast number of Church buildings – no fewer than 150 in Rome itself. Ronald J Rychlak reports that by now as much as one third of the Jewish population of Rome was hidden in buildings owned by the Catholic Church.[67] As many as 500 Jews were concealed in the Pope's summer residence at Castel Gandolfo, where the Pope's private apartment had become an obstetric ward.

In late September, the SS Commander in Rome, Herbert Kappler, ordered the city's Jews to hand over 50 kilograms of gold within 36 hours or 200 hostages would be deported. The Jewish writer Pinchas E Lapide comments: 'As soon as the Vatican found out about this, it discreetly informed the leaders of the Jewish community that, if the required quantity of gold could not be collected within the stipulated time, it would furnish whatever was missing.' Lapide then quotes Professor Oscar Halecki who stated: 'Pius XII instructed the Vatican treasurer to raise whatever gold was still required. This was accomplished in less than a day, probably by melting down religious vessels.'[68] The Germans had given assurances that their sole interest was in the gold. Despite it being paid over, the rounding up of Italy's Jews began in the following month. It meant that between October 1943 and January 1944 over 3,000 Italian Jews were sent to Auschwitz. Only 46 survived the War. When the process got under way, the Pope immediately instructed Secretary of State Maglione to protest vigorously to von Weizsäcker, Germany's Ambassador to the Holy See. He also ensured that all locations receiving fugitives bore a sign that they were under Vatican protection. Without the Church's intervention, the slaughter would have been even worse.

The year had been fateful for the Nazis. The surrender at Stalingrad

---

66. E C Helmreich, op. cit., p. 364.
67. R J Rychlak, *Hitler, the War and the Pope*. Columbus, 2000, pp. 202-04.
68. P E Lapide, op. cit., pp. 258-59.

on 2 February had been followed by defeat in North Africa in early May. The Allies invaded Sicily on 10 July and Mussolini was deposed on 25 July. On 3 September came the Allied invasion of the Italian mainland and Italy's subsequent armistice (8 September), which led to the German occupation of Rome and the rest of Italy two days later. The projected encirclement of the German homeland highlighted for the Nazi government the importance of national unity. So from this point it began to ease down on any policies contributing to internal tension. In Germany, at least, there was some consequent improvement in the situation of the Catholic Church – clerics and monastic priests were exempted from tasks of national defence, agitation in the Labour Service against the Church was expressly forbidden, a proposal to reduce the State's support for the training of priests was abandoned, and where schools had been evacuated due to heavy bombing, religious instruction was restored to its former levels. Even the hated Poles came in for some improvement of their lot for, on 5 June, German priests were permitted to participate in baptisms and burial for Polish forced labourers and, in August 1943, confession and the last rites were also allowed for Polish civil workers. Even so, as we shall see, there were still difficult times ahead for the Church.

1944 began on a bitterly ironic note when, in February, many of the fugitives in Castel Gandolfo were killed by Allied bombing. April was to bring more strain in the Vatican's relationship with the Allies, this time concerning a charitable project for starving Rome. The scheme was intended to bring food supplies, principally flour, from ports in northern Italy and in ships flying the Papal flag. Detailed logistical work was completed by the Vatican on sea and road transport and the vessels to be purchased but in the end the scheme was turned down because it would 'place severe restrictions on Allied operations in an area of military importance.'[69] The fall of Fascism had left a number of Italian officers and men stranded behind the German lines. Since they would not fight for Mussolini and his new Fascist state, located at Salò on Lake Garda, they were likely to be shot as traitors. Some were hidden in the Vatican and a Monsignor Moscatelli headed a group of five Jesuit priests who distributed money to families willing to

69. F.O. 371/50084, Annual Report for 1944 from Sir D'Arcy Osborne, April 1944, reported in Rhodes, p. 282.

conceal these fugitives. The German Security Service (RSHA) itself calculated that as many as 180 political refugees from the North were being concealed in the Vatican City State. Interestingly, these included the composer Pietro Mascagni. It should be noted that the Church did not discriminate among the asylum seekers on political grounds – a number of leading Communists and Socialists were hidden in the Basilica of St John Lateran. It was enough that they were being hunted by the Germans.[70]

Helmreich points out that in Germany the Concordat had been successful in keeping most Catholic clergy from serving in the armed forces.[71] This was of great benefit to the Church but also to Germany itself. The work of the clergy had increased tremendously. It now included Masses for men killed in action, Masses of intercession for soldiers in combat, ministration to the homeless and other victims of bombing, and the pastoral care of an extensive foreign labour force, much of it Catholic. The numerical strength of its clergy also meant that the Catholic Church was better placed than the Protestant groups to help address the problems of the post-war world. Although, in a general sense, as noted earlier, the changing fortunes of Hitler's Reich had led to some amelioration in the persecution of the Church, this did not mean that Nazi hatred of it had abated. The archival reports of the RSHA reveal much that is relevant here. Rhodes, for instance, notes the use of the word *ausrotten* (exterminate) in secret memoranda between Reinhard Heydrich and his chief Heinrich Himmler.[72] In a general circular to his staff, Heydrich had said: 'We should not forget that in the long run the Pope in Rome is a greater enemy of National Socialism than Churchill or Roosevelt.' It is also noteworthy that in RSHA reports to Heydrich is the comment that the Japanese were fully aware that 'Catholicism must be exterminated if a truly New Order is to arise in Asia.'

Heydrich himself had died on 4 June 1942, assassinated in Prague, but some of the best evidence that his hatred of Catholicism lived on is revealed in the stories of individual Catholics who opposed the

---

70. A Rhodes, op. cit., p. 301.
71. E C Helmreich, op. cit., pp. 352-5.
72. A.A. Pol III Informationsberichte über die politischen Kirchen, May/June 1943; see Rhodes, p. 309.

Nazi regime. Dr Max J Metzger, Catholic theologian, was beheaded in April 1944. His story is told in Chapter Six but here a detail from his martyrdom is very revealing. After his death, the nuns of the convent he had served were sent a bill for the costs involved in killing him. With acknowledgements to Helmreich,[73] the details are set out below:

Charge for death penalty	R.M. 300.00
Expenses	
Postal charge	.12
Prison charges June 29, 1943-April 16, 1944	
293 days at R.M. 1.50	439.50
Total charges	739.62
Covered by his own money	368.36
Amount still due	R.M. 371.26

On 15 February 1945, Father Alfred Delp SJ, a member of the Kreisau Circle (profiled in Chapter Six), was executed, allegedly for taking part in the bomb plot (20 July, 1944) to assassinate Hitler. To the very end, Father Delp steadfastly maintained his innocence. On 15 January 1944, 'Père Jacques' (Lucien Bunel) was arrested for sheltering some Jewish boys in his school. They had been passed on to him by the nun in charge of another school (Chapter Six q.v.). He was subsequently imprisoned in various camps and died on 2 June 1945 shortly after his liberation. The general 'climate' for the Church may have improved somewhat, but for individuals such as these there was no respite from the Nazi terror.

1944 was a significant year for the Catholic Church in Hungary. The country's Prince Primate, Cardinal Jusztinián Serédi had been hated by the Nazis from their very beginnings as a political party. When the Second World War came Hungary, fearing the threat of Soviet Commuism, had joined the Axis Powers. The Cardinal, however, was implacably opposed to Nazi ideology. In his Lenten Pastoral letter of 1942, he spoke of the 'attempts being made to force mankind to abandon God . . .' He also made a pointed reference to 'the withdrawal of the conditions of existence from certain members of the community.' This was clearly a reference to the Jews and, in St Stephen's Cathedral on New Year's Day, 1943 the Cardinal had been even more blunt, warning that there was no master race, no nation

73. E C Helmreich, op. cit., pp. 366-7.

was inferior to another. He had continued: 'Murder is murder, and he who, for political reasons, orders mass executions will not receive the rites and consolations of the Church. Nor will the Church grant the sacraments to those who, on ideological grounds, abduct human beings for forced labour.'[74]

His attacks led to complaints by the German Foreign Office to the Hungarian government. It replied that, under the terms of the Hungarian Constitution, the Prince Primate had complete freedom of speech. Then, on 23 March 1944, the Germans arrived in force. Up to that point, although they had suffered much prejudicial treatment, the actual lives of Hungary's 750,000 Jews had not been in danger. Now, however, as the deportation began, the Vatican telegraphed the Nuncio in Budapest, Archbishop Angelo Rotta, on 28 March and 5 April. The Holy See made clear to him how perilous the situation of the Jews had become and urged him to do all he could to protect them.[75] From the onset of the deportations, both the Cardinal and the Nuncio protested but were assured that the Jews were being moved for forced labour only. In the light of this, on 5 June, the Nuncio felt he had to ask two questions: since seventy- and even eighty-year old men were being expelled, along with women, children and invalids, what type of work would they be expected to do? Secondly, since non-Jewish Hungarians, off to work in Germany, were not allowed to take their families with them, why were the Jews being granted this special privilege?

It was clear that the 'labour camps' were, in effect, extermination camps and this was confirmed in April by two Slovak Jews who had escaped from Auschwitz and managed to reach Bratislava. There they gave information to Papal representatives about the gas chambers and crematoria. They also reported that the gas chambers were being enlarged and that the Nazi gaolers were boasting that 'soon we shall have fat Hungarian sausages.'[76] Plans to stop the deportations came to Admiral Horthy, Head of State, from Pope Pius, the King of Sweden,

74. A.A. Pol III Akten Repetorium, p. 0035, report from the German Legation, Budapest, (RSHA Obersturmbannführer Mylius, 25 January 1943).
75. M Burleigh, op. cit., p. 280.
76. These details are reported in the book *I Cannot Forgive* by RudolfVrba, one of the escapees (see Rhodes, p. 303).

the President of the International Red Cross, the diplomat Raoul Wallenberg, Cardinal Francis Spellman of New York, and the Papal Nuncio, Angelo Rotta. At that time Archbishop Rotta was making repeated visits every day to government headquarters. Westminster's Archbishop Griffin also made a significant contribution to the stream of protest as did the Hungarian Catholic prelates, under instruction from Vatican Secretary of State Maglione.

On 5 July the deportations ceased but in October when Horthy, who had a creditable record of frustrating German intentions, announced an armistice with the Russians, he was deposed. He was succeeded by a Nazi puppet, Ferenc Szálasi, leader of the Fascist Arrow Cross. The Germans sent their 'Jewish experts' to Budapest under Adolf Eichmann, head of the 'Jewish Evacuation Department' of the Gestapo, and the hunt for Jews could now be resumed.

The subsequent efforts of the Catholic Church and other organisations are shown in numerous examples. For instance: under the leadership of the Nuncio an 'International Ghetto' was established in Budapest. It consisted of several blocks of flats in which thousands of Jews were given sanctuary. The buildings were protected by the national insignia of the Vatican, Switzerland and Sweden. Secondly, very many religious houses in Budapest hid Jews, at great risk to the religious communities, male and female, involved. Father Ferenc Kálló was shot for issuing certificates of baptism for the safe conduct of Jews. Burleigh records that Dominican priests and other clergymen visited air raid shelters 'to carry out perfunctory baptisms which brought the all-important certificate that would enable the Jews to evade destruction.'[77] Thirdly, from Istanbul, Apostolic Delegate Roncalli sent thousands of these certificates to Hungary while Archbishop Rotta issued 15,000 protective passes to Jews requesting notional conversion to Catholicism. He also allowed a Red Cross official to take heaps of blank, but signed, letters of safe conduct to be used for the protection of Jews. Burleigh writes: 'As a result of these rescue efforts 55,000 Jews survived alongside the 69,000 in Budapest's "Big Ghetto".'

One of the most appalling entries in the catalogue of Nazi crimes was Eichmann's 'Death March' of Hungarian Jews. By now, trains and

77. M Burleigh, op. cit., p. 282.

'other means' of transport were extremely scarce. But Eichmann was not to be outdone. With his subordinates, he decided that the 20,000 Jews remaining 'at their disposal' should be marched from Budapest to Theresienstadt, a concentration camp thirty-five miles from Prague. Setting out on this difficult journey were many old and infirm people alongside mothers carrying babies. Cardinal Serédi and Archbishop Rotta, the Nuncio, organised relief vehicles to accompany them. These contained food and medicines and were protected from requisition by their Papal insignia. The commander of the relief convoy also carried with him several thousand blank Papal safe conduct passes. These were signed by the Nuncio together with a letter authorising the commander 'to find and help on the roads and in the camps all persons of Jewish origin who enjoy the diplomatic protection of the Holy See.'[78] It has been estimated that on this march alone, a further 2,000 Jews were saved as a result of the Catholic Church's efforts. We should note here also that the Nuncio personally hid 200 Jews in buildings available to him. He instructed all priests to do the same.

At the dawn of 1 January 1945, troops of the Allied forces were massed at the eastern and western frontiers of Germany. The Nazi government now most definitely had preoccupations other than religious persecution to engage it. But, as we have noted earlier, down to its final days the regime continued to kill all the clerics who had opposed it. These included the Protestant pastor Dietrich Bonhoeffer who, on 9 April, was executed in the concentration camp at Flossenbürg. And so, in Europe at least, on 8 May, the War came to an end, but Nazism was not yet done: Father Jacques Bunel died on 2 June, Father Rupert Mayer SJ on 1 November and on 28 March 1946 the 'Lion of Münster', Clemens von Galen, by now a cardinal, was laid to rest. We shall learn more of them, and many others of heroic virtue, in the chapter which follows.

78. A Rhodes, op. cit., p. 306.

Chapter Six

'HEROIC VIRTUE'

Individual Opposition to Nazism

Introduction

People labelled as 'progressive' hold fast to the notion that a secular society, purged by 'science' and 'reason' of the baleful influence of religion, will put the Age of Faith well behind it and enter a future where peace, humanity and justice prevail. The evidence, of course, is all against this, as the twentieth century, the most violent in history, has taught us. One historian of Christianity reminds us that because of a number of utopian, strictly secularist ideologies, wars on a hitherto unimaginable scale have been waged in the century just passed.[1] These conflicts have resulted in the deaths of perhaps 150 million people. On the other hand, he states that the Inquisition of the Spanish Crown, the worst abuse of ecclesial authority in Christian history, resulted, over three centuries, in possibly 30,000 deaths, all subsequent to a legal process which produced vastly more acquittals than convictions. He adds that the Soviet Union and the People's Republic of China have killed the same number of their own citizens in three days and that without any trial at all.

Another radically atheist political movement spawned by the century was Nazism, of course. And in scope and extent it was arguably the worst of all. Its revolutionary evil resulted in the most cataclysmic event in human history, the Second World War. And we have to remember that this title was accurate: it was a world war, one which raged over Europe, Africa, Asia, the Pacific and all the

---

1. D B Hart, *The Story of Christianity*. London, 2007, p. 238.

other oceans. It involved as participants every state which existed in the world in 1939, except Sweden, Switzerland, Portugal, Spain, the Irish Free State, Iceland, Greenland, Afghanistan, Tibet, Mongolia and Yemen.[2] Even within the century's unparalleled bloodletting its savagery was unique for it destroyed over fifty million people and left millions more scarred and destitute. So much for blood and as for treasure, much of Europe's cultural heritage was obliterated, its political systems viciously effaced and the very basis of its civilisation brought low. It was unique, moreover, in that it set about, by industrial means, the eradication of an entire race of people.

In this book, the nature of Nazi ideology has been outlined and evidence has been offered of the Catholic Church's unrelenting opposition to it. Now we turn from institutional to individual opposition. The Greek word *martys* means 'witness'. By the second century 'martyr' slowly took on the technical meaning of one who died or suffered for the public confession of the Christian faith.[3] In this chapter we meet fifteen Catholics who, in their witness to Christ, repudiated National Socialism. Most of them, quite quickly, paid for this with their lives. Others, at a later stage, 'died of their wounds', as it were. All of them have the power to inspire us and to shame us if our zeal is wanting. They range from a simple peasant, Franz Jägerstätter, to the brilliant academic, Edith Stein, but in their love of God and fidelity to Christian belief they have a common identity.

We also meet three members of non-Catholic denominations who suffered for their ideals. In *Ut unum sint*, his encyclical on Christian unity, Pope John Paul II said: 'These brothers and sisters of ours, united in the selfless offering of their lives for the Kingdom of God, are the most powerful proof that every factor of division can be transcended and overcome in the total gift of self for the sake of the Gospel.'[4] So their stories are briefly told here and perhaps someone will be motivated to produce a volume on the witness of men and women from other Christian denominations in those appalling times.

There are, of course, many other known martyrs who could have

---

2. J Keegan, *The Battle For History – Refighting World War Two*. London, 1995, p. 31.
3. J Bowden (ed.), *Christianity – The Complete Guide*. London, 2005, p. 726.
4. Pope John Paul II, Encyclical *Ut unum sint*, para. I, reported in *Bible Alive*, January 2009, p. 52

been added to our chapter and very many others whose stories are known only to God. As you read, in order to grasp the enormity of the courage and sacrifice being described, you have only to ask yourself: 'what would I have done?' Then listen to the sound of silence which will grip your heart and mind.

BLESSED TITUS BRANDSMA

Friesland (Fryslân in Frisian) is the province situated at the north-west tip of Holland, where it faces the onslaught of the sea. Its people have been involved for centuries in fishing, farming and the repair and maintenance of ships. By nature Friesians are hardy, independent and serious minded, tempered by the ages-long struggle with their environment. Not only had they to protect their land from the sea, they had to rescue it. They did this by building 'terpen', massive mounds of mud, and in the lee of these the continuous process of reclamation went on. The reward for their labours can be seen today – a flat, verdant landscape occupied by the famous Friesian black and white cattle. The guidebooks describe it as 'a scene to grace any milk carton.' What the description lacks in grace it makes up for in accuracy.

Close to the Frisian town of Bolsward is a place called 'Oegeklooster', where once stood a religious house (the name means convent of St Hugo). At the end of the nineteenth century the Brandsmas lived there. They owned a dairy herd and operated a factory producing milk and cheese. Devoted to their Catholic faith they attended Mass daily. The depth of their piety is illustrated by the fact that of the six children (four girls and two boys) five were to enter the religious life. These vocations meant the parents had to forego their children's labour on the farm and fund their ecclesiastical education for several years. In spite of harsh economic times, the elder Titus and his wife Tjitsje shouldered the responsibility willingly.

One son, Anno Sjoerd Brandsma, was born at Oegeklooster on 23 February, 1881. He was baptised in the parish church of St Martin, Bolsward, where he began his early schooling. Following the custom of the time, Anno made his first Holy Communion when he was eleven. Even before this he had told his parents he wished to become a priest. A little while later his brother, Henry, subsequently a Franciscan, expressed the same wish.

So Anno left home for Megen in the southern province of Brabant where he attended a Latin school for boys. This Franciscan junior seminary provided for anyone considering a religious vocation, Franciscan or otherwise. At the school he was popular and made good progress, particularly in history and literature. He was a small boy with a severe intestinal disorder so his health was a constant cause for concern but home visits always restored him and he completed his studies, with his tutors noting his independent mind, intellectual gifts and sense of humour.

At that stage it was felt his health might preclude him from the Franciscan life. He turned to the Carmelite Order, strongly attracted by its spirituality and special devotion to Mary, The Mother of God. At Boxmeer, in September 1898, he entered the Carmelite novitiate taking his father's name Titus for his own religious name.

As a student he was extremely active mastering Italian, Frisian, Dutch and English. Moreover, he began to translate several of the works of St Teresa of Avila from Spanish into Dutch. In 1901 these were published as *Selected Writings from the Works of St Teresa*. His literary leanings motivated him to encourage fellow students to write religious articles. He helped to get these published and also organised an in-house magazine for the Carmelites. Subsequently he published it for all Dutch Catholics.

Though constantly plagued by poor health he was allowed to make his first vows in 1899. In December 1901 he suffered a severe haemorrhage but in September 1902 he left Boxmeer for Zenderen where he began a four-year course in theology. One year at Zenderen and two years at Oss saw him ordained. He completed the course one year later.

Then the Provincial of the Order decided Titus should go to Rome. There, in addition to philosophy, he studied geometry, mathematics, physiology and astronomy. To this weighty list he was allowed to add sociology. Familiarisation with social science was significant in his spiritual formation helping him to discern how best Christianity could be brought more fully into national life. Though health problems meant that he missed many months of study, in 1909, at the age of twenty-eight he received his doctorate from the Pontifical Gregorian University.

On his return to the Netherlands he undertook an astounding amount of work. For fifteen years he taught in the Catholic Seminary at Oss. He initiated a journal of Marian devotion, edited a Catholic newspaper, set up a Catholic library and founded a Catholic secondary school specialising in the sciences. He led the translation of more of St Teresa's works into Dutch and helped to translate *The Imitation of Christ* into Frisian. He was involved in the rebuilding of the Carmelite church in Mainz and the opening of a Carmelite house in Nijmegen, of which he became the first Prior. Renowned for his gentleness, simple goodness and good humour he was much in demand as a confessor and devoted great efforts to his apostolate for the Reunion of Christendom.

His name will always be associated with the City of Nijmegen where in 1923 he helped to establish its Catholic University, subsequently taking up the post there of Professor of Philosophy and the History of Mysticism. He became an internationally recognised authority on mysticism, lecturing (in France, Italy, Spain, Germany and the USA) and organising conferences on the subject. In 1932 he was appointed Rector Magnificus of the University, and beyond the University his work in the City included the re-introduction of a traditional event 'Maria Omdracht', an ancient procession in honour of The Blessed Mother. His documentation of Middle Dutch mysticism is at the heart of Nijmegen's Titus Brandsma Institute, which is dedicated to the study of spirituality.

This absolutely tireless priest also organised the first pilgrimage in Friesia to Dokkum where St Boniface, Apostle of Germany, was martyred. He established the shrine there and the Stations of the Cross (St Boniface is generally believed to have been born in Crediton, Devon, and educated at Exeter and Southampton).

By 1935 Father Brandsma had become well known as a writer and journalist and was appointed by the Dutch Hierarchy as the National Spiritual Adviser to Catholic Journalists. Here it is interesting to note that, from the accession of Adolf Hitler to the German Chancellorship in 1933, he had always viewed the spread of Nazism with alarm denouncing it as 'pagan'. Its menace arrived in Holland in 1940 when the German Army invaded without warning. Now the persecution of the country's Jews and its organised religions began. The denunciation of what was happening by Dutch Catholic Bishops only intensified the terror.

Titus Brandsma, spiritual director of the country's thirty Catholic newspapers, came into direct conflict with the occupiers when they tried to place Nazi advertisements and press releases in them. In December 1941, Jan de Jong, Archbishop of Utrecht ordered that their requests should be flatly refused. For the Church this was clearly a matter of conscience. Titus was asked to explain to the editors that they could not feature Nazi advertisements and continue as Catholic newspapers. In view of its obvious dangers he was given permission to refuse the assignment but he would not contemplate doing so.

From 1937 his health had become much worse. He informed his Prior that he could no longer stand for any length of time. His exhaustion was plainly visible. He suffered recurring giddiness and deterioration of his memory. A diagnosis revealed that his spinal marrow had become infected and to worsen matters he developed a serious infection of the urinary tract.

In spite of all this he began his tour of Holland to see the Catholic editors. As he moved around, this 'dangerous little friar' was shadowed by the Gestapo. He had already become known to this organisation when he had travelled, at the request of the Catholic Education Council, in defence of the Jewish children being educated in Catholic schools. One of his dictums was: 'He who wants to win the world for Christ must have the courage to come into conflict with it.' And during those earlier journeys he had told the Nazis 'The Church in carrying out her mission makes no distinction between sex, race or people.'

In Nijmegen on 19 January 1942, Titus was arrested by the Secret Police. Overnight he was interned at Arnhem and then taken to the prison at Scheveningen near The Hague. It was at Scheveningen, in Cell 577, that he composed 'Never were you, O Lord, so near . . .', the poem on solitude, and his experience of the presence of God, which became famous. When earlier, during his travels to Catholic editors, he had been warned he was liable to arrest, he had jokingly replied that he had always wanted a cell of his own. Now, in his prison cell, after an intensely active life, he was able to experience the joys of contemplation once more: '. . . never has the good Lord been so near to me . . . He is now my sole refuge and I feel happy . . . Rarely have I been so happy and contented.'

Under interrogation he was asked to explain his 'sabotage'. His reply was: 'When measures are taken which are irreconcilable with Catholic teaching, the Church is obliged to refute them. I am told that I am under arrest until this affair is cleared up. But one thing I must make clear: the attitude of the Dutch Hierarchy is my own.' He also affirmed that if a similar situation arose in the future he would act no differently. On 12 March, 1942 he was transferred to the concentration camp at Amersfoort near Utrecht.

The regime at Amersfoort was brutal and degrading. Here Father Brandsma was stripped naked and left standing for hours in the bitter cold. Shaven headed, clad in an old uniform and issued with wooden shoes, he became prisoner No. 58. The misery and humiliations of the camp, its overcrowded conditions, the freezing cold, exhausting labour, the beatings by the guards, dysentery and starvation became his daily lot.

Before long everyone knew this Carmelite. Many prisoners approached him for solace and comfort. He brought an awareness of goodness, love and peace into the horrors of the place and prayed for God's blessing on his jailors. His Good Friday meditation on the Passion of Christ, given to a large audience including starving workmen, professors, doctors, priests and lawyers left everyone dumb with wonder for he had given them supernatural insight into their imprisonment.

On 16th May he was transferred to a transit camp at Cleves, for he was now en route to Dachau near Munich. At Cleves conditions were somewhat better although food was still perilously short. Though ravenously hungry he gave some of his own food to the Italian who shared his cell. On Saturday 13th June Titus, in chains, was put on a train to Dachau. The unspeakably miserable journey there lasted six days.

If you stand today outside the camp, viewing the pleasant suburban housing and the dense civilian traffic beating its way to and from Munich, it is difficult to imagine this was the site of a murderous hell-hole. Although Dachau concentration camp, the first of many built by the Nazis, was not intended as a mass extermination camp, hunger and illness, arbitrary killings, mass executions and the pseudo-scientific experiments of the SS doctors, resulted in the continuous extermination of prisoners. Dachau was established initially as a 'model' or training camp where the SS might perfect the systems they subsequently used for the extermination camps at Auschwitz, Majdanek, Treblinka and other places.

In the twelve years of Dachau's existence (1933-45), 206,000 prisoners were brought there. On 29 April, 1945, the camp was liberated. About 30,000 prisoners, of 31 different nationalities, were discovered. Bearing in mind that the camp was built to house 5,000 prisoners only, the disastrous conditions resulting from inhuman overcrowding were beyond description. About 10,000 other prisoners were found at Dachau's satellite camps. So the estimate that 40,000 survived from a total of 206,000 seems accurate though, of course, the number of non-registered arrivals and victims will never now be known.

When Titus Brandsma arrived he was already a very sick man. It was clear he would not long endure a daily schedule, which began at 4.00 am with dressing and roll call until 5.00 am, work without food, rest or water from 5.30 am to 11.00 am, a thirty minute break for a bowl of watery soup, then further work until 7.00 pm. A further roll-call followed, lasting perhaps for one hour and then the victims could collect their rations which consisted of three and a half ounces of bread, a little butter and two potatoes. Priests ('the hated ministers of God') were not allowed to retire until about 9.00 pm for they were forced to do an extra half-hour of marching and press-ups.

Because of his physical condition, worsened by large ulcerating wounds on his feet, Titus was unable to comply with the barbaric routine. So he became the continuous target for the camp guards. On one occasion he was struck to the ground and beaten repeatedly because he had crept back into the barrack block to retrieve his spectacles. On another he was beaten in the face with his own soup bowl leaving him a ghastly, bleeding sight.

There was one concession to reason in this malignant place: the German priests were allowed to build a small chapel and offer Mass daily. A stealthy system was developed to distribute consecrated hosts to other prisoners and Titus played a significant part in this process. Unfortunately while he was carrying the Blessed Sacrament the head of the SS Guards went berserk for no apparent reason and began to beat and kick him. Titus endured the pain and kept the Sacrament safe in his spectacle case which he had tucked under his left arm.

In the end, the combination of barbaric beatings, untreated uremic poisoning and his severe foot infection forced Titus' body to give way. He was assigned to the place all prisoners dreaded – the camp 'hospital'. Only the constant vigilance and support of another Dutch Carmelite, Brother Raphael, had kept him out of the place for so long. These days, only the footings remain of this block where biochemical experiments and deliberate infections were administered. Yet even as Titus lay on his bed of stinking straw other prisoners made their way to him for words of comfort. He blessed them and asked them to pray for the guards that they might return to God and recover their basic humanity.

Father Brandsma died by lethal injection on Sunday, 26 July 1942. He was 61 years old. How does one summarise the significance of this intrinsically holy, incredibly industrious, intellectually gifted, humorous, lovable Frisian? Perhaps two dates will serve as his epitaph: in 1985 he was beatified by John Paul II as a martyr of the Catholic Church, fittingly, his feast day is 26 July. Secondly, in 2005, he was chosen by the inhabitants of Nijmegen, the oldest city in the Netherlands, as the greatest citizen to have lived there.

FATHER JACQUES BUNEL

Throughout the German occupation of France, Catholic convents, monasteries and schools were very much involved in concealing Jewish people from the Nazi terror. A number of authors have drawn attention to the valour of the priests and religious who risked their lives in doing so. Prominent among these writers is Sir Martin Gilbert, Winston Churchill's official biographer and a leading British historian. In his book *The Righteous – The unsung heroes of the Holocaust*, he provides examples of how Franciscans, Benedictines and Jesuits, among other Catholics, saved Jews from deportation and death. An example which came to wide public notice was that of Lucie Dreyfus, the widow of Captain Alfred Dreyfus, 'arguably the most famous French Jew of modern times.'[5] She survived the war as 'Madame Duteil', hidden

5. M Gilbert, *The Righteous. The Unsung Heroes of the Holocaust*. London, 2003, pp. 354-5.

within 'Le Refuge', the convent of the Sisters of the Good Shepherd in Valence. Another example, which was also rightly publicised, is the story of Father Jacques Bunel. The famous film-maker, Louis Malle, was a pupil in Père Jacques' school and he produced *Au revoir les enfants* as a tribute to him. Released in 1987, the film was awarded 7 'Césars' in the Cannes Film Festival and 1 'Golden Lion' at the Film Festival of Venice.

Barentin is one of the suburbs of Rouen, in Normandy, and 'Père Jacques', baptised Lucien, was born there in 1900 to a family which was, like so many of the families mentioned in this chapter, devoutly Catholic, hard-working and poor. His father Alfred was a textile worker and his mother Pauline, formerly the daughter of a shepherd, was fully occupied in rearing their eight children, of whom Lucien was the fourth. The oldest son, also Alfred, was killed in World War I and the Bunels lost a daughter in infancy. The six surviving children were André, Lucien, Madeleine, Gaston, Maurice and René. Lucien's biographers, Tolansky and Scott,[6] describe the family as loving and merry despite their penury, with clear induction in the faith, through father's example (he would say the rosary on the way to work) and mother's pious diligence (she taught the children to pray as soon as they could talk).

While Lucien was still an infant, the doctor pronounced that he was incurably ill. Though Pauline was five months pregnant with her next child, his parents took him to the shrine of St Germanes in Normandy. A novena was also said for his recovery. The story is told[7] of how, when they had walked the twelve kilometres to the shrine, the rain-soaked mother asked God to be allowed to keep her child until he was twenty when she would then offer him back to God. From that moment Lucien stirred, smiled and recovered. From when he was told the story, Lucien always felt that he had been spared so as to fulfil some specific purpose. Until then, his life was on loan. The happening may also have influenced his aspiration to become a priest, but this posed a problem for the Bunels, not only because of the costs involved but because the loss of any potential wage earner

---

6. E Tolansky and H Scott, 'Johann Gruber' and 'Jacques Bunel' in *Victims of the Nazis*. London, 1999, p. 31.
7. Ibid., pp. 31-2

would mean an extra burden for the other children. Finally his parents relented and it appears that the costs involved were shouldered by Mr Bunel himself.

In October 1912, Lucien began his studies in the junior seminary at Rouen. He spent seven years there, then moved on to the senior seminary. At Rouen he had emerged as deeply prayerful, conscientious in his duties and a natural leader though a keen sense of injustice and a somewhat waspish temperament meant he sometimes had to struggle at self-control. His great love of God and pride in his vocation, however, were sufficient to see him through. The First World War posed a great threat to Lucien's vocation, for his elder brother, Alfred, was killed, his father was called up and his brother André, serving at Verdun, was taken prisoner. This left Pauline with four children, struggling to keep the family provided for. It seemed that Lucien must return home but then father Alfred was demobilised and found work with a new employer, Mr Badin, who, alerted to Lucien's problem by a caring nun, provided funds for the boy to remain at the junior seminary. Subsequently Mr Badin supported him throughout the remainder of his studies for the priesthood and even provided the vestments for Lucien's first Mass. This good man was remembered ever after in the daily prayers of the Bunels, not least by Lucien himself.

From the time he went to the diocesan seminary in 1919, the solitude of his cell made such a powerful appeal to him he wondered whether he was intended to serve God through a life of uninterrupted prayer as a Trappist monk, but having, in November 1921, attended a three-day retreat at a Trappist monastery, he was still unsure of the specific way in which he could best serve God. Only six months after arrival at the seminary he was called up into the Army for his three years' statutory military service. While he was undoubtedly shocked by the immoral atmosphere he found there, he turned the experience to positive, spiritual benefit. A non-commissioned officer, he showed great care and concern for his men, sharing their privations and seeking no special comfort for himself. By his example he sought to bring them near to God, organised study groups for them, gathered groups of boys from the surrounding area and organised forest walks yet managed to keep up his own studies in philosophy, theology, Greek and Latin. When he left the Army in 1922, his fellow-soldiers had such respect and affection for him they accompanied him to the station.

Military life had seasoned him for his life as a priest and in the Seminary he quickly earned the respect of his fellows through the power of his preaching, in which he was able to transmit God's love for each individual with integrity and clear devotion. And though he practised little acts of mortification, in eating, drinking and even the way he sat, he shared with the rest of his family a well-developed sense of humour and zest for practical jokes. Despite the tremendous attraction of the spiritual life, he still placed great importance on his life as part of the Bunel family, walking eight kilometres whenever a half-day's leave from the seminary gave him the chance to spend a few hours at home with them. His biographers record[8] that at Maromme in Normandy, where the family had now settled, his devotion to God through service to his fellow human beings was becoming evident for all to see. During his holidays at home, for instance, after an early morning Mass and the reading of his Office, he would work from 8 am in a crèche he had devised for the children of factory workers. His interest in the love and care of children was a sign of things to come.

His total confidence in God was demonstrated by an incident in 1926 involving his mother. He was just about to say Mass when his brother René burst into the Church imploring him to come to his mother who was dying. Calmly, Lucien replied: 'She won't die. I'll bring her the last Sacrament and Communion and God will cure her.' René returned home and presently Lucien arrived with the Blessed Sacrament. He anointed his mother and gave her Communion. She went to sleep and woke up feeling much better. Soon her health was fully restored. When the family expressed their joyous surprise, he said, simply: 'God is so good. He can do anything.' Of this incident, Tolansky and Scott say in their excellent biography: 'The episode was like the counterpart of Lucien's own cure in answer to his mother's prayers, in his infancy.'[9]

Lucien was to distinguish himself as a teacher, preacher and youth leader. He had his formal introduction to teaching while he was still studying for the priesthood. This was at St Joseph's School, Le Havre, where he was engaged first as a supervisor then as a teacher. There

---

8. Ibid., pp. 40-1.
9. Ibid., p. 42.

he was noted for the conscientious way he carried out his duties but his approach was based on a strategy of trust rather than punishment. Coupled with his sense of humour, this made him popular with students. Rather than respond repressively to one rather rebellious pupil, Lucien wrote to him: 'I would be really happy if you got good marks.' It was a note the pupil treasured long afterwards. This was where Lucien became keenly interested in education as a process. Later he would have opportunities to put his ideas into practice, as we shall see. In the meantime his charismatic approach to the pupils, their parents, the people of Le Havre of all social classes, his brother Gaston, then doing military service near Le Havre, and his fellow soldiers, meant that his room at the school was rarely empty. His love for everyone, a manifestation of his love for God, made him a great force for good.

On 11 July 1925, Lucien was ordained a priest and in addition to his own family, his benefactor, Mr Badin, and his family, were among the large congregation for his first Mass. Father Bunel continued his work at St Joseph's at this stage and his abundant energy and commitment extended beyond the school. He organised a scout group for the poorer children of the area and spared no pains to find the necessary resources for its activities. Through begging on the group's behalf and the sale of some of his own books, he was able to take his scouts to a camp near Plymouth, in England. His impact there can be gauged from the fact that though most of the scouts and their leaders were Anglicans, some of them would attend his Masses for the French Catholic boys and at the end of the camp, its leader asked him to give them all a special blessing.[10]

In spite of his efforts, and success, as both teacher and preacher, the best way in which he could serve God had not yet become clear to him. But 12 July was a fateful day. He had said Mass at the Carmelite convent in Le Havre and following this introduction began to learn more about the nature of Carmelite vocation and its way of life. At that time, the Carmelite monks were returning to France and in the process of setting up monasteries at Paris, Fontainebleau and Lille. He also learned that while the Carmelite nuns never left the cloister, the monks combined monastic life with apostolic work and, in order to

10. Ibid., p. 46.

work at their pastoral ministry, could leave their enclosure at definite times under specific conditions in accordance with their Rule. As he studied them still further, he realised his way was clear: for him, the ideal religious life was within the ranks of the Carmelite Order. Although he had to wait three years for his request to be granted, he finally entered the Carmelite monastery at Lille as a novice in 1931, receiving the brown habit on 14 September. He took Father Jacques of Jesus as his religious name.

In September 1934 the Carmelites established a new boarding school at Avon, near to Fontainebleau. Known as 'The Little School,' perhaps because of its dedication to St Thérèse of Lisieux, the Order appointed Father Jacques as its headmaster. Now he was able to put his educational ideas more widely into practice. His aim was for Avon to provide an educational experience to foster freedom, initiative and responsibility. In developing the child beyond examination requirements, its objective was also to open up a cultural, aesthetic and spiritual awareness in each pupil. The 'curriculum', in fact, was everything that affected learning and could be found in the forest, the playing field and the decoration and furnishings of the classroom. Physical punishment was taboo and the strategy of trust prevailed. Father Jacques told the pupils they were on their honour when unsupervised and anyone having a problem with that was free to discuss it with him. His aim was to assist the pupils to be happy and fulfilled as well as academically successful. In the following five years he won the respect and affection of the pupils and a staff which had been initially unsure.

In September 1939 the War began, the school was closed and its premises taken over by the Red Cross for a hospital. Father Jacques was one of many priests drafted into the French army. He was given the rank of warrant officer and did all he could to see that his men were adequately housed and fed and beyond this, through talks and discussions, did his best to alleviate boredom and sustain morale. He came to be much loved and admired, among officers as well as men, and was successful in bringing back to the faith a number who had ceased to practice. After France's surrender in June 1940 he was sent to a prisoner of war camp and spent his five months there ministering to his fellow prisoners. In November 1940 he was released and returned to the Little School which reopened in January 1941.

With the German occupation came the persecution of the Jews. Father Jacques abhorred this anti-Semitism from its onset and instilled in the pupils that as a sign of respect to Jews they were to take off their hats when they saw anyone wearing the yellow star, standing aside to let that person pass. Though in no sense political he also hated the law compelling men of working age to be available for compulsory labour in Germany. In many cases this resulted in Frenchmen going into hiding or joining the Resistance. Now Father Jacques asked his Superior for permission to help Jews and those men who had been ordered to Germany for forced labour. Permission was readily forthcoming for the new Provincial of the Carmelites in France, Father Philippe, was a non-belligerent member of the local Resistance committee. So there developed in the area of Avon, as in other parts of France and other occupied countries, a group of houses, individuals and institutes willing to provide support, guidance, ration books, false documents and general help to those 'on the run' from the Nazis. Prominent locations in the Avon network were the Little School of Father Jacques and the convent of Our Lady of Sion, whose parent organisation had strong links with Jewish people.

Father Jacques now began to employ, as a physics and chemistry teacher, Lucien Weil, a Jew unable to find employment elsewhere. He employed a Jewish boy, Maurice Bas, in the school kitchen and found shelter for his 13 year old brother, Simon Bas. In the academic year 1942-43 he found places in the school for three Jewish pupils: Hans-Helmut Michel (entered in the records as 'Jean Bonnet'), Maurice Schlosser ('Maurice Sabatier') and Jacques-France Halpern ('Jacques Dupré'). He also succeeded in finding a safe place on a farm for Arthur Schlosser, the father of Maurice. Although he was alerted in October 1943 that word about the boys might leak out he could find no alternative hideaway for them and so continued to give them shelter. By 13 January 1944 he had the clear feeling that danger threatened and he wrote to his brother René: 'Quite possibly something serious is about to happen to me. If I am shot you must all be happy for me, because I will have fulfilled my ambition: to give my life for those who suffer.'[11]

Two days later the Gestapo arrived and took away the three boys

11. Ibid., p. 57.

and Father Jacques. When he bid everyone goodbye (they had been assembled in the school yard), the pupils yelled 'Goodbye, Father' and burst into spontaneous applause. That same day, the school was closed down. The three boys, together with the teacher, Lucien Weil, and his mother and sister were gassed at Auschwitz on 6 February. Since the Gestapo had known exactly where to look for the boys it seems certain they had been informed. One theory pointed to a collaborationist group in the area, another to a former pupil who had joined the Resistance, been captured and then forced to give the information under torture. Father Jacques was taken to the prison at Fontainebleau where he met Paul Mather, a local government official at Avon and a key figure in the Resistance network there. He had been arrested on the same day. Though efforts were made, unavailingly, to secure their release, Father Jacques was quite detached about this, saying to Father Philippe, the Provincial, 'You have no idea how badly priests are needed in the prisons.'

On 6 March 1944 Father Jacques was taken in chains to the transit camp at Compiègne, and in a letter to a Carmelite Prioress nearby he told of his joy in being thus transported because he had sheltered three boys from the same race as Jesus. Relatively speaking he found the regime there quite relaxed and he was able to celebrate Mass every day. His life was otherwise taken up with offering spiritual comfort and support to fellow prisoners, particularly those who were isolated and near to despair. He also provided classes in Christianity to whoever was interested. He noticed that each week fifty of the prisoners, fearful of their fate, were transported to some unknown destination. Father Jacques told a friend of his wish to go with them since he sensed that these men were now in need of even greater help. On 28 March he was among a group detailed for the transport and subsequently arrived at Neue Breme, a transit camp, near to Sarrebruck in Germany.

Conditions at Neue Breme were appalling. The prisoners were frequently beaten and provided with no more than a starvation diet. Tolansky and Scott[12] record that of the fifty prisoners who had arrived with Father Jacques only seven were alive three weeks later. The man in the Carmelite habit was made to carry a heavy wooden beam on

12. Ibid., p. 62.

his back and, for hours, was made to walk or run along a narrow wall which separated two pits full of water. During this inhuman treatment his uppermost thought was of Christ carrying his Cross. Now there was no prospect of saying Mass or offering spiritual comfort. Like other prisoners he was forbidden to converse with his fellows and in his case it was decreed that he must have no contact with anyone he had known hitherto, including his family. In spite of the brutality already meted out to him he endured a further beating when he asked for permission to look after the sick. In the end his persistence won through and the first task he gave himself was to wash down the filthy ceiling, walls and floor of the so-called 'infirmary'. Then he washed the sick and their clothes. His ministrations also included the making of bandages from whatever clean rags were to hand and the daily begging of scraps and left-overs from the kitchen for his beloved sick. In these tasks he was helped by a Communist prisoner. On 20 April 1944 he found himself on a list of men to be moved on. Despite the fact that no-one lived for more than four months at Neue Breme, he risked another beating by directly approaching the officer in charge of the camp and asking to stay so that he could continue caring for the sick. The request was refused.

Three days later he arrived at the Mauthausen concentration camp where his habit was taken away and replaced by the striped rags of the camp prisoner. Before leaving for the Gusen I satellite camp on 18 May, he spent the intervening time in 'quarantine'. He shared this experience with three hundred others crowded into a room meant to house fifty, was given food which was revoltingly inedible and provided with straw mats to sleep on, alive with lice and fleas. This misery was punctuated by endless roll-calls in the prison yard and Father Jacques was to be seen moving everywhere so he could give comfort, sustain the morale of those around him and, through prayer, help others to associate themselves with Christ's sufferings.

Although he strove to be optimistic and did all he could to foster hope in others, Gusen was a place of the watchtower and the crematorium chimney, of ferocious guards and their dogs and a pervading sense of death and terror, truly a slough of despond. In all of this, for the sake of his fellow prisoners, he had to show them he was steadfast in prayer with a capacity to endure. Often he would beseech the help of another Carmelite, St Thérèse of Lisieux. Because his presence meant so much to the prisoners they succeeded in getting him moved from heavy construction work to lighter work checking the output of Gusen I's armaments factory. His place at the end of the inspection line was where other prisoners made for, if only for a fleeting visit. There he would talk to them about all manner of things – themselves, their homes, the world outside to which, by God's grace, they would return, his theories on education – anything to lift their spirits and remind them that there was a world beyond the beatings and the barbarism of their daily pattern. He said Masses, heard confessions, gave talks, ministered to the sick, gave away his food and even tried to foster some type of intellectual activity in that hell-hole, although knowing that if ever he was discovered exercising his priestly ministry, torture and death would be his reward.

The other prisoners revered him but could see that his health was failing. There was fluid in his lungs and by now, his agonised coughing indicated that tuberculosis held him fast. The other prisoners begged him to rest but he would not listen, visiting the sick in the darkness of the early morning telling them of his belief in the coming victory and their release. Victory did come that spring but before it did, with the rest of the French prisoners in Gusen I, he was marched the five kilometres to the Mauthausen main camp on 28 April 1945. The rain poured down on that sick and starving cohort and ten of them died on the march. By now, Father Jacques had contracted pneumonia and was completely exhausted. Even so, on two occasions, he gave his morsel of food to a fellow prisoner.

When Mauthausen was finally liberated on 5 May, Father Jacques Bunel weighed 75 pounds. It was clear he would never survive the journey back to France so he was taken to the St Elizabeth's Hospital in Linz and was cared for by the Franciscan Sisters there until he died on 2 June. From the balcony of the Town Hall at Linz his French comrades bade an official good-bye to his mortal remains. They felt he had provided living proof of God's love for them and his greatest triumph had been to sustain their morale so that they were now able to go home.

At a special ceremony at the Yad Vashem Holocaust Remembrance Centre in Jerusalem, since he had suffered imprisonment and death for sheltering Jewish children and adults, Father Jacques was accorded the title of 'Righteous among the Gentiles.' The cause for his beatification and canonisation was opened in 1997.

BLESSED MARCEL CALLO

Like many of the martyrs we meet in this chapter, Marcel Callo was born of devout Catholic parents. They had left the Morbihan, a rural part of Brittany, and come to Rennes, its capital, in search of work. Monsieur Callo, who had served with the French army in World War I, obtained a low-paid job with the Department of Public Works and his wife worked in domestic service. They had nine children and Marcel, the second, was born on 6 December 1921 and baptised two days later at the Church of St Aubin. Jean, the eldest child, became a priest and although the family was poor it did manage to survive. In fact, the father was prudent enough to move his family from rented accommodation and obtain a State loan to purchase an old house which he refurbished for his large family. That house, at 8 rue des Tanneurs, is apparently still in existence.

Marcel was of a happy disposition and untypical of young boys for he willingly assisted with household tasks and the care of the younger children. With brother Jean, he also served Mass every morning at the Church of St Aubin, where he made his Solemn First Communion when he was ten and a half, having previously made a Private Communion as a seven year old at the Convent of the Adoration. His early role shepherding his siblings obviously helped him to develop his nascent leadership skills. When he was thirteen he became apprenticed to a printer and although he was very much a healthy extroverted young teenager, loving football, wrestling, table tennis and bridge, the moral standards at his workplace repelled him. His colleagues reviled the Church and took delight in shocking Marcel with tales of their sexual adventures. He had been brought up with a deep respect for women and so was particularly appalled to find his female colleagues were among the worst for bad language and behaviour.

It is not difficult to imagine the effect all this had upon him. He had looked forward to working, for he believed that honest work was pleasing to God and it would enable him to make a contribution to the family's income. He was a daily communicant, brought up in a home where the father made the sign of the cross on each child's forehead before he went to his rest, where they could see him kneeling by his bedside and where the family Rosary and a set form of night prayers were part of the unchanging pattern. Now it was part of Marcel's daily burden to run the gauntlet of the sneers and lewd comments directed at him in the printing works. Yet, there is evidence from another apprentice, Roger Renoncet,[13] that gradually the workers came to respect Marcel and curb their crudities in his presence because he clearly believed in the inherent worth of each one of them and he wanted them to recognise this in each other.

In this 'dark night' period Marcel found enormous support through his membership of the *Jeunesse Ouvrière Chrétienne* or 'JOC' ('Young Christian Workers' or *Jocistes*). 'Jocism', an important part of the Catholic Action movement, had been developed in Belgium and France from 1912 onwards by a Belgian priest, Father (later Cardinal) Joseph Cardijn. It drew upon the directives of Pope Pius XI that Catholic lay people be organised for apostolic action in society. Cardijn initiated the formation of Young Christian Worker groups in the belief that the young would respond to clubs in which they would receive religious instruction, undertake constructive activities and benefit from the fellowship thus available. A fundamental principle, to guard against meetings becoming 'talking shops' with little tangible achievement, was the 'see – judge – act' approach. A group would undertake to survey some work or social situation, decide how it could be improved and report back at the next meeting on the action taken. A starting point, for example, could be group study of the New Testament. This might be productive in restoring a more Christian spirit within the working classes. This had steadily declined since the days of the Revolution and the advent of secularism.

In the St Aubin's parish, a JOC group had been established by Father Jules Martinais, who was very popular with young people. He provided a meeting room behind the presbytery and Marcel persuaded Roger Renoncet, his fellow apprentice typographer, to join him in the group. An example of their faith in action related to the open witness they planned for Good Friday. At three o'clock in the afternoon they turned off the

13. M Couve de Murville 'Edith Stein', 'Marcel Callo', 'Titus Brandsma' in *Victims of the Nazis*. London, 1997, p. 34.

electricity at the printing works and called for one minute's silence to commemorate the death of Jesus. In his biography of Marcel, Archbishop Couve de Murville[14] reports that the workers were so astonished they cooperated fully. Another action the group took, spiritually more 'venturesome', was to visit the cinema on All Saints Day to counteract the gloom that usually descended on this day which was also, in the afternoon, the First Vespers of All Souls. Not everyone appreciated this singular way of marking a great feast day of the Church.

Marcel's time with the Jocistes at Rennes was also fruitful in another way for through the group he met and fell in love with Marguerite Derniaux. She was a chaste girl who matched his own piety and it was therefore a chaste courtship. According to the profile of Marcel on one website[15] it was one year before he declared his love for her and a further four months before they first kissed. He had met Marguerite at the end of 1941 and by the end of 1942 the couple, who had loved each other at first sight, became unofficially engaged. From this point they agreed on a strict spiritual way of life by which they would say the same daily prayers and go to Mass and the Sacraments as often as possible (when one considers the culture inculcated in the classrooms of Britain today, the example of Marcel and Marguerite indicates what is meant by the moral decline of the West). Marcel was now enthused with the idea of finding a home and marrying this lovely girl. Tragically he was to do neither.

The first blow fell on the Callo family on 8 March 1943 when the U. S. Army Air Corps made a daylight raid on the railway station at Rennes. Collaterally, some of the nearby office buildings also received hits. Marie Madeleine, the eldest of the Callo sisters, was working nearby. When Marcel heard of the damage he raced from the printing works and was soon clawing at the rubble in search of his sister. He it was who found her body and he it was who returned home to break the news to his family. Marie Madeleine was buried on 10 March and it did not seem fitting for him to tell his parents that on that very morning he had received papers instructing him to report for forced labour in Germany. In mid-May 1940 the Germans had surprised the French by attacking through the Ardennes. Their blitzkrieg ('lightning

14. Ibid. p. 35.
15. http://www.savior.org/saints/callo.htm (4 August 2009).

war') had proved too much for the Allies and by 22 June the French had had no option but to sign an armistice with Hitler at Compiègne. Since then, life in Rennes, as in so many French cities, had been conducted under the constant surveillance of German troops. By the third year of the occupation the forcible abduction of men to serve the German war industries was well established. Rather than this happen, many young men had gone into hiding and some of these had joined the Resistance. It would have been possible for Marcel to have hidden with Breton relatives near Redon but he saw this as no alternative, fearing reprisals against his family and the possibility of Jean, now within a few months of ordination, being sent in his place. The misery of leaving was exacerbated by being parted from Marguerite but he tried to be positive about it. After all, there was clearly an outlet for his JOC (Young Christian Worker) experience among his compatriots in Germany hence his comment: 'I am going as a missionary, you know'. It is difficult to know what prompted her but before he left, Marguerite said: 'You will be a martyr'. He had replied: 'I will never be good enough for that'.

Marcel was sent to the small town of Zella-Mehlis, in the province of Thuringia, eastern Germany. There, along with about 1,000 other foreign workers, mainly from France and Belgium, he worked at the assembly of rocket-firing armaments in the *Carl Walther Waffenfabrik*. His 'accommodation' was a bunk in a crowded wooden hut, the food was depressingly poor, the wages were low and there was no mechanism at all for the redress of grievances. His prospect of leave was extinguished by the non-return of another French worker and in 1944 when the war worsened considerably for the Germans, all home leave was cancelled henceforth. Marcel was miserable and extremely homesick. His JOC activity provided a life-line, however, and he applied himself energetically to it. Other 'Jocistes' in the camp agreed to meet and pray with him each day, in spite of their exhaustion, and soon he had persuaded all the other men in his room of the hut to attend the Masses provided once or twice each month by a visiting German curate, Father Steinberg, who spoke French. The JOC group in which Marcel was active did a great deal to build up the morale of the other forced labourers. In his biography, Archbishop Couve de Murville[16]

16. Couve de Murville: op. cit., p. 42

outlines how they organised a football team, established a lending library and prepared special meals for the weekends. And Marcel was doubly happy because he could save his meagre wages and send them to his family. The Archbishop describes the development of a network within which 700 Jocistes and 300 priests were providing apostolic care for the 700,000 Frenchmen forced to work in Germany.

Of course, the Nazis hated the Church and saw members of Catholic Action and its offshoots as no more than subversives. Moreover it was galling to them to realise that the faith they had done so much to suppress was being reinvigorated in their own country through the agency of foreigners. For their part, the Jocistes knew the Gestapo were carefully monitoring their activities but it did not deter them for continuing with their programme. It was a programme that was working wonders, for Marcel as well as others. Whereas previously he had been depressed through lack of Mass and the Sacraments, missing his family and being unable to see Marguerite, now his disposition had changed. He said: 'Finally Christ reacted. He made me understand that the depression was not good. I had to keep busy with my friends and then joy and relief would come back to me'.[17] Sadly, however, his health and the poor diet could not sustain him against the inhumane rigours of forced labour. By now he was suffering from the pain of boils, headaches and infected teeth and once he physically collapsed but he forced himself to continue his work for, and leadership of, the Jocist programme.

The Gestapo now made their move. By 1943 they had already arrested several hundred German priests for their resistance to National Socialism. In June, they followed this by a ban on German priests providing special Masses for foreign workers. Later that summer came the first arrests of unauthorised priests ministering to French workers. In December Catholic preaching of any kind for French workers was completely banned. Matters worsened in 1944 when the Gestapo turned to Thuringia. On a list of the details of JOC section leaders, uncovered by their searches, they found the name of Marcel Callo. When they moved to arrest him, a fellow French worker asked why. He was told, astoundingly, it was because Marcel was 'far too Catholic'. Perhaps this

---

17. See reference 15, above.

says everything about what the Church had to endure in those times.

Along with other Jocistes and Father Jean Lecoq, of the diocese of Rennes, who had been charged with the 'crime' of saying Mass, Marcel was interrogated. They all denied political motivation of any sort, but were imprisoned in the Gotha gaol pending a decision on their fate from Berlin. There was some compensation for them in their daily schedule at this time for they were taken out to work on highways and farms. There they met prisoners of war and through them they were able to send letters home and receive messages and food from other Jociste groups which, in spite of the dangers, were still active. Marcel continued to be unwell, however, having to work in spite of continually increasing stomach pain. It seems likely that this was due to lead poisoning resulting from his work as a printer. In his letters home, however, though he told his family of his concern they might be caught up in the fighting after the Allied invasion of June 1944, he still tried to be positive. They must be assured that he prayed every day for Christ to spare them and Our Lady to protect them. He tried to get nearer and nearer to God and dreamed of the fine home he would build for Marguerite when he returned.

Matters improved in Gotha somewhat when he was moved to a larger cell on the first floor of the prison. He shared this with Father Lecoq, three seminarians and seven other Jocists. They held and shared everything in common, including food, cigarettes and whatever else the local Jocistes were able to give them. They managed to acquire a Missal and two New Testaments. This larger cell which became known as 'the Church' and 'the Upper Room' because a Lutheran chaplain had formerly used it for services, was also now adorned by a cross which had been fashioned from dried flowers. Sadly, of the twelve disciples in that 'Upper Room' only four would ever return to France. Although local Jocistes tried to obtain hosts which they would then have smuggled into the prison, it was only possible, during his entire time at Gotha, for Marcel to receive Holy Communion once. From a scribbled note he left, this was on 16 July 1944 and he records the immense joy this brought to him. It seems probable that this was the final time he received the Sacrament.

On 25 September 1944 the sentence on Marcel, and the Jocistes interrogated with him after their arrest, was received from Berlin. They had all been found guilty during their work service of 'constituting a threat to the State and to the German people' because of their Catholic action among their French fellow workers. Accordingly, on 8 October, manacled to four other prisoners, Marcel was sent to Flossenbürg concentration camp and, at the end of the month, to the camp at Mauthausen. In the introductory chapter of this work some details were given of the main camp at Mauthausen, but Marcel stayed there only long enough for registration. On the 26 October he was sent to a satellite camp just a few kilometres to the west. This was K Z Gusen I where he was detailed to sort rivets for the Messerschmitt aircraft industries located there. This work was cruel enough for a man in Marcel's rapidly deteriorating physical condition but on 7 November 1944 he was sent to the dreadful satellite K Z Gusen II which its survivors have titled 'hell on earth'. There, in tunnel No. 4 of the St Georgen (Bergkristall) underground installations, he was detailed to rivet aircraft parts using heavy pneumatic tools.

He endured this until 5 January 1945 when he was so seriously ill and exhausted he had to be moved into the vile and disgustingly overcrowded camp 'hospital'. By now he was suffering from bronchitis, dysentery, starvation and its accompanying swelling of the body, and a high fever. His misery at the welding process had been made worse because someone had stolen his spectacles and peering at the work had caused both eyes to become terribly bloodshot. The inhumane conditions reduced some of the inmates to the level of animals and there were instances of them killing each other as they fought for an extra bit of space. Theft was also endemic and in addition to his spectacles, Marcel had also lost the small prayer book which he had kept carefully hidden from the guards and, bewilderingly, the letters and photographs of Marguerite. Marcel Callo spent the final months of his life in a degradation designed to break the spirit of the inmate, a world of frequent beatings and roll calls, sometimes in the middle of the night, where it was common for captives to be left standing for hours in freezing temperatures.

Yet, in spite of all this he worked unceasingly to sustain the morale of his comrades imploring them not to give up, since God still watched over them. He drew them into a hastily convened 'Hail Mary' in any brief moment when they were out of sight of the guards. When it was apparent that death was near he was moved back to the central camp at Mauthausen, and the indescribable conditions of the 'Sanitaets-Lager' (sanitary camp) just beyond its walls. In the early morning of 19 March, 1945, the feast of St Joseph, he was finally called to his rest.

Archbishop Couve de Murville[18] tells of a former Colonel in the French Army, Albert Tibido, who also lived in Rennes and who had been with Marcel in his final hours. He survived the camp and at the beginning of June 1945 went to the Callo home to tell them of Marcel's death. Unfortunately they were not at home so he left his address with neighbours. The next day brother Jean, now an ordained priest, went to see the Colonel who told him what had happened to Marcel. The premonition of Marguerite Derniaux had proved to be well founded and it was perhaps fitting that it was Father Callo who told the family of his brother's martyrdom. It is reported that, insistently and with emotion, Colonel Tibido had this to say: 'I am an old pagan. I have seen thousands of prisoners die, but I was struck by the look on the face of Marcel Callo because there was something really extraordinary about him. It was a revelation to me: the look on his face expressed the deep conviction that he was going towards total bliss. It was like an act of faith and hope in a better life. I have never seen anything like it anywhere else with any dying person . . . nothing like what I saw in his gaze.'[19]

Soon afterwards, Father J-B Jego, also of Rennes, wrote the biography of the young man killed for being 'too Catholic'. Later his book was translated into English, German, Hungarian and other languages. Movingly, it was German Catholics who quite quickly recognised Marcel Callo as a model of Christian life and courage, and they began to support the call for his Beatification. They were joined in this cause by 'Catholic Action' groups in many countries and by all the bishops of Germany and Austria. It appears that these efforts gave rise to the beginnings of reconciliation and even friendship between former enemies. Accordingly, the name Marcel Callo is said to stand for international understanding and peace in Christ.[20]

---

18. Couve de Murville, op. cit., p. 50ff.
19. Ibid. p. 55.
20. http://www.nizkor.org/hweb/camps/gusen/pers/callo01x.htm (4 August 2009).

At St Peter's in Rome he was beatified by Pope John Paul II, on 4 October 1987. On 4 October 1997, the Diocese of Linz, supported by hundreds of pilgrims from all over Europe, celebrated the tenth anniversary of his Beatification. These celebrations were conducted at the sites of his martyrdom in St Georgen, Gusen and Mauthausen.

ALFRED DELP SJ

On 15 September 1907 Maria Bernauer held and gazed at her new-born son. It is reasonable to suppose she was asking herself a question: will Friedrich marry me now? Maria herself had been born of devout Catholic parents and the tiny boy was her second child – the first, Justina, had been given to Maria's childless sister to raise as her own. Both children had been fathered by Friedrich Delp, an office worker and a Lutheran. So, at this time, Maria's life must have been anything but smooth, hence her concern about her lover's intentions. Fortunately, Friedrich married Maria a month after his son's birth and, in time, the boy Alfred, baptised as a Catholic, was joined by two further sisters, Gerda and Greta and two brothers, Ewald and Fritz.

At the time of Alfred's birth, the couple were living in Mannheim but in 1914 the Delps moved to the town of Lampertheim, close to the Rhine river and south of Frankfurt. They settled very near to the Catholic Church of St Andreas but although Friedrich had permitted a Catholic baptism for Alfred he insisted that he be educated at the Lutheran school and receive instruction in that faith. The child, obviously intelligent, was soon making his mark as an Evangelical scholar but during these years he also became friendly with Father Johannes Unger, the parish priest of St Andreas. When he was already a hefty thirteen year old and confirmed as a Lutheran, a significant incident occurred. One day he arrived late for a religious lesson and the Lutheran pastor wanted to know why and was told he had been with Father Unger. Alfred had already acquired a reputation for lapses into an insolent attitude. Whether it was because of his visit to the Catholic priest or because of his manner in explaining his delay, it prompted the pastor to slap his face. Vowing never to return, Alfred marched out of the Lutheran church, and crossed over to the Catholic Church in search of Father Unger.

In June 1921, after receiving instructions from this priest, Alfred

Delp made his first communion and nine days later was confirmed in the Catholic Church. A little to the north of Lampertheim was the minor seminary at Dieburg. Alfred entered there in 1922 with the half-formed idea of being a Catholic priest. After his closely knit family life and the Lutheran milieu, Catholic culture, its colourful liturgy and his boisterous fellow-pupils made a decided impact and expanded his thoughts to new ideas and new ventures. As a reaction to the chaos and privations of the post-Versailles era, youth movements proliferated. Notable among these was Neudeutschland, a Catholic movement whose founding concepts derived from: Catholic social principles as expressed in the encyclical of Pope Leo XIII (*Rerum Novarum*); service to the Fatherland, and the repudiation of class and political conflict. Before long, Alfred Delp was a willing disciple. He matched Neudeutschland's ideals, its rallies and its marching songs with his own great fervour and limitless energy. Alfred's intellectual energy was also notable and thanks to his friend and mentor Father Unger and the support of the local bishop, Alfred was soon on his way to the Germanicum in Rome, Germany's seminary for 'high fliers', destined for the diocesan priesthood. To Johannes Unger's disappointment, however, and based on Alfred's introduction to the saints of the Society of Jesus and the *Spiritual Exercises* of St Ignatius Loyola, he announced that he wished to join that Order for 'I think I can best serve the Saviour there.'[21] After his school examinations, and now eighteen, he moved to the Jesuit novitiate at Tisis, near Feldkirch in western Austria.

In the words of Mary Frances Coady, teachers and students found in Alfred Delp 'a compelling mixture of piercing intelligence, high-energy zest for life, and loudmouthed bravado.'[22] Tisis offered him a rich eclectic experience, including the silence, meditation and reliance on God's will nurtured by the monastery, the mountains of the Voralberg with its hiking in the Alpine air, and a rich variety of spiritual readings including, significantly, *The Imitation of Christ* by Thomas à Kempis. Above all, of course, he was now being schooled by intellectually gifted men including a young but already notable theologian called

---

21. M F Coady, *With Bound Hands. A Jesuit in Nazi Germany*. Chicago, 2003, p. 6.
22. Ibid., p. 10.

Karl Rahner. With a deep appreciation of God as the centre of all things he was next sent to study philosophy at Berchmanskolleg in Pullach, south of Munich. Now he was a 'scholastic' i.e. a candidate for the priesthood. The Berchmanskolleg offered him powerful spiritual and intellectual sustenance. From his abiding interest in history, and particularly that of political change, sprang forth his preoccupation with Catholic social teaching, with special regard to the Papal encyclicals *Rerum Novarum* (1891) and *Quadragesimo Anno* (1931). With gusto he entered the pulling and hauling of debate sometimes with scant respect for the sensibilities of others and during the 1930s he became perceived as an expert in this field, particularly with regard to *Quadragesimo Anno*.

Unfortunately, Alfred was a complex character who combined a fine mind and deeply zealous prayer life with a scant, and sometimes cruel, disregard for the thoughts and feelings of others. This led occasionally to the doubts of his superiors as to whether Alfred, with his lack of control, would ever 'fit in' to the Society's norms of behaviour. However, in 1931 for his 'regency period of apostolic work' he arrived at the Stella Matutina school at Feldkirch where he became prefect to a group of 87 late-teenage boys. They appreciated his participative style of teaching and his Neudeutshland approach to their physical education. It was at the school that Alfred met Augustin Rösch, the head prefect who later became the school's rector. The two were closely associated in later years, as we shall see, but at this stage, while admiring Delp's intellectual ability, Rösch was wary of his highly informal approach to his duties which clashed with his own rigid discipline in the Jesuit tradition. In the meantime there was some tension in the school as Hitler's accession to complete power in Germany unfolded.

It was not long before Nazi policy made itself felt when it was decreed that 1,000 Reichsmark had to be paid to the German government for every German citizen living outside its borders. It was therefore decided to close the German section of the school and re-establish it at St Blasien in Germany itself. Alfred accompanied the long files of German boys as they marched from the Stella Matutina. Not long after his arrival at St Blasien, he was sent to the Ignatiuskolleg at Valkenburg in Holland . . . it was April

1934. With the advent of the Nazi currency laws preventing the dispatch of money beyond Germany, the Ignatiuskolleg soon found itself in dire straits with difficulties in maintaining its library and science departments, paying taxes to the Dutch government and even providing necessities for its 250 students. Related to this, it is reported that Dutch Catholics tried to help 'through food drives and special Sunday collections.'[23] Stories were now reaching Valkenburg of the Nazi persecution of its own citizens – the harassment and murder of the Jews, the dissolution of many Catholic organisations in violation of the 1933 Concordat, the monitoring of priests' sermons. In company with other Jesuits, Alfred published a book called *The Rebuilding*. It outlined the kind of society which should emerge after the destruction of National Socialism. His fertile mind and boundless energy also led to the publication of *Tragic Existence*, a work on the philosophy of Martin Heidegger.

On 24 June 1937 Alfred Delp was ordained priest at St Michael's Church in Munich. He celebrated his first solemn High Mass in the church of St Andreas in Lampertheim, his home town, on 4 July. Almost exactly one year later, having completed his studies in Frankfurt, he received his licentiate in theology. In September 1938 he left for Starnberger See, south of Munich, to complete his final year of formation as a Jesuit before formal entry into the ministry of the Church. Following the public distribution and reading from the pulpits of *Mit brennender Sorge*, the highly critical Papal encyclical, the Nazis increased their persecution of the Catholic Church. The Jesuits were especially suspect, for they were very well educated, were esteemed educators and were well connected. The word went forth that continuous reports had to be submitted by the regime's spies on their activities and a campaign of constant vilification was also well established. Father Augustin Rösch, Alfred's former rector at the Stella Matutina and now the Jesuit's provincial superior of the Upper German province, emerged as an arch-opponent of the Nazis. He liked to remind the Gestapo during their continuous harassment that he was a hero of World War I. He was quite clear that they intended to destroy Christianity and so was not surprised when, following Hitler's annexation of Austria, the Stella Matutina was

23. Ibid., p. 21.

forced to close in spring 1938.

Consumed with hatred for the Jesuits, the Nazis had now begun to persecute some individual members of the Order, including Father Rupert Mayer whom, at this time, they regarded as their arch-enemy (a profile of Father Mayer is provided later in this chapter). The 'atmosphere' for Catholic priests was hostile and when in the later Spring of 1939 Alfred was given permission by the Order to work for a doctorate in philosophy, the University of Munich refused his application: 'permission could not be granted to him for studies in philosophy or in any other academic faculty . . .'[24] He then volunteered to become an army chaplain but again, was turned down. At this point he joined the staff of Munich's Jesuit publication, *Stimmen der Zeit* ('Voice of the Times'), working as a writer and editor, until it was suppressed by the Nazis in April 1941. He also became involved in the 'Mission to Men' conferences, to spiritually fortify Catholic men in those forbidding times. Now he became acknowledged as a most effective speaker – biographer Mary Coady describes him as 'subtle and clever in naming the crimes of the regime without getting himself into trouble.'[25] He also introduced his audiences to his 'Third Idea'. Both capitalism and Communism were grossly deficient in serving the economic and psychological needs of the individual. But there was a third way – in a new social order which derived from the social teaching of the Papal encyclicals.

It was at this stage that Delp became rector of the St Georg parish in Bogenhausen, a salubrious part of Munich. He also worked at the Heilig Blut Church, preaching, giving religious instruction and working with the youth of the parish, which delighted him. The two churches became, in effect, one parish but when the newer, larger Heilig Blut Church was bombed and burned to the ground, the parish had to concentrate on St Georg. Father Karl Adolf Kreuser SJ whose family became firm friends with Father Delp was once asked for his impressions of Delp's preaching. He replied: 'It was thrilling. The Church would be full. And after the loss of the larger church building, the little church of St Georg was even more crowded than before; not everyone could get in. He really had something to say to the people

24. Ibid., p. 31.
25. Ibid., p. 34.

living at that difficult time.'[26] Immediately after he joined the parish as its rector Alfred became highly visible in the protest of parish youth when, in the Summer vacation of 1941, all crucifixes were removed from Munich schools. Father Delp blessed the replacement crucifixes when the mothers and youth of the parish took matters into their hands. It is also reported,[27] from more than one source, that his address became a 'safe house' for Jews escaping to Switzerland through the 'underground'.

We must now consider how Father Delp's link with the Kreisau Circle[28] led to his eventual arrest and execution. The Circle was a resistance group named after the estate of its leader, Count Helmuth James von Moltke, great-great-nephew of the famous Helmuth von Moltke, Prussian military hero. The primary objectives of the Group were based on establishing fundamental principles upon which a new Germany might be founded, for it was obvious to many Germans, after the reverses of 1942, that Nazism, sooner or later, would collapse. Though 'Kreisau' could be termed a resistance group, it did not support a coup d'état against Hitler nor did it take part in the July 1944 Bomb Plot (though many members, as individuals, knew of it and concurred with what was to be done). The 'Kreisau' membership was drawn from Protestant, Catholic and Socialist circles and von Moltke, a Protestant himself, was convinced that if *Gleichschaltung* and all it entailed was to be completely reversed, the new Germany must be based on a moral code emanating from religious belief. He had been greatly encouraged by the 1941 sermons of Bishop von Galen (see profile later in the chapter) and was now looking for a Catholic who might persuade the German bishops to align themselves with his group. Through a mutual friend, Baron Karl Ludwig von Guttenberg, the Count was introduced to Father Augustin Rösch, Alfred Delp's former rector at the Stella Matutina and now a Jesuit provincial superior. At a gathering of the Circle, von Moltke explained to Rösch that though he was acquainted with the Catholic stance on social justice, through the

---

26. http://www.ignatiusinsight.com/features2006/frakreuser_intervw_oct06.asp (4 August 2009).
27. See, for instance, http://www.columbia.edu/cu/augustine/arch/heroes.htm (4 August 2009).
28. Taylor, J and Shaw, W, *Dictionary of the Third Reich*. London, 1997, p. 164-5.

Papal encyclicals, an expert in this field was needed – enter Father Alfred Delp.

Alfred's response to the invitation was already clear for he had earlier written that: 'Whoever doesn't have the courage to make history is doomed to become its object. We have to take action.'[29] Fathers Rösch and Delp were joined by a third Jesuit, Lothar König. Through their participation they were able to provide close contact between the Circle and the Catholic bishops, with the social encyclicals as a basis in establishing much common ground between the churches and the Social Democrats and trade unionists. From October 1942 onwards Munich was repeatedly bombed by the Allies and destruction, smoke, dust, fire and escaping gas provided the backdrop to daily life. Alfred did what he could to mitigate the suffering and sadness. This included no small amount of emergency repairs at which he was adept. Mary Frances Coady describes his efforts in these words: 'Delp became known for his mechanical skills and for his fearlessness in the face of the bombing raids: after the sounds of the planes had died away, he often left the basement before the all-clear signal, rushing from one demolished house to another, digging and sifting to reach those buried beneath the rubble. He reportedly took over the rescue operation after one attack, yelling orders to the men from the fire department who were supposed to be in charge. This overenthusiastic effort earned him an official warning.'[30]

In January 1944 von Moltke was arrested and sent to a prison attached to Ravensbrück concentration camp. He had been phoning a colleague to warn him he was under surveillance, not knowing that the Gestapo had tapped the colleague's phone. Now the work of the Kreisau Circle began to wind down. At this stage, Alfred had been a Jesuit for almost eighteen years and was looking forward to making his final vows. This normally occurred after about sixteen years but as a result of the vetting process which preceded the vows he had been told in 1943 that the final vows were to be deferred in his case until 15 August 1944. Speculation on the reasons for this is probably futile for the vetting process is confidential but it may be that Alfred's cigar-smoking ebullience and his independent-mindedness may have

29. M F Coady, op. cit., p. 48.
30. Ibid., p. 52.

caused some concern within the disciplined ranks of the Jesuits. However it seems probable that the postponement made him think and he intensified his efforts to be acceptable to the Society.

Nevertheless, he was frustrated at the curtailment of his resistance activities and on 6 June 1944, the date of the Allied landings in Normandy, while he was in the town of Bamberg to give a lecture, he decided to visit the home of Count Claus Schenk von Stauffenberg, the army officer who would place the bomb at Rastenburg on 20 July in an attempt to assassinate Hitler. While Stauffenberg received Delp courteously enough, he was secretly furious because the visit ran the serious risk of endangering the Stauffenberg family. It is virtually certain that he did not disclose any details of the bomb plot to Alfred including his own key role in it. After the abortive attempt, Hitler's retribution was swift. Stauffenberg was shot immediately and thousands of others were put to death. Victims of the purge included some leading members of the Kreisau Circle – von Moltke, von Trott zu Solz and Yorck von Wartenburg. Well-wishers, including Jesuit priests, warned Alfred Delp he was in mortal danger and should go into hiding. He wished to stay with the people of Bogenhausen with whom he had endured the Allied bombings and he reasoned that flight might convey he knew more about the bomb plot than was actually the case. Most of all, he did not wish his final-vow ceremony, scheduled for 15 August, to be postponed once again.

On Friday 28 July, Father Delp was arrested by the Nazis. On 7 August he arrived in Berlin and was taken to Moabit, the Gestapo prison on the Lehrterstrasse where he remained for seven weeks. Through bomb damage, the security of Moabit became compromised and so he was moved to Tegel prison in the north of the capital. It has been recorded that Franz Sperr and Nikolaus Gross, members of resistance groups linked to the Kreisau Circle, had stated under interrogation that Delp had known of the bomb plot.[31] Anyone knowing of the plot beforehand and failing to report it would incur the death penalty. To the end Alfred Delp maintained he knew nothing of the plot and throughout his internment was extremely concerned that Sperr and Gross should retract their statements. While Gross was prepared to do this, Sperr (codename 'Donaustrasse') seemed to have closed his mind

31. Ibid., p. 78.

on the issue and communication with him was virtually impossible as he was being held in another prison. In the end it did not matter, as we shall see. Despite the brutality of his captors' interrogations, the fact that his hands were manacled throughout his captivity and his narrow cell permitted him no more than three strides to the left or right, when the Gestapo offered him his release if he left the Jesuits and joined the Nazis he rejected this.

There are a number of moving aspects of his imprisonment. One of these concerns the compassion and support of 'the two Mariannes.' Alfred had met Marianne Hapig and Marianne Pünder a year before his arrest. When they learned he was imprisoned they searched Berlin to find him. Subsequently they washed his blood-stained clothing and returned it many times. Their baskets also invariably contained shaving supplies, cigarettes and food. Hidden in the folds of the clothing, among the supplies, were pen, ink and writing paper together with incoming letters. His outgoing mail was smuggled within his dirty laundry. Most significantly, through bribes to the head guard, they supplied Father Delp with Communion hosts and altar wine so that he could say Mass. Another touching aspect concerns the conduct of these Masses. Mary Frances Coady writes: '. . . with his bound wrists, he knocked on his wall to the left and to the right when Mass was beginning, and the others in turn knocked on their walls and so on until the entire block of prison cells became alive with the great offering, the cosmic prayer of thanksgiving. Here, religious differences vanished.'[32] There is also the poignancy of the manner prisoners communicated during their limited exercise periods. Forbidden to talk to each other they would speak to the corners of the walls of the yard, hoping that the sound would reverberate and reach the ears of the prisoner behind them.

Another steadfast friend at this time was Franz von Tattenbach, a Jesuit priest who acted as the Order's courier working between Berlin and Munich. He was Delp's main link with the Society of Jesus. On 8 December, the Feast of the Immaculate Conception, he brought a document for Alfred to sign. At last he had been authorised to receive his final vows and the date had been brought forward from 15 August. The Latin document was incomprehensible to the guard who had no objection therefore in Alfred receiving it. When he had signed, Father

---

32. Ibid., p. 80.

Franz explained that for the vows to be valid the formula had to be read aloud. Though he was sobbing, Father Delp managed to do this down to its final words. He had achieved a major spiritual goal at last.

On 9 January 1945 he was taken with three other prisoners to Berlin's *Volksgerichtshof* or 'People's Court', another euphemism. Roland Freisler, its President, was a notorious Nazi whose pursuit of justice consisted of his reading the appropriate file on the night before the hearing, deciding on the verdict, then launching a cruel onslaught on the defendant for the enormity of his crimes. The court procedures were a grotesque pantomime in which the accused was stripped of every vestige of dignity – for example, braces, belts and neckties were removed from the defendants and they were forced to grab their trousers to prevent them from falling down. Since some of the Court's activities were filmed it is possible to hear Freisler's hysterical ravings in television documentaries even to-day. Here is an example of the learned judge's technique, based on a chaplain's recollection of one of his interchanges with Father Delp: 'You miserable creep, you clerical nobody – who dares to want the life of our beloved Führer taken ... a rat – that should be stamped on and crushed ... Now tell us, what brought you as a priest to abandon the pulpit and get mixed up in German politics with a subversive like Count Moltke and a troublemaker like the Protestant Gerstenmaier. Come on, answer!'[33]

Predictably Alfred was brought back into the Court on 11 January, with five other defendants, for the verdict and sentencing. All were found guilty, three received prison sentences and the other three, Delp, Moltke and Sperr were sentenced to death by hanging. Yet in Father Delp's case, whether or not he had prior knowledge of the Stauffenberg bomb plot was not explored. He was to die because of his link with the Kreisau Circle, his work as a Jesuit priest and his Catholic-social concepts. He was taken from Tegel to the Plötzensee prison on 31 January. On Friday, 2 February, the feast of the Purification, Catholic Chaplain Peter Bucholz went to cell 317 where a wreck of a human being, pale, emaciated and with eyes sunken in his head smiled almost playfully. 'In half an hour, I'll know more than you do,' he said. He was then taken to the execution chamber and hung from a meat hook.

33. Ibid., p. 162.

It is likely that Alfred Delp's ashes, like those of all others allegedly involved in the bomb plot, were strewn over sewage waste. In cell 317 were his effects – a pair of broken spectacles, a rosary and a copy of *The Imitation of Christ*.

Germany never forgot Alfred Delp. A school in Bremerhaven is one of many named after him. A Catholic student residence in Mannheim also bears his name as does the guesthouse on the campus of the Canisius College in Berlin. In Dieburg are many commemorations: a street is named after him as are the Alfred Delp School and the Catholic Community Centre (Father Delp House). In Donauwörth the Bundeswehr has named its barracks the *Alfred-Delp-Kaserne*.

BLESSED CLEMENS AUGUST CARDINAL von GALEN[34]

Clemens August was born on the 16 March, 1878 to Count Ferdinand Heribert von Galen and his wife Elisabeth, by birth a Countess von Spee. He came into the world in the bedroom of his parents at Dinklage Castle, near Oldenburg, which at that time had been the seat of the von Galen family for three hundred years. To say it was a devout Catholic family is hardly to do it justice. In the words of Brigadier Sedgwick: '. . . the holy Catholic faith was the foundation and the never-questioned guide of the thought and life of all the inmates of Dinklage Castle.'[35] The descendants of Count Matthias, Clemens August's grandfather, included two bishops, eight priests, two theologians and sixteen nuns. Like his father before him, Count Ferdinand found his marriage blessed by thirteen children. Clemens August and his siblings were rigorously educated. As they grew it was made clear that obedience, order, punctuality and industry were

---

34. A biography of Count Clemens August von Galen, the 'Lion of Münster', was published in Germany in 1953. This was written by his chaplain, the Reverend Dr Heinrich Portmann. It was translated into English, adapted and provided with an Introduction by Brigadier R L Sedgwick, a convert to Catholicism, who at the end of World War II was appointed Controller-General of Religious Affairs in Germany's British Zone of Occupation. I am greatly indebted to both Reverend Portmann and Brigadier Sedgwick for the details set out in this biography.

35. H Portmann, *Cardinal von Galen*. London, 1957, p. 36.

perpetually required of them. They developed in a world without luxury for there were neither bathrooms nor even running water in the old castle. There was no heating in most of its rooms.

Thus was the man who became the 'Lion of Münster' tempered from his earliest days for his role as an arch-opponent of the Nazis. Describing Clemens August, R L Sedgwick writes: 'plain and simple he remained all his life, straightforward and hard, strong and reserved, positive and angular, unyielding and inflexible, he was typical of the world of his childhood and youth.' He adds: 'A faith which the scepticism of the time never infected, and on which nothing made any inroad, was handed down to him as a priceless inheritance.'[36] So we see how he acquired the armaments for the struggle ahead.

On 27 April 1890, with his brother Franz, he made his First Communion in the parish church of Dinklage. They then followed their elder brothers Friedrich and Augustinus to the Stella Matutina Jesuit school at Feldkirch in the Vorarlberg, where at six foot six inches, Clemens August was easily the tallest pupil. For the young giant, the clear mountain air was a delight and he was very happy but in the summer of 1894 the two brothers had to leave the Stella Matutina because the school was not recognised by the Prussian government. Four blissful years came to an end and the last two years of school life were spent at the Catholic public school of Oldenburg at Vechta. But there were compensations for Sundays were passed at the Castle of Dinklage, a mere ten miles away. They took their leaving examination in the summer of 1896.

Count Ferdinand decided that before choosing a profession the boys had to 'learn to think' so in the spring of 1897 they were sent for two terms to the Catholic University of Friburg in Switzerland where they studied philosophy and history. A year later at the end of the winter term the brothers visited Rome for the first time. Clemens August ('Clau') found his faith further deepened and his appreciation sharpened of the extent of the Catholic Church as a universal organisation. He also had the unforgettable experience of hearing the Papal Mass said by the 88 year old Leo XIII. On the way home, and after a retreat at the Benedictine Abbey of Maria-Laach, Clemens August told Franz he had decided to become a priest. The inseparable

36. Ibid., p. 37.

brothers were now to go their different ways. The following Autumn found Clemens August at the Canisianum, the Jesuit Theological College in Innsbruck.

Apart from his towering stature, his intellect, humour, empathy, self-possession and modesty marked him out as a natural leader. So he was appointed *bidellus*, or link-man, between the teachers of the College and its 250 students. Significantly, his curriculum interests centred on such practical issues as the relations between Church and State, State and science, the State and education and the State and the family. Social questions also engaged his interest, doubtless fuelled by his innate love for the poor and the marginalised. In 1903, he was admitted to the ecclesiastical seminary of Münster and was consecrated priest in its great cathedral on 28 May 1904.

The following month he was appointed an assistant priest at Münster Cathedral with the specific duty of attending on his uncle, the auxiliary bishop. In 1906 he was sent to the church of St Matthias in Berlin, in order to take up parish work. His Rector was to later report on how he excelled in pastoral work. His biographer writes: 'Day by day he set out upon his visits both to cellar dwellings and attics and to elegant residences on the Kurfürstendamm, but he preferred the poor quarters. He dried many tears: many petitioners came to his door; his liberality was known; in this way he became the father of the poor.'[37] He became President of the capital's Catholic Young Men's Association and was especially pleased to assist significantly in the creation of its new building. He loved the family atmosphere of the Association, which reminded him of the gatherings at Dinklage, and lived in a flat above the Association's hostel. As was his rule, he cared nothing for personal comfort – his two rooms were furnished with 'monastic simplicity' and he shared the plain fare of the Grey Nuns who looked after him, along with three other priests in the hostel. His only concession to indulgence was the row of long pipes he kept in a corner.

He served the Clemens-Hofbauer Church (St Clement's) which included deputies from the Imperial and Prussian parliaments among its daily worshippers. He spent nine years at St Clement's as its *Curatus* and loved it deeply. Then, in 1919, he returned to St Matthias as its

37. Ibid., p. 46.

Parish Priest, taking his few household goods with him. By instinct, his ideals were monastic so he consumed little by way of daily food and drink, which seemed not to impair the vitality of his giant frame but he derived much pleasure from his long pipe which he scarcely abandoned even in times of fasting. His humility in the faith was a basic element in his character. Each Saturday evening he would go to the room of one of his senior assistant priests, kneel down and make his confession. Preparing for his annual retreat he would ask his confessor what he ought especially to guard against and what faults he ought to correct.

Though he loved his pastoral work, the revolutionary atmosphere after the Great War disturbed and worried him. He was pained to see Germany's young growing up without regard for authority and without reverence. This decline of authority fed the clear decline in morals. As we have seen earlier, a godless state was developing which would prepare the way for Hitler. With the unswerving logic derived from his fully Catholic ideals he fought every pernicious tendency without compromise. He insisted, for example, that the Decree of the bishops against the continually increasing licence in women's dress should be immediately read and acted upon. He loathed from his heart every un-Christian tendency and sensed that in the western world 'a terrible avalanche would fall upon the institution of marriage and upon family life.'[38] How prophetic these feelings were!

In 1929, after 23 years of dedicated service to the people of Berlin, Father Clemens August was called home to the diocese of Münster. There was a sad leave taking of the congregation and the assistant priests. When he offered his hand to each priest, he then knelt before him, begged for his blessing and asked forgiveness for any wrong he may have done to him. On the 24 April he took up his post as Parish Priest of St Lambert's, the municipal and market church of Münster, capital of Westphalia. The Burgomaster and the town councillors were among the great congregation there to greet him – furnishing proof of the Catholic foundations of public life in Münster. After the Mass they visited his residence to give him their sincere address of welcome.

By 1933 the Nazis were announcing their ascendancy to the people of Münster and the Parish Priest of St Lambert's felt forced to write

38. Ibid., p. 53.

in his Parochial Chronicle: 'On Monday, March 6th, notwithstanding the unanimous protest of the town council, the flag of the Hitler party, a red flag with a swastika, was flown from the council house.'[39] After the death of Bishop Poggenburg in January 1933, Clemens August was summoned to Berlin by Nuncio Monsignor Orsenigo and told that the Holy Father intended to appoint him Bishop of Münster. It is recorded that upon his return to the diocese: 'The hearts of the faithful were full of pride and joy. They trusted the bishop-elect absolutely. They knew of his piety and the Catholic strength of the race of von Galen.'[40] Under the terms of the Concordat, the new bishop had to take the oath of allegiance before the Prussian President of the Council of Ministers, Hermann Göring, who emphasised to him the necessity of ensuring the clergy supported National Socialism. He was rebuffed for his efforts. Later, when Göring was still enjoying a 'honeymoon period' with the German people, von Galen declared him to be not one whit better than the rest of the Nazis.

In his Lenten and Easter Pastoral letters of 1934, the Bishop lost no time in expressing his distaste for National Socialism and particularly for its fundamental worship of race. Two SS men came to him for a copy of the Easter Pastoral. He handed it over and told them to read it carefully. The NSDAP were worried for, well beyond the diocese, his writings were having dramatic impact. On 5 July, addressing the Knights of Malta he described how 'ruthlessly one-sided propaganda of novel ideas and dazzling slogans could lead whole masses into error by its dominating influence . . . The danger to the Catholic faith in Germany could not be neglected.'[41] In 1935, at the Nazi Party rally for the Münster region, the Bishop was abused by Alfred Rosenberg before an audience of SA 'Brownshirts' especially drafted in from a wider area. The reply of the Catholics came the next day at their Great Procession. The attendance of the previous year had been 7,000. Now it had become 19,000 and the Bishop received a tremendous ovation. Someone remarked to a companion that the 'brown men' were blind to arouse the Lion of Münster.

He noted with deep sadness that so much literary output was

39. Ibid., p. 57.
40. Ibid., p. 58.
41. Ibid., p. 65.

being made to serve the propaganda of a new paganism. Catholic publications, which could have offered resistance, had been crushed. Now only the pulpit remained and that would be his way. On 22 March 1936 he refuted the allegation that the Christian faith was a hindrance to German restoration and on 6 September he preached powerfully against totalitarianism denouncing it as the crudest form of slavery. At last, in the Spring of 1937, the Papal Encyclical *Mit brennender Sorge* exposed National Socialism to the world for what it was. He attached much importance to his links with the theological students of his diocese but he could not always succeed in getting to grips with the more recent theology nor did he hold that the less intelligible a statement, the more profound was the writer's thinking. He even found what was hazy and extravagant in the language of modern prayer, saying: 'I talk to God in a simpler way. It seems to me that men of today like to walk on stilts.'

There was a close bond between the Bishop and his priests. They would come to him with all their worries. Now, as they fought the new heathenism he was heartbroken to hear of a priest called before the Gestapo, another taken into 'protective custody', another expelled from a school and prohibited from giving religious instruction, another banished from the region. Scandalous imputations would be made against a priest's character and in some cases they were offered bribes to give up their vocations, then good jobs would await them in government. Courageously they refused so their captors went to work on them without mercy. In many cases the Bishop could do little but pray for them for his very name infuriated the Nazis and only increased the persecution of the priests. But he was not to be cowed and in two great sermons of June 1941 he spoke of the cellars of the Gestapo and the concentration camps where his priests were held captive. Whenever he heard of the death of one of his priests in Dachau he was heartbroken.

In July 1941 on the Feast of the Visitation, at the Church of Our Lady of the Seven Dolours in Telgte some 7 miles north east of Münster, he read out the general pastoral letter of the German bishops against the measures of euthanasia applied to the mentally sick. Because of Allied bombing on the previous evening, long streams of people left Münster for the little township on foot. On Saturday 12 July news reached him that the Jesuit institutions in Münster's Königstrasse and at Sentmaring were being taken over by the regime. He hurried to both buildings and caught the Gestapo driving members of the Order from their properties. He railed at them calling them and their leaders thieves and robbers. Returning to his residence he vowed he would no longer be silent. Shortly afterwards, from the pulpit of the parish church of Überwasser he gave his famous sermon in which he likened the National Socialists to a 'hammer', adding that 'we are the anvil' and 'the anvil is harder than the hammer.' On 30 July, by order of the Führer, the practice of forcing their way into religious houses by the Gestapo was ended. Hundreds of thousands of copies of the Bishop's sermons were now being distributed throughout Germany. In Leipzig several of the distributors were sent to concentration camps where some died.

The family motto of the von Galens was *nec laudibus nec timore* (Neither men's praise nor fear of men shall move me). Despite the persecution, what was now evident was that the Bishop of Münster was totally free of fear and would continue, come what may, his strict interpretation of the rights and duties that had been entrusted to him. He was completely oblivious to propaganda or threats in maintaining his Catholic standpoint against 'the brown gang', as he called them. And as time went on he grew more irascible with them. Once, at an educational conference the chairman had suggested that a wife and mother was more valuable to the teaching process than a spinster. The Bishop believed the statement derived from the heathen and materialist concepts of the Nazis. He banged the table and said: 'I won't listen to talk like that; Germany is not a stud farm.'[42]

On Sunday 10 October 1943, the Cathedral at Münster was severely damaged by Allied bombing. The Bishop's Chaplain tells of how he and his colleagues, rushing around the bomb craters and over the ruins, could see the Bishop covered with dirt and dust, standing in the doorway between his bedroom and his study on the second storey. To reach the ground the Bishop had to lie down and slide along steeply sloping beams. Many of his flock believed he had been saved from death as by a miracle. Since he paid too little attention to himself, it was a week later, when the pain and lameness could

42. Ibid., p. 118.

no longer be hidden, that it was discovered he had a wound in his left thigh. His biographer found it ironic that he had been 'pursued and endangered by the bombs of those very countries which, in their wireless propaganda against the Third Reich, had broadcast his sermons round the world.'[43] The Bishop and his Provost had, like thousands of others throughout Germany, now to contend with a primitive form of life in which there was no piped water supply, no artificial light and windows and doors were boarded up against the cold. The biographer comments: 'It hurt one's feelings to watch those elderly gentlemen groping about in all this muddle with a candle.'[44]

Whatever privation and danger he shared with the rest of his flock this did not mitigate the hatred the Nazis felt for Bishop von Galen. The following comments are attributed to Heinrich Himmler, Head of the SS, by Lieutenant General Faeckenstedt in his report on a conference held near Oldenburg on 30 September 1944: 'The whole set are enemies of the State. We couldn't settle accounts with the traitor Galen for reasons of foreign policy. We shall catch up with him later on, and the whole Church with him and the gang that is backing it. There will be a thorough liquidation in that quarter.'[45]

When the bomb plot of 20 July 1944, led by a Catholic, Colonel von Stauffenberg, failed to assassinate Hitler, and after which nearly 5,000 people were executed, including Stauffenberg, the Bishop became gloomy. Now it seemed the dictator would only be deposed by the continued advance of the Allied armies. This had its brighter side, however, for Münster had not been bombed for a whole year and as the Allies progressed through France and Belgium the bombing of German cities had been wound down. Then on 12 September, Münster had its greatest air raid and much of the city became a landscape of craters and dust. Though the Bishop fought against leaving the city, others insisted that the cellar of the Theological College did not provide him with adequate shelter. He could no longer risk his life and the welfare of the diocese impelled his immediate evacuation. Bitterly resigned, he was taken to the St Joseph Institute at Sendenhorst, a town lying 22

43. Ibid., p. 129.
44. Ibid., p. 137.
45. Ibid., p. 145.

kilometres to the south-east. Heinrich Portmann[46] paints a touching picture of how, during the following winter the church embroidery guilds at Emsdetten, Greven, Borghorst, Oelde and Ibbenbüren worked feverishly to produce new vestments and how through the snow and ice young people on bicycles brought vestments and sacred vessels to their bishop at Sendenhorst. It was in the Institute there, on the afternoon of Easter Sunday, 31 March 1945, that he heard the first heavy Allied tanks rolling slowly past its doors.

On 12 April, he returned to Münster to protest publicly about the Russian and Polish workers who, seemingly unrestrained, were plundering, torturing and murdering the inhabitants. In the months that followed, either at Sendenhorst or at Münster, he worked at his desk trying to mitigate the chaos that ensued after the War's end. Sometimes he worked until the early hours of the morning because regular queues of visitors were bringing their problems and anxieties to him. Following his interviews with individuals and families he had then to enter into lengthy negotiations with the occupying powers. His health had hitherto been unassailable. Now it was being steadily undermined. Of this time, Father Portmann writes: 'In the streets of the Münster province one saw wretched people from the great industrial areas trekking out into the countryside in long columns (as a protection against the foreign workers) to try and find there the barest necessities to keep body and soul together.'[47]

Despite its pain and privation, Münster became ecstatic on the evening of the last Sunday before Christmas – the radio announced the appointment of no less than thirty-two new cardinals. Among them was Bishop Clemens von Galen. Apparently the Romans were astonished at the sight of this giant bishop attending the Consistory but they took him to their hearts and feted him wherever he went. When he returned to Münster, fifty thousand people congregated at the massive mountain of rubble by the west door of the cathedral. Through their Lord Lieutenant, Lord Mayor, and the speakers for Catholic committees and youth organisations, the Cardinal was assured of the love and loyalty of his faithful. During the next few days he was unwell and on the Tuesday following his first Pontifical High Mass, on the insistence of

46. Ibid., pp. 147-8.
47. Ibid., p. 169.

his doctors, he was admitted to the Franciscan hospital for diagnosis. He told those assembled around his bed that the day was the anniversary of his baptism and also the Feast of St Joseph, the patron of the dying. The subsequent operation revealed perforation of the caecum and intestinal paralysis. Subsequently, each day's bulletin was worse than the last and on the afternoon of Friday the Lion of Münster breathed his last.

At the tolling of the city's bells, people stood stunned in the streets, wept openly or hurried to the nearest church to pray. On 28 March 1946 he was taken to his ancestral resting place like a king. Three cardinals, including Cardinal Griffin of Westminster, and many bishops accompanied him on his final journey. And the priests who, just a few days ago, had walked in triumph before him now sang the Miserere for their beloved master.

Clemens August von Galen was once described by a professor at the University of Munich as 'a giant with the heart of a child'. He was respected and trusted for his boundless courage but he was loved for his humility and his sensitivity. He was a strong man who could cry like a child, particularly in situations charged with devotional feeling. Tearfully he once spoke of how two Bavarian soldiers told him that whenever they approached the Church of St Servatius they always went in to say the rosary for their wives and children at home. The humble never escaped his notice. He once spoke movingly of an old charwoman who for many years had peeled the potatoes in one of Münster's ecclesiastical buildings. On many an afternoon he had seen her, with her back deeply bent, go into the cathedral to make the Stations of the Cross. He described her as the most devout person in all Münster. Once he took a grieving father by the hand and prayed with him at the grave of his young child. So many people had their own stories of his compassion. Brigadier R. L. Sedgwick, who came to know him extremely well, says simply, in his introduction to the Portmann biography, that he was: '. . . the greatest German I have ever met'.[48]

BLESSED NIKOLAUS GROSS

In 1891, Pope Leo XIII published *Rerum Novarum*, one of the Catholic Church's most notable encyclicals. In it he demonstrated

---

48. Ibid., p. 29.

his advanced social thinking, giving his clear and unmistakable views on the exploitation of the poor in the newly emerged industrial society. In his opening words he laments that: 'a small number of very rich men have been able to lay upon the teeming masses of the labouring poor, a yoke which is very little better than slavery itself.' He believed that the labouring classes had the right to the membership of unions and also the right to strike, though here he thought it the duty of the state, through legislation, to remove the grievances at the root of strikes.[49]

Rerum Novarum ('Of new things') has influenced Catholic social thinking throughout the twentieth century and down to the present day. It was a logical development of the views of such Catholic churchmen as Wilhelm Emmanuel, Baron von Ketteler, Bishop of Mainz, who believed he was well within his rights as a bishop to speak with authority on social issues. In his book *The Labour Question and Christianity* (1864), he had advocated labour associations and suggested that Christian capitalists should generously aid their establishment. At the September 1869 Fulda conference of the German bishops he believed the Church, in the name of faith, morals and charity, had a clear role in the removal of economic exploitation.[50] Working men had a right to legal protection. He also urged that in every diocese some priests should be selected to study economic questions. Such ideas were still influential several decades later among such Catholic churchmen as Alfred Delp and Max Metzger, both of whom are featured in this chapter.

Two Catholic laymen who undoubtedly heard the voice of the Church down the years, both toilers in the industrial relations field, were George Woodcock in Britain and Nikolaus Gross in Germany. Since their formative years were very similar, it might be useful to say something about George Woodcock before moving on to Nikolaus Gross, the subject of this profile. The son of a cotton weaver, George Woodcock was born at Bamber Bridge, Lancashire in 1904. He began to work in a cotton mill, as a 'half-timer' at the age of twelve. One year later he was working full-time at the mill. Forced to stay in bed due to a

---

49. E Duffy, *Saints and Sinners. A History Of The Popes*. London, 3rd ed. 2006, pp. 311-12.
50. http://www.newadvent.org/cathen/08629c.htm (4 August 2009).

long illness, he discovered books and in 1929 won a T.U.C. scholarship to Ruskin College, Oxford. In 1931 he moved to New College where he took a first-class honours degree in philosophy, politics and economics. He joined the T.U.C. in 1936, becoming 'the outstanding trade union leader of his time'.[51] Elected its General Secretary in 1960, within his first year he oversaw the expulsion of the then Communist dominated Electrical Trades Union. Under his leadership, from being a body of protest, the T.U.C. became an organisation with an accepted role in the making of economic policy.

Nikolaus Gross was born in Niederwenigern, near the city of Essen, on 30 September, 1898. The son of a colliery blacksmith, his educational opportunities were limited to attendance at Niederwenigern's Catholic school from 1905-12. The Ruhr valley, dominated by its coal and steel industries, offered little beyond manual labour to working-class boys such as Nikolaus. First he was employed in a plate rolling mill and next as a grinder. Then he worked at the coal-face in one of the Ruhr's many mines. He did this for five years and we have to remember that coal extraction was not then the capital intensive process it subsequently became. Mining the coal was then largely a matter of the miner kneeling in the dirt and danger and swinging his pick at the coal seam. Alternatively, the coal was 'won' by controlled explosions, which intensified the dangers of working underground.

Like George Woodcock, Nikolaus Gross was bent on self-improvement and devoted the little spare time he had to study. He also perceived that the lot of the labouring class could best be improved through solidarity with others so, in 1917, he joined the Christian Miners' Trade Union, following this by membership of the (Catholic) Centre Party in 1918, and, in 1919, membership of the St Anthony's Miners' Association. This last Association was the leading union for Catholic miners and it had a powerful voice on Catholic issues. When he was 22, he became the secretary for young people in the Christian Miners' Trade Union. Organisationally and administratively he must have found his feet in a remarkably short time for one year later he was appointed assistant editor of the union's newspaper, *Bergknappe* ('The Miner').

In this role he was required to travel throughout Germany but his journeys and his studies were no bar to his interest in a Niederwenigern

---

51. *The Times*, obituary of George Woodcock, 19 June 1979

girl named Elisabeth Koch. They married and produced seven children. From a number of sources, it is reported that the marriage was a very happy one. At his beatification on 7 October 2001 Pope Paul II said in his homily that 'Nikolaus loved his wife and children very much' and it is evident that in Bottrop, the Ruhr Valley town where he settled his family, he was an outstanding husband and father, dedicated to their spiritual, educational and material well-being. Yet, while family life was one of the principal ways in which he could serve God, his work was the other. Here, he once wrote that the poor and the sick had a special claim to our love and, echoing St Thérèse of Lisieux, that the great things are accomplished through the little, routine things being done willingly and well.

His success at his job led to him being appointed, in 1927, assistant editor of the *Westdeutsche Arbeiterzeitung*, the newspaper of the St Anthony's Miners' Association and before long he became its editor-in-chief. In this role he often had to give guidance to Catholic workers on social and labour questions. For this he was well suited because, in the tradition of Bishop von Ketteler, with his view that social reform had to begin with the interior regeneration of the soul, and Pope Leo XIII's contribution to the evolution of a moral landscape for economic activity, Nikolaus Gross firmly believed in the moral claim underlying all political issues and the necessary spiritual effort required for the solution of social problems.

This was the standpoint he brought to his work. Through his life itself, he was an outstanding witness for the Catholic faith. On both of these counts his views on the emergence of the Nazis were abundantly clear. He believed that only 'political immaturity' and 'lack of discernment' could account for their burgeoning popularity. In fact, after moving to Cologne's Ketteler House in 1929, he described the Nazis as 'mortal enemies of the present state.' On 14 September 1930, as editor of *Westdeutsche Arbeiterzeitung* he wrote: 'As Catholic workers we reject Nazism not only for political and economic reasons, but decisively also, resolutely and clearly, on account of our religious and cultural attitude.'[52]

Earlier in this book we have noted that through the process of *Gleichschaltung* ('co-ordination'), Hitler set about creating a highly

52. http://www.savior.org/saints/gross.htm (4 August 2009).

centralised one-Party Reich by dismantling the political, social and cultural institutions of the old Germany. For a time, only industry and the armed forces were exempt, while with the Protestant faith organisations he was not totally successful and the Catholic Church gave him so many headaches he decided to ignore it until after the War. It follows then that the trade unions were never destined to escape his clutches. After the election victory of 1933 he appointed Robert Ley as the leader of the new Labour Front (DAF). Hitler promised this would 'bring peace to the world of labour'.[53] The assets and offices of every trade union were taken over by SA men and the single Labour Front was then established with Nazi Party members filling every official post. It is worth noting that Hitler's promise of industrial peace resulted in workers being deprived of any bargaining mechanism. The employer was the 'leader' and the workers 'followers.' Wages were set by the Front and a 'pay freeze' was established in spite of increases in the cost of living. Compulsory deductions were made from pay, for income tax, obligatory charities and instalment payments for the future Volkswagen. Over 330,000 workers subscribed 280 million Reichsmarks for the 'Beetle' car but only a handful were ever produced before 1946.

Robert Ley, a violent anti-semite with a reputation for drunkenness, coarseness and unrefined ostentation, immediately declared that the *Westdeutsche Arbeiterzeitung* was 'hostile to the state'. And so the lines were drawn. No doubt by now Gross's office at the Ketteler House in Cologne was being carefully watched, as were his travels throughout Germany and the contents of the newspaper he edited. In commemoration of the former Bishop of Mainz, his newspaper had been retitled *Ketteler's Watch*. Gross's task now was to keep the newspaper from being suppressed by the Nazis whilst not compromising its editorial. This must have been a formidable burden for, unlettered as he was, he had to proceed by inference rather than strident prose. His success in doing so may be gauged from the fact he managed to keep it in being until November 1938.

During the next phase he became more actively resistant to the regime and his motivation sprang not from political beliefs but from

53. J Taylor and W Shaw, *Dictionary of The Third Reich*. London, 1997, p. 167.

his religious convictions. He believed ardently that man must obey God more than men, declaring that: 'If something is demanded of us that goes against God or the Faith, then not only may we but we must, refuse obedience (towards men).' He was one of several Catholic labour leaders of the same mind. Some others were Bernhard Letterhaus of the Christian Textile Workers and Otto Müller, a priest who headed the West German Workers' Union. Significantly active at this time also was the layman Erich Klausener, who was head of Catholic Action in Berlin from 1928. (Klausener organised protest rallies one of which, in 1933, was attended by 45,000 Catholics. Another Catholic rally, in 1934, was attended by 60,000. Shortly afterwards Klausener was shot to death in his office by an SS officer). Nikolaus Gross believed that Hitler was so uniquely bad for Germany, people would come to realise this and vote him out of office. When he saw they would never have the conventional opportunity to do so he joined the resistance movement. After his newspaper was banned he distributed pamphlets critical of the regime. Two of these, *The Great Tasks* and *Is Germany Lost?* were later discovered by the Gestapo and used as evidence against him when he was brought to trial towards the end of the War.

With Bernhard Letterhaus, Nikolaus formed in Cologne, a resistance group, the Catholic Workers' movement. A parallel grouping, of Bavarian Catholic lay people, known as the Sperr Circle, also emerged at this time. Through Father Alfred Delp SJ, both groups established links with the Kreisau Circle.[54] By 1940, the Gestapo were interrogating Nikolaus and searching his home. Although his pamphlets were primarily intended to strengthen the critical faculties of the workers through their faith, his opposition to the regime was also clear. The fortitude of Nikolaus and others has been remarked upon by the well-known workers' chaplain, Mgr Caspar Schulte of Paderborn. In his memoirs he writes:

> In my many conversations, especially with Nikolaus Gross and the association's head, Otto Müller, I got to know and admire these men's moral greatness. They did not stumble into death. They went their way also prepared to bear a painful death for the sake of freedom. I said to Nikolaus Gross on the day before the assassination attempt on Hitler of

---

54. M F Coady, *With Bound Hands. A Jesuit in Nazi Germany*. Chicago, 2003, p. 53.

> 20 July 1944: "Mr Gross, remember that you have seven children. I have no family for which I am responsible. It's a matter of your life." To which Gross made a really great statement to me: "If we do not risk our life today, how do we then want one day to justify ourselves before God and our people."[55]

In 1943, Nikolaus Gross set out his credo in a booklet. His words were prophetic and for a man whose education was hard won, eloquently enough expressed. An extract reads:

> Sometimes my heart becomes heavy and the task appears insoluble if I measure my own human imperfection and inadequacy against the greatness of the obligation and the weight of responsibility. If a generation must pay the highest price, death, for its short life, we look for the answer in ourselves in vain. We find it only in Him in whose hand we are safe in life and in death. We never know what problems are waiting to test the power and strength of our souls . . . Man's ways lie in obscurity. But even darkness is not without light. Hope and faith, which always hasten ahead of us, already have a presentiment of the breaking of a new dawn. If we know that the best thing in us, the soul, is immortal, then we also know that we shall meet each other again.[56]

In addition to his writing, Nikolaus opposed Hitler through his work as a courier among various resistance groups, which inevitably brought him into close contact with Count Helmuth von Moltke and the Kreisau Circle – the group of philosophers, educators, journalists, businessmen and trade unionists bent on devising a plan for a post-Hitler government.[57] As has been remarked in the profile of Alfred Delp although these members wished to rid the world of Hitler as quickly as possible, most of them were opposed to his assassination since this was contrary to the mainly Christian ethos of the Circle. Their best hope for Germany was that it would become a leading nation within a European Community, which ideally would also include Russia. Each nation would have limited individual power thus enabling the Community itself to be a great collective force for good and for peace.

---

55. See reference 52.
56. Ibid. p. 2.
57. S Ottaway, *Hitler's Traitors. German Resistance to the Nazis*. Barnsley, 2003, pp. 138-9.

Even though Nikolaus Gross was not in any way implicated in the Bomb Plot of 20 July 1944, it did not avail him in the slightest when Hitler's vengeance fell upon those who had given the least cause for his suspicions. Nikolaus Gross was arrested on 12 August 1944 and taken first to Ravensbrück and then to the Berlin-Tegel prison. When Elisabeth Gross visited him in Berlin she could see clearly the signs of torture on his arms and hand. There is evidence of his belief in the power of prayer: in his letters to his family he asked for their continual prayer while Father Peter Buchholz, his prison chaplain, has attested to how prayer was a source of comfort and strength to Nikolaus. Prayers were to attain even greater significance as his ultimate fate steadily became clearer. In the notorious 'People's Court' on 15 January 1945, showing the inherent disregard for human life becoming of Hitler's favourite legal executioner, Roland Freisler, its President, sentenced Nikolaus Gross to death. With ghoulish matter-of-factness he reflected that Nikolaus: 'swam along in treason and consequently had to drown in it.'

The devout family man and devoted trade unionist was hanged in Plötzensee prison on 23 January 1945. Nazi hatred of him extended beyond death for he was denied both grave and Christian burial. In a final Nazi act of extirpation, he was incinerated and his ashes spread across a sewage farm. Father Peter Buchholz, the Chaplain who was to be with Father Alfred Delp at his execution just over a week later, had accompanied Nikolaus on his final walk to his death. As he had blessed the victim, Father Buchholz later reported: 'Gross bowed his head silently . . . His face already seemed illuminated by the glory into which he was getting ready to enter.' At his beatification, Pope John Paul II said: 'In the Blessed Martyr Nikolaus Gross was accomplished what the prophet foretold – "The just man will live on account of his faith." '

BLESSED FRANZ JÄGERSTÄTTER

I began to prepare this profile on Friday, 26 October, the date of Austria's National Holiday. That year (2007) it possessed added significance as the day Franz Jägerstätter, a farmer, was beatified at St Mary's Cathedral in Linz. Comparatively, his recognition was belated, coming sixty four years after he was beheaded by the Nazis. The process of his cause had been difficult, not to say controversial, for Franz was an unusual martyr.

Before we consider the philosophical/theological aspects of his cause, let us look at the bare bones of his story.

He was born in 1907 at St Radegund which is no more than a cluster of houses and a tiny church with an onion-shaped steeple. The village is located on the Austro-German border and is about forty miles north-east of Salzburg. Linz, where Hitler spent his early years, is not far away. Ironically, Linz is also closely associated with Adolf Eichmann, the orchestrator of the Final Solution.

Franz's mother was Rosalia Huber and his father Franz Bachmeier. They are said to have been too poor to marry and when Bachmeier was killed in World War I the boy was cared for by his grandmother and attended St Radegund's primary school. When he was ten his mother married Heinrich Jägerstätter, a local farmer. Heinrich adopted Franz who, there being no other children of the marriage, inherited the farm when Heinrich died of TB in 1933.

Though he practised the outward forms of his Catholic faith he was later to describe his adolescent years as centred on no more than 'half-baked' Christianity for he rapidly gained a reputation as a young tearaway invariably spelling trouble for the villagers, chasing the local girls without let up and battling violently with any rivals for their affection. The village inn was his staging-post and he and his 'gang' even fought a pitched battle with some mercenaries who were policing the border area around St Radegund. For that escapade he spent some days in gaol. When he was twenty he left home to work in the mines of the Steiermark area and was away for two years during which period he earned enough money to buy a motor-cycle. The local people remember him zooming around the area with unabashed pride and they too were impressed for this was the first motor-cycle they had seen.

On 1 August 1933 a child was born in St Radegund to Theresia Auer and, according to Mary Cole, one of his biographers, the father was Franz Jägerstätter, whose mother vehemently opposed his marriage to the girl, so it did not take place.[58] However, Cole relates that Franz was a very good father to his little daughter who deeply mourned his execution ten years later. In 1936 he met and married Franziska

58. M Cole, 'Nein! "Better my hands fettered than my conscience."' in *Crusader* magazine. Manchester, July 2007, p. 4.

Swaninger and their first action was to offer to adopt Theresia Auer's child, but the mother was not prepared to give her up. Among his poignant letters before being guillotined are those saying farewell to Theresia and her daughter.

His marriage with Franziska was very happy and significantly the wedding was marked, not by the traditional big celebration, but by an immediate pilgrimage to Rome. At first Franziska was the more devout Catholic but, still alive, she repudiates the idea that she worked the change in him and is adamant that they 'helped each other to grow in the faith'.[59] Also, we should note that some observers suggest the change in him was becoming apparent on his return from the iron-mines in Styria. In spite of his joy in the motor-cycle, inwardly he had decided material goods were not enough in his quest for contentment.

Three daughters were born to them in rapid succession and Franz proved a wonderful father, again breaking with tradition by pushing a pram proudly around the village, which was simply not done by St Radegund men in those days. The seven years the family were spared to each other were blissful and, time and again, Franz told Franziska he could never have imagined that marriage would be so wonderful.

Reverting to the time of his return from the mines, it was then that Franz had expressed an interest in joining a religious order. Father Karobath, the village priest, had dissuaded him, reminding him of his mother's reliance on him for the operation of the farm now that his foster-father was ageing. Yet from this point a change could be discerned in his outlook and behaviour – the tearaway was becoming a thoughtful and zealous Christian. Daily he attended Mass and received Communion, which was somewhat singular for a man in a rural culture. He would pause from his labours in the field to read passages from the Bible or to say the rosary. He sang hymns while he worked and on his way to and from church. He noted down pious reflections as they occurred to him. Some villagers were critical, all were bemused.

In 1938, the Nazis carried out the Anschluss, the 'protective' invasion of Austria and in April the Austrians were asked to legitimize what had

---

59. Ibid., p. 4.

already taken place, in a plebiscite. They signalled their approbation overwhelmingly, for Hitler was seen as the 'strong man' to fight the Communist threat and he had repudiated the hated Versailles treaty and significantly increased employment in Germany. Franz Jägerstätter was one of the very few people in Austria, and certainly the only one in St Radegund, who voted against the action. At first he was determined not to vote, for he regarded Hitler not only as a threat to his beloved Austria but also as a dedicated and dangerous enemy of the Catholic Church which he loved even more. Franziska threatened that if he did not vote she would no longer love him (the only time, as she later testified, that she had tried to pressure him). So he attended the plebiscite, and voted 'No'. It mattered little, for the authorities destroyed his ballot paper.

Franz was resolutely opposed to the 'New Order' and made no attempt to conceal his attitude. He was completely open and direct in his arguments with the villagers about the 'Führer' and would respond to the virtually obligatory 'Heil Hitler' greeting with an emphatic 'Grüss Gott'. He carried his detestation of the Nazis into his private life for he refused to accept their benefits including the family allowance to which he was entitled and the government assistance available after his crops, with others in the area, had been destroyed in a severe hailstorm. When he was criticised by his mother and others for selling off part of his land, he replied: 'My few kernels won't save Hitler.'[60]

He made a practice of filling a knapsack with meat and farm produce to take to poor people in the area. Though this was undoubtedly an act of charity, Gordon Zahn, another biographer, has suggested it may have been 'his way of evading Nazi regulations and keeping at least some of the fruits of his labour out of the wartime economy'. Perhaps this and the sale of land were an indirect method of sabotage.

Franz was sacristan at the village church and a good friend of its pastor, Father Karobath. They would spend many evenings together discussing the state of the world and the political situation under Hitler's hegemony. Both men were dedicated opponents of Nazism but Father Karobath counselled the farmer on the dangers of expressing his opinions so freely when the regime's spies were everywhere. At the time of the Anschluss plebiscite he intimated that for his friend

60. See G Zahn, 'Jägerstätter – Martyr For Conscience'. Erie, 1994, p. 2.

to vote 'No' was merely making a pointless gesture. So it is ironic that it was Father Karobath who suffered the more for his imprudence at that stage, in that he was arrested and imprisoned for making critical comments in one of his sermons.

The War began and in May 1940 Franz received his call-up papers but the village mayor intervened stating that he was 'indispensable', that his wife was ill, that his third child was about to be born and that there was no one to run the farm. The application was successful but when his call-up was renewed in October 1940 he told his wife to resist any move to defer it as he wished to know what life was like in the army. When the village leaders succeeded in getting him discharged in April 1941 he had certainly satisfied his curiosity. His army experience had appalled him for everything possible was done to prevent him practising his faith or going to Mass and he had been the butt of the officers' aggression because of his Catholicism. He had also become acquainted with the Nazi euthanasia programme in a mental asylum.[61]

In December 1940, despite the restrictions placed on him, he had been received into the Third Order of St Francis. Returning to the village in April, Franz was quite clear about National Socialism and its leadership – his country had been taken into an unjust war and every action supporting the war was a criminal offence. He could not in conscience carry out any orders which were unjust, criminal, and therefore sinful. In 1938 he had had a dream in which the Nazi party appeared to him as a railway train. Laughing men, women and children hastened to clamber aboard, not knowing it was taking them to hell. He believed the dream to be a message from God in answer to his question: 'Should I be a Nazi or a Catholic?' His 'No' vote in the Anschluss plebiscite had followed.

Next he sought the advice of priests and even Bishop Fliesser of the Linz diocese who was extremely guarded (for Franz may have been a Nazi spy) and warned him to think of the effect of his conscientious objection on his wife and children. Other counsellors pointed out that thousands of Catholics were already fighting and dying and he should bear this in mind. Yet his mind was made up – his duty was to God and not to the demands of a secular ruler. He

---

61. M Cole, op. cit., p. 5.

had expressed his standpoint some years before in a letter written to Franz Huber, his fatherless godson. In it he had warned against people who take the sixth commandment lightly and urged young Huber to fix his eyes on the eternal homeland adding: 'Though we must bear our sorrows and reap little reward in this world for doing so, we can still become richer than millionaires – for those who need not fear death are the richest and happiest of all.' In February 1943, he received further call-up papers. Taking a sad and painful parting from his wife he set out on 1 March for the barracks in Enns. As he left the village, a neighbour called: 'God go with you Franz!' Quietly he said: 'You will see no more of me.' The following day he told the military authorities that he did not intend to serve in the army. He was immediately arrested and taken to the prison at Linz. While there he suffered something of a crisis of faith as pleas came from every quarter, including his dear friend Pastor Karobath, for him to abandon his stand and remember the needs of his dependants and his moral duty for their well-being.

Contrary to expectations he was not badly treated in prison or by those presiding at his trial. They are reported as being touched by the sincerity of this simple man and they explored ways to resolve his dilemma offering the promise that if he relented then unarmed, non-combatant duties would be found for him. If he withdrew his refusal, his life would be spared. This compounded his problem for it raised the question that if he rejected the opportunity to live might that be a serious sin? In effect, would he be guilty of suicide? He decided to persist in his refusal and in his last days he described the primacy of his conscience thus: 'These few words are being set down here as they come from my mind and heart. And if I must write them with my hands in chains I find that much better than if my will were in chains . . . For this reason I am convinced that it is still best that I speak the truth even if it costs me my life. For you will not find it written in any of the Commandments of God or of the Church that a man is obliged, under pain of sin, to take an oath committing him to obey whatever might be commanded of him by his secular ruler.'[62] When he had been sentenced to death he was transferred to Berlin's Tegel prison to await execution. On her last

---

62. B Kent, *Franz Jägerstätter*. London, 1997, p. 27.

visit to Franz, Franziska had pleaded with him to change his mind for 'I did not want my husband to die.' Even so, she resigned herself to the fact that it was his decision. And he was convinced that no-one could dispense him or anyone else from acting according to his conscience. For him the logic of his position was inescapable: 'God's commandments teach us that we have to obey our secular superiors even if they are not Christians, but only to the extent that they do not command something wrong. For we have to obey God more than man.' Reading the Jägerstätter story is like re-visiting the trial of St Thomas More ('I die the King's good servant but God's first'). Both provide a model of a correct decision in conscience. In Franz's case, how could he choose to serve a monster hell-bent on creating a godless empire in preference to God himself?

At the last, Father Jochmann, a prison chaplain, entered his cell and, still trying to save him, pointed to the document lying on the table. He had merely to sign it for his life to be spared. Smiling, Franz pushed it aside. How could he take an oath in favour of an unjust war? The priest then offered to read to him from the New Testament or to bring in some devotional booklets. Franz thought not, explaining: 'I am completely bound in inner union with the Lord and any reading would only interrupt my communion with my God.' Father Jochmann commented later that as Franz spoke his eyes shone with such joy and confidence they would be fixed in his memory for the rest of his life.

At 4 pm on 9 August 1943, facing the guillotine and without a blindfold, Franz Jägerstätter stepped forward and was executed. Later the prison chaplain said to some Austrian nuns: 'I can only congratulate you on this countryman of yours who lived as a saint and has now died a hero. I say with certainty that this simple man is the only saint I ever met in my lifetime.' Franz did not expect his death to be remarked upon; known only to his family and the villagers of St Radegund, he considered himself unimportant. Yet his decision was not upheld by a number of people: for example, Franziska and Father Karobath, the parish priest returned from imposed exile, had to struggle to have his name included on the village war memorial. When Father Karobath worked to keep his memory alive by references in his sermons to Franz as the only one who had lived up to his responsibilities as a Christian, he is said to have alienated a large part of his congregation. There was nothing printed about the local martyr in the diocesan paper and the then Bishop of Linz averred that while one might honour Franz for his fidelity to his conscience he was not a model for others to follow – that place should be accorded to the real heroes who had fought and died.

So Franz's story had seemingly passed into obscurity until it was discovered by Gordon C Zahn, the National Director of America's Center on Conscience and War. Zahn's 1964 book, *In Solitary Witness: The Life and Death of Franz Jägerstätter* brought Franz's story back into public notice. It led to a 90-minute drama/documentary by the Austrian television network. Entitled *Der Fall Jaegerstaetter* (*The Jaegerstaetter Case*), it was presented in prime time on Austria's major patriotic holiday. After a linked discussion by 500 groups on the question 'Did he do the right thing?' he was recognised as an authentic, if unusual, hero.

After the execution, a prison chaplain had gathered Franz's ashes for burial in a private cemetery in Berlin and at the end of the war these were transferred to St Radegund and ceremoniously re-buried beside the wall of the church where he had served as sacristan. Hundreds, from political dignitaries to labourers, now began to visit the spot. A call emerged for the beatification of Franz Jägerstätter with the Pax Christi organisation prominent in this. In 1993, Bishop Maximilian Aichern of Linz began the diocesan process to examine the case.

Of course, the road to Franz's recognition was already long because, for decades after the war, he was a controversial figure. Christa Pongratz-Lippitt, correspondent of *The Tablet* in Austria, sees nothing surprising in this. She writes:

'Jägerstätter was a provocation they could not yet bring themselves to face. Catholic priests who had survived the concentration camps were seldom welcomed when they got back to their parishes. People felt uncomfortable in their presence.' So Franz was an enigma to many, even the devout.

It is perhaps reasonable to ask two questions. Firstly, was he a fanatic? Hardly, for from the earliest days of Hitler's march to power Franz had voiced, quite openly, his detestation of the Nazis. Moreover, as the war progressed, he received reports from friends and relatives on leave from the Russian front of the atrocities being committed there by the Germans. Events at home also disturbed him: eight of the eleven priests in his deanery had been arrested by the Gestapo. Moreover, he had learned that, in the castle at Hartheim, disabled and mentally disturbed patients were being murdered because the Nazis considered them 'unworthy of life'. How then could he put loyalty to such a regime above the call of his conscience? The next question is: did he act with callous disregard of Franziska and the children? Anyone who reads the letter of August 1943 to his family would not entertain such a notion. He explains how he would have liked to spare them the pain and sorrow they must bear but that 'we must lose everything dear and worthwhile on earth rather than commit even the slightest offence against God.' He asks his children to be good and obedient and to pray for him so that they may soon be reunited in heaven. The depth of his faith is profound.

On 26 October 2007, Pax Christi members from the UK, Ireland, the USA, Germany and Italy travelled to Austria to take part in the Mass for the beatification of Franz Jägerstätter. The celebrant was the current Bishop of the Linz diocese, Dr Ludwig Schwarz. This is what he had to say:

> Franz Jägerstätter was a prophet with a global view and a penetrating insight which very few of his contemporaries had at that time. He is a shining example in his fidelity to the claims of his conscience, an advocate of non-violence and peace, a voice of warning against ideologies, a deep believing person for whom God really was the core and centre of life. His prophetic witness to Christian truth is based on a clear, radical and far-sighted analysis of the barbarism of the inhuman and godless system of Nazism, its racial delusions, its ideology of war and deification of the state, as well as its declared programme of annihilating Christianity and the Church. His educated mature conscience led him to say a resolute 'No' to Nazism and he was executed due to his consistent refusal to take up arms as a soldier in Hitler's war.

The story is also a reminder of the fleeting nature of earth's glories for there are no memorials to Hitler or Eichmann in Linz or anywhere else ... but not far away, where Franziska Jägerstätter and her three daughters still live, tiny St Radegund has become a place of pilgrimage.

BLESSED RESTITUTA KAFKA

When it was clear to the world that Hitler, after his successful reoccupation of the Rhineland, had become infected with the dictatorial disease of galloping expectations, it saw him turn his attention to Austria. He had this predominantly Catholic country in mind for annexation to the 'Greater German Reich' and began his move against her in July 1934 when he incited Nazi comrades in Vienna to murder Engelbert Dollfuss, the Austrian Chancellor. At that stage, government forces, led by Dr Kurt von Schuschnigg speedily re-established order.

In 1938, his patience at an end, Hitler summoned Dr Schuschnigg, by now Austrian Chancellor, to his mountain retreat at Berchtesgaden. In a predominantly one-sided conversation he ranted that Austria had done everything to avoid a friendly policy with Germany then added ominously: 'The German Reich is one of the great powers and nobody will raise his voice if it settles its border problems.'

Schuschnigg, a Jesuit-trained intellectual, regarded Hitler's threats as an unwarrantable interference in Austrian sovereignty. However, he tried to remain conciliatory, pointing out that Austria's contribution to German history had been considerable. With his own warped version of events, Hitler snarled: 'Absolutely zero. I'm telling you, absolutely zero. Every national idea was sabotaged by Austria throughout history; and indeed all this sabotage was the chief activity of the Habsburgs and the Catholic Church.'

After the Anschluss (i.e the union of the two countries in a Greater Germany) had taken place the Austrians were to discover that life would increasingly become a matter of repression, arbitary arrest and the blood purge. And this was the context in which Blessed Restituta Kafka, though not a well-known martyr perhaps, provided a particularly poignant example of fidelity to the Cross of Christ.

Helene Kafka was born near Brno in 1894. Brno was then within the Austro-Hungarian Empire but is now in the Czech Republic. She was the sixth daughter of Catholic parents, her father being a shoemaker. In 1896, to improve the family's fortunes, the Kafkas moved to Vienna settling within a working-class district populated by thousands of other Czech immigrants. Until she was fifteen Helene attended local schools and then there is evidence that for four years she went into domestic service and also worked as a salesgirl. However, she cherished the idea of entering a nursing Order so as to help those who were sick and suffering.

Helene was nineteen when the Hartmann Sisters, a German Order, were asked to provide the nursing staff for a new hospital at Lainz, a district of Vienna. In order to obtain some first-hand appreciation of nursing work she joined the hospital staff as an unskilled general assistant. Her vocation became unmistakably clear to her and she asked her parents for permission to join the Order. To her surprise this was refused. One writer suggests that the Kafkas may have nursed anti-German sentiments.[63] As we shall see, Helene was very strong-minded and ran away to the motherhouse of the Hartmann Order. Consequently her parents gave their consent and her dowry was provided by bequest from the diocese. It is grimly ironic that she chose Restituta for her religious name after Restituta of Sora who was beheaded for her faith in the time of the Emperor Aurelian.

The novice nun soon found herself helping to cope with the flow of First World War casualties streaming into the hospital and felt drawn to work in the operating theatre. As her experience grew she became extremely skilled at this, becoming a theatre Sister and anaesthetist. She gave many years of dedicated service at the Modling hospital, south of Vienna. Her name was a byword for care and concern and she was much loved by both the patients and the members of her Order. A clue to her character is provided by the fact that she was often called Resoluta rather than Restituta. And the human side of her character gives us a clue perhaps to the affection she generated for, after a hard day's work this short, stout nun usually called for 'a goulash and a pint of my usual.'

When Hitler seized Austria, mindful of world opinion, he claimed that disruptive elements had reduced Austria to chaos and its government had requested Germany to send in troops to restore order. It was a monstrous lie. Sister Restituta made her abhorrence of him quite plain, calling him a madman and writing a poem which ridiculed him. Among the many repressive measures of the Nazi regime was the abolition of all religious observance in hospital wards. A down-to-earth woman, Restituta denounced the regime in two of her writings

---

63. P Burns, *Butler's Lives of the Saints*. London, 2003, p. 143

and continued to pray with dying patients. It so happened that the surgeon she assisted was a zealous Nazi. At that stage he did nothing, but continued to watch her. The powerful emblem of the Nazis was the hooked cross or swastika, which appeared in all propaganda, on uniforms and ceremonial banners. In time it was to be regarded throughout the world as the hated symbol of a monstrous tyranny.

The cross which Restituta Kafka kept in her heart, as Pope John Paul II was later to affirm, was the Cross of Christ. And so, when a new wing was built at the Modling hospital, she made sure that a crucifix hung in every room. This was too much for her surgeon who then informed the Gestapo. And so, as she emerged from the operating theatre on Ash Wednesday in 1942, it was to find them waiting for her. Her arrest bemused the Sisters in her Community. At first they believed that she would be released after three weeks or so. When this didn't happen they surmised it might be about three months before she returned. When she still did not reappear they organised a petition for her release . . . to no avail.

Unbelievably, on 29 October 1942, she was sentenced to death by the Nazi court (euphemistically titled the 'People's Court' or *Volksgerichtshof*) for 'aiding and abetting the enemy in the betrayal of the Fatherland and for plotting high treason.' So here we have it – the might of the 'Thousand Year Reich' in mortal peril from a small, plump, middle-aged nun whose principal 'weapons' were her healing hands and her love of Christ and his Cross. The sentence handed down by the Court left even the Nazis with stirrings of conscience for they promised her freedom if she left her religious congregation. She refused.

It is recorded[64] that she was imprisoned for over a year and during that time she lost half her own body weight because she gave most of her rations to others. She was thus able to save the life of a pregnant mother and her baby. The regime had a variety of methods to dispose of its 'enemies' – from the pistol shot to the gas chamber. The infamous Martin Bormann, head of Hitler's secretariat, decided that Restituta was to be guillotined as a dread example to others. Thus, 30 March 1943 provides us with the picture of a tiny nun, clad only in a paper shirt, and with her hands tied behind her, being led to her death. Shortly before she had asked the prison chaplain to make the Sign of

64. Ibid., p. 144.

the Cross on her forehead. Her words at the last were: 'I have lived for Christ. I want to die for Christ.' The chaplain heard the thud as the blade fell upon her and because her body was consigned to a mass grave it has never been recovered.

It is significant to note here how strong a threat the Cross posed for Hitler and his henchmen. He had perceived first the disillusion and then the resistance of many Christians towards his regime. So he envisaged the establishment of a 'National Reich Church'. A thirty point programme for it was drawn up by Alfred Rosenberg, a scornful pagan. Its essence is made clear by a few of its articles:

18 The National Church will clear away from its altars all crucifixes, Bibles and pictures of saints.
19 On the altar there must be nothing but *Mein Kampf* (to the German nation and therefore to God the most sacred book) and to the left of the altar a sword.
20 On the day of its foundation, the Christian Cross must be removed from all churches, cathedrals and chapels . . . and it must be superseded by the only unconquerable symbol, the swastika.

On 21 June 1998, in Vienna's Heroes Square, Sister Restituta was beatified by Pope John Paul II. The only relic of her that could be found to give him was a small piece of her habit. He told the crowd gathered there he wished to speak not of the heroes of this world, but of the Church. He said that Sister Restituta had risked her life for her witness to the Cross and went on: 'And she kept the Cross in her heart. Many things can be taken away from us Christians. But we will not let the Cross as a sign of salvation be taken from us . . . Thank you, Sister Restituta, for swimming against the tide of the time.'

With her beheading and the casting away of her body no doubt the Nazis hoped to expunge her memory too. But this did not happen for the district hospital in Modling, with its large maternity unit, now stands in 'Sister Restituta Street', renamed in her honour in 1995. Thus, every baby born there has a birth certificate with her name on it.

SAINT MAXIMILIAN KOLBE

On 8 January 1894 at Zdunska Wola, near Lodz in Poland, a second son was born to the family of a poor cloth weaver. The child was given the baptismal name of Raymond though in September 1910, when he was received as novice, he took the new name of Maximilian. Like many other in Lodz, Raymond's father, Julius, was a 'home worker', toiling up to sixteen hours a day and selling his output to the merchants from Lodz who arrived at his door. From this back-breaking work he was able to eke out an existence for the family. Raymond's mother, originally Maria Dabrowska, was, like his father, deeply religious with a great devotion to the Virgin Mary. Her first ambition had been to become a nun. Unfortunately, however, the times were against her because Poland was at that time partitioned by three occupying powers: Prussia, Russia and the Austro-Hungarian Empire. Little Zdunska Wola was controlled by the Russians who closed several of the Catholic convents. Raymond's parents decided to marry and became members of the Third Order of St Francis. Five children were born to them of whom three sons survived: Francis, the eldest, Joseph, the youngest, and Raymond.

To accommodate the growing family, the Kolbes moved from their poor, one-bedroomed dwelling in Zdunska Wola to, in turn, Lodz, Jurzkowice and Pabianice. Each abode was slightly better than the last and at Pabianice it was large enough to rent part of it to another weaver. Maria Kolbe opened a second-hand shop and also worked as a nurse and midwife while Julius improved their living standards a little through his labours on three vegetable plots. Like their parents, the boys were industrious and since he began to display a gift for numbers, Raymond helped out his mother in the shop. However, Francis was the lucky one who was intended for schooling. But – as in countless other cases down the centuries – the Church stepped in to save Joseph and Raymond from a lifetime of illiteracy. Their local priest, Father Waldimir Jakowski, taught them to read and write, to learn their Catechism, and to acquire a little Latin.

This last point had a happy outcome for Raymond. One day he was sent on an errand to the local pharmacist, Mr Kotowski. The boy handed him the prescription asking for the item by its Latin name. The pharmacist was astounded and began to question Raymond. As a result, the good man offered to tutor him without charge so that he could go to school the following year. He started at the local school and when he was thirteen, without doubt, he had further evidence that

God was on his side. Some Conventual Franciscans had come to the parish to give a mission. Both Francis and Raymond were interested in becoming Franciscans and, since the piety of their parents was well established by then, the boys were thought to be good candidates. This was undoubtedly a tremendous opportunity because the Franciscan school at Lwow provided room and board as well as tuition. The fact that the Kolbes were living in the part of Poland controlled by the Russians, whereas Lwow was in the sector under the aegis of the Catholic Hapsburgs, did not deter Julius in the least. He disguised his sons as farmers, smuggled them across the border and enrolled them at the school.

At this stage, Raymond was about to make his first confession and receive Holy Communion when something of great significance took place. Like most boys, he was given to pranks and after one of these his mother said exasperatedly: 'I don't know what's going to become of you.' It may have been a commonplace remark but it struck home and Raymond prayed intensely to the Virgin Mary, seeking to know what, in fact, would become of him. Subsequently, he told his mother that the Virgin had appeared to him holding two crowns, one white and the other red. She had smiled beatifically and asked him if he would accept either of them, explaining that the white one meant he would remain pure and the red one, that he would become a martyr. He told her he wanted them both. Doubters might dismiss this as youthful imaginings but it is interesting that from then on his mother was always sure he would become a martyr.

What he remembered of those years at home was the devotion of the people to the faith and their desire to see their beloved country free from foreign rule. Nearly every morning at five o'clock his parents attended Mass. In the Kolbe home there was a small altar dedicated to Our Lady of Czestochowa. When the family prayed before her picture they were often joined by friends and neighbours. It was a happy house but unfortunately the shop did not prosper. A lot of money was owed to them for goods sold on credit which was never paid, so they were forced to close. Though this was a grievous blow it did not destroy the harmony of the household. Sadly, however, the Kolbes did pay a heavy price for their patriotism. To support the call for liberty, Julius used to circulate an underground newspaper. On one occasion this led to his brief arrest, but worse was to follow. When the First World War commenced he joined a Polish legion. His unit ultimately became surrounded by Russian forces. Since Kolbe was leader of the unit he was executed.

Some years earlier, Francis and Raymond had joined the junior seminary of the Franciscans at Lwow. Studies were a joy to Raymond, particularly in mathematics and physics, and at that stage the parents, feeling they had made the best provision they could for their children, announced that they also were to enter the religious life. Of course they were not to know then what tragedy the War would bring. In 1910, Raymond Kolbe was received as a novice with the religious name of Maximilian. In 1912, he was sent to the Gregorian College in Rome to study philosophy. He completed the course in 1915. He was then admitted to the Collegio Serafico where, until 1919, he studied theology. By the end of this period he had completed doctorates in each subject and was ordained in Rome on 28 April, 1918.

This had been a highly creative, deeply satisfying period but now he began to discern the evil present in the world and to perceive how the disquiet of sin sought to disturb the serenity of even devout souls. He felt it necessary to take some action and so, with six companions, on 16 October 1917, he founded the Crusade of Mary Immaculate. Their aim was the conversion of sinners, heretics and schismatics, particularly freemasons, whom they regarded at that time as the chief enemy of Europe's Catholics, and to bring all men to love Mary Immaculate.

It was now that an otherwise euphoric existence was threatened by his state of health for he was found to have contracted tuberculosis and the disease had reached an advanced stage. It is said that the shadow of death only intensified his love for the Holy Mother and that, from this point on, he became determined to devote his entire life, long or short, to bringing souls under her protection. In 1919 he returned to a Poland liberated once more from her oppressors and was overjoyed to learn that the Holy See had acceded to the petition of Polish bishops that there be established the Feast of Our Lady Queen of Poland. Maximilian now felt it the mission of the Crusade to capture every Polish heart for her. Even though by now his tubercular condition had been pronounced incurable and he had one lung collapsed and the other damaged he saw this as no impediment to this mission. In fact, it stirred him to begin the work of the Crusade without delay. Soon its cells and circles were appearing throughout Poland. Now it was a question of how to carry the fight forward.

He concluded that much of the secular press was not only trivial and synthetic, for both readers and journalists it was also positively sinful. Couple this with the exaggerated respect of many for whatever they saw in print and it was obvious the press was a medium which could do lasting damage to the moral underpinning which should support every aspect of life. So the Crusade would fight the dark forces with its own weapons. In January 1922, a monthly review, the *Knight of the Immaculate*, appeared with a print run of just 5,000 copies – which was all that the available funds allowed. It became obvious almost immediately that extra working space would be required, hence the move to a friary in Grodno where it also became possible to acquire a small printing organisation. This enabled the venture to grow and by 1927, 70,000 copies of the journal were being printed. This meant that now the Grodno friary was no longer adequate. Also, it seemed important for the sizeable organisation which had developed to be located in the Warsaw area. Prince Jan Drucko-Lubecki owned some land at Teresin, to the west of the capital, and generously offered this to the Crusade. They immediately began to develop the site, watched over by the statue of Mary Immaculate they had erected there.

Beginning with no more than a few shacks, the Friary at Teresin was to flourish. The move from Grodno to Teresin was completed by 21 November 1927. By 8 December the Friary had been consecrated and named *Niepokalanow*, the City of the Immaculate. Maximilian declared that Niepokalanow had been chosen by Mary Immaculate and was dedicated solely to her veneration. Everything that was, or would be, located there would belong to her. Within the monastic spirit of St Francis, the Crusade members would work there, practice obedience and be poor. The scale of subsequent development is difficult to comprehend. Estimates showed that, in just a short time Niepokalanow had become one of the largest, if not the largest, friaries in the world. By 1939, it comprised 13 priests, 18 novices, 527 brothers, 122 junior seminarians and 82 candidates for the priesthood – 762 members in total. This number included doctors, dentists, farmers, mechanics, tailors, builders, printers, gardeners, shoemakers and cooks so that the *City of the Immaculate* was completely self-supporting.

The latest techniques of typesetting, photogravure and binding were being employed by now and more modern printing machines had been installed. Consequently the circulation of the *Knight of the Immaculate* had reached the staggering monthly figure of 750,000 copies. Other publications were also being printed – a daily Catholic newspaper, *The Little Daily*, had achieved a weekly circulation of 137,000 copies and a Sunday/Holy Day circulation of 225,000 copies. Moreover, it was decided that since secularism was by now using all manner of media of mass communication, the Crusade must do likewise. So on 8 December 1938, a radio station was established at the Friary. Its signature tune was the Lourdes hymn, played by the Friary's own orchestra. Gratifyingly, in the years immediately before the Second World War, parish priests were reporting that the Crusade's literature had been instrumental in the most marked increase in faith they had noted in their congregations. Maximilian and his colleagues were especially proud of the campaign against abortion they had conducted in 1938 through the columns of the *Knight of the Immaculate.*

As early as 1929, Crusade members had felt there was work for them to do in the mission fields. In February 1930, with the blessing of their Father General, Maximilian and four of the brothers left for Japan. They had absolutely no finance for their venture but were glad to leave the matter to Jesus and his Mother. As it happened, they were greeted enthusiastically by Bishop Hayasaka of Nagasaki who not only gave them formal permission to remain but also agreed that they could print their literature in exchange for Maximilian's work as professor of philosophy in the diocesan seminary. They had immense problems in acquiring suitable accommodation and equipment for their venture, but eventually located themselves on the steep slope of Mount Hikosan. Their Japanese home became *Mugenzai no Sono* (*The Garden of the Immaculate*) and the Japanese version of the *Knight* had become *Seibo no Kishi*, with an initial printing of 10,000 copies. By 1936 it had attained a circulation of 65,000. The other landmarks of this venture were the founding of a novitiate in 1931 and a junior seminary in 1936. At that point Maximilian was recalled to Poland and, although his health was now poor, he left Japan with great sadness.

When the Germans invaded in September 1939 they took over

Niepokalanow almost immediately. Most of the community were sent to Germany but by early December were released. Back in the priory they then began to take in about 3,000 Polish refugees. Two thirds of these were Jews. The friars recognised that now their mission was among Jews as well as Christians and accordingly shared everything with them – food, clothing and shelter. In the meantime, the Germans kept them under constant surveillance and in early 1941, as a result of Maximilian's writings in the only edition of the *Knight* they had allowed to be published, he was arrested and sent to the Pawiak prison in Warsaw. He had written that beyond occupation and the camps, the real conflict was between good and evil . . . that the victories on the battlefield were one thing but the real battle was the personal one between wickedness and love . . . it was important not to lose this. The occupiers were very angry and in the prison they made this quite plain. One guard beat him repeatedly. He had seen the rosary around Maximilian's habit and asked him if he believed in Christ. The answer was 'Yes' so the guard attacked him to make him change it but he would not.

On 28 May 1941 Maximilian Kolbe was transferred from Pawiak to Auschwitz. A crematorium was being constructed and along with others he was made to carry blocks of stone for it, as well as large, heavy tree trunks. The work continued through each day and the blows of the guards ensured the prisoners ran while they worked. The leader of these guards, Krott, formed an intense hatred for Father Kolbe and continually sought him out for special attention. Because he was sick, he could barely sustain this barbarism but he deterred his colleagues from helping him lest they came in for more punishment. He assured them that the Mother of God was with him and that all would be well.[65] One day Krott, who was an ex-criminal and was nicknamed 'Bloody', was almost berserk with anger. He loaded Maximilian with the most heavy planks and ordered him to run. Soon, his victim had collapsed. Krott kicked him in the stomach and ordered the guards to give him fifty lashes. Maximilian lost consciousness and thinking him dead, Krott threw him in the mud. Secretly, some of the other prisoners carried him back to the camp hospital.

Maximilian saw this as a great blessing for while he was there he

---

65. M Craig, *Maximilian Kolbe*. London, 1997, p. 15.

was able to hear confessions and speak of God's infinite love for all of them. He knew that the great hope in life of the prisoners was to return to their families and he felt his own mission was to help them do just that. He felt it his bounden duty to sustain the prisoners' faith and to share his food with them so that they might survive their ordeal. The comments of his fellow prisoners attest to his love for them. Here are some examples: 'He made us see that our souls were not dead, our dignity as Catholics and Poles not destroyed' (Mieczyslaus Koscielniak).[66] 'When he spoke to us of God, we had the impression that the speaker was someone not of this earth' (Alexander Dziuba).[67] 'Each time I saw Father Kolbe in the courtyard I felt within myself an extraordinary effusion of his goodness. Although he wore the same ragged clothes as the rest of us, with the same tin can hanging from his belt, one forgave this wretched exterior and was conscious only of the charm of his inspired countenance and of his radiant holiness' (Father Zygmunt Rusczak).[68] 'I can only say that the way he was is beyond words. I am a Jew by my heritage as the son of a Jewish mother, and I am of the Jewish faith and very proud of it. And not only did I love Maximilian Kolbe very, very much in Auschwitz, where he befriended me, but I will love him until the last moment of my life' (Sigmund Gerson).[69]

Prisoners entering Auschwitz knew that their stay there would not be a long one. They were told that if any among them were Jews they had no right to live beyond two weeks. For priests the time span was one month and for all others three months. The crematorium chimney was their only exit though they were free to leave at once by throwing themselves on the fences. On 31 July 1941, driven no doubt by the sadism, the intolerable, degrading conditions and the interminable atmosphere of dread fear, one of the inmates managed to escape alive. Like Father Kolbe, he was from Block 14. That night the guards withheld the food of the prisoners from the Block and interrogated them endlessly for what they might know of the escapee's plans and whereabouts. Throughout the whole of the next day, still without

66. R Royal, *The Catholic Martyrs of The Twentieth Century*. New York, 2000, pp. 209-10.
67. Ibid., p. 210
68. M Craig, op. cit. London, 1997, pp. 16-17.
69. R Royal, op. cit., p. 207.

food and water, they were made to stand to attention in the heat while the guards searched. By evening, Fritzsch, deputy commander of the camp, told them that, as a reprisal, ten would be chosen to die in the Starvation Bunker.

As if extending the horror of the selection was some part of the retribution, Fritzsch and his men did not hurry over it. One prisoner, having been selected, stepped out of the ranks as ordered. He began to cry and explained that he was leaving behind a wife and children. When he murmured 'good-bye' to his fellows, his anguish was heart-rending. Father Kolbe, feeling impelled to act, stepped out of his own line and told the nearest guard that he wished to speak to the officer. He was waved away but stood his ground and insisted on seeing the deputy commandant. When his SS colleagues pointed out to Fritzsch what was happening, he turned towards Maximilian: 'What do you want?'

In German, Maximilian explained that he wished to die in the place of one of those selected. 'Why?', he was asked. Since he knew it to be a Nazi principle that the sick and the weak be liquidated, Father Kolbe replied that he was an old man and good for nothing. His life was no longer of use to anyone. He was then asked which prisoner he wished to replace. He pointed towards the tearful man with the wife and children. Fritzsch scrutinised Maximilian and his squalid rags: 'Who are you?' 'A Catholic priest', he replied. It was not the rule of course for concentration camp staff to accede to any request from a prisoner and certainly not one of such a nature. Perhaps because he was one of *die schweinerischen Pfaffen* ('priest swine'), second only to the Jews in the order of Nazi hates, Maximilian's identity turned the scales. Fritzsch called over his assistant, Palisch, instructed him to delete the weeping prisoner's number from the death list and replace it with Father Kolbe's. They then motioned Maximilian to join the others destined for the Starvation Block. As they marched away, it amused one of the guards to tell them that soon they would look 'like dried up tulips'.

In the following two weeks a great deal happened in the block. Each day Maximilian organised prayers. He and the others destined to die sang hymns and recited the rosary. These victims became so absorbed in their devotions they scarcely knew when the guards opened the door and carried out the dead. Only when the guards yelled at them to stop was there any pause in their praying and singing. In that wretched place where Christ and the religion he had founded were hated so much, the hymns and prayers were more than the SS men could bear, the more so since the devotion of the condemned had been taken up by the souls in the neighbouring cells. The whole complex had become like a church.

It would have been understandable for these victims to have cursed their captors, letting themselves be degraded by the appalling experience. In the camp above them they had known poor creatures who had stolen from each other and even killed each other in order to survive, for existence often meant an extra bit of bread or bed space. Even in the bunker, which they had now come to see as a sanctified space, they had been forced to yield to the unspeakable forces seeking to destroy their serenity. Lack of water had driven them to drink their own and each other's urine. Now that had gone they were constantly enduring the physical and mental agonies which signalled the collapse of their physical systems.

From the moment he had arrived in the camp Maximilian had reminded his fellows of Jesus' wish for them to love one another. From those who thought him a 'holy fool' there were many wild curses. No doubt he thought that to be a fool for God was good. As for their tormentors, he had to remind the prisoners that Jesus had not said: 'Father, destroy them . . .' but 'Father, forgive them.' Each of their captors were uniquely important to God and so deserving of their love. Because words come easily enough he had to demonstrate what they meant. An earlier illustration of this was on one of the days when the prisoners were dealing with manure. Maximilian did not react when an SS man struck him several times in the face. He then set his dog on Father Kolbe who tried to bear its bites and torments with calm and endurance. When the attack was over, he climbed back into the ditch and continued to move the manure. Throughout the whole episode he had managed not to complain or to speak evil of the guard. Occurrences such as these made it easier for the others to listen when he advised them to place themselves under the protection of Mary Immaculate and to bear the miseries inflicted on them with patience, forbearance and prayers for their tormentors.

God had chosen a tubercular priest with a single lung to minister to those whom He loved, here in the bunker. And no doubt Maximilian saw with great gladness how God worked his wonders because every day, though under the shadow of a tortuous death, soul after soul became ready to witness to God's presence among them. At the end of two weeks, only Father Kolbe was left alive but the authorities were impatient since the cell was needed for more victims. So the shouts began, signalling the arrival of the guards. One of them had a needle. It went to its mark and prisoner number 16670 was called to his reward.

It had been reported that Maximilian once said at Auschwitz: 'If I have to die I would like it to be on the Feast of Our Lady.' He was given the fatal injection of phenol on 14 August 1941, the vigil of the Feast of the Immaculate Conception.[70]

On 17 October 1971, Father Maximilian was beatified by Pope Paul VI. On 10 October 1982 he was canonised in Rome by Pope John Paul II. Several former concentration camp prisoners were among the massive crowd at the Mass of Canonisation in St Peter's Square. Among these was former Sergeant Francis Gajowniczek, prisoner 5659, the man replaced by Saint Maximilian in the selection for the Starvation Bunker.

BLESSED KARL LEISNER

This is the story of a young man who went to prison, and eventual death, for no more than a casual remark. This same young man became a Catholic priest who said but one Mass, never preached a sermon and never heard a confession. His name was Karl Leisner and in the 1930s he and three of his friends, members of a Catholic youth group, set off from the Lower Rhine and cycled to Switzerland, revelling in the beauty of the river, the forests and the mountains. As Karl surveyed the splendour and vastness of nature he could not credit that anyone would doubt the existence of a living God who had created it all.

Born at Rees-am-Rhein in February 1915, of a fervent Catholic family, Karl moved with his parents and their four other children, to the city of Cleves when he was six. Cleves is notable for at least two reasons – first, because Anne of Cleves, who became Queen of

70. Ibid., p. 210.

England, hailed from the city. Secondly, during the Second World War its medieval buildings had to be completely destroyed and very many of its civilians killed as the only effective way of defeating Hitler's armies and saving thousands of Allied lives.

Making his first Holy Communion at ten and being confirmed when he was twelve, Karl was soon to display the leadership qualities that led to him being made Deanery Youth Leader in Cleves. This brought him into early contact with the Nazi movement which had begun to recruit the young of both sexes into its own youth organisations. It is recorded that in order to shield his own members from Hitler's ideologues, Karl took them to Dutch and Belgian locations for the summer camps of 1934 and 1935.[71]

When he was nineteen and having passed his Abitur examinations (equivalent to our GCE 'A' levels) he came to the decision that his future lay in the priesthood. Cleves is in the diocese of Münster and its bishop at the time was the formidable Clemens August von Galen. No one was more alert to Nazi perils than Bishop von Galen who not only admitted Karl as a Church student at the Collegium Borromeum in Münster but also appointed him Diocesan Youth Leader. The Bishop could see that the Nazi plans for the destruction of Catholic youth groups were making the post too dangerous for a layman whereas the seminary afforded the Leader some protection at least. Obviously, Karl was very gratified to be given this responsibility but in addition to the strain of much travel in the role, there was the pressure of maintaining the morale of group members in the face of Nazi persecution.

He studied philosophy for two years at the 'Borromeum' then went to the University of Freiburg for his two 'free semesters' where he read Dogmatic and Moral Theology as well as the Old and New Testaments. During the 'free semesters', which are meant to widen the student's educational experience through contacts with a new university, new students, new professors and new subject areas, students lodge outside the university, typically with local families. Karl was placed with a devout Catholic couple and their twelve children. He looked forward to his year of living in a home again but was soon confiding to his diary of his deepening feelings for one of the daughters of the house. So he struggled with a dilemma: was he meant for marriage or the

71. Archbishop M L N Couve de Murville, *Karl Leisner*. London, 1997, p. 38.

priesthood? When in March 1937 he left Freiburg he had decided his vocation was in the priesthood. No doubt it was fortunate the girl was a Catholic for when he wrote to tell her this she replied that she understood.

Before he could resume his studies he was called up for six months compulsory work service and was posted to Saxony for labour on the land. He had to endure from the Nazis a barrage of defamation of the Catholic Church but this did not deter him rallying his fellow Catholics to their faith and organising their Mass attendance in an area where, unlike the diocese of Münster, Catholic churches were few. This brought him to the notice of the Gestapo who labelled him as one to be watched. In late October 1937 they raided his home in Cleves, taking away all his personal papers including his diaries which, of course, contained details of his feelings for the girl in Freiburg. Though this caused him much anguish, his biographer, M N L Couve de Murville, has pointed out that their action proved fortuitous for after the War and despite the destruction of Cleves, the diaries were found intact in the Gestapo vaults of the City.

Although now a 'marked man', Karl was able to resume his studies and on 25 March 1939 he was ordained deacon and looked forward to his priestly ordination. However, his health became problematic. In Saxony he had had an attack of pleurisy. Now, in the seminary, other students noted that in spite of his happy disposition, he had a persistent cough and seemed perpetually lethargic. His mother's anxiety led him to a medical examination where it was revealed he had tuberculosis (TB) in both lungs. At that time, and without the drugs to combat the disease which were developed later, such a diagnosis was extremely serious. Long hospitalisation, a nutritional diet, fresh air and rest in special sanatoria typically constituted the regime to combat TB. Karl was sent to Sankt Blasien in the Black Forest and a sanatorium there under the care of nuns. Since he was basically fit he seemed to be making great progress.

Here we must divert a little for on the evening of 8 November 1939, Hitler made his annual speech to the Party's 'Old Guard' in the Bürgerbräukeller in Munich. The speech was shorter than usual and immediately after it, he left the building. Twelve minutes later a bomb exploded killing seven people and wounding 63 others. It had been planted in a pillar directly behind the speaker's platform and was obviously intended for Hitler. On 21 November, Himmler announced that the British Intelligence Service was implicated and the actual perpetrator was Georg Elser, a German communist carpenter. Since then there has been argument as to whether the whole action had been orchestrated by the Nazis themselves to increase the Führer's popularity and to sharpen the German people's appetite for the war he had just started.[72] This need not detain us here, for what is important in this profile is the significance the incident had for the future of Karl Leisner.

When the news reached the sanatorium at Sankt Blasien a young patient came to Karl's room with the news. Referring to Hitler, Karl said: 'Pity he wasn't there!' The messenger was somewhat mentally retarded and he raced around the sanatorium, this time with news of Karl Leisner's response. It has been estimated that membership of the Gestapo itself, at its largest, was no more than 45,000 but that it was supported by at least 100,000 informers. There must have been at least one of these in the sanatorium for within the hour Karl was being questioned. Had his comment been referring to the assassination attempt on the Führer? It was not in his nature to lie or dissemble and he stated this was so. Karl's name had been on the Gestapo's books since his early days as a Catholic youth leader. Now they could move, and they did so quickly, for that same afternoon their transport came to take him to Freiburg prison. As he was taken away, the youth who had spread the word of Karl's comments was distraught but was assured that he was forgiven.

Long months of imprisonment in a cold cell at Freiburg depressed Karl but he was heartened by his mother's visits and her complete trust in God's will. Inspired by her example, he thanked God for his serious illness and his imprisonment and asked forgiveness for his enemies as well as himself. With complete disregard of any of his legal rights, for he was never charged with any breach of the law, he was sent to Sachsenhausen concentration camp on 16 March 1940 and was then transferred to Dachau on 14 December. He was to remain there for the rest of the War and, as part of the process of degradation,

---

72. W Shirer, *The Rise and Fall of the Third Reich*. London, 1995, Vol. 3, pp. 35-36.

be known as Prisoner No. 22,356. Dachau was not an extermination camp like Auschwitz, where death came quickly, but a 'work camp' where death also came but at a slower, agonising rate – brought on by overwork, overcrowding and starvation.

Statistics on the general overcrowding in Dachau were given in the profile of Blessed Titus Brandsma. For specific data on ministers of religion we are indebted to M N L Couve de Murville,[73] who notes that, in all, 2,700 of them were imprisoned in Dachau of whom 1,072 died. He estimates that at any one time there would be about 200 German priests, 1,400 Poles, 60 Lutheran ministers and 150 priests of other countries, mostly Belgium and France. He adds: '. . . it is an indication of the spiritual resistance to Nazism in Europe.' When I visited the camp recently I was most moved to see evidence of the efforts made to maintain the Faith in that abominable location. From little scraps of metal and strips of cloth, the prisoners fashioned chalices, patens and rudimentary vestments. It stirred one's pride but heightened one's sadness that since the War we Europeans have all but squandered the spiritual legacy left to us by such heroic virtue.

When Karl Leisner arrived at the camp he discovered that Blocks 26, 28 and 30 had been designated for priests. Himmler had ordered that Block 26 should house a chapel for the regular celebration of Mass but, in keeping with Nazi imponderability, its use was restricted to German priests only. The distribution of Holy Communion to others became a clandestine affair courting brutality and death. Karl did all that he could to maintain a happy Christian outlook and his qualities of leadership were not subdued even in that hell-hole for he gave physical sustenance to some by handing them his meagre bread ration and spiritual sustenance to others, including priests, with his constant dictum that: 'We bear all this for the sake of our young people.' When he arrived at Dachau he had somehow managed to bring his guitar among his possessions. He persuaded one of the guards to release it and he organised evening sing-songs for his fellow-inmates.

So this deacon with the power to fortify priests had become a beacon of resistance and hope from his first days. This development had been noted by the guards and one night they visited Block 26 and beat him unmercifully. He lay unconscious on the floor of the

---

73. M L N Couve de Murville, op. cit., p. 50.

Block for many hours and shortly afterwards he had a haemoptysis, which is a continuous spitting of blood. There was nothing for it but admittance to the dreaded Infirmary Block, where as we noted in his profile, Blessed Titus Brandsma was to die by lethal injection on Sunday, 26 July 1942. In contrast to the conditions in the sanatorium in the Black Forest where his chance for life had been returned to him, he was now confined to a room with up to 150 other TB patients. When a prisoner was seriously ill it was the camp commandant and not a doctor who decided on his admittance to the Infirmary. Typical illnesses were frost-bite, abscesses, tuberculosis, starvation oedema, and circulatory diseases. Epidemics in the camp were of dysentery, scabies and typhus (which resulted, for example, in 967 deaths between January and March 1943). No prophylactic medication was given for these conditions. The official causes of death were usually notified as 'general debility', 'heart failure', 'circulatory collapse' and 'pneumonia'. The medical experiments performed by SS doctors usually had fatal results and to add to the terror of the place there was a regular selection of prisoners for the 'invalid transports', the euphemism for the dispatch of incurable patients to the gas chamber at Schloss Hartheim near Linz.

At times it was all too much, even for such a buoyant and pious personality as Karl Leisner. He had made a friend of Father Otto Pies SJ, who used to visit him as often as possible. Sometimes he would find Karl weeping with despair and asking why he had to suffer so. Why did his prayers go unanswered? Here we must remember that, in addition to the horrors of the Block, and despite the strong constitution of Karl, the TB was ravaging his body. During 1942 and 1943 the disease virtually destroyed his lungs and, twice, loving and willing hands took him back to the priests' block lest he be pronounced incurable and sent to the gas chamber. During 1944 the disease penetrated his gut and intestines, sapping more and more of his strength. Then, as the Allies progressed across France, following the June invasion, it soon became necessary to transfer to Dachau prisoners from a concentration camp in Alsace. Among these was Catholic Bishop Piguet of Clermont-Ferrand.

Earlier we noted that Karl had been ordained deacon on 25 March 1939 and looked forward to becoming a priest. That ordination had been due to take place at the end of that same year so his illness and subsequent imprisonment must have only intensified his anguish and sense of loss. When Bishop Piguet arrived in Dachau (he had originally been imprisoned for issuing false papers to assist some people to evade detention by the Germans) it was suggested that in secret he might ordain Karl to the priesthood. He was willing to do this but first the authority of Karl's bishop must be obtained and all the liturgical rubrics for a priestly ordination would have to be observed. The next part of the story is especially stirring and the market gardens near the camp where the priest-prisoners worked served as an important conduit.

One of the garden's regular customers was a postulant called Mädi who purchased supplies for a convent nearby. A priest in the packing department of the shop outlined the problem to her and asked whether she would act as an intermediary. At great risk to herself and supported by her Superior, Mädi succeeded in dispatching letters to Bishop von Galen of Münster and Cardinal Faulhaber, Archbishop of Munich. Chrism for the anointing and the Pontifical book containing the Latin text of the rite were smuggled into Dachau. Prisoners in the workshops clandestinely produced the Episcopal vestments, the mitre, a wooden crosier and a ring. I like to think that these items were among those I saw when I visited the camp. Not knowing the story of Karl Leisner at the time, to my chagrin I never enquired.

The ordination took place on 17 December 1944 in what has been described as 'an intensely moving and unique ceremony.'[74] It was made all the more poignant since Karl was now so weak he had to be taken back to the infirmary immediately after the ceremony. A fellow prisoner painted his ordination card: it showed two hands in chains, elevating a chalice and bore the words *Sacerdotum oportet offerre* ('a priest must offer up'). It was 26 December before Karl was able to say his first Mass. This beautiful Mass (the 'Primiz') is usually an occasion of great civic rejoicing with scores of people seeking an individual blessing from the new priest. It might be thought that there could be no party in Dachau but this was not so. Lutheran ministers had prepared one, complete with begged and borrowed pottery, coffee, cake and floral decorations. And all of this unknown to the guards, by

74. Ibid., p. 54.

now no doubt preoccupied with the advance of the Russians from one direction and of the Allies from the other. In that abominable, desolate place, Karl Leisner, priest, had triumphed – by God's grace and the courage of others, some known, many unknown, he had been ordained.

Tragically, his first Mass was to be his only Mass: he was so weak it was clear he was in the terminal stages of his illness. When the camp was liberated by the Allies he had been a prisoner of the Nazis for just ten days short of five and a half years. On 4 May 1945 he was taken into the care of the Sisters at the Planegg sanatorium near Munich. He was overwhelmed by their care and concern and overjoyed, in his own words, to be 'Restored to human dignity.'[75] However all that could now be done for him was to help him to meet death as comfortably as possible. His dear friend, Father Otto Pies SJ, gave him the last Sacraments on 30 May but until his death on 12 August he was able to give visitors his blessing, which made him deeply happy. His joy was immense when his parents, having somehow managed to traverse a chaotic landscape, reached his bedside on 29 June. His mother was able to be with him until he passed away.

When Pope John Paul II came to Berlin in 1996, he beatified Karl Leisner and Bernhard Lichtenberg. The diocesan process for Karl's canonisation was completed at Münster in 1982 and his cause is now at the Vatican. It is true that here was a priest who never administered a parish, never gave a sermon or heard a confession, and celebrated only a solitary Mass. But a priest is no mere functionary and it could be argued that by his example to others and his pastoral care he had exercised some of the most sublime elements of the priestly office.

In the weeks before his death he was able to write once more, which he loved. On 16 June, he wrote: 'Poor Europe, return to your Lord, Jesus Christ! . . . let me contribute to this, in however small a way.'[76] Since then, in the grip of secular liberalism and moral relativity, Europe has distanced itself from God. We can only pray that through the advocacy of Karl Leisner and the example of his life and death, it may one day come home again.

---

75. Ibid., p. 56.
76. Ibid., p. 57.

BLESSED BERNHARD LICHTENBERG

In his latest work *The Righteous – The unsung heroes of the Holocaust*, Sir Martin Gilbert tells of the efforts of several hundred Jews to obtain public recognition of those who had saved their lives by hiding them. He mentions these as including 'Roman Catholics – among them Franciscans, Benedictines and Jesuits.' There is no better example of the Church's compassion and concern for its Jewish brethren than the story of Blessed Bernhard Lichtenberg, an unsung hero even perhaps among his fellow Catholics. Let us now look at that story.

Bernhard was born on 3 December 1875, to Catholic parents at Ohlau, which is about 30 kilometres from Breslau. In some documents his father is described as 'a merchant on a minor scale', in others as 'the keeper of a food shop'. We may safely conclude then that the family was involved in the grocery trade. Bernhard was the second oldest of its five children.

At that time Ohlau was in the Prussian province of Lower Silesia and Catholics were less than one third of its population of 16,000. Significantly there was a tiny minority of Jews (less than 1%). So it may not be implausible to suggest that Bernhard grew up with a clear idea of the pressures of life within a minority group. Here we must remember that from 1871 to 1880 Chancellor von Bismarck carried out a series of repressive measures against Catholics. Labelled *Kulturkampf* ('Struggle over culture') it meant that Catholics in Protestant Prussia were regarded as an alien grouping which owed its loyalty to a 'foreign potentate' (the Pope in the Vatican). The suspicion and mistrust thus engendered may well have given the young Lichtenberg insight into the plight of the Jews for whom, from time immemorial in most parts of Europe, alienation had become their daily burden.

After local schooling, Bernhard obtained his Abiturium (as noted, roughly equivalent to GCE 'A' levels) and decided that the priesthood was his vocation. He studied theology at Breslau and Innsbruck and, with Cardinal Kopp, Bishop of Breslau, presiding, he was ordained priest on 21 June 1899 – along with 88 other deacons (an example, perhaps, of how repression has always stimulated the faith).

Subsequently, his duties were always based at or near the city of Berlin. His priesthood began with more than 10 years service as Minister of the Heart of Jesus Community in Charlottenburg. In 1932 he was then designated Cathedral Rector (*Dompfarrer*) at the Church of St Hedwig. By this time, he was also very much involved in politics. This may seem strange but we have to remember that at that time German Catholics had their own political party – the Centre Party. Catholics had been driven on to the defensive by the atmosphere of suspicion and mistrust generated by the *Kulturkampf* and the growing power of Protestant Prussia. There was also mounting liberal hostility to their faith. So Catholic members of the Prussian Lower House formed their own national party, the Centre.

This party was unique for it drew support from all social strata: the aristocracy, middle class and working class. By 1871 it was the second largest party in the Reichstag with fifty-eight seats and it was pledged to defend the Church, support confessional schools and oppose civil marriage. Prior to the Unification of Germany, a host of small states and princedoms had operated independently in the old Confederation. The Catholic Centre Party resisted extensions of imperial power, favouring decentralisation and greater autonomy for these states.

Until 1920 Bernhard Lichtenberg served as a Centre party representative in the District Assembly of Charlottenburg. Then for ten years he was a member of the regional parliament of Wedding. He had served as a military chaplain in World War I and its horrors no doubt seared into his make-up the importance of peace between races and nations. So it is no surprise that at this time he became a member of the Peace Association of German Catholics. In 1929 he was also elected to the directing board of the Inter-Denominational Working Group for Peace.

His work for peace included vigorous protests against the revival of militarism, the glorification of war and the issue of war threats linked to demands for the recovery of former German territories. This brought him into direct conflict with the rising Nazi Party. In 1931, its hatred for him intensified following the release of the film *All Quiet on the Western Front*. This was the famous anti-war film based on Erich Maria Remarque's novel of the same name (which I saw as a small boy and still remember vividly). The film aroused furious opposition from the Nazis and other ultra-nationalists who considered its pacifist message unpatriotic. Passionately, Monsignor Lichtenberg called upon

Catholics to see it. For this he was viciously attacked in *Der Angriff*, a newspaper controlled by Dr Joseph Goebbels, who was to become Minister for Propaganda when Hitler came to power. From that point on, Bernhard Lichtenberg was under surveillance.

Immediately Hitler became Chancellor in 1933, the Jews of Germany were viciously persecuted and, as we know, this was subsequently extended to all parts of occupied Europe. Taking their cue from the hysterical rantings of *Mein Kampf*, Goebbels and the notorious 'Jew baiter', Julius Streicher, began to orchestrate physical violence against the Jews, who were attacked on the streets and whose property was smashed. They were banished from the civil service and the professions by an enactment of 1934 and a year later the Nuremberg Race Laws initiated a systematic programme of ruination and death. In 1936 Germany hosted the Olympic Games and there was a lull in the persecution which was resumed when the foreign visitors had departed.

Only two months after the Nazi takeover Bernhard arranged for the Jewish banker, Oskar Wassermann, to meet Cardinal Bertram, Catholic Archbishop of Breslau, to request his intervention in the boycott of Jewish businesses planned for the following day. This produced no results but it was the beginning of Monsignor Lichtenberg's sustained struggle to protect Jewish people, their property and their livelihoods. He signalled clearly his belief that as a Catholic priest he felt bound to intervene when his Jewish brethren were being robbed of every vestige of their civil and human rights.

No doubt his experience of the pulling and hauling of politics had tempered him for the fight, because from this point on Bernhard was a tirelessly outspoken critic of the Nazis and their anti-Semitism. He filed formal complaints against the regime's policies, organised protests outside concentration camps and led public prayers for the ending of the torment. Interestingly, the documents of the Potsdam State Police for February 1936 indicate he held a religious meeting with two rabbis, two ministers of the Protestant Confessing Church and a number of Jewish laymen. The meeting concluded that 'the German people will have much to atone for with regard to the Jews.'

In 1937, Lichtenberg was elected Cathedral Provost (*Domprobst*) at St Hedwig's and in August 1938 took charge of the Relief Office of the Berlin area. In this role he assisted many Catholics of Jewish origin to emigrate from the Third Reich.

On the night of 9-10 November 1938, using the assassination of a German diplomat in Paris as an excuse, the Nazis carried out violent anti-Semitic attacks. The pogrom became known as Kristallnacht (night of broken glass). One hundred Jews were killed, Jewish homes were smashed, shops and businesses were looted and synagogues were burned and desecrated. No fewer than 30,000 Jews were arrested and imprisoned. Subsequently, the greater number of them were sent to concentration camps. Reviewing the night's results, Hermann Göring, Hitler's second-in-command, cruelly observed: 'We should have killed more Jews and broken less glass.'

Publicly and fearlessly Monsignor Lichtenberg denounced this fearsome brutality. These were some of his words: 'We know what happened yesterday, we do not know what lies in store for us tomorrow. But we have experienced what has happened today. Outside burns the temple. This is also a place of worship.' From this point on he prayed day after day from the pulpit of St Hedwig's – for Jews, for Jewish Christians, for those consigned to concentration camps and for other victims of the regime. When war broke out he even contacted the Berliner Luftschutzleiter (official responsible for air raid shelters) to protest against the racial segregation in shelters resulting from a decree of 14 December 1939.

On 23 October 1941, he was arrested, because two women students had heard him pray publicly for Jews and concentration camp inmates and had denounced him to the authorities. That same day the Gestapo searched his home. They found a pulpit message he had prepared for the following Sunday. It was a response to a leaflet devised by Goebbel's Propaganda Ministry. This warned against offering help to Jews even by so much as a friendly greeting. Lichtenberg's proposed homily contained the following comment: 'An anonymous slander sheet against the Jews is being distributed to Berlin houses. This leaflet states that every German who supports Jews . . . be it only through friendly kindness, commits treason against his people. Let us not be misled by this un-Christian way of thinking: but follow the strict command of Jesus: "You shall love your neighbour as you love yourself."' Under interrogation he refused to retract his statement. The

Gestapo had found an annotated copy of *Mein Kampf* in his possession. They pursued him on this and he stated the *Weltanschauung* set out in Hitler's book was in complete contradiction of Christianity. As a Catholic priest he was bound to oppose it. He was also prepared to accept all the consequences of his opposition (in effect, *Weltanschauung* means a 'world view'. With quasi-religious fervour Hitler was bent on instilling it into the German people).

Once again, Bernhard made it plain that he rejected the deportation of the Jews and its effects from the core of his being. It refuted 'love of neighbour', a fundamental tenet of Christianity. In a Jew he saw his neighbour, possessed of an immortal soul and made in the likeness of God. He realised, of course, that he had no power to defeat Nazi policies and had therefore decided to accompany both Jews and Christian-converted Jews into exile so he might minister to them spiritually. He asked the Gestapo to give him this opportunity.

In May 1942 he was arraigned before the Berlin District Court and sentenced to two years imprisonment for 'abuse of the pulpit' and 'insidious activity'. Asked for his response to the charges he said: 'I submit that no harm results to the State by citizens praying for Jews.' He was committed to Berlin's Tegel prison and towards the end of his sentence, during a visit by Count Konrad von Preysing, Catholic Bishop of the city, an offer from the Gestapo was relayed to him: provided he promised to refrain from preaching for the duration of the War he would be allowed his freedom. He would not, however, give any such undertaking and requested the Bishop's support in his wish to accompany the Jews into exile. The Bishop tried earnestly to dissuade him for he had been worried about Bernhard's health since well before his arrest when heart myasthenia, coronary sclerosis and angina pectoris had been diagnosed. At that stage he had been warned to guard strenuously against excitement and over-exertion.

After his release he continued his vehement protests against the treatment of the Jews and ultimately the State Security Service found him too much to cope with, so his internment at Dachau concentration camp was ordered. While en-route to Dachau on 5 November 1943, he collapsed and died.

In Berlin's Olympic Stadium on 2 July 1994 Pope John Paul II declared Monsignor Lichtenberg as 'Venerable'. On 23 June 1996 in the same stadium Pope John Paul declared his Beatification. There is an important supplement here in that a non-Jew who had saved Jewish lives during the Holocaust (as did another, Oskar Schindler) would be eligible for formal recognition as 'Righteous Among the Nations'. This is accorded by Yad Vashem, the Holocaust Martyrs' and Heroes' Remembrance Authority in Jerusalem, as laid down in the law of the State of Israel. It is only awarded after the rigorous examination of each case for recognition. On 7 July 2004 Yad Vashem declared Blessed Bernhard Lichtenberg as 'Righteous Among the Nations'. It is also worth adding that the reverence of Berliners for Bernhard was such that they made efforts to recover his body and brought it back to the city.

This point provides a small personal addition to the story. About three years ago I attended a Saturday Vigil Mass at St Hedwig's Cathedral (and was overawed by the ardour of the congregational singing). I recounted this to John Davies, editor of the Parish Magazine at St Austin's, Liverpool. He told me that if I had descended to the crypt of St Hedwig's I would have found, within an appropriate memorial, the remains of Bernhard Lichtenberg. How I wish I had known.

BLESSED RUPERT MAYER SJ

Rupert Mayer was born in Stuttgart on Sunday, 23 January 1876. His father, Rupert 'the First', was a skilled and successful merchant who hailed from the Black Forest. His mother Emilie (née Wehrle) was born in Pforzheim where her parents owned a glassware and jewellery factory. It was, in fact, business interests which brought the Mayer and Wehrle families together and led to the subsequent marriage of the couple, both of whom were devout Catholics in a Protestant city. They brought up six children (2 boys, 4 girls) in a just, friendly and loving household with a deep loyalty to its faith. It is interesting to perceive a connecting thread in the lives of the individuals described in this chapter which is that so many came from happy, caring and pious families. This was certainly so in Father Mayer's case: one of his biographers, Anton Koerbling SJ records that 'Father Rupert Mayer thanked God his whole life long, in public lectures and from the pulpit too, that He had given him such a good start in life in his excellent family.'[77]

77. A Koerbling SJ, *Father Rupert Mayer*. Cork, 1950, p. 7.

One also finds instances in lives such as Rupert's where the individuals concerned gave very early signs of their inclination towards the religious life. For instance, although Rupert was a no more than average scholar, who had to work hard to succeed at his studies, religion was his favourite subject and his teachers could always rely on 'Mayer' to supply an answer when the question was beyond the rest of the class. His sister Hermanna has described his profound reverence in prayer and related how sometimes a fit of laughter would overcome the children but if it happened during prayers, then despite his tender years, Rupert would put out the candles and say: 'When you can control yourself again, we'll go on with our prayers.' Amusingly, we are told[78] that religious ritual also played its part in his childish fancies as when he would 'hear confessions' through the little windows in the wicker work of an old beach chair.

We must take account of another trait which could be clearly discerned, even in his childhood – his indomitability. Though he matured into a tall, strong man, he was a small and delicate child. He literally willed himself to become agile and enduring in athletics, swimming, bar-climbing and ball games, leaving taller, stronger competitors in his wake. He also became proficient in horse-riding, which he loved, and fencing with both foil and sabre. His father, Rupert 'the First', had grown up in Tübingen in entirely Protestant surroundings. This nurtured in him a deep piety, strong faith and deep respect for the Catholic priesthood. He was by all accounts a loving son of Holy Mother Church. His own son Rupert had a parallel experience in Protestant Stuttgart where he had to endure anti-Catholic jibes from his schoolmates and his history teacher. This man was given to spouting the most slanderous tales about the Church and its religious orders. In preparing his rebuttals, Rupert consulted both his father and his teacher of religion then returned to the classroom and attacked the history man fearlessly. He himself linked the experience of these early years to the love he developed for apologetics and Catholic doctrine, the fundamentals of his success as a preacher.

It is important to touch upon these aspects of his beginnings because they were to serve him and the Church so well in his encounters with

---

78. Ibid., p. 14.

the Nazis, in which he has been described as 'stunningly heroic.'[79] In their quasi-religious propagandising they had depicted themselves as courageous and bold, these being typical Nazi virtues whereas Christianity with its sense of sin, of asceticism and humility, was weak and ineffectual. They were to discover in Father Rupert Mayer a man with a clear mind on right and wrong and an uncommon courage in saying so. He ranks alongside Cardinal von Galen therefore in his resolution to confront Nazism head-to-head and this explains why the regime took the steps it did to silence him.

To finish his high school education he was sent to Ravensburg. There he met a number of former students of the 'Stella Matutina' Jesuit school of Feldkirch, Austria and became friendly with them. When he returned home on vacation he announced that he was going to be a Jesuit. So his father probed for his reasons. He explained that though the Order was persecuted everywhere it gave its students the best possible training. Since he wished to go 'well-armed into the fray'[80] the Order seemed to him the logical choice. His father counselled caution. A year after his ordination, Rupert could make his choice with his blessing. By then Rupert would be able to take full responsibility for the path he had chosen. The son agreed to be bound by his father's wish and later expressed his gratitude for it.

In addition to his moral courage he was the personification of generosity, a virtue he displayed from his earliest childhood. It distinguished him in his youth and became the hallmark of his priesthood. For example, he was an enthusiastic altar-server and especially liked to serve Mass for those priests who gave no payment for the service. One day his father asked him what he did with the money he did receive. He explained that he gave it to the other boys so that they would let him serve more often. He noticed that the railway-porters in Stuttgart had a difficult time in delivering heavy loads by handcart, particularly when they had to negotiate the steep hills of the city. He used, therefore, to run behind the carts and push them up the hills, dodging out of sight whenever a porter looked around in pleasant surprise. He was ordained at the same time as a good friend

---

79. R Royal, *The Catholic Martyrs of the Twentieth Century*. New York, 2000, p. 151.
80. A Koerbling SJ, op. cit., p. 21.

from his schooldays. Rupert knew that his friend's family were not as prosperous as his own and worried in case the arrangements being made for his own first Mass might overshadow those of his friend. He chose therefore to have his own Mass on the first week-day after ordination so as to let his friend have his Mass on the Sunday.

In his youth, with two of his sisters, he visited the family of a manufacturer in the Bohemian border district. At parties, with the daughters of that family and with other visitors, Rupert played his part in the fun and games. One of the girls said subsequently: 'He always joined in all our fun, and yet in his presence, we felt the awe of something holy which still fills me with joy.'[81]

After his ordination Father Mayer was assigned to Spaichingen in Württemberg. On 10 June, 1899, he took up his duties as curate at the new church of St Joseph in the suburb of Hofen. Of this time, Father Anton Koerbling wrote: 'They were dear, good people who bared their hearts in trust to their new pastor and were never disappointed in his love and care. Nor did they ever forget this curate, although he only lived and laboured among them for a single year.'[82] The poor and the sick of Spaichingen found a special place in Rupert's heart and although his apostolic zeal inspired them they also remembered how he worked in the local bakery for a few hours each day when the baker was on a pilgrimage to Rome and how he helped the sacristan with his haying, leading the animals in front of the hay cart. In 1926 when he returned to Spaichingen for a fiftieth birthday celebration of certain parishioners much love and honour was bestowed on the young priest who had left them 27 years before.

When he had completed his training as a Jesuit, he was sent to Munich in 1912 to serve as a 'freelance' parish priest, more specifically to minister to new arrivals in the city. There was a great movement at that time from the country to the cities and the population of Munich was increasing by more than 20,000 per year. Munich was already feeling the tremors of revolutionary change, which were to gather such momentum from 1918 onwards. Within the turbulence, neo-paganism and venomous hostility to Christ and his Church were taking root. Rupert's first job was to organise a programme of visits to the

81. Ibid., p. 22.
82. Ibid., p. 30.

new arrivals so as to bring them into parish life. With his background of prosperity and culture he had no difficulty with Munich's rich and eminent but he also felt especially at home among the cab drivers, the truckers, porters and streetcar conductors, the market stall holders and the housewives who bought from them. Another biographer, Paul Reisterer SJ,[83] describing Father Mayer's work among the arrivals tells of how, armed with a torch, he climbed the steps leading to dark and dingy slum dwellings to welcome the newcomers, often receiving a stream of insults for a reward. Then he would visit the workers' clubs to join discussions, often about their daily jobs and to give lectures on burning issues of a religious and ecclesiastical nature.

As his popularity and appeal increased so did the pressures upon him. For example, prompted by his parishioners, the parish priest of the Holy Cross in the suburb of Geising asked him to conduct a one-week mission. He gave three sermons daily to packed congregations, for by now many wanted to see 'the Jesuit'. At 5 o'clock each morning he began hearing confessions before making a schedule of housecalls on those wavering in their faith. His evening confessions went on to midnight and beyond. He established a monthly Communion for the young girls of Geising. Despite early scepticism it proved successful with 46 girls attending at the start and the numbers increasing from then on. It spread to other parishes and Father Mayer always gave the sermon at each one of the Communions.

In company with two other priests he founded a new society which was to be called 'Sisters of the Holy Family.' Its founding principles were that the sisters were to train young working women for a Catholic family life; they were to foster the spirit of Catholic living among women; and they were to provide a family life for those separated from their families because of their employment.

Father Mayer looked upon this Community with both pride and joy as he observed them bringing cleanliness and good order to the slum dwellings, tending to the sick children and sorting out the family feuds and quarrels. He saw how many women were rescued from the depths of despair and set up for a better life. The Sisters, with deep respect, found ways and means of sending small gifts to their founder even when he was imprisoned by the Nazis. This prompted him to say to them:

---

83. P Reisterer SJ, *Rupert Mayer*. London, 1997, p. 63.

'Should I ever be free again and should I live to be as old as Methuselah, I should never be able to repay all the loving kindness you have shown me during these hard times.'[84] In the meantime, Rupert's generosity to anyone in need continued without pause. A story from the period will illustrate this. His mother came to Munich and was distressed to find that all his cupboards and drawers were bare. What had happened to all the new linen which she had provided? He looked at her and said: 'So many people come to me in need.' Mother Mayer had no option but to send a fresh batch as, apparently, she had often done before.

When war broke out in 1914, Father Mayer immediately volunteered for duty as an army chaplain. This was not due to a personal surge of patriotic fervour but derived from his zeal as a pastor. Men called to military service still needed pastoral care . . . only the context had changed. The history of his military career abounds with examples of his incredible courage and boundless love, particularly for the wounded and the dying. In August 1914 he was assigned to pastoral duty in a field hospital of the 1st Bavarian Army Corps. His tireless work led to his being appointed divisional chaplain of the 8th Bavarian Reserve Division. He retained the post when, in January 1915, the Division became part of the 19th Reserve Infantry Regiment. With the Regiment he saw service in the Munster Valley region of Alsace, in the summer of 1915 in Galicia on the eastern front, and again in Alsace in the autumn of that year. In the 1916 Battle of the Somme, his unit took part in the heaviest fighting and by the Autumn, it was at Siebenbürgen in Rumania.

There are innumerable stories of the way in which Father Rupert exposed himself to danger in order to be with the men, for he refused to take shelter, even in the heaviest barrages. He had to seek out and comfort the dying. There was, for example, the incident when a soldier who had lost both legs was lying in the open under a hail of shells. Father Mayer threw himself on top of the man, assuring him that if they were hit it would now strike him first. There was also the occasion when soldiers crept though a barrage to dugouts which were almost buried. They came upon Father Mayer who had collected some men together to say the Rosary. In a space lit by a single candle he was praying with the men before a very small picture of Our Lady. It has been said that

84. Ibid., p. 63.

because he insisted on taking part in every danger to which others were exposed and because of the nature of his pastoral care, he opened up the well-springs of religion in many a heart. So esteemed was he for his endeavours that Protestants too came to him with their spiritual needs.

On 30 December 1916 in Rumania, Father Mayer, tired of waiting in a reserve position, joined an officer on his way to the front. He was crossing a weak bridge in the Sulta Valley when he was wounded, his left leg being shattered from the knee down. One of the doctors in the dingy dressing station remembers that, as they tried to fortify the faint beating of his heart by injections, Rupert, in a scarcely audible voice, apologised for his continual moaning and groaning. The doctor records that even as he lay there in a pool of blood, Rupert seemed amazingly detached from himself. That evening the leg was amputated and early in February 1917 his family learned that he had undergone a second amputation above the knee. On 27 October it was a skeletal, crippled priest who said Mass again, this time at the Chapel of Ignatius in the invalid training centre at Landsberg. Before long he was ministering to the soldiers once more. Cardinal Count Konrad von Preysing of Berlin said of him at this time: 'His absolute love of truth was most convincing. One had the feeling that his entire personality stood behind every word and every sentence that he uttered.'[85] Pouring with sweat from his labours, Father Mayer was to walk about on a sorely irritated stump as he returned to pastoral duties with his burning zeal for souls. For his courage and devotion he had received no less than 4 decorations including the Iron Cross, 1st Class, held at the time to be the equivalent of Britain's VC.

He returned to a Munich ripe for revolution. Many, bitter at losing the War after their sacrifices, looked to Communism to bring them out of the misery of their destitution. Father Mayer would go to their Communist meetings denouncing the arguments of the speakers. 'A country without religion will perish,'[86] he warned. He frequently met with vile abuse but never faltered, even when his life was threatened. To pleadings for restraint, for his safety's sake, his reply was: 'If no one has the courage to speak then I must. God is with us.'[87] Operating from

85. A Koerbling SJ, op. cit., p. 80.
86. Ibid., p. 83.
87. P Reisterer SJ, op. cit., p. 67.

his room in the Jesuits' house in the Ett Strasse he organised retreats for the army, the police, women and girls and was deeply committed to mission work in the Munich parishes. Following a visit to Rome, Cardinal Faulhaber reported that the Holy Father had almost lost faith in Bavaria but his eyes had lit up when told of Father Mayer's apostolic work in the city. In 1921, he became President of the Munich Congregation of Mary. A men's congregation, founded in 1610, it had 2000 members. It was divided into parish groups at the close of the First World War. Among Rupert's work for it were monthly visits to each group, celebration of the Mass and Benediction and sermons which are reported as being 'downright and unequivocal.' In the Holy Year of 1925, Cardinal Faulhaber led a pilgrimage of 600 men to Rome, 200 of whom were from the Congregation. 'They're all men!'[88] was the admiring cry of the Romans. At an audience, Pope Pius XI thanked Rupert Mayer deeply for 'all your labours and sufferings.'[89]

He was still very much in demand as a confessor, for in addition to confessions after daily Mass he was hearing penitents on Sundays and holy days of obligation from 3 pm until often as late as 10 pm with no more than a short break for supper. The pain of his wound from these long sittings frequently made him sick and exhausted but there was never any let up in bringing love and care to penitents many of whom stated that through him they felt the love of God. The privations of the War and the subsequent staggering inflation had left many destitute. He was instrumental in bringing food, clothing, housing and even jobs to vast numbers of Munich's needy. Father Paul Reisterer SJ[90] tells of how the files of Munich's Caritas, the Catholic relief agency, disclosed that one third of the 70,000 people in the lists had received assistance of some kind from Father Mayer, be it a monthly benefit payment, a job of work, an arrangement for convalescence and so on. He would make 'hoarding journeys' to the country, returning with food, clothing and substantial sums of money, not a pfennig of which he kept for himself. His helpers claimed that he often went without food to help others and regretted being unable

88. Ibid., p. 69.
89. Ibid.
90. Ibid., p. 71.

to give away his underpants for these now had only one leg per pair! It is also said that when he made his house calls people came to life again because of '. . . a warm heart that really cared and realised how bitter the struggle for their daily needs was . . .'[91] In 1935, he stood his ground, box in hand, when during a street collection for Caritas he was surrounded by Nazi thugs chanting: 'Down with Caritas! Not a penny for Caritas! Everything for the National Socialists.'[92]

At a meeting in 1919 he had inveighed against the evils of Communism. He was followed on the platform by Adolf Hitler, who declared that now that the priest had attacked Communism on religious grounds he would oppose it on political grounds. Any adversary of Communism was of interest to a Catholic cleric, so Father Mayer subsequently attended a number of Hitler's meetings. Through their sloganism on the deification of state and race and its call for the banning of the Old Testament, the true nature of Nazism soon became apparent to him. His opinion was then given fearlessly: though Hitler was an effective public speaker he was essentially an agitator who didn't always stick to the truth. He made his feelings even more clearly known when he attended a 1923 meeting on the theme 'Can a Catholic be a National Socialist?' When he declared at the outset that the answer was 'never', in true Nazi fashion he was howled down and barred from further comment. Not long afterwards, the NSDAP suffered its first defeat and Father Mayer was held to be responsible for it. Thus, he had now become, in the eyes of the NSDAP, an enemy and a marked man.

Another important social aspect of Rupert's pastoral work was the institution of Masses at the City's railway station. He felt after a long week at work people should have access to the countryside, or to sport, without running the risk of missing Mass. The room used for employee training was made available by the transport authority on Sundays and holy days. Having persuaded a doubtful Vicar General, Rupert posted the timetable – there would be Masses at 3.10 am, 4.05, 4.40, 5.15, 5.50 and 6.25 am. This was another development which endeared him to the citizens of Munich. Travellers seeking a day's recreation were joined by postal and railway workers, hotel employees, night

---

91. A Koerbling SJ, op. cit., p. 95.
92. P Reisterer SJ, op. cit., p. 72.

watchmen, cab drivers and policemen. In the year 1925/26 there were 130 Masses, 13,797 participants and 820 attending Communion. The comparative figures for 1936/37 were 364 Masses, 62,852 participants and 5,408 Communions. In time, additional Masses were instituted at Munich's Eastern Station and at the Hotel Schneefernerhaus at the summit of the Zugspitze Mountain. All this sprang from the mind of a crippled priest in constant pain who became endeared to Munich to the extent that the SS did not begin to disrupt this development until the end of 1937.

Father Mayer was a fighter: one not interested in war and killing but a fighter for faith and charity. His entries in the police records were quite extensive – there were 77 of these before his first arrest. When the Nazis finally came to power, as we have seen earlier, the persecution of the Church began. As it intensified so the fervour of 'the Jesuit' increased. While the Gestapo sat beneath his pulpit, or in the shadow of the organ, making notes, his rock-hard antagonism was clear. He publicly denounced the Nazi threats that had been made to Cardinal Faulhaber, he spoke of the evidence to hand which destroyed readers' faith in a large part of the German press, and his protest against the violence done to parents at the 1937 Munich voting on parochial schools contained these extracts: 'Catholics in Munich entitled to educational privileges have been deprived of their parochial schools in contravention of all law and justice. In these school battles such flagrant lies were uttered as would bend the stoutest rafters. All civil and Party offices worked together. The whole thing looks as if the government concluded the Concordat just to have it sabotaged ... It was a terror, a victory of force, a victory which certainly does no credit to those who achieved it.'[93]

When Catholicism as an ethos was expunged from the principles of the Catholic Students' Association he severed his contacts with it and when the war veterans associations were taken over by the Nazis he terminated his subscriptions to them and ceased to wear his war medals. The regime hated him but because of his popularity was perplexed as to how best to proceed against him. So on the 8 May 1936, he was given a warning as to his future conduct. Father Mayer simply continued to preach so that on 16 May 1937 came notice that

93. A Koerbling SJ, op. cit., p. 144.

any further public 'utterance' was prohibited. This too he ignored on the basis of two standpoints: (1) that he did not give political speeches but spoke entirely on religious and moral grounds and that (2) under the terms of the Concordat only his religious superiors could withdraw his permission to speak. This resulted in a more precisely worded prohibition of 'preaching activity' on 28 May, but he did not abide by this either.

On 5 June 1937 he was arrested and subsequently brought to trial. A large collection of his sermons was spread before the judges but it was, in effect, superfluous for he was more than ready to admit, indeed to reiterate, the 'offences' with which he was charged. He challenged the court with such vigour that the chairman of judges asked finally: 'Do you think it is pleasant for us to sit here and listen to you?'[94] Wryly, Father Mayer answered: 'I'm far happier to be the defendant here than one of the judges.'[95] He was sentenced to six months in prison but this was set aside. His religious superiors were advising him, no doubt for his own safety, to stop preaching and he was willing to obey them. However, the following jibe reached Rupert's ears: 'That's the way these pastors all are. You just have to threaten arrest and rattle the keys to the concentration camp a bit, and then they'll lie down and shut up.'[96] This was too much and he asked for, and was given, permission from his superior to preach again. When he did so, he was rearrested and committed to prison first at Stadelheim then at Landsberg am Lech to serve out his original six-month sentence. An interesting point from this period was that when he was attending the Courts of Justice for his trial he was even denied the use of the building's lift. 'Let him walk!' had been the order of the police lieutenant.

After an indifferent attempt at making paper bags, due to brutish tuition, he was transferred to the invalid section of the prison where he was able to apply himself to intellectual activities. There was Mass on Sundays and holy days and the food was adequate. He was also delighted to be able to go each week to the prison chaplain for confession. At the beginning of May, 1938 he was told he was to be released. When he departed, this chaplain wrote: 'Our beloved Father

---

94. Ibid., p. 147.
95. Ibid., p. 147.
96. Ibid., p. 148.

Rupert Mayer must become our patron saint in the Landsberg prison, and indeed he will become it; of that I am convinced . . .'[97]

When World War II commenced the regime was determined to silence any subversive influences on the home front, so on 3 November 1939 he was arrested yet again and sent to the concentration camp at Sachsenhausen. Though he was not molested he could hear the sound of other prisoners being flogged. The Nazis believed he was in touch with monarchists and other opponents of their regime but he regarded any conversations with anyone as confidential. The priest must win trust through his secrecy. Despite their efforts he would not even comment on their suggestions and, in the end, frustrated, they stopped their interrogations. The food, consisting mainly of soup, was obviously inadequate and he was now on the way to starvation. As a result of his incarcerations the stump of his leg no longer fitted into the artificial limb. He could only improve matters by putting on more stockings, one over the other. In the end he had on four heavy stockings at once and despaired that he could not pull on a fifth stocking for a proper grip on the artificial leg.

Of this period it has been written: 'The authorities at Sachsenhausen had a problem on their hands in Mayer. They could not brutalise the rock-hard priest as they did other prisoners. His very presence in the camp set a bad example.'[98] The regime decided to negotiate with the Church on his future. It was agreed that he would now be confined to the monastery at Ettal, on condition that he refrained from all manner of public activity, so on 7 August 1940 he left Sachsenhausen. To the doctor who saw him first after his release he presented a typical picture of starvation. Extracts from his notes read: 'Six feet tall, weight 110 pounds; fatty tissues of body nearly all consumed; musculature reduced, skin dry and wrinkled; in his leg – starvation oedema, twice normal size; slight cardiac noise; blood pressure 180/90; severe cough, symptom of bronchitis.'[99]

In the monastery he was looked after by Father Abbot and the monks, being given the spacious, elegantly furnished guest room, which brought him the joy of his own wash-basin. When he was

---

97. Ibid., p. 163-4.
98. R Royal, op. cit., p. 154.
99. A Koerbling SJ, op. cit., p. 173.

strong enough he was able to swim in the monastery pool, which delighted him. But severe restrictions had been placed on both him and the monastery by the Gestapo: his correspondence, reduced to a minimum, must deal only with personal matters; only a physician and most immediate family members were to visit him; he was not to conduct services if there was a possibility of outside persons attending and he was absolutely forbidden to hear confessions. He was not to have any contact with the outside world in any way, shape or fashion. The ecclesiastical authorities must ensure that he never left the monastery. The abbot and his community did all they could to restore him to health and they tried to interpret the strict conditions of his stay in every way that was helpful to him. Even so, a Protestant clergyman who was visiting him wrote: 'Father Rupert Mayer seemed to me like a caged lion whose strength had only been subdued by force. He would have liked most to leave the monastery and take up the fight against the Nazis publicly and in person again. He was prepared to take the consequences, death as a martyr.'[100] Of this time, Anton Koerbling SJ wrote: 'No exertion or trouble was too great for him to bring the sick people in the monastery Holy Communion after his Holy Mass. He often had to climb stairs in doing so . . . With truly heroic courage he bore the pain which the stump of his amputated leg caused him.'[101]

On 11 May 1945, with the War just ended, he was taken back to his beloved Munich. He had taken leave of it with tears in his eyes not thinking he would ever return. Before long he was hearing confessions again, celebrating Holy Mass, preaching to huge audiences, making house calls in the ruins and sick calls in the cellars, appealing for the release of fathers of families held as prisoners of war and helping the victims of concentration camps return to their former jobs. On Thursday 1 November, he began the eight o'clock Mass in the Chapel of the Cross in the ruins of St Michael's Church. He read the Gospel and began to talk of the saints in Heaven. Nearing the end of the talk he began a sentence three times with the words: 'The Lord . . . The Lord . . . The Lord . . .' but did not complete it. He remained

100. Ibid., p. 180.
101. Ibid., p. 181.

standing, leaning against the altar unable to say more. A woman cried out: 'Father Mayer . . . Father Mayer!' Two priests who had been hearing confessions hurried to him. He was carried in his vestments from the chapel. A stroke was diagnosed and he died just before 11 am. Thousands in Munich saw the fact that it was All Saints Day as symbolic. 'Father Mayer was called to join the Saints in Heaven. Father Mayer never fell down in his whole life, not even when he died!'[102]

So many people visited his grave in Pullach that it was decided to prepare a special tomb for him in the crypt of Munich's Bürgersaal. It has been recorded that about 300,000 people lined the streets as six horses drew his coffin to its last resting place.[103] It was 23 May 1948 and the watchers saw that 30,000 men had come from all over Germany to walk behind him. On 3 May 1987, in the Olympic Stadium in Munich, Rupert Mayer was beatified by Pope John Paul II.

FATHER MAX JOSEF METZGER[104]

Max Metzger was born on 3 February 1887 at Schopfheim, Baden, Germany. Schopfheim is a small, secluded village in the Black Forest where, in their fervently Catholic home, Freidrich August Metzger and his wife Anna, raised four children, Max being the eldest child and the only boy. Friedrich was a teacher of History, Latin and French and a particularly competent and devoted one. Unfortunately Anna suffered from asthma so that her health was never robust but the home was a happy one, Friedrich Metzger, with his dry sense of humour, being able to tell the most improbable stories with a straight face. In addition to being fluent in French, Friedrich was also a skilled pianist and organist and music was an important element in the life of the happy Metzger household – one of Max's biographers records that he sang well and enjoyed composing music. There are examples in this work of pious boys who, from their earliest days showed great enthusiasm for acting out elements of the Holy Mass and other

102. Ibid., p. 195.

103. P Reisterer SJ, op. cit., p. 86.

104. All the references in this profile are drawn from an unpaginated internet copy of *Bloodwitness for Peace and Unity – The Life of Max Josef Metzger* (Copyright 1977) by Leonard Swidler and published by Ecumenical Press, Philadelphia, Penn. This author tenders his deepest thanks for sight of all the most valuable information contained in the book.

Catholic devotions, and Max was another of these. As a small child he announced that he wished to be either a missionary or a doctor and his uncle, a Father Gaenshirt, promised to help him if his vocation lay in the missions.

Though Friedrich Metzger was undoubtedly a loving father, he paid particular attention to Max's development – he was to be a 'model' boy and only first place at whatever he undertook was good enough, so there were some tearful episodes along the way. For three and a half years, Max attended the grammar school at Schopfheim, progressing to the Realschule there. His father was his teacher for French and History and expected the highest possible standards from him. He also taught him Latin in his spare time. From the Realschule, but still in the Black Forest, he next became a pupil at the Progymnasium at Donaueschingen. After one year he moved again, this time to the gymnasium at Loerrach on the German-Swiss border. He was at Loerrach to complete his fifth and sixth years of secondary schooling and commuted there from his home at Schopfheim. Although he did well at Loerrach, writing to Father Gaenshirt that he had headed the first year class academically, he was nevertheless reprimanded for boisterous behaviour which resulted in injury to another pupil.

In 1902 his father obtained a post at Meersburg's pedagogical academy which meant another move for Max, this time to the gymnasium at Constance. He lodged at the St Konradi Haus, a type of minor seminary. Interestingly, the rector there was Dr Conrad Gröber who, after Max's ordination, would become his archbishop at Freiburg and who was his archbishop in 1944 when he was executed. He studied the Humanities with a strong emphasis on languages and at the 'Abitur' state examinations he passed 'sehr gut', the highest rating. In 1905 he began his theological studies at the University in Freiburg. By this time, the family's economic situation had deteriorated so badly that Friedrich August was considering the rationing of bread, milk and meat for them. Max did well at his theological studies but his assessment contained reference to his high spirits, pointing out that he would need to curb these if he was to become a good priest.

In May 1908 he was permitted to study for a doctorate and he devoted several semesters to this at Fribourg in Switzerland, returning to Freiburg in Germany where, in completing the task, he devoted much time to the study of church history. He was awarded a prize for his doctoral thesis which was considered to be 'an admirable contribution to liturgical scholarship'. As a student he had enjoyed drinking with his fellows but during his stay in Fribourg, Switzerland, he had spent quite a lot of time, as a member of the S.V.P., working with poor children in the run-down areas of the city. He saw that a great deal of the misery visible around him was caused by drunkenness and pledged himself to total abstinence from alcohol for the future. He also intended to actively promote the virtues of abstinence. In June 1911, Max Josef Metzger was ordained priest and he celebrated his first Mass at his uncle's church in Oberhausen.

Unfortunately his early pastoral work was not trouble-free. This was due to his impulsive and over-enthusiastic advocacy of temperance. It led to adverse reports on him by the parish priest of St Peter and St Paul, Karlsruhe, where he served for some months, and by the incumbent at a parish in Mannheim where he had served as an assistant from 12 October 1912 to 27 January 1914. Both priests found his lack of balance in approaching his duties, devoting too much time to the temperance movement, more than irritating. He was found unwilling to take advice and too ready to undertake initiatives without proper consultation. On the other hand, Monsignor Wilhelm Baumeister, a significant figure in Catholic social work and charitable activities, believed that the Archdiocese of Freiburg should be grateful for his efforts in helping to establish temperance organisations. When Max left Mannheim it was to assist his uncle, Father Gaenshirt, at Oberhausen who was struggling with a cancer which was later to claim his life.

When the Great War began on 3 August 1914, Max Metzger immediately wrote to his archbishop seeking permission to volunteer for service as a front-line chaplain. This was granted and on 16 May 1915 he was awarded the Iron Cross for 'self-sacrificing actions and particularly for courageous work in the front-line trenches of the 42nd cavalry brigade'. At about this time he was approached by a Professor Johann Ude, a Catholic priest well acquainted with his earlier work on temperance. He wished to recruit him as the general secretary of the Austrian *Kreuzbündnis* (League of the Cross), also a temperance organisation. While he would have liked to have taken on the work he was hoping to return to university for preparation to undertake social and urban pastoral work. He wrote to his archbishop seeking advice on the route to choose but was testily told that he must make up his own mind and that he would be granted leave of absence accordingly.

In the end he decided to take up the offer from Professor Ude whom he would join at the end of the war. However, in the autumn of 1915 he was discharged from the army because of a severe lung condition and so, in October, left for Graz to become general secretary of the Kreuzbündnis and of the Priests' Abstinence League. Much of his work consisted of writing and editing but he also undertook a grinding schedule of lectures: in one year, 1916, he gave no fewer than 119 talks and lectures on alcoholism in an area ranging from Graz in Austria to Berlin in Germany. Yet, though for Father Metzger alcohol was a critical problem, for society as a whole he was alive to the need for reform in many other aspects of life, believing that this should be rooted in spirituality.

In this regard his connection with Father Wilhelm Impekovin, of the Divine Word Missionaries (and afterwards known as 'Brother Gottwills') was most important. Together they established the World Peace League of the White Cross ('White Cross' was derived from the small cross usually impressed on the Mass host and signalled the devotion of the organisation to the Eucharist). The White Cross movement declared its commitment to work of all kinds . . . pastoral, spiritual, works of mercy, work for peace and for the unity of the Church, work to promote healthy and simple living and assistance to the victims of un-Christian economic pressure. Through the charity of a prosperous gentleman they obtained substantial premises and were joined by a young Father Hasenbichler who became 'Brother Franz'. Father Metzger had taken the name 'Brother Paulus' and with Brothers Gotwills and Franz he set out to establish the 'White Cross' as successful and significant. Unfortunately by September 1923 Brother Paulus found himself the solitary leader for both his colleagues had died.

While the local hierarchy was somewhat circumspect about the movement, endorsement came from the Vatican particularly with regard to its work for peace. In spite of a number of problems the organisation grew so that its inner group, the Mission Society of the

White Cross, comprised 50 members. About half of these were sisters, the rest priests and brothers. There were houses, or members, in or near Graz, Vienna, Lausanne, Bruenn, Pettau, London and Frankfurt. By the time of Father Metzger's death in 1944 and despite the restrictions imposed on it by the Nazis, the organisation was still engaged in an immense variety of social and pastoral work, bible study, care for families and children, homes for the aged, work for peace and the publication of books and pamphlets. Its mother house had become established at Meitingen, near Augsburg. It has been recorded that the New Testament was a 'rule of life' for Max and even a Protestant Journal noted, in 1934, that Metzger had made a major contribution to the significant growth of the Catholic Bible Movement. In his lectures, books, pamphlets, conferences and retreats he repeatedly stressed the daily reading of the Bible.

By 1929, the organisation had become known as the Society of Christ the King, but it proved difficult to obtain ecclesiastical endorsement for the statutes of the Society. This hampered its movement to new dioceses and its capability of attracting vocations. At last, however, approval was obtained from the Bishop of Bruenn, Czechoslavakia for what was canonically described as an 'international pious union'. The early years of the 'White Cross' were certainly not easy but during the 1930s Father Metzger was able to expand membership of the Society and to recruit and train seminarians for it. In 1936, when he was looking for a major seminary to assist this expansion the diocesan seminary at Eichstätt agreed to help. At this time, the Society already had 61 male members (38 living in community) and as many as 176 sisters (97 living in community). His tendency to 'cut corners', particularly with regard to the canonical technicalities for ordination of the seminarians, led him into difficulties with the local hierarchy and his biographer interestingly sets out how, in 1938, he journeyed to see bishops as far away as South America to resolve these difficulties.

Metzger perceived the role of the Church as being one of service, a concept later endorsed by Pope John XXIII and Vatican II, the 'White Cross', and its successor, the Society of Christ the King, thus becoming a key provider of social service. Its work in the world unsurprisingly brought its founder under the surveillance of the police and he was arrested on 1 December 1939 for 'suspicion of complicity in political activities.' He answered the charge by drawing attention to a list of his recent publications which were anything but political. In a necessarily short profile it is impossible to encompass all the many interests and activities of this dedicated and energetic priest, so the rest of this outline will concentrate on his work for world peace and ecumenism. It was through his work for peace that he was to lose his life.

He envisaged the unity of Catholics world-wide in an international peace programme. The World Peace League of the White Cross aimed to join together all the local and national Catholic peace organisations. In 1918 the Peace League of German Catholics (*Friedensbund deutscher Katholiken*) was founded by Metzger but even earlier than that he had met many representatives from neutral and 'enemy' countries who shared his aspirations. Unsurprisingly, though the influence of the Friedensbund had grown considerably through the 1920s, within months of the advent of Hitler in 1933 it had been crushed. From the time of the Nazi accession, Father Metzger had opposed Nazi ideology and in May 1933 his publication *Christkoenigsbote* featured a whole front-page editorial on the new government. In it Max Metzger made his past and present objections to the party abundantly clear. In March 1935, Hitler repudiated the Treaty of Versailles, sent his troops into the Rhineland and announced the rearmament of Germany. *Christkoenigsbote* ran a front-page picture and article under the headline 'Give us peace Lord in our days!' and within days, the publication had been suppressed.

By then, Dr Metzger was working tirelessly not only for peace and social reform but also for the unity of Christians. In this last cause he founded the 'Una Sancta Brotherhood' in 1938. The purpose of its 'Ecumenical Meeting Circles' or 'Una Sancta Circles', as they came to be called, was 'to promote a rapprochement and mutual understanding between believing Christians of different confessions in fulfilment of "the last wish of the common Lord . . . that all may be one." ' The success of the movement was such that by Christmas 1940 Metzger was writing to Archbishop Gröber, seeking the establishment of a theological ecumenical commission to assume responsibility for the entire Una Sancta movement.

In 1941, Father Metzger published an article 'Breakthrough to Una Sancta' which was revolutionary for its time. It held that 'the blind apologetics of the past' which saw everything as either black or white, with all the black on one side and all the white on the other, was now a cause for shame, and that there was at that point the beginning of a real spiritual meeting in genuine Christian freedom.[105] Metzger's writings on ecumenism are said to be prophetic and even to have influenced what emanated from Vatican II. Documents reveal that he travelled throughout 1941, 1942 and even 1943 to disseminate his ideas. His work for ecumenism was highly significant and generated an amazing response but now we must turn his conflict with the Nazis, whose ideology was one of hate. Since Metzger's propagated a gospel of love, conflict was inevitable.

Max Metzger made himself known to the Nazis soon after their accession for in late 1933 he published a pamphlet *Die Kirche und das Neue Deutschland* (The Church and The New Germany) in which he strongly re-emphasised the incompatibility of a Catholic *Weltanschauung* and the National Socialist system. The Gestapo imprisoned him at Augsburg from 23-26 January and confiscated some of his publishing equipment. Just after the War began he was arrested twice. On 4 September 1939 came the ludicrous charge that his Society of Christ the King (the successor to the White Cross movement) was suspected of being no more than a 'front' for a monarchist party in Bavaria. The humour of the situation had not escaped even the Nazis for his imprisonment lasted for one day – 5 September. In October he was again questioned and more of the Society's materials and equipment were confiscated.

He was arrested again and imprisoned from 9 November to 4 December but without charge. He immediately wrote to find out why and was told by Augsburg's police commissioner that, along with 120 others, he had been arrested for the attempt on Hitler's life in Munich's Bürgerbräukeller and that his foreign correspondence revealed his complicity. His reaction, sent by post to colleagues was: 'That is so dumb.' He would not let the matter rest and on 1 December he wrote to the state police insisting that he had no interest in politics and asking again, why he was imprisoned. Released on 4 December, he continued to ask of what he had been accused. The answer came that he ought to be happy he was free again.

---

105. L Swidler, *Bloodwitness for Peace and Unity,* 1977.

His complete lack of fear and indeed his recklessness emerged unmistakably in the autumn of 1942. It was clear that the war was now going badly for Germany. Unbelievably, he drafted a letter to the Führer asking him to step aside in favour of a government which could then negotiate an honourable peace. At the beginning of 1943 he showed the letter to a Dr Matthias Laros who immediately took him to task for being so naïve. Laros eventually persuaded him not to send the letter, an extract from which, according to the memory of Dr Laros, read as follows:

> 'Herr Chancellor, if you really love our people and are prepared to give your life's blood as you have insisted, then you must step aside and make room for another government which will still be able to conclude a peace which is honourable, since our armies on the borders of the empire still present a considerable force which will not be easily overrun. As the enemy does not wish to and will not negotiate with you, the only alternative, as in every law-abiding nation, is your stepping aside in order to save the nation, even if you must lose your life in the process; now still in honourable battle, later, however, in shame and degradation.'[106]

Whilst Metzger's artlessness is seemingly unbelievable, we have to grant that his bravery was indeed breathtaking. And while he was persuaded not to send the letter he would not let the matter rest and despite the warnings of Dr Laros he prepared a memorandum along similar lines to his friend Archbishop Eidem, the Lutheran Archbishop of Uppsala in neutral Sweden. In January 1943, Field Marshal Friedrich von Paulus had surrendered his 6th Army to the Russians at Stalingrad. This intensified Father Metzger's feeling that Germany was on the way to collapse. The memorandum to Archbishop Eidem was then to be forwarded to English bishops and through them to Allied commanders in order to obtain some mitigation in the peace conditions which would be imposed on Germany.

A Swedish woman, Dagmar Imgart, now enters the story. She had married a German, lived in Germany and had become interested in the Una Sancta movement. She had gained Father Metzger's confidence and since she travelled periodically to Sweden she occasionally carried mail, albeit of a religious nature, from Father Metzger to Swedish clerics. He had come to trust her completely and so explained his

---

106. Ibid.

plan to her. She immediately volunteered to carry the memorandum to Archbishop Eidem on her next visit to Sweden. Accordingly, in the spring of 1943, the memorandum was handed to Frau Imgart. On the second of two visits to Dr Metzger's Berlin residence on 29 June 1943 she was accompanied by several Gestapo agents. Imgart herself was a Gestapo agent (and by 1944 her husband Otto was serving with an SS company at the Bergen-Belsen concentration camp). She had been determined to betray him.

Initially, Father Metzger was taken to Gestapo's infamous prison on Berlin's Prinz-Albrecht-Strasse. On 11 September he was transferred to the Plötzensee prison to reduce the overcrowding, and hence the vulnerability of this city-centre prison, during air attacks. The move to Plötzensee meant a worsening of conditions – poorer food, fewer visits, the wearing of prison clothes for the first time and, of course, the misery of constant air attacks on the capital. On 14 October 1943, Father Metzger appeared before the People's Court, whose president was Dr Roland Freisler and who, in that court, fully justified in case after case, the nickname 'raging Roland'. He liked nothing better than to torment those brought before him with a mixture of sarcasm, fanaticism and cunning. As Father Max was outlining his career, Freisler sneered: 'So then you founded the Una Sancta, and then, isn't it right? . . . there will of course come the Una Sanctissima!' Metzger had been accused of 'conspiracy for high treason' and 'giving aid and comfort to the enemy.' He was later to write: 'It soon became very clear to me that all human hope was in vain' . . . 'the judgment gavel fell even before I could justify myself.' Freisler had screamed at him: 'How do you get the idea to doubt our victory when the whole German Volk is filled with the certainty of victory?' and later: 'We believe in victory and whoever doubts it must be wiped out!'

It took ten minutes for the court to reach its decision. Max Metzger was condemned to death with absolute loss of honour. With his hands chained behind him he was led down to the cellar of the building. When he returned to Plötzensee that evening, it is reported that he: 'knelt down and thanked God that He had taken me so intimately into the discipleship of Christ and I prayed to him to strengthen my heart to the end.' On 22 October, because of the bombing raids on Berlin, he was transferred to the prison at Brandenburg-Goerden, some 67 miles distant. There he found his sorrows alleviated somewhat by the beautiful view of the forest which his cell afforded him. On the other hand he missed the friendship of Plötzensee's chaplain, Father Peter Buchholz. From Leonard Swidler's biography, and from other sources consulted in the research for this book, Father Buchholz emerges as a very fine priest.

While waiting for death, Max Metzger wrote a 138 page long theological treatise on the Church. Its composition, despite his chains, is said to be immaculately set out and contains 394 footnotes (an inspiration to any writer weary with reference-hunting). Despite the long journey accomplished in difficult wartime conditions, Father Buchholz visited Dr Metzger on 28 December 1943 and again on 12 April 1944. The latter was to be his last visit, for at 3.26 pm on Monday, 17 April 1944, Max Josef Metzger was beheaded. Afterwards, his executioner told Father Buchholz: 'Never have I seen a man die like that.' At mid-morning on Friday 21 April, prison officials brought his body in a hearse to the old city cemetery in Brandenberg. It was a wet and weary day, but as the casket sank into the grave, the sun came out.

FATHER FRANZ REINISCH

It is one thing to understand that we have a conscience but quite another to be able to describe how it works. To put it simply we can say that we have a conscience since we stand by certain convictions that we ignore or repudiate only at the risk of losing our integrity. Once we have decided that it is morally right to do something, then the dignity of the primacy of conscience requires, if the conscience is correctly formed, that we adhere to our decision.[107] The era being described in this book provides us with examples of martyrs for conscience – we saw how Franz Jägerstätter refused to conform to the standards of the Nazis for he thought that what he was being asked to do was against the will of God. We noted the story of Nikolaus Gross and his belief 'that one must obey God more than men.'

In his pursuit of god-like status, through *Gleichschaltung* ('co-ordination'), Hitler strove to create a highly centralised one-Party Reich by destroying the privileges and traditions of the old German

---

107. J Bowden (ed.), *Christianity. The Complete Guide*. London, 2005, pp. 277-78.

states. The political, social and cultural institutions of the former Germany were swept away, along with the rights of the individual – there was even an Oath of Loyalty to the People's Chancellor, Adolf Hitler, for German Poets.[108] And ultimately, industry and the armed forces were 'co-ordinated' too, in the name of the 'Secure Unity of the Party and the Reich.' However, one of the people who opposed this lunacy was Father Franz Reinisch and he is reported as being the only Catholic priest who refused to serve in the German army during World War II.[109] The established procedure was for priests to serve as non-combatants, in the medical corps, but Franz Reinisch was appalled to realise that joining the forces in whatever capacity would entail taking the oath of allegiance to Hitler, something his conscience could not allow. Moreover, he did not mince words in his refusal. Among other things he said: 'The present government is not an authority willed by God, but a nihilistic government that has attained its power only through force, lies and deceit... The National Socialist principle, 'Might before Right', has forced me into a position of self-defence. Hence for me there can be no oath of allegiance to such a government.'[110]

Who was this man of such staggering courage? Franz Reinisch was born at Feldkirch-Altenstadt in the Austrian Tyrol on 1 February 1903. His father, also Franz, was a local tax official who was moved a number of times before being stationed in Innsbruck. Again, as we have seen so often in these profiles, Franz the younger, along with his siblings (in this case, three girls and another boy), was cradled in the faith by devout parents. Franz also shared another characteristic with a number of the martyrs in this chapter in that he was a delicate child and his health was a problem throughout his life. Even so, he was mischievous and given to feats of derring-do, his roguishness leading one teacher, an uncle, to declare: 'No good will come of him!'

His devil-may-care attitude meant that throughout school and university he did no more work than was minimally required, but Franz had winning ways and became very popular with his fellow

---

108. I Kershaw, *Hitler 1889-1936: Hubris*. London, 1998, p. 481.
109. M Cole, 'Fr Franz Reinisch – Martyr of Conscience' in *The Crusader*, February 2007, p. 4.
110. M Gollwitzer et al. (eds.), *Dying We Live*. Glasgow, 1974, pp. 47-8.

students at Innsbruck University where, like his brother, he read law. A good-looking boy who danced well, he had many admirers among the female students but an initial romance came to nothing when the girl and her family left the area. He seems to have survived the blow and readily transferred his affections to another girl. Since, unlike the first girl, she was not a Catholic, the Reinisch parents were dismayed but Franz would not give up this girl whose feelings apparently matched his own.

During the first year of his studies, he was approached by fellow student Kurt von Schuschnigg. This was the Doctor Schuschnigg who would become the Austrian Federal Chancellor in 1934 when his predecessor, Engelbert Dollfuss was murdered by the Nazis. Dr von Schuschnigg came to personify independent Austria during the Anschluss crisis in 1938 and for his resistance he was committed to a concentration camp where he remained until after the War. As a young friend of Franz Reinisch, however, he too was involved in an affair of the heart but one much less fraught. Quite simply, he was becoming engaged, but had previously reserved a place on a four-week retreat conducted near Basle by the Jesuits. Would Franz Reinisch take his place? Schuschnigg pointed out that Franz could always leave the retreat if it was not to his liking. The retreat must have made an impression on him for the following semester found him at Kiel University studying medical law and while there it brought him in touch with a sordid world he hardly knew existed. From that point, his vocation was clear – in Franz's own words: 'I saw the religious and moral misery of the harbour city with the eyes of the retreat. A great longing broke through in me to win souls for Christ. In July 1923 I returned home having decided to become a priest.'[111] Naturally his girl friend was greatly upset but his family, once over its initial surprise, adjusted to his decision. His kind father, in agreeing, told him the option to return to his legal studies would still be open if he had been mistaken in his calling.

When he took up his studies in theology, there was no great change in his work habits: he did just enough to 'get by'. His introduction to smoking was to become a torment to him but he managed alcohol quite well. There was one early overt sign of his fervour: he changed

111. M Cole, op. cit., p. 5.

the motto of the Students' Association, for his own purposes, from 'As immovable as the mountains of home' to 'Our Faith in Jesus Christ and Mary is as immovable as the mountains of home' and, according to writer Mary Cole, 'it became his compass in life.'[112] In 1926 he entered the seminary at Brixen and, as a result, came to know the Pallottine Fathers, becoming a close friend of one of them. The Pallottine Fathers and Brothers are a religious society founded by Vincent Pallotti who was canonised in 1963. St Vincent was born in Rome in 1795. His formative years were a time of diminishing faith and he felt committed to revive it. His key concern was that each baptised person is an Apostle of Jesus Christ and in 1835 he founded the Union of Catholic Aspostolate, an organisation of both religious and lay people acting in unison to spread God's word. It is said that the ideas with which he infused the Church were reflected in the work of the Second Vatican Council.

So the Pallottines made their mark on Franz Reinisch. Another landmark in his spiritual formation resulted from a pilgrimage to Rome at Christmas 1926. At an audience with the Pope he experienced such 'wholehearted love' from Pius XI, he became an enthusiastic devotee of the Papacy thereafter. Even so, the final decision to become a priest was not easy and led him to wonder whether he should abandon the idea. Even when he had taken Minor Orders his struggle continued but he persevered and on 29 June 1928 (the Feast of Ss. Peter and Paul) he was ordained priest. It was then that his mother disclosed a secret to him: 'It was in Bozen on Corpus Christi 1903. You were not even six months old. As the Blessed Sacrament was carried through the streets I stood at the roadside with the pram. As the Lord went by, I took you out of the pram and lifted you up, saying, "Lord, if you want this child to be a priest, I give him to you with all my heart." '[113] She had not told him of this previously lest he felt obliged in some way to seek ordination whatever his feelings.

Even now he did not think that his spiritual quest was at an end but in November 1928 he applied for admission to the Pallottine Society. And still his turmoil continued, but from physical rather than spiritual

112. Ibid. p. 5.
113. Ibid., p. 5.

causes. He had by now become addicted to tobacco but was astounded to learn from the Novice Master that all tobacco products were denied to members of the novitiate. He was obliged to hand over about 150 cigarettes and spend the following weeks in misery. In the end he decided to leave the Pallottines altogether, but because he felt ashamed to give the real reason for this, he decided to leave clandestinely. When his attempt to get beyond the walls was unsuccessful he paced the grounds in frustration. However, as he approached the Lourdes grotto his anguish so intensified that he wept and in the aftermath of his tears, he found his addiction had disappeared. Now he was sure that this was his turning point and at the end of 1930 he was professed as a Pallottine and sent to its Provincial House near Augsburg in order to work with youth.

One day he discovered a publication which was issued by the Schoenstatt Movement, a Catholic organisation founded in 1914 by Father Joseph Kentenich, also a Pallottine priest. Father Kentenich conceived this Catholic Marian Movement as a means of spiritual renewal within the Church itself. The literal meaning of *schoenstatt* – 'beautiful place' – did not provide the Movement's title, which is derived from the small village of that name close to the town of Vallendar, near Koblenz. The Schoenstatt Movement emphasised a deep devotion to the Blessed Virgin Mary, who is upheld as the perfect example of love and purity. Members of the Movement are encouraged to possess the faith and purity of children and to think of Mary as their mother. When he had read about the Schoenstatt Movement, Franz Reinisch confided to his diary that now he had found what he had been searching for and, as he read everything he could obtain from Schoenstatt, he longed to visit the shrine there. He realised his ambition in August, 1934.

By that time the Nazis were increasing their hold on Germany. Father Reinisch found this unbearable and did not hesitate to say so. Mindful of what might happen to him, his superiors moved him from place to place. It was a development he found irksome and in the end he was sent to Schoenstatt and charged with the task of generating support for the missionary work of the Pallottines. He travelled throughout Germany conducting retreats and days of recollection and he was also asked to take charge of the groups for men at a time when the religious persecution was gathering momentum, so his role was far from easy. This did not deter him from saying what he thought of the current situation with the result that in September 1940 he was forbidden to preach or speak in public. The quality of their adversary was not lost on the Gestapo, who said to him, astoundingly: 'Come over to us, we need men like you.'[114] At about this time, the Gestapo at Fulda sent a report on the Movement to its headquarters at the dreaded Prinz-Albrecht-Strasse in Berlin.

Franz himself had no illusions. Very soon he would be recruited to the Army, which meant taking the oath of allegiance to Hitler which he knew he could never do whatever the consequences. He had no doubt that his refusal would find favour with God and His Blessed Mother. Father Kentenich, his spiritual director, listened carefully to what he had to say about his belief. In effect, he replied that each person should reach his own decision according to his conscience before God. Colleagues had tried to persuade Franz to change his mind and they appealed to Father Kentenich, who would not alter the view he expressed to Franz. Here the sublime courage of Father Kentenich himself should be noted, for he was arrested on 20 September 1941 and, after solitary confinement in Koblenz for one month, and despite having a medical certificate attesting he was unfit to be sent to a concentration camp, he chose freely to go to Dachau and remained there for nearly four years, returning to Schoenstatt at Pentecost 1945. While in the camp, despite the appalling conditions, he continued to work for the Movement. In 1943, he was presented with the Silver Cross of Pope Pius XII.

In 1941 Father Reinisch had been to see his parents to acquaint them with his decision and to prepare them for the inevitable outcome. Instead of recriminations he found only understanding and support, a testimony to the family's faith. In April 1942 he received his call-up papers. He was to report to the barracks at Bad Kissingen on 14 April. He returned home to say farewell to his parents. After celebrating Holy Mass, with his father as server, he blessed his parents and left them. He chose, however, to visit a friend, deliberately reporting to Bad Kissingen a day late. This upset the receiving sergeant considerably who shouted: 'You don't seem to

---

114. Ibid., *The Crusader*, March 2007, p. 4.

want to become a soldier', to which Father Franz replied: 'I would want to if I could serve a different regime.'

While he had expected to be shot out of hand, instead he was pressured to change his mind by the commanding officer of the unit, by the examining judge and by a good friend acting as an emissary from the Provincial of the Pallottines. It was all to no avail, this last effort being made on 20 April, which happened to be Hitler's birthday and also, as Franz recorded in his journal, the anniversary of: 'the day I first decided in all seriousness to follow Christ.'[115] He was sent to Berlin, arriving there on 8 May and the outgoing prison chaplain refused to give him Holy Communion in the hope that it would make him realise how serious it was to go against the wishes of bishops and superiors. However, when the new chaplain, Father Kreutzberg arrived, Franz was delighted to discover he was a Schoenstatt diocesan priest. He took this as a sign that the path he had chosen to follow was the right one.

On 14 April 1942, he had written a moving farewell letter to his parents. In it he thanked them for all they had done for him. They had brought him into life so that he could give honour and glory to God. They had had him baptised and reared in the Catholic faith so that he could be drawn into the life, suffering and glorification of Christ. It was largely thanks to them too, that he had been able to receive priestly orders and for fourteen years been permitted to celebrate Holy Mass and administer the Sacraments for the salvation of many souls. He then thanked the Holy Trinity, the beloved Mother of God and all his benefactors, spiritual and material, whether living or dead. To be called into the Pallottine Society and to work at Schoenstatt so as to extend the Marian kingdom of Christ throughout the world he regarded as 'a great gift of grace.' He asked his parents to join with him in a glorious and joyful Magnificat and Te Deum when they heard that his mission in this world was ended, only really to begin in the next. He wished for sorrow and joy to be reconciled in the boundless love of the Father, the Son and the Holy Ghost. Then he blessed again his parents and also his brothers and sisters, their children and 'all of my country, the Tyrol.'[116]

115. Ibid., p. 5.
116. M Gollwitzer et al (eds.), op. cit., pp. 48-9.

The new chaplain, Father Kreutzberg, asked him to outline in writing the reasons for his decision. Franz was not sure he wished to do this but yielded to the chaplain's argument that by doing so he might well help others. At great risk to them both, Father Kreutzberg smuggled the writing materials into the cell and Franz's written pages out of the prison. He pleaded with the chaplain not 'to make a saint out of me!'[117] Faced with the confinement and brutality of the prison Father Reinisch was depressed and fearful lest he might waver in his intention, conjuring with the idea of attacking a guard so that he might be shot. Father Kreutzberg proved a loyal friend for he brought Holy Communion and a picture of the Schoenstatt shrine to Franz. Later he even took the risk of arranging for him to say Mass in secret. He was also fortified by a note from the concentration camp at Dachau. It was from Father Kentenich and it urged Franz to sell his life 'as dearly as possible'.

His trial was held on 7 July 1942 and strangely the doubts and uncertainties experienced in his cell were banished: in the courtroom he was completely resolute and began to give his religious reasons for refusing to take the oath. That done, he was interrupted and therefore could not give the political reasons. He interpreted this as a sign that he was being guided by God for it meant that he was being condemned solely for his religious convictions. Now he was handcuffed to prevent suicide, for the Nazi regime was determined to exact its retribution, but before long Father Kreutzberg intervened again and his hands were freed. From this point Father Reinisch continually re-examined his decision knowing that if he went back on it, he would be freed. The more he thought the more he felt certain that he could not deviate from the path he had chosen. During this final phase of intense mental anguish, he was sustained by the words of Cardinal Newman's 'Lead kindly light'.

His sentence was confirmed on 25 July and on 11 August he was transferred, for execution, to the prison in Brandenburg. There he was attended by Father Tick, who had travelled from Schoenstatt to be with him, and Father Jochmann, the prison chaplain. Franz fondly hoped that by the Feast of the Assumption (15 August) he would have been called to his Maker. This did not happen, but finally, Father Reinisch was guillotined at 5.05 am on 21 August so that, after his

---

117. M Cole, op. cit., March 2007, p. 5.

initial disappointment, but in accord with his further hope, he died within the octave of the Feast. Writer Mary Cole provides a moving outline of the procedures entailed in his execution.[118]

Franz Reinisch made a powerful last statement which, thankfully, has been preserved. He begins by adverting to the struggle against bolshevism and for the preservation of a Christian Europe in which Germany is engaged. But, he states, the war was being used chiefly to tear from the hearts of the people, especially the young, the belief in God incarnate, Jesus Christ. He goes on: 'This seriously undermines the will to fight of the men at the front. Soldiers on leave and wounded men, all of them fathers, on coming back from Russia have said to me – "What is the point of our fighting? We fight *against* the bolshevism of foreigners and *for* bolshevism in our nation." '[119] To support this last point he instanced the removal of crucifixes from the schools, the suppression of monasteries, and the closing of churches. He stated he was not a revolutionary – an enemy of the state and of the people – but a Catholic priest using not violence, but the weapons of the spirit and of faith. And he knew what he was fighting for.

Those who were bringing about the disintegration of the armies should be rendered impotent and condemned to death, but the present regime did not restrain these forces, it actually favoured them. So he believed that in refusing to give his oath of allegiance he was more genuinely loyal to the German nation in its fight for survival than he would have been in taking the opposite course. He was therefore ready and willing to sacrifice his life for Christ the King and for the German Fatherland, in order that Christ the Lord might defeat the anti-Christian and bolshevist powers and principalities not only abroad but also especially at home so that Germany might become once more a strong and free nation of God.[120]

ST EDITH STEIN – TERESA BENEDICTA OF THE CROSS

She was small, frail and easily overlooked, but intellectually, colleagues and students found Dr Edith Stein a formidable proposition. On 12 October 1891 she had been born into a prosperous Jewish family in

118. Ibid., p. 5.
119. M Gollwitzer et al (eds.), op. cit., pp. 49-50.
120. Ibid., pp. 49-50.

Breslau, Germany (now Wroclaw, Poland). The Steins' wealth came from the timber trade and with their devotion to the ceremonies and prayers of the Jewish faith they added another Jewish trait – reverence for scholarship. Edith was the youngest of seven children and much loved in that happy home. It is said[121] that when Paul, a brother keenly interested in literature, carried her about, he would talk to her about Goethe, Schiller and Heine so that at four years of age she could recite the key facts about the major German poets.

Edith's father died when she was three years old and this might well have threatened the comfort and elegance of the large Stein home but for the willpower and energy of Edith's mother, Frau Auguste Stein. To ensure the family's survival, this strictly pious woman assumed full responsibility for the family business, mastering not only the intricacies of commercial management but also the technical aspects of timber itself. Under her stewardship the business did not merely survive, it prospered. But this meant that little 'Jitschell' (Edith's nickname) was necessarily denied the close motherly love her infancy warranted. Thrown back on her own devices she sought the company of other children but found herself marginalised because she was small and delicate. She then turned to her sisters, who were extremely conscientious students, and this intensified the capacity for hard work she had inherited from her mother so that intellectual achievement became the all-consuming goal of a dedicated soul who devoted her life to the pursuit of truth.

Throughout her school years her progress was outstanding, so much so that on graduating from grammar school her headmaster, summing up her achievements, chose the German proverb: 'Strike the stone ['Stein' = stone in German] and wisdom will leap forth.'[122] It should not be thought, however, that her drive for perfection and her phenomenal will-power hardened her nature for she is described[123] in her school years as being warm, loving, patient, kind and helpful, an unfailing source of support and advice to her school friends. Nonetheless, when she was about thirteen years of age she lost her Jewish faith. Secretly regarding herself as an atheist, she continued to go to the synagogue with the family and to observe the rituals at

---

121. L Knowles, *Modern Heroes of the Church*. Huntington, 2003, pp. 105-6.
122. R Royal, *Catholic Martyrs of the Twentieth Century*. New York, 2000, p. 170.
123. M Matthew, *Edith Stein*. London, 1997, p. 8.

home but though the purpose of this was to please her mother, it did not impress Frau Stein who perceived that Edith lacked conviction, or even interest, in Judaism. What we now know was that she was moving out of the shadow of her family in order to begin an intellectual journey in search of the truth. The truth would be her fulfilment and the quest would take her far beyond unbelief.

At the onset of her intellectual journey, now enrolled at the University of Breslau, she began to study German language and literature and also psychology. Philosophy was a compulsory subject. Psychology she found too mechanistic – its inferential statistics and psycho-physical measures held no appeal, but philosophy appealed to both her head and heart and almost by chance she discovered *Logical Investigations* by Edmund Husserl. In effect he had developed an entirely new school of philosophy, phenomenology. Its fundamental proposition is that the truth can be discovered by looking at all the 'phenomena' in the world, that is, by examining those things that can be apprehended directly by one or more of the senses. Among these phenomena are the experiences that have led to the historical development of religion and spirituality.[124] The assertion of phenomenology that there is 'a real and objective world that can be known by the human mind' is said to be '. . . a view more in tune with traditional Catholic philosophy than other modern schools of thought' and Pope John Paul II, a former professor of philosophy has been described as an expert on Husserl and his work.[125]

When Edith entered the Philosophy School at Breslau she and her professor, Dr Karl Stern, immediately became soul mates and he, in fact, on the same spiritual/intellectual journey as herself, was later to become a Catholic. As for phenomenology, which had exercised an immediate and lasting impact on her, it is interesting that Edmund Husserl joked from time to time that he ought to be canonised since so many of his students became Catholics. After two years at Breslau, she was able to continue her studies at Göttingen University where Husserl was her Professor. He was mightily impressed from the first for she told him that she had read the whole of *Logical Investigations*, including its 'difficult' second volume. Before long they were to

124. R Royal, op. cit., p. 171.
125. L Knowles, op. cit., p. 107.

become personal friends. She also became personal friends with Husserl's assistant, Professor Adolf Reinach and his wife, and this was to be significant for her religious formation.

At about this time, on a hiking journey with friends through the mountains she stayed for the night at a farmhouse. The following morning she was moved to see that before the owner and his men set off to work they gathered together in prayer. Later she commented that this introduction to the Catholic faith had impressed her deeply. A little later she attended a series of lectures given to the Philosophical Society by Max Scheler, who had a European reputation for his force and brilliance. He was a Jewish convert to Catholicism who drew crowds of students fascinated by his spiritually invigorating views. He considered himself a Roman Catholic first and a philosophy lecturer second. Edith understood phenomenology as an attempt to reason dispassionately and to record faithfully all human experiences. And there was no denying that the sense of religion was a major human experience. Now here was Scheler propagating '. . . Catholic ideas with all the brilliance of his intellect and power of expression. This was contact with a world which had so far remained unknown to me.'[126] She had to concede that he had revealed to her a whole region of phenomena which she could no longer ignore.

Edith had arrived at Göttingen, significantly, on Easter Sunday 1913. She had completed her doctorate in 1916, which was awarded *Summa cum laude*. It was no surprise that 'the Master', as Husserl was known to colleagues and students, asked her to accompany him as his research assistant to the University of Freiburg where he was to become Professor of Philosophy. When war had been declared in 1914, her friend and early mentor at Göttingen, Adolf Reinach, had volunteered for active service. Stein herself was a patriotic German and feeling she was not, as a student, making much of a contribution to her country she dropped her studies temporarily and became a nurse in a military hospital. There she became noted for her warmth, compassion and patience. When she returned to academic life she found assisting Husserl arduous for he was innately disorganised and it was proving extremely difficult for her to keep the corpus of his work in any kind of order. Even so she found the intellectual experience

126. M Matthew, op. cit., p. 10.

extremely rewarding. Nevertheless, one biographer[127] reports that in the hospital she had encountered phenomena which were hard to ignore or rationalise and among these was the lesson that: '. . . it was good to be smart, but even better to do good.'

In 1917 she was provided with another reminder that life should extend beyond academic distinction when the war claimed Adolf Reinach among its victims. Now she was full of trepidation, for she scarcely knew how to comfort her friend, Reinach's widow. The experience surprised her for she found this young woman, full of Christian hope for her husband in the after-life, well able to comfort her own intending comforters. Edith wrote of her visit: 'It was my first encounter with the Cross and the divine power that it bestows on those who carry it.'[128] (It is useful to note here that the widow Reinach later converted to Catholicism and that her daughter entered a convent). One of her former student friends, Hedwig Conrad-Martius, owned, with her husband, a fruit-farm at Bergzabern where Edith was often invited to stay at the weekends. For her, this was a return to the family life she had loved. One weekend the couple were called away urgently but encouraged her to stay and make use of their library. Though both Protestant, they had a number of Catholic books on their shelves one of which was the autobiography of St Teresa of Avila. In choosing it to read Dr Stein was about to take the next step on her spiritual journey.

She began to read the lengthy work and '. . . was at once captivated and did not stop until I had reached the end. As I closed the book I said: "That is the Truth." '[129] Of this incident one biographer, Monk Matthew, says this: 'A remarkable thing happened that weekend, when you consider that, at the conscious level, Edith was by now a former atheist groping around in the uncertain world of agnosticism. Consider the spirituality of St Teresa. It is of the highest order of mysticism. It is the language of the soul and it communicates itself only to those in whom spirituality is alive – even if, as in Edith's case at the time, that inner life is unrecognised by the conscious mind.'[130] Suddenly she recognised the emptiness of her intellectual atheism and

---

127. R Royal, op. cit., p. 174.
128. Ibid.
129. M Matthew, op. cit., p. 13.
130. Ibid.

resolved to become a Discalced Carmelite living a life of prayer and contemplation.

Early the next day she purchased a Roman Catholic Catechism and Missal and having read these went immediately to the church in Bergzabern to request that she be baptised! She arrived in time for Mass and although this was her first entry into a Catholic church found that nothing was strange to her. She understood what was going on down to the finest detail. The priest was astonished at her request, explaining that the Sacrament could only succeed after careful preparation and instruction. Edith then invited him to test her knowledge with the result that the priest arranged for her to be received into the Church on New Year's Day 1922 for he was not only amazed by her knowledge, he was deeply impressed by her 'feeling' for Christ. She chose the baptismal name 'Teresa' and spent the whole of the preceding night in prayer. Edith now had to face telling her mother who was not angry but clearly heartbroken. It was the first time that the Stein children had seen their mother weep. Edith prayed that her conversion would not disrupt the stability of her family and, in spite of her anguish, Auguste Stein was able to confide to a friend that she had never seen anyone pray like Edith.

By now Edith had left the service of Husserl and returned to Breslau, staying at the family home for six months. Later in 1922, she was confirmed in the Cathedral at Speyer and a Canon Schwind became her spiritual director. In spite of her pleas he would not countenance her entry into the Carmelites at this stage and suggested she apply for the vacant post of principal teacher in Speyer's Dominican convent, a girls' teacher training college. Dr Stein, a former significant figure at Freiburg, the centre of excellence for philosophy, now came to serve the Catholic Church in a more modest role. For the next few years, esteemed by both the sisters and the students, she served the Convent well and was personally rewarded by the intensification of her prayer life and her studies of St Thomas Aquinas. Subsequently her writings on St Thomas drew favourable attention and she became much in demand as a speaker, as well as a Catholic writer. Nevertheless, she yearned for a life of contemplation for, as she expressed it: 'prayer and sacrifice, in my opinion, are much more crucial than anything we can say.'[131]

---

131. R Royal, op. cit., p. 178.

In 1927 Canon Schwind died and Father Raphael Walzer, Abbot of the Benedictine Abbey of Beuron, became her new spiritual director. He too withstood the force of her requests to enter the Carmel for while he was overwhelmed by her mystical gifts, coupled with her lovable simplicity, he could not be dissuaded that her abundant talents would be best used in the service of Catholic Truth through her literary work for the glory of God. In the early 1930s she was travelling widely in Germany and Switzerland giving her lectures and in the spring of 1932 had moved in with the Sisters of Notre Dame at the Collegium Marianum in Münster. Here she impressed everyone with the intensity of her devotion and her asceticism. With the accession of Hitler and the steadily developing persecution of the Jews she wished to bear the Cross of Christ which she perceived was now being laid upon them. By offering her own life as an oblation she might help to save her people from the wrath of their persecutors. Even so, Dom Raphael Walzer still maintained that her greatest contributions to God and country were to be outside the cloister.

Her premonitions concerning the Jews now took on a personal aspect for in the spring of 1932, influenced no doubt by her spiritual director, she had accepted a lectureship at Münster's Catholic Educational Institute but as the National Socialists became increasingly repressive she was asked, discreetly, to leave the Institute until the waves of anti-Semitism had abated. In April 1933, she rose from intensive prayer convinced that it was God's wish she should enter the Carmel. She was unwavering in her intention which, inevitably, meant another explanatory meeting with her mother. It would be agonising to both of them. And this time it would be even worse for Frau Auguste to bear, for the Carmel clearly meant separation from the family. Edith, however, matched her mother's iron will with her own – she was determined to become a Carmelite. The confrontation may have been fraught enough, but intriguing to anyone appreciative of Jewish humour, for finally the exasperated mother, referring to Christ, remarked 'Why did you have to get to know him? . . . He was a good man – I'm not saying anything against him. But why did he have to go and make himself God?'[132] Edith herself made no distinction between being a Christian and being a Jew. For all her fervour as a Christian

132. Ibid., p. 182.

she was proud to be a Jew, saying later: 'You don't know what it means to me to be a daughter of the chosen people – to belong to Christ, not only spiritually, but according to the flesh.' Although Edith's deep piety was clearly evident to her, Frau Stein could not resign herself to the situation. Even so, as her daughter left home on 12 October 1933, she did manage to say: 'May the Eternal One be with you.'

On 15 April 1934, she was admitted to the Carmelite Order at Cologne as Sister Teresa Benedicta of the Cross – 'Teresa' with reverence to the great Saint of Avila, 'Benedicta' with gratitude for the guidance and support of the Benedictine Abbey of Beuron and 'of the Cross' to signify her wish to share in the sufferings of her Lord. On this last point, when the Prioress at Cologne had seemed reluctant to admit her, Edith had said: 'It is not human activity that can help us but the Passion of Christ. It is a share in that, that I desire.'[133] So now the brilliant philosopher became the novice nun and she laughed as heartily as anyone at her lack of skill in needlework and scrubbing floors. The solitary scholar also had to adjust to the bustle of life in a community. Two years later at the exact time her mother died, Edith was waiting in choir to renew her vows and wrote afterwards that at that moment she could distinctly feel her mother was beside her. On Christmas Eve 1936 her sister Rosa, having been received into the Church, received her first Communion at the Midnight Mass in Cologne.

By this time the Nazi venom not only towards the Jews but to any Christian opposing their will, was becoming abundantly clear. Convents and monasteries, as well as synagogues, were being attacked or closed. Nazi hatred for things sacred extended to anyone who had chosen a celibate life; this was unpatriotic since the role of women was to bear large numbers of children for the Fatherland. In the 1938 elections, some of the Sisters argued that it would be pointless to vote against Hitler. Since he would win anyway, this was no more than a dangerous gesture. Sister Teresa Benedicta could not subscribe to this – one should be loyal to the truth, however good the motives were for doing otherwise. The Nazis barred the Sisters from going to the polling stations and visited the convent to collect the ballots.

133. M Matthew, op. cit., p. 22.

When doing so, they made a note of the fact that 'Dr Edith Stein' was a non-Aryan. As a result of Kristallnacht, on 8 November 1938, it was apparent that no Jew was safe in Germany and several members of Edith's family left for the United States and other countries. The Prioress at Cologne fearing for Edith's safety, even though she had converted to Christianity, decided she should be moved to the Carmel at Echt in Holland. It was 31 December 1938.

Although there had been no thought that the Nazis would invade Holland they did so in 1940 and on the 15 May the country surrendered. Sister Teresa Benedicta seems to have had premonitions of her fate for in 1939 she wrote her last Testament in which, in submission to God's holy will, she joyfully accepted in advance the death ordained for her – for the honour and glory of God and his Church, for the Carmelite Order and the Carmels of Cologne and Echt, for the Jewish people and for her relatives living and dead so that none of them be lost. In the Summer of 1940, after passport difficulties, she was joined in Echt by her sister Rosa who was given accommodation outside the convent and received into the Third Order of Our Lady of Mount Carmel. Monk Matthew reports that the two sisters then spent long hours daily in prayer and contemplation within the convent chapel. Whatever happened now, at least they would be together. Edith also received at this time a commission from the Echt prioress which she regarded as a great blessing. She had developed a profound interest in the life and work of St John of the Cross, friend and ally of St Teresa of Avila. The prioress instructed her to write a study of St John and it transpired to be the last of her writing. It was published after her death as *The Science of the Cross*.

In Chapter Five of this work, we have noted that in July 1942 the deportations began of the Jews of Holland which led to a formal protest from all the major Dutch denominations, followed by the Pastoral letter of the Archbishop of Utrecht. These led to the arrest of all baptised Catholic Jews. In May 1942, Sister Teresa Benedicta and Rosa had already been summoned to appear before the Gestapo. 'Praised be Jesus Christ' was Teresa Benedicta's greeting to them. Still bemused, after a rigorous examination of the sisters, the Gestapo allowed them to return to the convent. However, following the Bishops' protests it was a different matter and on 2 August members of the SS burst into the convent and arrested them. Teresa Benedicta asked the Sisters to pray for them, then turning to Rosa she said: 'Come, we are going for our people.'

They were taken to the transit camp at Amersfoort and within days to a camp at Westerbork where they were badly treated and left without food. A fellow Jew who later escaped told of how Teresa Benedicta gave comfort to mothers among the captives, who were so terrified they were even unable to look after their children properly. On 7 August the train taking these prisoners to their extermination stopped at Schifferstadt on its way through Germany. One of her former pupils waiting on a platform heard her name being called and recognised the voice of her former Professor, Doctor Stein. 'Give my love to the Sisters of St Magdalena's' was the request, then Teresa Benedicta added: 'I am going toward the East' – the euphemism for Auschwitz, its gas chambers and crematoria. No one ever heard from the sisters again but Robert Royal[134] indicates that according to Nazi records, Sister Teresa Benedicta perished in an Auschwitz gas chamber on 9 August 1942. Her sister Rosa undoubtedly shared her fate.

During his visit to Germany, Pope John Paul II beatified Edith Stein at Cologne on 1 May 1987. He canonised her in Rome on 11 October 1998 and the Church celebrates her feast day on 9 August each year. She had been blessed with a brilliant mind. While at Speyer, for instance, she had translated John Henry Newman's letters and journals into German and completed a similar task with Thomas Aquinas's treatises, under the title *Disputed Questions on Truth*. She invariably kept fully abreast of developments in her own specialism and her published work *Finite and Eternal Being* draws upon her mastery of Aristotelian and Thomist philosophy. Yet it is not enough to see her as a glittering academic, a strict and demanding teacher and a powerful writer and lecturer. This tiny woman learned, like Saint Teresa of Avila, to laugh loud and frequently, sometimes until tears ran down her cheeks. When she was ministering to her fellow captives it is said that she moved among them like an angel. In the end, however, we come to see that her single most important attribute was her love of Christ and his Cross. In Alasdair MacIntyre's volume *Edith Stein,*

134. R Royal, op. cit., p. 191.

a philosophical prologue, he argues that while the lives of philosophers are one thing and philosophy itself quite another, '. . . she deliberately and intentionally brought her philosophical thinking to bear on the practices of her everyday life and drew upon the experiences afforded by those practices in formulating philosophical problems and arriving a philosophical conclusions.'[135] Here we might add that it was, therefore, her development as a philosopher that led to her quest to discover and live the truth . . . a quest that ultimately brought her to sainthood.

PROTESTANT OPPOSITION

In the early pages of this book the point was made that it was being written to affirm Catholic opposition to Nazism and to honour some Catholic martyrs of that era. However, while Protestant opposition to Hitler was less in evidence, there certainly was opposition, in fact, and this needs to be remembered. It would be ungracious to close this chapter without drawing attention to at least a few of the key figures within that opposition. In affirming their Christian faith they avowed their resistance to National Socialism and its hideous results, being prepared to suffer and, in some cases, to die as a consequence.

Among the twelve million people killed by the Nazi regime, Dietrich Bonhoeffer was one of its great Protestant victims. He was born on 4 February 1906 a few minutes before his twin sister Sabine. The Bonhoeffer family was cultured and wealthy. Dietrich's father, Karl was a well-known neurologist and professor of psychiatry. Paula, his mother, daughter of a chaplain in the court of Kaiser Wilhelm II, raised their eight children as devout Lutherans. From the time of Hitler's accession, the Bonhoeffers felt he meant doom for Germany. Through their support of Jews, they resisted him from the start and it is noteworthy that a number of the family later married Jews or became members of the German Resistance.

While a boy, Dietrich decided he wished to study theology which, at that stage, did not win the wholehearted support of his father. When later, at the age of nineteen, Dietrich was awarded his doctoral degree with distinction and his father heard his first sermon, which revealed the young pastor's heart as well as his mind, Karl Bonhoeffer

135. A MacIntyre, *Edith Stein – a philosophical prologue* London, 2006, p. 6.

came to realise his son had chosen wisely. While writing the thesis which would qualify him as a university lecturer, Dietrich witnessed the hunger, homelessness and desperation brought on by the Great Depression. In the two theological works he published at the time, *The Communion of Saints* and *Act and Being*, he made clear his credo that Christianity could not detach itself from the pressing human problems of the day but must work to mitigate their misery.

In 1930 he was appointed lecturer in Systematic Theology at Berlin University and, being granted leave of absence for one year in order to study in America, he accepted a scholarship from the Union Theological Seminary in New York. While he appears not to have gained much academically from his stay in the US, he was able to glean powerful insights into the lot of the poor and the oppressed, through his perception of how, at that stage, America's black population was treated. Also, he was able to take a detached view of what was happening in Germany and this sharpened his awareness of the Nazi menace. On his return to Germany he was alarmed to discover that some of his friends were being deluded by Hitler, and his promised support for the churches, which Bonhoeffer saw for the lie it was.

Ordained as a Lutheran minister he became completely immersed in pastoral work and, though elected youth secretary (Germany and Central Europe) by The World Alliance for Friendship through the Churches, he resigned the post in 1937 for he felt that the Alliance had failed to support German Jews. In his University lectures he emphasised that the Evangelical Church had aligned itself with the privileged rather than the oppressed and he could not credit this was Christian, for Jesus was to be found among the homeless, the prisoners and the persecuted Jews. His fidelity to the Jews found no favour with some students who began to boycott his classes. At this time he met the renowned Swiss theologian, Karl Barth, and they were to become firm friends.

In 1933, Dietrich had broadcast a radio message denouncing the Hitler cult and this was purposely interrupted by the authorities. Before the church elections of that same year he had also inveighed against the concept of the 'national church' of the German Christians, imploring the Evangelical Church to 'remain a church'. While the Nazi flag, with its Swastika, was beginning to appear at Protestant services, an underground movement began to take shape within the Nazified German Evangelical Church, led by Bonhoeffer and Martin Niemöller. This was the Pastors' Emergency League which had a membership of 6,000. It became the basis of the Confessing Church (Chapter Three gives an outline of both organisations). At this stage, Bonhoeffer spent sixteen months in England and aided by his friend, Bishop George Bell of Chichester, he urged ecclesiastical leaders in several Western nations not to accept the German National Church.

In 1935, the Confessing Church established its first Training College at Finkenwalde in Northern Germany and Dietrich became its Director. Before long the Gestapo began to persecute the Confessing Church, arresting some of its pastors, including Martin Niemöller. In September 1937, they ordered the closure of the Finkenwalde seminary. Since Hitler's entry into government the Jews of Germany had been systematically oppressed, the culmination of which was Kristallnacht on 10 November 1938 which revealed to the world the nature of Nazism. From the beginning, Bonhoeffer had spoken out against this persecution. It had a particular, as well as a general importance to him, for his twin sister, Sabine and her Jewish husband had been forced to escape to Switzerland.

By now he had become disappointed in the Confessing Church, feeling it had not done enough to expose the unjust way in which Jews were being treated. He had always believed words were not enough for Christian belief – that action was necessary. Frustrated at the closure of Finkenwalde, and the ban placed upon his preaching, he accepted an invitation to revisit America. After only one month there he told his host, Reinhold Niebuhr, the eminent theologian, that his visit had been mistaken. He had to return to Germany, for if he did not share the trials of his people he would have forfeited the right to participate in the reconstruction of Christian life in Germany. Through his brother-in-law, Hans von Dohnanyi, he was appointed a civilian agent of the Abwehr, the German military intelligence organisation. In this way he avoided enlistment in the German army and the oath of allegiance to Hitler which, in any event, he would never have taken.

During his time with the Abwehr he passed on secret information to the Allies, tried to negotiate a peace plan between the German resistance and Britain and also became involved in 'Operation 7', a clandestine scheme to rescue Jewish people. In 1943, after a failed attempt on Hitler's life, it became clear to the Gestapo that the Abwehr had been involved in German resistance activities and the smuggling of Jews into Switzerland. Among those arrested were Hans von Dohnanyi and Dietrich Bonhoeffer. After the bomb plot of 20 July 1944, Hitler vengefully had 5,000 officers and civilians executed. Although Bonhoeffer had played no direct part in the 20 July plot, the Gestapo did discover material linking him with the conspirators. He was transferred from Berlin's Tegel Military Prison then to the city's main Gestapo prison in the Prinz-Albrecht-Strasse. When this was destroyed in an air raid in February 1945 he was transferred to Buchenwald concentration camp.

With the Russians advancing he was moved again and finally hanged at Flossenbürg concentration camp on Low Sunday, 9 April 1945. The camp was liberated 11 days later. The doctor attending the hanging said of Dietrich: 'I have hardly ever seen a man die so entirely submissive to the will of God.' Although his body was never found, he left a lasting memory of his worth as pastor, theologian and philosopher, through his life and writings particularly the best seller *Letters and Papers from Prison*, first published in English in 1953.

Martin Niemöller, born in Lippstadt, Germany, on 14 January 1892, was the son of a pastor. He became an officer-cadet in the German Navy at 18 years of age and saw service in the First World War. When it ended he had come to be regarded as among the most successful of his country's U-boat captains and was awarded its Iron Cross, first class. After the war, he became keenly interested in politics and, concerned about the possibility of Communist ascendancy in Germany, joined its Freikorps. He supported the aborted Kapp putsch, the right-wing move to take control of Berlin and he was also in charge of a battalion of the Freikorps in Münster.

In February 1919, a national assembly met in Weimar and it drew up, in Weimar's National Theatre, a new constitution for Germany. The assembly had met in Weimar, a town 150 miles south-west of Berlin, because of the political turmoil raging in the capital. Thus the new state became known as the Weimar Republic and it lasted until the Nazi accession of 1933. It was as 'Weimar' came into being that

Martin Niemöller turned to the study of theology. Even so, he did not forsake his interest in politics and, in fact, continued to believe that his country needed the strong leadership personified by Hitler. Niemöller was one of many sincere men who, in 1933, believed that the programme of the Nazi party was a 'renewal movement based on a Christian moral foundation.' To Hitler's attempts to unify German Protestantism into a single Reich Church, and his decision to appoint Ludwig Müller 'Reich bishop' as a prelude to this, Niemöller was, however, strongly opposed.

In January, 1934, Hitler called a meeting with Müller and some of his opponents, including Niemöller. He asked Göring to read out the substance of a telephone conversation intercepted that morning. In it, Niemöller had stated he hoped to play off Hitler against Hindenburg. Hitler then shouted at Niemöller: 'You leave concern for the Third Reich to me and look after the Church!'[136] So Müller's status was thereby affirmed and now the German Christians set to the task of forming the Reich Church with a will. The lines had already been drawn for, in the autumn of 1933, Niemöller, supported by Dietrich Bonhoeffer and Karl Barth, had formed the Pastors' Emergency League which by 1934 developed into the Confessing Church. Its 'Barmen Declaration' rejected the concept of the Evangelical Church as an organ of the state and asserted that 'the Church must remain the Church'.

Niemöller was particularly alarmed by Hitler's stipulation that Jewish converts should be expelled from the Evangelical Church. He took the view that, by conversion, their place in the Protestant confession was secure. On 27 June, 1937, Niemöller spoke out because the secret police had penetrated the closed church of Friedrich Werder and arrested at the altar eight members of the Council of Brethren. On 1 July, he was arrested by the Gestapo and was held, without trial, for eight months. The court then found him guilty of 'abusing the pulpit' and he was fined 2,000 marks. On leaving the court he was re-arrested by the Gestapo and committed to the Sachsenhausen concentration camp. The objective was that he be 're-trained' in respect of his views. However, Niemöller held firm to his beliefs of right and wrong and

---

136. M Burleigh, *Sacred Causes*. London, 2006, pp. 206-7.

so was transferred to Dachau, where he languished without trial until 1945. As the War was coming to an end he was transferred with other notable prisoners, among them Kurt von Schuschnigg and Leon Blum, to the Austrian Tyrol where he was to be executed. Fortunately, in the very last days of the War, he was rescued by Allied troops.

He had remained alive thanks to the tireless advocacy of George Bell, Anglican Bishop of Chichester. Bell had argued in the British press that the Nazis' treatment of Niemöller clearly illustrated their attitude to Christianity. It seems this was one of the rare occasions when Hitler and his followers were sensitive to world opinion. Also there was dissension among the Nazi hierarchy, for Goebbels urged that Niemöller be executed whereas Rosenberg maintained that to do so would be grist to Bishop Bell's mill. For once, Hitler sided with the moderating view.

After the war, Martin Niemöller became a leader in Germany's Evangelical Church, president of the World Council of Churches, and a highly significant figure in the World Peace Committee. He died on 6 March, 1984, and will forever be regarded as one of the torchbearers of Christianity in the dark days of the Nazi era.

Corrie ten Boom: Anyone wishing to know what life was like under the Nazis can do no better than read the 'astonishing memoir'[137] of Cornelia (Corrie) ten Boom. It is easy to see why her publisher claims her story to have been 'an inspiration to millions' and 'one of the greatest Christian testimonies of our time.'[138] It is now almost four decades since its publication and it is, apparently, still a bestseller. Written in conjunction with John and Elizabeth Sherrill, *The Hiding Place* tells the story of Casper ten Boom, a gentle, courteous old man who was a watchmaker in Haarlem, Holland and his family. Devoted Christians and members of the Dutch Reformed Church, they risked everything for the sake of others and for the love of Christ. At the time of the Nazi occupation and despite the risk of betrayal or discovery the ten Booms offered shelter and succour to many Jews of their region. The Beje, a crooked little Dutch house just one room wide, was full to bursting with people being hunted by the Nazis. It was both home to

137. *The Hiding Place*. London, 2004, back cover.
138. Ibid.

the ten Booms and their business premises where watches were sold and repaired. Each morning at 8.30, with his employees and children gathered around him, old Casper would take down the big brass-hinged Bible from its shelf and start the day with a Scripture reading. He emerges from the memoir as a most lovable man. For instance, Corrie says of him: 'Father was as innocent of business know-how as his father had been before him. He would work for days on a difficult repair problem and then forget to send a bill.'[139] The more rare and expensive a watch, the less he was able to think of it in terms of money. 'A man should pay for the privilege of working on such a watch!'[140] he would say.

When the Gestapo raided the Beje, Corrie records that, in all, 35 people were arrested. And the family's activities were not confined to their quaint house on Haarlem's Barteljorisstraat for it was the centre of a network of 'safe houses' in the vicinity where others fleeing Nazi persecution were also hidden. Proof that their Christianity was not confined to Bible reading was personified by Casper's remarks at his arrest. The Gestapo chief told him that because of his advanced age he would like to send him home again – provided he could take Casper's word that he would not cause further trouble. Casper's reply came evenly and clearly: 'If I go home to-day, tomorrow I will open my door again to any man in need who knocks.'[141] Ten days later he was dead.

His two daughters, Corrie and Betsie, both well into their middle years, were sent to the concentration camps at Vught and Ravensbrück. Betsie died in captivity but not before she had sustained Corrie's spirits and those of many others around her by her fidelity to Christ. She emphasised that they had been sent by God into indescribable conditions and treated brutally so that they could spread His word and help others to endure. She saw an opportunity to thank God for even the most hideous of their miseries. For example, the barrack block where they were kept at one stage was so infested with fleas none of the camp guards would enter it. This meant nights without rest because of the torment but it also, for some space of time, freed

139. C ten Boom, *The Hiding Place*. London, 2004, p. 17.
140. Ibid., p. 17.
141. Ibid., p. 131.

the prisoners from the ill-treatment of the guards. So God must be thanked – even for the fleas.

Willem ten Boom, a Protestant pastor and their brother, also shared their saintliness. He had, according to Corrie, 'scrimped and saved' to build a home for the elderly of all faiths, for he was against any system of segregation. Nevertheless, in addition to the elderly Jews he housed there, after the Nazi accession he found the home deluged with younger arrivals – all Jews and all from Germany – 'And still the frightened, homeless people kept coming, and with them tales of a mounting madness.'[142] Also a result, Corrie records that: 'Willem and his family had given up their own living quarters and were sleeping in a corridor.'[143] He had been arrested with the rest of the family and survived the horrors of interment but when Corrie was released at the beginning of 1945 she made her way back to Holland and saw Willem once again. He too had been released, but was dying. No examination of the Nazi era is complete without acquaintance with the inspirational story of the ten Boom family. It reveals the depths to which some human beings can sink and others can rise.

There were other Protestant figures, of course, who gave witness to Christ at this time. They include Heinrich Gruber, Dean of Berlin, who established a number of organisations for the relief of persecuted Jews and survived brutal treatment in Dachau concentration camp. And, of course, Hans and Sophie Scholl, leaders of the 'White Rose', a student resistance movement they organised in Munich University. They were taken to Stadelheim prison, along with Christoph Probst, who became a Catholic, where all three were executed in the courtyard. The White Rose group, consisting of five students and one staff member of the University, came together in 1942 through their horror of Nazi brutality in Germany and occupied Europe. They distributed a set of leaflets to draw attention to the atrocities being carried out in Germany's name. After the disaster of Stalingrad in January 1943, the final leaflet before their arrest began as follows: 'Fellow Students! The nation is deeply shaken by the destruction of the men of Stalingrad. The genial strategy of the World War I corporal has senselessly and

142. Ibid., pp. 18-19.
143. Ibid., p. 18.

irresponsibly driven three hundred and thirty thousand German men to death. Führer, we thank you' (18 February 1943).[144]

The cool courage of White Rose members was astounding for they must have known that what they said, and how they said it, was courting disaster. So it proved when they were betrayed by a porter at the University. Within weeks all six of them had been arrested, tried and decapitated. The President of the court was the notorious Roland Freisler who, according to Dumbach and Newborn 'has gone down in the unsavoury history of the Third Reich as one of the most repellent figures in the constellations of power.'[145] Before their deaths, Hans and Sophie Scholl were visited by the Protestant chaplain and read some of their favourite psalms. Christoph Probst, though a student, was married with children and had, for some time, considered becoming a Catholic. Now he asked for a priest. After they had spoken and prayed together Christoph made his First Communion and received the last rites.

---

144. M Lynch, *Nazi Germany*. London, 2004, pp. 165-6
145. A Dumbach and J Newborn, *Sophie Scholl & The White Rose*. Oxford, 2006, p. 156.

Chapter Seven

THE PAPACY IN THE NAZI ERA

Introduction

During the last two thousand years, empires, kingdoms and cultures have come and gone. Only one institution, established in the time of Christ, remains: the Catholic Church. At its head is the Pope, a figure of undisputed global significance, a source of immense moral authority. The Papacy also has remarkable capacity to endure and historian Paul Johnson succeeds brilliantly in conveying this: 'We may reject the dogma of Papal Infallibility. But we cannot dispute that the papacy itself, purely as a human institution, is unique. The historian bows his head in humble respect at its antiquity, continuity and durability and observes in awe its endless splendours and shadows as they flicker across the centuries. It has now survived two entire millennia with its essential functions intact. It is granitic in its capacity to endure. "Thou art Peter and upon this rock I will build my Church." The Church is still there.'[1]

Not only is it still there, it continues to grow. Catholics are to be found in virtually every corner of the globe. There are now 1.1 billion of them. Half of this number are in North, Central and South America, a little over one quarter are in Europe while Africa has 12 per cent, Asia 10 per cent and Oceania the remainder. In an attempt to negate its importance and influence, the critics of the Catholic Church often use the word 'Roman' in a pejorative, limiting, sense; yet only prejudice can fail to acknowledge it as the historical universal

---

1. P Johnson, *The Papacy*. London, 1997, p. 6.

Christian Church. And at the head of it is the Pope, who, whatever the storms, is expected by his loyal flock to exercise that quality of institutional, charismatic and intellectual leadership necessary to secure its integrity and the survival of its faith.

Yet the Church, as Paul Johnson reminds us, is a human institution and so we must bear in mind that its head is also human. Another distinguished historian, Professor Eamon Duffy says: 'And that is why we do no service to the gospel by pretending that our bishops or popes are superhuman, that they never commit sins or make mistakes.'[2] He speaks of the special error of refusing to see the pope as a man like other men and adds: 'We are all guilty of this to some extent, we all want the pope to be a hero, a genius, a saint, a star.' So very often in the history of the Church we find the Pope having to confront and overcome some appalling threat to its existence. Perhaps no event was more appalling than the accession to power of Adolf Hitler and what followed it. And maybe this was the greatest test of character ever to fall upon a human frame. In the light of dispassionate scholarship, it is clear to many that the two men who kept watch for the Church in those years should be forever revered for what they did.

The writer of 'bestsellers out of bad history'[3] would challenge this, of course, particularly in the case of Pope Pius XII, but this book will have failed in its aims if it does not provide some rebuttal to the defamation of these great and good men. In this chapter we are going to take a closer look at both of them.

POPE PIUS XI

Desio, on the way to Lugano, is a small town twelve miles north of Milan. In 1850, young Francesco Ratti arrived there from the countryside. By now, Milan, the capital of Lombardy, was fast becoming industrialised, specialising among other things in the manufacture of silk. This lured peasant families, for jobs were to be had both in the capital and the small towns clustered around it. Which is why Francesco left Alta Brianza and made for Desio where he was to be manager of a silk factory.

---

2. E Duffy, *Faith of our Fathers*. London, 2004, p. 64.
3. D G Dalin, *The Myth of Hitler's Pope*. Washington DC, 2005, p. 3.

Recently he had married Teresa Galli, also a poor peasant and they were to make their home in part of the factory. Before long they had five sons and one daughter. Most of them were to make their mark in the burgeoning commerce of the region but surprisingly, the fourth Ratti son, Ambrogio Damiano Achille, seemed to have a distinct appetite for study.

Sadly, the firm employing Francesco became bankrupt but during the child-rearing years he managed to find other jobs. However, he never earned a great deal and was only able to provide a rudimentary education for the children. Since there was no municipal educational provision at that time the alternative was the private tuition given in his own house by an old priest, Don Giuseppe Volontieri. However, Francesco could afford the fees for no more than one year. Fortunately, there had been priests in the Ratti family for generations and Achille's uncle, Don Damiano Ratti, was the parish priest in nearby Asso. Sensing Achille's promise he agreed to pay for his studies and obtained a place for him as a seminary pupil.

Asso, on the Bellagio promontory looking out on the Lombardy plain, was spectacularly beautiful with its superb lawns, its sheltering chestnut groves and sublime views of Lake Como. The Rattis looked forward each summer to leaving the sweltering Lombardy plain and holidaying among the Alpine lakes and the snowy peaks, which formed the backdrop to the village.

Don Damiano was well-known and respected for, as part of his ministry, he had built a hospital and also an orphanage. He watched over Achille's progress carefully taking great delight in the boy's intellectual gifts. In the family tradition he was clearly bound for the priesthood. Consequently he was moved to the larger seminary at Monza and from there to the Archbishop's college at Milan for a stay of three years as a theological student. Being the most outstanding student of his year led to the offer of a lectureship in mathematics at Turin.

However, Achille's progress was also being carefully monitored by Monsignor di Calabiana, Archbishop of Milan, who would hear no talk of a lectureship in mathematics. Accordingly the twenty-two year old was sent to Rome to complete his theological studies. A few months after his arrival at the Lombard College there he was ordained priest.

The next three years were divided between studies at the College and the Gregorian University. It was a jubilant Ratti family that learned, towards the close of 1882, that his labours had been rewarded with the supremely distinctive award of three doctorates – in Philosophy, Theology and Canon Law.

He had received his early training at St Peter's Seminary in Milan. Now he returned there as its Professor of Sacred Eloquence and Dogmatic Theology. Beyond his duties in the post he spent time in historical research at Milan's Ambrosian Library. One of Achille Ratti's earliest biographers,[4] in describing the Ambrosian as one of the most important libraries of the world explains that it then (1932) contained 250,000 printed volumes, which had been accumulated through centuries of scholarship. By that time also, its 15,000 manuscripts contained a larger number of palimpsests (i.e. a parchment manuscript on which a more recent text has been written over an older one) than any other library possessed. It was among these palimpsests that Cardinal Mai discovered the long-lost text of Cicero's *De Republica* and they have yielded up many other important discoveries.

Don Ratti had been a professor for five years when a vacancy occurred among the Doctors of the Library. The Ambrosian's Prefect, Monsignor Ceriani, one of Europe's most famous Oriental scholars, urged his young friend to apply for the vacancy. Ratti had already been admitted as a member of the Oblates of St Charles, to whose care and custody the Library was entrusted. When he was elected to the band of Ambrosian Doctors, a noted and honourable company, it fortified his deep desire to devote his life to scholarly research and he relished the thought of publishing original work. A specialist in ecclesiastical history he now set out to compile a comprehensive record of the Church of Milan . . . an undertaking requiring vast research. It is reported[5] that his ambitions were entirely scholarly and he paid little heed to the ecclesiastical promotions being secured by his contemporaries.

His days began at 4.00 or 5.00 am and were taken up with the treasures of the Ambrosian. There was, nevertheless, an aspect of his religious life, which he took care to protect. When he had returned from Rome,

4. D Gwynn, *Pius XI*. London, 1932, p. 37.
5. Ibid., pp. 39-40.

the Archbishop had made him chaplain to a religious community, which had originated in France and recently arrived in Milan. This Order, The Ladies of the Cenacle, divided its activities between the contemplative life and the teaching of Christian doctrine. At their convent he was required to organise and supervise catechism classes for children, to prepare them for their first communions, to deliver weekly sermons and to hear confessions. He was an accomplished linguist, able to speak German, French and English in addition to his native Italian and on returning from Rome he had speedily taken up the study of Hebrew. Consequently, outside his confessional a notice stated he could hear the confessions of German penitents, a service needed and appreciated at the time. His generous devotion to the convent was among the factors leading to the Order's search for larger premises before long.

There was also an 'external' interest, and one that led to public acclaim, for he was a daring and skilled Alpine climber. All his family had been capable climbers and elder brother Carlo was a notable member of the Italian Alpine Club. Father Achille had been appointed an associate and almost immediately acquired a reputation for extreme bravery and remarkable powers of endurance. His extraordinary physical strength became a byword when, by holding on to a heavy alpine guide who had fallen from the topmost ridge of a notorious glacier, he managed to save the man's life. Among his remarkable achievements was the ascent of the highest peak of Monte Rosa from the Italian side. Long regarded as completely impossible it had, only three years previously, claimed the lives of two famous mountaineers.

Accompanied by another learned Milanese priest, Professor Grasselli, he set off up the mountain. They were forced to spend two nights in the open, sheltering as best they could from the icy winds. Ultimately they reached the summit: before them lay the comparatively easy descent into Switzerland. Both were keen to achieve what had never been achieved so they decided to create a double record by being the first climbers to find a descent into Italy. Milan was waiting to fete them and when Achille completed his report for the review of the Alpine Club it was considered one of the most compelling descriptions in the literature of mountaineering. Professor Ratti's first concern had been to set out for climbers complete and accurate information on the project. But the report went beyond that for it encompassed, in beautiful prose, the wonders of God's creation, as they had stood beneath the stars on a narrow ledge close to the summit and witnessed them.

While still at the Ambrosian he completed his history of the Church of Milan: it comprised three large volumes. In the archives he had discovered a vast amount of documents relating to Charles Borromeo. Among the stream of publications emanating from the indefatigable Achille was a closely detailed study of the Saint's life and times. Beyond this, he was proving a tower of strength in assisting the Prefect, Monsignor Ceriani. Though immersed in the Library's day-to-day administration and its constant cataloguing he was always at the disposal of visitors. These ranged from anxious students preparing learned theses, antiquarians with their arcane enquires and eminent scholars seeking to view old manuscripts and scrutinise its works of art.

This small, quick, neat, robust figure with the broad smile was the antithesis of the bookworm. Requests for assistance met with highly methodical and energetic response. It is said[6] that many students paid tribute to the generosity of his assistance – for they frequently found that the investigations they intended had been completed for them: the fruits of Achille's hard work would be cordially handed over.

In spite of all pressures he continued his work as Chaplain to the Convent of the Cenacle, taking particular delight in the children and their catechism classes. By now his sermons there were attracting sizeable audiences and for many years he preached in German for the many Germans now working in Milan. His fluency in French led to his being sent to Paris to assist the Papal Delegate. While there he made sure to visit all its principal libraries. In fact, visits to foreign libraries were a bonus to him in his duties. On his two visits to England he visited the John Rylands Library in Manchester, the Bodleian at Oxford (where he spent much time among its treasures), the British Museum Library in London and the London Library in St James's Square.

In 1907, Monsignor Ceriani died. In keeping with the esteem in which he held his devoted friend and master, who had paid him the

6. Ibid., p. 53.

supreme compliment of choosing him as his confessor, Dr Ratti made arrangements for a funeral worthy of the old priest. Achille was now appointed to succeed him, with the title of Monsignor. In Ceriani's final years, his assistant's work on the restoration and renovation of the Library was so praiseworthy that it had led to an award for him of the Order of Saints Maurice and Lazarus by the Italian government. Now that he had become its Prefect the Ambrosian flourished with renewed vitality. Sadly, the pressures on him were so great he had at last to relinquish his Chaplaincy at the Convent of the Cenacle.

Here it is important to add that his services to Italian art were almost as significant as his contributions to written scholarship. This remarkable man had by now become immensely interested in the latest developments in restoring pictures. Consequently he was able to render valuable assistance in the saving of Leonardo da Vinci's 'Last Supper' in the Dominican Convent of Milan. The restoration of old manuscripts also claimed his close interest and he so mastered this delicate work he often preferred to carry it out personally.

When he had been Prefect for four years he was unexpectedly called to Rome – it was November 1911 and he was 54 years old. In a private audience with Pope Pius X he was told that under the Bavarian Jesuit, Father Ehrle, he was to be Vice Prefect of the Vatican Library, with right of succession. Of course, his links with Milan were so long and cherished he could only be saddened at the thought of leaving it. However, he had to do as he was directed and, moreover, there were wonderful compensations, not least access to the treasures of the Vatican Library itself. Also, when he had succeeded Monsignor Ceriani at the Ambrosian he had left the Doctors' House and chosen to live in the Library itself, sleeping in a room for the storage of old manuscripts. Now he could live in Vatican City, among its palaces and gardens. This was an added joy.

He brought his customary zest and methodical skills to his new duties and had soon published several important new catalogues. Even in his first year a number of his essays appeared together with one of his most important works, the *Missale Ambrosianum Duplex*, the fruit of his years of study in Milan. At fifty-six, he imagined the Vatican Library was to be his home for the rest of his life but when he returned from one of his visits to England, Europe was moving towards war. When war came, Father Ehrle, a Bavarian, felt he was not the best person to ensure that the collaboration of the scholars of all nations could be sustained. Moreover, his secondment had not been entirely favoured by the Jesuits whose Rule ran counter to such exceptional appointments. Accordingly, he offered his resignation and this was reluctantly accepted. Almost immediately afterwards, Pope Pius X died from the strain of trying to avert the war and the Vatican found itself with a new Pope, Benedict XV, and a new Prefect of its Library, Protonotary Apostolic Achille Ratti.

The destruction and death raging across Europe caused Pope Benedict much pain and Prefect Ratti witnessed the many appeals he made to the belligerents that the madness should stop . . . all to no avail. The wholesale slaughter of Europe's peoples and its culture cast a shadow over the Vatican and the destruction of Louvain's priceless library was a tragedy for learned men everywhere. Yet, despite the increasing tumult and interruptions of those bitter years, the Prefect's work of research and reorganisation continued. Also, the Library gradually became an adjunct to the Vatican's diplomatic services and significantly, the private passage which connected the Library with the Pope's own chambers became an important element in this development.

Consequently Benedict increasingly consulted his Librarian on countless questions affecting international relations. He came to perceive that Monsignor Ratti could provide valuable help on many issues. Moreover, this widely known and respected man, one of the best linguists in the Papal Court, had won a reputation as a shrewd judge of men. Benedict's Secretary of State, Cardinal Gasparri, was also constantly concerned with historical precedents and he was coming to appreciate that Achille Ratti was one of Europe's most erudite historians. His extensive scholarship and wide reading were now an important resource. In addition, with the situation in Poland becoming increasingly tense at the beginning of 1918, Gasparri was intrigued to discover the Librarian could talk with an exceptional grasp of the problems of that unhappy country.

In the Spring of that year, with the country at last free from the grip of an anti-Catholic tsardom, the Polish bishops had asked the Pope to send them a high official with whom they could discuss the religious restoration of their country. When Monsignor Ratti was chosen for the task, he was astonished, as were many others, but as one of his early biographers records[7] all the Pope would answer to his protestations was: 'What day can you leave?' His lack of diplomatic experience notwithstanding, he was to proceed at once to Poland as its Apostolic Visitor. There was nothing for it but to accept. As he journeyed through Munich, Vienna and on to Berlin he was appalled to see the ravages of the war. Exhaustion and starvation were everywhere evident. Determined to affirm the religious character of his mission, his objective was to reach Warsaw in time for the festivities of Corpus Christi.

When he reached Berlin he was astounded to find that a deputation from Poland had come to meet him. The rest of his journey was a triumph – at Wloclawek, for instance, on the eve of Corpus Christi, the whole town turned out to greet him. In Warsaw on the next day, though poverty and distress were to be seen everywhere, he was overwhelmed by the jubilation and deep emotion. Investigating the history of that time leads one to appreciate Pope Benedict XV for the great and good man he was. In addition to his constant prayers and pleadings for peace he had done all he could to ameliorate the sufferings of the War's wounded, refugees and displaced persons. As a result, every safe in the Vatican was empty and on learning that the Vatican's finances were by now non-existent Benedict gave away all of his own money. He told Achille Ratti to expect a tragic situation and had said: 'Spend whatever you think is necessary, for We are proud of Our dignity though We are poor.'[8]

While the War went on, the Church's yearly collection for 'Peter's Pence' amounted to very little. Typically, Benedict had ordered that what had been offered in Belgium, and other countries grievously affected, should be spent in situ for the relief of local distress. When Monsignor Ratti arrived in Poland he brought with him substantial supplies of comforts and a large donation from the Pope himself. He immediately handed these into the care of the Archbishop of Warsaw. Ratti wanted to set an example of simple living and in this he was helped by the pious Monsignor Brzeziewicz, whose home became the

7. P Hughes, *Pope Pius The Eleventh*. London, 1937, p. 68.
8. D Gwynn, op. cit., p. 81.

Apostolic Visitor's headquarters.

Immediately the modest presbytery was besieged by countless visitors whom he received with patience and understanding. Nevertheless he fully appreciated his duties as Apostolic Visitor, the first for more than one hundred years and he was determined to move beyond Warsaw. So in spite of the transport difficulties in Poland's straitened circumstances he travelled without pause. A key responsibility arose from the fact that nearly one dozen Sees were vacant and though he had not yet been appointed to a titular See himself, Rome looked to him for his recommendations on the filling of these posts. In fact, when summer came he had completed the task.

As he moved about the country two things stood out for him: the plight of the people and the depth of their Catholic faith. In Jasna Gora, for example, he had witnessed a crowd of forlorn, starving pilgrims praying before the miraculous statue of the Madonna. In the autumn he moved south. When crowds of war-worn peasants ran to his train wherever it passed he looked out over their religious banners and, deeply moved, he said: 'Now I begin to realise what the Pope really is. I am only a poor librarian but look how these crowds throw themselves at my feet since they know that the shadow of the Pope follows me.' He reflected that the first few months in Poland had taught him more about the universality of the Church than had even the seven years he had spent at the Vatican.

Perhaps only he could have withstood the terrible pressures on him at this time for his continual comment was: 'It is only proper that I should give every one the right to see me or to speak to me.' Here it is also important to bring out the Jewish question, which would clearly play an important part in the resurrection of Poland. He made it abundantly clear that the Holy See would not countenance persecution of any kind and in distributing the relief sent to him by the Pope he made no discrimination between Jews and Catholics. No doubt he was pleased to have studied Hebrew in his early days in Milan for it meant much to him that he could speak to the Rabbis in their own language. One of the stories told about him at this time was of his coming upon an old Jewish woman crying by the roadside. She explained that she had lost her only cow. He gave her the money to buy another.

In June 1919 Monsignor Ratti was raised to the rank of Papal Nuncio and given the title of Archbishop of Lepanto. It was clear that the historic See had been bestowed on him as a mark of special friendship. At the same time he realised now that any hope of returning to the Vatican Library was illusory. His early mission as Nuncio was to prepare a Concordat between the Holy See and post-war Poland. Then, in July 1920 the Bolshevik armies attacked northern Poland and before long they were sweeping forward. It appeared that Warsaw was threatened, for the Polish government seemed unable to marshal any effective resistance. Nuncio Ratti sent his secretary to safety with the archives of the Nunciature but he ignored any question of his own personal safety. Next he made formal application to the government to safeguard the departure of other diplomats but announced his intention of staying in Warsaw as long as any member of the government remained there. A wave of enthusiasm and gratitude swept the city. On the eve of the Feast of the Assumption the Polish army determinedly stood its ground outside Warsaw and on the Feast day itself 100,000 people processed through the streets reciting prayers. That evening the Poles counter-attacked, the Bolsheviks retreated and Warsaw was saved. When the Prime Minister jubilantly proclaimed the triumph of the Polish armies he declared that the courageous example of the Nuncio had contributed markedly to sustaining the morale of the population.

In February 1921 another member of the hierarchy worn down by ill-health and overwork passed away. He was Cardinal Ferrari of Milan. Nuncio Ratti's prestige at the Holy See had grown greatly and Pope Benedict recalled him from Poland for he intended to appoint him Archbishop of Milan. Achille Ratti was now sixty-four and at this juncture there was hardly a more important post in the whole of Europe, for Milan was a much troubled city. It had become a political storm centre riven by riots and street fighting. Communists had seized many of its factories, and to regain control the Italian government had called in Mussolini's Black Shirts. What the Church needed was a man of proven ability and great courage at the helm in the region and Benedict summoned Nuncio Ratti once again in terms that brooked no argument. He was told that he must return to Rome no later than May for, at a Consistory in June, he was to be made a Cardinal.

It is said that his entry into Milan was like a pageant from the Middle Ages but after a banquet with many speeches he made his way to where a thousand of the city's poor were assembled. 'Let no one ever prevent your coming to me,' he said to them, for the door of this once poor boy would always be open to the poorest. The weeks went by with personal visits to colleges, hospitals, orphanages, charitable institutions and very many religious communities. A plan of action was being prepared with which all the Catholic forces in Milan were to be organised and co-ordinated. Soon it was 1922 and on 22 January, after just one week's illness, Pope Benedict died. Cardinals from all over the world, Cardinal Ratti among them now converged on Rome. By 2nd February the Conclave had commenced to elect Benedict's successor. This followed the usual nine days of mourning.

If his appointments to Poland and Milan had surprised him, Cardinal Ratti was astounded by the results of the Conclave for, after only six months as Archbishop of Milan, on 6th February 1922 he was elected Pope. Choosing the name Pius he designated 'Christ's peace in Christ's kingdom' as the Papal motto. Clearly, he was as devoted as his predecessor in seeking peace on earth but the motto has also been interpreted to mean that while the Church should be active in society it should not be protected from it.[9] He believed that, in essence, life was action and, as Pope, a man of action he certainly became. The outline below of some of his achievements merits our recognition and deep respect.

Conceptually and organisationally Pius XI introduced 'Catholic Action'. Referring to it as the apple of his eye, he defined it as 'the participation of the laity of the work of the hierarchy.'[10] Of course, when he became Pope, Catholic parishes had already developed all manner of organisations including youth clubs, mothers' unions, savings banks, prayer groups, nursing associations and even film centres. The movement set out to encourage lay men and women to do work for society previously allotted to the priests. Catholic Action would unify local initiatives into an instrument of lay evangelism subject to the leadership of the Pope and the bishops. In the period 1930

9. P Hurley SVD, *Pope of the Missions*. Cheadle Hulme, *Catholic Life* Nov. 2007, p. 26.
10. Ibid., p. 26.

to 1960 it became very strong and took various forms in different countries. After Vatican II its influence waned, though the Association of Catholic Workers is still influential.

Justifiably, Pius XI is regarded as the 'Pope of the Missions'. He believed that missionary work 'surpasses all other works of charity'. For him, the missions were his 'special duty and obligation'. Paul Hurley SVD, points out that when Pius became Pope not a single mission diocese had a local bishop. Seventeen years later there were 40 and the number of mission priests had trebled, to over 7,000.[11] Their Catholic populations had increased from 9 to 21 million. Other landmarks were: the ordination of the first Chinese and Japanese bishops; the inauguration of 31 congregations of local priests and brothers and 160 of local sisters; and the establishment of no fewer than 2,178 mission dioceses in total. Under this heading we must also include the inception of the Fides Missionary News Agency and, of course, of Mission Sunday.

Though undoubtedly a man of action in temporal matters, e.g. the reconstitution of the Pontifical Academy of Sciences, he was also greatly committed to the enrichment of the Church's spiritual life. Here we should note the establishment of the feast of Christ the King and his inauguration of three Jubilee Years and no fewer than nine international Eucharistic Congresses. Don Bosco, Thérèse of Lisieux and Thomas More are among the 34 saints he canonised in his 17-year reign. He regarded St Thérèse (the 'Little Flower') as his second guardian angel, turning to her whenever he was troubled.

The 30 encyclicals he produced were not only remarkable in number but also in scope. Christian education, marriage, the priesthood, the arms race, the evils of totalitarianism and even the cinema were some of the subjects he addressed. His encyclicals concerning fascism, Nazism and communism belong among the outstanding ones of the recent century while his denunciation of savage capitalism in *Quadragesimo Anno* (1931) became widely known and highly regarded. Its message on the concentration of economic power ('no one dare breathe against the will of the rapacious few') is, if anything, even more pertinent today.

Upon his election, in expressing his intention to give his

11. Ibid., p. 27.

benediction from the outer balcony of St Peter's, he sent an important psychological message to the Church and the World. The isolation and seclusion were over – no longer would the Pope be regarded as the 'prisoner in the Vatican'. He would immediately be seen as diplomat and negotiator. His efforts resulted in the 1929 Lateran Treaty and Concordat with Italy. The Holy Father was now able to exercise his spiritual powers freely through the establishment of a small pontifical State under his sovereignty. The 108.7 acres of Vatican City and its extra-territorial dependencies of the Lateran and Castel Gondolfo were the result of three years of hard bargaining with Mussolini. With its own post office and radio station the Vatican was that much better able to fulfil its role in the world. The hard-won concessions included compensation of 1,750 million lire for the loss of the Papal states, recognition of the Church's Canon Law, Church control of Catholic marriages, the teaching of Catholic doctrine in schools and the important symbolism of crucifixes in classrooms. Pius also concluded Concordats with eleven other countries, Austria, Poland, Portugal and Germany among them (though as we saw in Chapters Four and Five, the last of these was to give him continual heartache).

We run the risk of hagiography, however, unless we consider the less attractive aspects of Pius' character. Firstly, he had little time for ecumenism. The Catholic faith was the one true faith and he was the keeper of Christ's word. This left no room for discussion. As he asked in his encyclical of 1928, *Mortalium Animos*: 'can we endure . . . that the truth revealed by God be made the object of negotiations?' As Eamon Duffy wryly observes,[12] his stance with other denominations was: 'Come in slowly, with your hands above your head.'

Fear of his towering rages permeated the whole of the Vatican. He concluded, for example, that *Action Française*, an extreme anti-republican movement, exploited religion in the service of the politics of its leader, Charles Maurras. Pius saw to it that Maurras and his movement were condemned, its newspaper and all Maurras' writings placed on the Index of Prohibited Books and, in 1927, all its supporters excommunicated. When the Jesuit, Cardinal Billot, reportedly the most influential theologian in Rome at that time, sent

12. E Duffy, *Saints and Sinners. A History of the Popes*. New Haven and London, 3rd ed., 2006, p. 344.

a note of sympathy to the movement, he found himself no longer a Cardinal. Another supporter of Maurras was the Rector of the French Seminary in Rome. Pius summoned the elderly Superior of his Order and instructed him to sack the Rector. 'Yes, Holy Father, I'll see what I can do,' was the reply. At this, Pius exploded: 'I didn't say see what you can do, I said fire him.' It is reported that in making his point, Pius grabbed the old man's beard.[13] On another occasion, when a curial Cardinal asked if he might give the Pope some advice, the retort was: 'You may, when you are asked for it.'

As we saw in Chapter Four, the Concordat with Germany was a mere prelude to Nazi persecution of the Church. With respect to treaties, Hitler once confided to Joseph Goebbels: 'I always break them, I can't help myself.'[14] This was certainly true of the Concordat. The biggest bone of contention was Article 31, which had seemingly secured protection for Catholic organisations and societies. As a conduit for its status and operations, the Church had always clung to these. Now, the Third Reich with equal fervour was doing everything possible to exterminate them.

From their Conference at Fulda on 20 August 1935, the Catholic Bishops sent a lengthy memorandum to Hitler himself. This set out in detail all their grievances which were manifestly at variance with the statements and promises previously made by his regime. Pope Pius was deeply pained by the attacks on the Church and its faith. He was appalled that the State appeared to condone these attacks and, in fact, did everything possible to prevent the Church from defending itself. An analysis of the documents emerging from the Vatican at that time makes clear the sympathy Pius felt for German Catholics, his admiration for the sacrifices they were making for their religious ideals and his acknowledgement of the truly supernatural spirit which inspired them.

On 6 May 1935, he said this to a German pilgrimage: 'Almost daily We receive reports which show how loyal Catholics in Germany are persecuted and hindered from the exercise of their Faith. In the name of so-called positive Christianity efforts are being made to de-Christianise Germany and lead her back to a

13. Ibid., p. 337.
14. E L Woodward, and R Butler (eds.), *Documents on British Foreign Policy 1919-1939,* 3rd series, vol. VII, no. 314. London, 1954; and in F McDonough, *Hitler and Nazi Germany*. Cambridge, 1999, p. 84.

barbarous paganism.'[15] The Papal encyclical of 14 March 1937 (*Mit brennender Sorge*) makes clear the fundamental errors at the root of National Socialist opposition to the Church. This encyclical insisted on the Christian conception of God, the recognition of the Divinity of Christ and all which that entailed. It also stressed the position of the Church and the Papacy in relation to the moral order. *Mit brennender Sorge* has recently been described as 'an immensely astute critique of everything the Nazis stood for. It anticipates virtually all of the themes that contemporary scholars of Nazism, especially in continental Europe, are currently pursuing to comprehend this phenomenon.'[16]

It took only five days from the ratification of the Concordat for it to be completely violated with the passing of the Nazi sterilization law. Within another five days, Dr Erich Klausener, the leader of Catholic Action in Germany, had been murdered. The next four years were to see the arrest of hundreds of Catholic priests. It has been recorded that at least 127 of these were sent to concentration camps. In addition to the dissolution of all Catholic political and senior political parties and the widespread confiscation of Church property, over 200 Catholic publications were suppressed.

It was against this background that in 1936 Pius XI asked: 'How can the Catholic Church do other than complain, protest and pray when she sees that at every step she takes in her approach to the family, to youth, to the people, that is to those very quarters . . . that have most need of her, she meets with contradictions and difficulties? How can the Church act otherwise when the Catholic press is fettered, ever more and more restricted and suspected?'[17] On 9 June 1937, he told another group of German pilgrims that times were not merely difficult but deplorable; indeed they were so bad, so menacing and so painful as to call for the loudest protests. Seven days later, speaking to a group of newly ordained priests from the German College he pointed out that the priestly formation they had received in the Eternal City would be an invaluable support in the difficult apostolate which awaited them

---

15. Burns Oates, *The Persecution of the Catholic Church in the Third Reich: Facts and Documents*. London, 1940, p. 5.
16. M Burleigh, *Sacred Causes*. London, 2006, pp. 190-91.
17. Burns Oates, op. cit., p. 5.

on their return to Germany which was in the midst of 'a blind and furious war against the Church of Christ.'

In his Christmas allocution of 1937 he condemned the persecution of the Church in the most severe terms: 'It shall not be said of Us, in the words of an ancient historian, that We have forgotten the real names of things. No, thank God, We have not forgotten how to describe things as they truly are and We intend to do so. In Germany there exists in very truth a religious persecution. For a considerable time efforts have been made to make men believe there was no persecution. But it is known that there is such a persecution and that it is a heavy one. Indeed, seldom has there been a persecution so heavy, so terrifying, so grievous and lamentable in its far-reaching effects. It is a persecution that spares neither force, nor oppression, nor threats, nor even the subterfuge of intrigue and the fabrication of false facts.'[18]

In the Spring of 1938 Hitler visited Rome. The Vatican newspaper, *L'Osservatore Romano*, made no reference to the fact and, meaningfully, Pius left the City for Castel Gondolfo. There, he said in an audience: 'Sad events are taking place, very sad, both at a distance and also near at hand; yes, saddening events indeed and among them one may well mention the fact that on the feast day of the Holy Cross there is openly borne the badge of another cross, which is not the Cross of Christ.'[19] Not only did Pius avoid meeting Hitler, he ensured that monasteries, convents, religious houses and ecclesiastical colleges were forbidden to fly the Swastika flag.

What has been described as the 'white heat' of his indignation over the persecution of the Church in Germany is amply demonstrated in the following extract from his comments to members of the Congress of Christian Archaeology (1938): 'These persecutions in Germany and in Austria are carried out with an audacity which is truly unique, and they are constantly intensified in their methods and their severity. We learn this from witnesses whom we have had before Our own eyes. This persecution affects the Pope very deeply, and his grief and anxiety are immeasurable. And this, not only in so far as he is Head of faithful Christendom as Pope but also because as a man he sees human dignity betrayed so basely, just as it was by Julian the Apostate and Judas

18. Ibid., p. 8.
19. Ibid., p. 11.

Iscariot; for this persecution extends even to the least layman.'[20]

It is bewildering to see the claims of some that the Catholic Church was in some degree complicit in the rise of Hitler when the evidence of the Pope's hatred of exaggerated nationalism is available for anyone troubling to find it. Also, it needs to be said that Pius was no racist and his concern for the Jews was also emphasised on numerous occasions. For example, in September of 1938 he drew attention to the fact that in the Canon of the Mass Abraham is described as 'our father in faith'. He reminded his listeners therefore that no Christian could be anti-Semitic for 'spiritually, we are all Semites'.[21]

Another telling fact in this regard is provided by *Humani Generis Unitas* which has been called 'the missing encyclical'. In the summer of 1938 Pius asked three Jesuits, John La Farge (American), Gustave Desbuquois (French) and Gustav Gundlach (German), to work on an encyclical denouncing the racial theories of Hitler and Mussolini. A draft was completed but not subsequently promulgated because on February 10, 1939, Pope Pius XI died. It had seemingly disappeared until 1997 when, thanks to the painstaking efforts of scholars Passelecq and Suchecky, several working manuscripts were skilfully reconstructed. The encyclical has been described as an unequivocal assertion of the unity of the whole human race, a denunciation of all racism and of anti-Semitism in particular.[22]

Achille Ratti was undoubtedly 'his own man'. When decided on a course of action he paid little attention to the views of others. He was also the man for his time, of the metal required by that perilous era for the Church. His rages were apparently terrifying and his presence enough to instil fear. Hermann Göring, buffoon though he became, was a man of physical courage, as his First World War record testifies. Yet he said after meeting Pius: 'He stood up to greet me; and before that little figure in white, for the first time in my life I was afraid.'[23] The burden that Achille carried caused him much pain and anxiety but he never flinched from denouncing injustice for, as he said himself: 'the tongue must always return to the tooth that is aching.'

---

20. Ibid., p. 12.
21. E Duffy, op. cit. p. 343.
22. Ibid., p. 344.
23. P Hurley SVD, op. cit., p. 27.

It is intriguingly fitting that this was the Pope who established the feast of Christ the King, since Christ exercised his Kingship by sending this tireless fighter for the faith to safeguard Holy Mother Church when She was in mortal danger.

POPE PIUS XII

From his earliest days, Eugenio Pacelli was marked out as exceptional. At school, where his high intelligence was matched by his commitment and intense concentration, it is reported that 'he was always winning academic prizes.'[24] As a young seminarian he applied his intellectual gifts to his studies, at both the Capranica College and the Gregorian University, so devotedly it was clear he would be eminently suited to the priesthood. His intense daily application to prayer and study in the end undermined his health. Such were his qualities that, unsurprisingly, he was granted the extraordinarily rare permission to live at home and continue seminary studies as a day student.

Born on 2 March 1876, he was ordained on Easter Sunday, 2 April 1899. Whilst still a seminarian he had taken courses in the history of philosophy as well as in Latin and Greek at the state university of Sapienza, at the same time pursuing a course in theology at the Papal Atheneum of Saint Apollinare, where he was subsequently to complete a doctorate. As a young curate he also completed a doctorate in canon law and civil law and only two years after that he completed doctorates in philosophy and in theology. His academic attainments can only be described as 'glittering'.

The Vatican knew full well how exceptional he was for in 1901 the 25-year-old priest was given his first delicate diplomatic mission – to convey to King Edward VII, on the death of his mother, Queen Victoria, the personal condolences of Pope Leo XIII. In 1904, Father Pacelli became papal chamberlain with the title of Monsignor, and in 1905 he was made a domestic prelate. In 1908 he was again sent to England to attend the Eucharistic Congress in London: another task in what was to become virtually forty years of diplomatic service to the Vatican. By now, the quality of his legal training had become readily apparent from the clear and well-founded drafts and reports

---

24. M Marchione, *Crusade of Charity: Pius XII and POWs (1939-1945)*. Mahwah 2006, p. 11.

he invariably produced. His capacity for hard work had also become a byword. When Pope Pius X asked Cardinal Gasparri to reduce the vast number of edicts, papal bulls, instructions and decrees into a coherent Code of Canon Law it seemed logical that he would call on Monsignor Pacelli to assist him in this task. They worked together from 1904 to 1916 on a monumental task of clarification and updating and, after scrutiny by the bishops of the Church, the Code was published in 1917.

During this period, in 1911, Monsignor Pacelli was appointed under-secretary for extraordinary ecclesiastical affairs and shortly afterwards he became the secretary, with responsibility for negotiating the terms of agreement with foreign governments. Still in his mid-thirties, it was a measure of the confidence of the Holy See in him. In 1917, Pope Benedict XV appointed him Nuncio to the kingdom of Bavaria. Before taking up his post, on 13 May 1917 he was consecrated a bishop by the Pope in the Sistine Chapel and elevated to the rank of Archbishop. On 28 May 1917 he presented his credentials to Ludwig III of Bavaria and on 22 June 1920 he was appointed the first apostolic Nuncio to Germany. He was to serve in Germany until his recall to Rome on 16 December 1929 when he was created Cardinal.

On 7 February 1930 Pope Pius XI appointed him Secretary of State and on 25 March he became Archpriest of the Vatican Basilica. The years up to 1939 saw him intensely active on Vatican affairs concluding Concordats with Baden (1932), Austria (1933) and the German Reich (1933). In October 1934 he was the Papal Legate at the International Eucharistic Congress, Buenos Aires. In 1935 he was at Lourdes in France for a jubilee celebration and in the same year he concluded a Concordat with Yugoslavia while in 1936 he undertook an 8,000 mile trip in the United States visiting 11 strategic locations and establishing a firm friendship with President Roosevelt. 1937 saw his return to France where he consecrated the new Basilica at Lisieux, and acted as Cardinal-legate to the Eucharistic Congress. In 1938 (25-30 May) he attended the Eucharistic Congress in Budapest.

From 1935 he had been designated as the Camerlengo of the next conclave to elect a pope. For almost ten years he had been the loyal 'right arm' of Pius XI, and when the Pope died, on 10 February 1939, no one felt the loss more deeply than Cardinal Pacelli. This might explain why he applied himself so energetically into the arrangements for the conclave. We find more evidence of Eugenio Pacelli's exceptional nature in the history of the conclave itself: it was the shortest conclave since 1623, lasting just 24 hours. After only two inconclusive ballots, and despite the fact that no Vatican Secretary of State had been elected Pope since 1667 and no Roman since 1721, it was the man who had never actually administered a diocese, Eugenio Maria Giuseppe Giovanni Pacelli, who, on his sixty-third birthday, became the 260th sovereign pontiff of the Catholic Church.

In tracing the brilliance of this great and good man's career there is the danger of lending credence to the jibes of much lesser men that he was remote, unfeeling, self-serving and opportunistic. Yet we have only to look at some of the recorded aspects of his character to rebut these unjust allegations. Were these brought out more frequently we should arrive at the truth more readily. First there was his humility. This was apparent from the beginning – as a boy he never felt superior to others because of his remarkable academic results, believing that since he was genuinely interested in the subjects themselves it was wrong to take credit for doing well in them.[25] As a man he continued to minimise his own worth: when Pope Pius XI informed him that he was to be Cardinal Gasparri's successor as Secretary of State he declared himself unfit for such responsibility. The Pope would not be contradicted at which the Cardinal said: 'Holy Father, I shall do what you wish but I'm sure you will be sorry for appointing me.'[26]

Neither will the charge that he was remote and unfeeling stand up to scrutiny. This was a man who, when Pope Benedict XV died in 1922, grieved as if it had been his own father; whose eyes brimmed with tears when news was brought to him of the sufferings of people in Nazi-controlled Europe and who prayed along with bereaved relatives among the ruins of a bombed church in Rome.[27] His love for humanity can be gauged from his encyclicals and from the immense efforts he made to organise relief for the victims of war and for prisoners-of-war and which he carried out in both World Wars. In fact, a French prelate, Bishop Fontenelle, stated that his visits to prisoner-of-war camps in

25. E Tolansky and H Scott, *Pius XII*. London, 2003, p. 10.
26. Ibid., p. 28.
27. M Marchione, op. cit., pp. 56-7.

World War I were carried out so conscientiously that many lives were saved because of him.[28] In furtherance of the Church's objectives, his primary aim was to save souls, but he was also concerned with the physical and material needs of humanity as we shall see later in this profile. He was anything but remote.

From his meteoric rise in the hierarchy, it becomes simple to fabricate a picture of him as a man beguiled by success, steering his way carefully to the next stage of preferment. This too must be challenged for he was never happier than when immersed in pastoral work. His first priestly assignment was as curate at Chiesa Nuova, the parish church of his family where he had served as an altar boy. Hearing confessions, teaching catechism, making sick calls, celebrating Mass and distributing Holy Communion, were all duties that he relished. The congregation of souls at the Chiesa Nuova came to love their curate and he returned that love. Two of his biographers write that: 'Those who knew him said that his whole ambition in life was to continue looking after the spiritual needs of those in the parish.'[29]

Nevertheless, when in February 1901 Monsignor (later Cardinal) Gasparri was looking for assistants for his work at the Vatican's equivalent of a Foreign Office, the Jesuits at the Gregorian University recommended Father Pacelli. When he was approached, the young man was dismayed. 'I had hoped to spend all my life on pastoral work,' he said. The Monsignor replied that all work in the service of the Church was pastoral activity and that there would still be time for more direct pastoral work.[30] So he had no option but to comply with the Church's request but he remembered the rider of Gasparri and even when he began work in the Vatican diplomatic service he continued to teach catechism, hear confessions, preach at the Chiesa Nuova, lecture in canon law at the Apollinare College, give frequent seminars at a girls' school and act as spiritual adviser at a home for working girls. Even as a Monsignor, he continued to give retreats, hear confessions, prepare children for their First Holy Communion, teach philosophy and act as unofficial chaplain to a religious community. So whenever implications of careerism

---

28. R McInerny, *The Defamation of Pius XII*. South Bend, 2001, p. 17.
29. E Tolansky and H Scott, op. cit., p. 12.
30. Ibid., p. 13.

arise it is perhaps well to remember that at the time when he was working for his doctorate in canon and civil law he was also teaching catechism to children.

Next we must address the charge that he was so pro-German it undoubtedly affected his readiness to condemn Nazism and the Holocaust. This is the most unjust of criticisms but quite simple to refute. Of course, there is no doubt that he loved Germany and the German people. That love was refined when from 1917 onwards he dedicated himself to bringing physical and spiritual assistance to Bavaria's sick and wounded. He also assisted prisoners of war to renew contact and communication with their families. After the First World War, representing the interests of the Church in the whole of Germany, he gave all the assistance he could to the nation's striving against revolution, counter-revolution, staggering inflation and political chaos. But none of this meant that he ever entertained a scintilla of doubt that Nazism was anything but evil and repugnant.

The best evidence for this comes from the Axis powers themselves. Scrutiny of the period prior to and after the election of Pope Pius XII discloses that in February 1939 the German and Italian Press campaigned vigorously to prevent his election. The Nazi journal *Das Reich* declared – 'Pius XI was a half-Jew, for his mother was a Dutch Jewess; but Cardinal Pacelli is a full Jew.' In Nazi minds it was the ultimate insult. The day after the election, we find in the *Berliner Morgenpost* – 'The election of Pacelli is not favourably accepted in Germany, since he has always been hostile to National Socialism.'

On 3 March 1939 the *Frankfurter Zeitung* said – 'Many of his [Pacelli's] speeches have made it clear that he does not fully grasp the political and ideological motives which have begun their victorious march in Germany.' The first quarterly report of 1939 from the Reich's Chief Security Service ('top secret') contains the following statement – 'Pacelli has already made himself prominent by his attacks on National Socialism during his tenure of office as Cardinal Secretary of State, a fact which earned him the hearty approval of the Democratic States during the papal elections.'

General Ludendorff, German national hero and a prominent Nazi from Hitler's earliest days wrote a book *On the Policy of the New Pope Pius XII 1917-37*. It contains the following observations:

(i) ... Pacelli was the live spirit which stood behind all the anti-German activities of Rome's policy (p. 12);
(ii) ... diligently Pacelli is active in reconciling England and Italy ... against Germany and in order to shatter the Rome-Berlin axis. (pp. 40-41);
(iii)... the condemnation of (Germany's) race theory was in the foreground of Pacelli's visits to France in 1935 and in 1937. (p. 47)

Freiherr Ernst von Weiszäcker, second in command of Germany's diplomatic service and the man credited with knowing more of Pius' attitudes to Nazism than anyone else, was appointed Ambassador to the Vatican in 1943. On the day that he left for Rome, he remarked to Hitler – 'I am actually leaving for enemy country.'[31]

Why, if Pius XII was so pro-German, did the Nazis make these observations? The question is rhetorical but undoubtedly pertinent. No doubt it was because his was the guiding hand behind that courageous Papal encyclical *Mit brennender Sorge* and 'for whose minimal observance he had laboriously to formulate fifty-five notes of unavailing protest.'[32] Or it may have been because: 'Of the 44 speeches which the Nuncio Pacelli had made on German soil between 1917 and 1929 at least 40 contained attacks on Nazism or condemnation of Hitler's doctrines.'[33] And, of course, reviewing his nunciature in Bavaria reminds us that the National Socialists recognised he was not wanting in physical courage. When every other diplomat had fled from the Communist mobs in Munich, Pacelli stayed on to distribute relief packages. This earned him the hatred of the Bolsheviks but despite their guns and the glass which flew across his desk from their grenades, he ordered them out of his home: 'You must leave at once! This house does not belong to the government but to the Holy See. It is inviolable under international law.'[34] When the socialist leader rammed his gun against the Archbishop's chest, it struck his pectoral cross. Abashed, the man retreated. Telling of this incident to a national television audience years later, the revered

31. P E Lapide, *The Last Three Popes And The Jews*. London, 1967, p. 123.
32. Ibid., p. 117.
33. Ibid., p. 118.
34. M Marchione, op. cit. p. 13.

American bishop Fulton Sheen declared: 'The cross that Pacelli wore that day is the cross that I am wearing now.'[35]

Then there is the accusation that he was indifferent to the fate of the Jews during the locust years of Nazi persecution. In fact, Eugenio Pacelli's fight to secure equal rights for Jews goes back to the beginning of the twentieth century. On 17 April 1916 the *New York Times* announced: 'Papal Bull Urges Equality for Jews.' This was as a result of an appeal on 30 December 1915 to Pope Benedict XV by the American Jewish Committee urging him to use his moral influence against anti-semitism. Secretary of State Gasparri signed a declaration prepared by Monsignor Pacelli. An extract from it reads as follows: 'The Catholic Church, faithful to its divine doctrine . . . considers all men as brothers and teaches them to love one another . . . [and] never ceases to inculcate among individuals, as well as among people, the observance of the principles of natural law and to condemn everything which violates them. This law must be observed and respected in the case of the children of Israel, as well as of all others, because it would not be conformable to justice or to religion itself to derogate from it solely on account of religious confessions.'[36]

In 2005, David G Dalin, an ordained rabbi and a professor of history and political science, wrote a book entitled *The Myth of Hitler's Pope – How Pope Pius XII rescued Jews from the Nazis*. In it he declares that the definitive work by a Jewish scholar remains *The Last Three Popes and the Jews*, first published in 1967. It was written by Pinchas Lapide, an historian and diplomat who had been the Israeli consul in Milan and who had interviewed many Holocaust survivors. His work has been described by Rabbi Dalin as 'meticulously researched and comprehensive'. In the book, Lapide sets out what Pius did for the Jews in Italy, Slovakia, Hungary, Roumania, Bulgaria, Greece, Spain, Poland, France, Holland and Belgium.

From his researches, he concludes that 'the Catholic Church, under the pontificate of Pius XII, was instrumental in saving at least 700,000, but probably as many as 860,000, Jews from certain death at Nazi hands', and adds: 'These figures, small as they are in comparison with

---

35. Ibid.
36. Ibid.

our six million martyrs whose fate is beyond consolation, exceed by far those saved by all other churches, religious institutions and rescue organizations combined.' He also asserts that the figures stand in startling contrast to 'the unpardonable foot-dragging and hypocritical lip-service of those outside Hitler's reach, who certainly disposed of far greater means to rescue Jews whilst there was still time: The International Red Cross specifically and the Western democracies in general.'[37] This forces us to remember that President Roosevelt made it perfectly clear that he did not wish to enter a European war over the persecution of Jews. He also made Jewish immigration to the USA 'almost impossible'.[38] Hence the tragedy of the *SS St Louis* which, in May 1939, carried 930 German-Jewish asylum seekers to Cuba, and then Florida, where they were refused entry. The vessel was therefore compelled to return these passengers to Europe, and many to their ultimate liquidation.

Movingly, in writing of those times, Pinchas Lapide invokes the following words of Sholem Asch: 'On the flood of sin, hatred and blood let loose by Hitler upon the world, there swam a small ark which preserved intact the common heritage of the Judaeo-Christian outlook; that outlook is founded on the love of God and love of one's fellow-men. The demonism of Hitler sought to overturn it in the flood of hate. It was saved by a handful of saints.'[39]

During the War itself, Jewish voices were raised in praise of Pope Pius XII's efforts. They included that of Albert Einstein who had managed to flee Nazi Germany. In 1940 he wrote that: 'only the Church stood squarely across the path of Hitler's campaign for suppressing the truth . . . I am forced thus to confess that what I once despised I now praise unreservedly.' The first President of Israel, Chaim Weizmann, also gave witness to the amount of assistance given by Pius, as did Moshe Sharett (who became Israel's second Prime Minister), at a wartime meeting with the Pope. The gratitude of Isaac Herzog, the Ashkenazi Chief Rabbi of Palestine, was conveyed to Pius at the time for the 'invaluable help given by the Catholic Church to the Jewish people' coupled with his assurance that . . . 'the people of Israel know how to

37. P E Lapide, op. cit., pp. 214-15.
38. K D Lewis, *The Catholic Church in History*, New York, 2006, p. 157.
39. P E Lapide, op. cit., p. 212.

value his assistance and his attitude'.[40]

After the War, a massive volume of thanks from the World's Jews was directed to the Vatican. Isaac Herzog sent a special blessing to the Pope and reiterated his thanks as did the chief rabbis of Egypt, France and London while the chief rabbi of Rome, Israel Zolli, converted to Catholicism and took the baptismal name Eugenio, in deference to Pius. Dr Joseph Nathan of the Hebrew Commission said in an address to the Jewish Community in September 1945: 'We express our heartfelt gratitude to those who protected and saved us during the Nazi-Fascist persecutions. Above all, we acknowledge the Supreme Pontiff and the religious men and women, who, executing the directives of the Holy Father, recognised the persecuted as their brothers and with great abnegation, hastened to help them, disregarding the terrible dangers to which they were exposed.'[41] Tolansky and Scott record that on 12 October 1945 the World Jewish Congress sent a gift of 2 million lire to the Vatican and they draw attention to the fact that in 1955 the Israeli Philharmonic Orchestra, on its first European tour, gave a performance in the Consistory Hall of the Vatican, playing a Beethoven symphony 'as a mark of the lasting gratitude of the Israeli people for the help given them by the Pope and Catholics throughout Nazi-occupied Europe during the war.'[42] It is worth adding that the orchestra was composed of musicians from fourteen countries, and that most of them had suffered from Nazi persecution.

On 9 October 1958, Pope Pius died. This generated a massive volume of condolences from all over the world, one in which the Jewish people were especially prominent. Among the countless messages reaching the Vatican was one from the World Jewish Congress representing Jewish communities and organisations in sixty-five countries. On the day of his death, Mrs Golda Meir, Israel's Foreign Minister, and later its Prime Minister, cabled these comments to the Vatican: 'We share in the grief of humanity at the passing away of His Holiness, Pope Pius XII. In a generation afflicted by wars and discords, he upheld the highest ideals of peace and compassion. When fearful martyrdom came to our people in the decade of Nazi terror, the voice of the

---

40. K D Lewis, op. cit., p. 152.
41. E Tolansky and H Scott, op. cit. p. 90.
42. Ibid., p. 91.

Pope was raised for the victims. The life of our times was enriched by a voice speaking out on the great moral truths above the tumult of daily conflict. We mourn a great servant of peace.'[43] In her speech to the United Nations she expressed the same sentiments.

On 12 October, Dr William F Rosenblum, in his sermon in Temple Israel, New York, described the late Pope as 'a great religious leader whose works for brotherliness and peace in a time of crisis in our history should remain as an example to emulate.' Leonard Bernstein, famous composer and the then conductor of the New York Philharmonic Orchestra, called for a minute's silence at the beginning of a concert in memory of 'a very great man'.[44] The adulation heaped upon the Pope would, of itself, fill a minor volume. Pinchas E Lapide who had, incidentally, fought in Italy with General Montgomery's Jewish-English brigade wrote that 'no pope in history has ever been thanked more heartily by Jews for having saved or helped their brethren in distress.'[45] Finally, despite the restriction of a short profile, space must be found for the editor of the *Jewish Chronicle*, who, on 10 October 1958, wrote: 'Adherents of all faiths will recall how Pius XII faced the responsibilities of his exalted office with courage and devotion... Confronted by the monstrous cruelties of Nazism, Fascism and Communism, he repeatedly proclaimed the virtues of humanity and compassion ... This attitude found practical expression during the Nazi occupation of Rome ... when many hundreds of fugitive Jews found sanctuary in the Vatican from massacre by the Nazis. Such actions will always be remembered.'[46]

The papacy of Benedict XV was marked by the efforts of the Holy See to bring the wholesale slaughter of World War I to an end. Despite the reluctance of the belligerents to listen, Benedict strove to free Europe from its function as a vast killing field. It has been suggested[47] that his strategy comprised 3 elements: a) the absolute impartiality of the Vatican, for only in this way could it be regarded as effective and credible as a peacemaker; b) to do everything possible to alleviate the sufferings of refugees, prisoners of war and others affected by the War;

43. P E Lapide, op. cit., p. 227.
44. E Tolansky, and H Scott, op. cit., p. 103.
45. P E Lapide, op. cit., p. 229.
46. Ibid., p. 228.
47. K D Lewis, op. cit., p. 155.

and c) to emphasise the futility of war and by prayer and diplomacy to work endlessly for peace.

Pope Benedict had no more fervent admirer or tireless supporter than the then Monsignor Pacelli. Between them they established an office in which the details of men who had been killed, taken prisoner or were missing in action, were registered, so that the anxieties of relatives could be allayed. They acted as negotiators with all the belligerents for the exchange of wounded and seriously sick prisoners as well as interned civilians. They arranged for priests who could speak an appropriate language to visit the camps, at the same time emphasising that no distinctions were to be made between prisoners on the grounds of race, religion or nationality. Through this work, which included the supply of medical resources and food to field and base hospitals, and to the refugees, and which was organised so superbly by Monsignor Pacelli, he became devoted to Benedict. And it is possible to identify the three strands of Pope Benedict's strategy in Eugenio Pacelli's own actions as Supreme Pontiff. Earlier in this book, reference has been made to Pius XII's courageous stand to safeguard Vatican impartiality and examples were given of his efforts for peace. But nothing has so far been said of the massive efforts he made to alleviate the suffering due to the War. This might be an appropriate point to do so.

When World War II began, it was clear that the organisation and policies established by the Vatican to relieve the distress caused by the 'Great War' would be needed again. So they were re-instituted, and quickly. Among contemporary writers, no-one has been a more loyal protector of Pius XII's reputation than Sister Margherita Marchione. She has been described as ranking among the most accurate and well-informed researchers of his life and times.[48] In her list of publications there are 11 books featuring him as the subject. Among the later ones are: *Pope Pius XII – Architect for Peace* (2000) and *Crusade of Charity – Pius XII and POWs – 1939-1945* (2006). It is with this latter work that we are concerned here. Resident in the United States, she travelled to Italy and applied for access to the Vatican Secret Archives in order to research the subject. This was granted and has resulted in a substantial work based on Vatican documents as source material.

48. M Marchione, op. cit., p. x

She discovered millions of documents, not only the original letters requesting help for prisoners of war, but copies of the responses and all other pertinent information relating to them, meticulously recorded on file cards. She relates how in some instances the research for a person's whereabouts was relatively simple but in other instances was 'etched in desperation.' It was the Vatican Information Office, acting on Pius XII's orders, which served as the information clearing house for the victims of the war and their families. Sister Marchione describes how at the onset the office personnel comprised two assistants which was quickly increased to 16. By 1943, more than a thousand letters were arriving daily and the 600 people then working on the project included volunteers from Rome's seminaries and religious houses. The Information Office concluded its great work on 31 October 1947 by which time there were 885 staff members in Rome and thousands of auxiliary personnel throughout the entire Catholic world.[49]

Her documentary research disclosed that the number of requests reaching the Vatican reached almost ten million and the reply communications reached the greater figure of 11,293,511. To this must be added 'the number of messages requiring research and those seeking to communicate with prisoners and refugees that were transmitted via Vatican Radio from June 1940 to May 1945 – all in all, a total of 1,240,720 requiring 12,105 hours of air time. Despite a vast array of obstacles the Church managed in all to transmit some twenty million messages.' Among those messages was one that became significant to this writer whose friend was a prisoner of the Japanese from the fall of Singapore (15 February 1942) to the end of the War. Eventually, his family learned of his whereabouts, not through official British channels, but via Vatican Radio. A recent television documentary recalled that during those years, desperate families would often answer a knock on the door to be told by an excited neighbour that a son or a husband was safe because 'it's just come over Vatican Radio.'

Requests for help came from all over the world, from people rich and poor and of every age: from the wife of a sailor, who had disappeared, the sister of an infantryman who was missing, the father of a missing pilot, from a French soldier on the beach at Dunkirk who leant on the knapsack of a fallen comrade and wrote to the Pope entrusting

---

49. Ibid., p. 48

him with the education of his children and the protection of his wife. To convey the actual nature of the messages, Margherita Marchione quotes directly from the documents on occasions, for example:

> 'Dear Pope, I am the little girl who sent you Christmas greetings last year. Now I am sending you greetings for this Christmas. I want news about my uncle . . . and I want to know how he is and send him many kisses. I pray every evening that all my uncles come home and also that Jesus will bless you.'
>
> 'I am not a Catholic but I am certain that you who are so good will endeavour to help me find my son.'
>
> 'My son is a prisoner of war in Egypt and . . . I have had no news about him. I am a poor widow with a large family. I cry day and night . . . I hope Your Holiness will have compassion on a poor woman who has no bread.'
>
> 'I am not a believer, but I am turning to you, Mr Pope.'

Marchione explains how, to the many thousands who wrote such letters, the Vatican became 'a beam of hope.' Her researches disclose that the human stories set out in these letters were not only carefully answered by the Vatican staff but that often the Pope would write on them in his own hand suggesting a remedy. She also appends many examples of the gratitude expressed by those seeking help, for instance: 'To whom am I indebted? To the most worthy and most charitable Head of the Church'; 'Thank you! Thank you! I pray so much for you'; 'Your charity will always remain in my poor prisoner's heart'; 'Our first thought was an enthusiastic acknowledgement of the truly unique and universal influence of the Holy Father and of his immense goodness.'

There was a moving tribute to the Pope when Cardinal Federico Tedeschini was speaking of the work of the Vatican Information Office:

> Who has not read – in periodicals and magazines – letters written by prisoners or by their families to the Pope? There have been rescues and resurrections; mitigations of pain and comfort; news and messages; visits and recommendations; material and spiritual help. The soul that suffers and is consoled is a noble one. And the soul that knows how to enjoy such an august intervention is noble and, at times, sublime! But this is not what is dear to the Pope's heart; because even if everyone were

> forgetful and everyone were ungrateful, the Pope would bless them; it is his mission, it is a necessity, it is his life.[50]

At the end of the War, thousands expressed their deep gratitude and venerated the Holy Father for his courage, his intercessions and his love for them. Whether Jew or Gentile, Pole or German, Catholic or Unbeliever, 'Holy Father' was no formal title but something that was felt from the heart. Then in 1963, with the appearance of a play *The Deputy* by Rolf Hochhuth, a German playwright, Pope Pius XII became, in the minds of far too many, a 'controversial figure'. Hochhuth depicts Pius as an aloof individual detached from the extermination of Jews, a moral coward who was 'silent' for fear of damaging the financial interests of the Vatican. This led to the emergence of a belief in some quarters that if Pius had 'spoken out', German Catholics would have ceased to support Hitler and this, in turn, would have brought the Holocaust to a stop. A left-wing writer and a former member of the Hitler Youth, Hochhuth wrote a play that was billed as 'the most controversial of our time'. It was fictional and offered no historical evidence for its attempt to destroy the reputation of one of the Church's greatest Popes.

However, the damage was done, for in its wake it drew a number of imitators each hoping, in the words of Rabbi David Dalin, 'to make bestsellers out of bad history'.[51] The mainspring of the attack seems to lie with Communist propagandists who declared that the Catholic Church and its hierarchy supported Hitler during the War because of the fear of Communism. The evidence to the contrary is enormous and it seems to have evaded these revisionists that during the War the weekly publication of the *Communist International* described Pius XII as 'the leader of the Catholic resistance movement' against the Nazis.[52]

Unfortunately, and perhaps saddest of all, the latter-day detractors now include Catholic ex-priests, ex-seminarians and other alleged Catholics. These latter usually have some personal agenda to service relating to the Church's teaching on sexuality, abortion, contraception, priestly celibacy or the role of women in the Church or some other

50. Ibid., p. 46.
51. Rabbi D G Dalin, op. cit., Washington DC, 2005, p. 3.
52. E Tolansky and H Scott, op. cit., p. 104.

issue for which only 'pick-and-mix' Catholicism can supply a remedy. I will not dignify these authors and other detractors or their titles by mentioning them further but their output has caused Rabbi Dalin to declare that 'this hijacking of the Holocaust must be repudiated. The truth about Pope Pius XII . . . must be restored.' He then continues: 'The liberal culture war against tradition – of which the Pope Pius XII controversy is a microcosm – must be recognised for what it is: an assault on the institution of the Catholic Church and traditional religion . . . It is astonishing that so little commentary exists about the extreme nature of the attacks on the Catholic Church. Books and articles attacking Catholicism have become a cottage industry of the mainstream media.'[53]

This is perhaps not the place to describe the contribution of the mass media to Europe's moral decay but it is self-evident to anyone with the sense to see it. The British press has played a highly significant part in this decline. Not only is it prepared, for example, to give extensive coverage to the works of Pope Pius' detractors it gives little or no room to his numerous defenders. Where, for example, are the editorials and the reviews for the work of Margherita Marchione, Pierre Blet, Michael O'Carroll, Pinchas E Lapide, Ralph McInerny, David G. Dalin and others? This lack of balance of the secular press and the so-called 'documentaries' on television betrays their ultimate motives.

Francis D'Arcy Osborne, as we have seen in earlier chapters, represented UK interests to the Holy See during the War and was obliged, because of hostilities, to live in the Vatican itself for most its duration along with a host of other diplomats. Few people outside the hierarchy and staff of Pius knew him better. When the Hochhuth play was first produced he sent the following comments to the press: 'Pius XII was the most warmly humane, kindly, generous, sympathetic (and, incidentally, saintly) character that it has been my privilege to meet in the course of a long life. I know his sensitive nature was acutely and incessantly alive to the tragic volume of human suffering caused by the War and, without the slightest doubt, he would have been ready and glad to give his life to redeem humanity from its consequences.'[54]

---

53. Rabbi D G Dalin, op. cit. p. 3.
54. E Tolansky and H Scott, op. cit., p. 106.

Such sentiments really expose the idiocy of the question: 'Was the Pope a Nazi?'

In 1964 Pope Paul VI initiated proceedings for the beatification of Pope Pius XII and, at this point in time, it seems that a Vatican pronouncement on the cause for his canonisation might be announced before long. Yet still attempts to defile his memory continue. *The Universe* newspaper reported on Sunday 21 September 2008 that Archbishop Rino Fisichella, then Rector of the Pontifical Lateran University in Rome spoke out strongly against a guide at the Holocaust Memorial in the Holy Land which emphasised 'the silences of Pius XII' when the Jews were being persecuted by Hitler. In the 26 September 2008 issue of *The Catholic Herald*, Pope Benedict XVI was reported to have launched 'an impassioned defence' of Pius XII who, the Holy Father emphasised, had worked courageously, secretly and silently to save Jews.

Pope Pius XII was not only a great Pope, he was a great figure of the twentieth century. My view is endorsed by other twentieth century figures. Field Marshal Viscount Montgomery of Alamein said after his death: 'He was a great and good man, and I loved him.'[55] President De Gaulle, reflecting on a Vatican audience of 30 June 1944, wrote in his *War Memories*: 'Pius XII judges everything from a perspective that surpasses human beings, their undertakings and their quarrels.'[56]

55. P Blet SJ, *Pius XII and the Second World War*. Leominster, 2003, p. 289.
56. Ibid., p. 289.

Chapter Eight

REFLECTIONS

Among the biographers of Adolf Hitler, Konrad Heiden has an esteemed place. His work *Der Fuehrer* was published in 1944 in both London and New York. Heiden witnessed the rise of Hitler at first hand and so had a decided advantage over the many others who came later with their biographies. He continues to be respected for, in the words of one eminent historian, who has described Hitler as 'the greatest mover of the masses in world history', Heiden's work is as 'powerfully imaginative and intellectually convincing as anything produced since the war.'[1] For instance, he succeeds brilliantly in conveying the economic desperation of the German people with the following single example: in the summer of 1930, gas broke through the walls of the Wenceslaus Mine near Waldenburg in Silesia. Three hundred miners died as a result. Rows of corpses were found with their faces raised to the roof: they had died trying to catch the last vestiges of air before the gas overcame them. The mine was closed. It was a death trap and ought to have been closed earlier. Heiden then describes how three thousand miners petitioned the government for it to be reopened, sending delegations to Berlin and issuing proclamations to the German people. They wanted Wenceslaus to be reopened because they felt it better to work under the constant threat of death than to have to face their starving families.[2] A sick joke circulated among the millions of those who had failed financially in those Depression years: 'Optimist: "next winter we'll go begging"; Pessimist: "from

---

1. R Overy in K Heiden, *The Fuehrer*. London, 1999, p. 5.
2. Ibid. pp. 310–11.

whom?" ' But this man Hitler, with his populist image, really seemed to understand the needs of the unemployed. That belief was a thread in the tangled skein of factors which enabled him to grasp supreme power. Moreover, things did get better: in January 1933 when he became Reichskanzler, there were six million unemployed; by 1936, there was full employment. So we should not rush to judgment on the German people for their part in the Hitler era, and also remember that the National Socialists never obtained an overall plebiscite majority.

Their personal faith in the Führer endured for much of the Nazi age. Not only had he provided work, he had smited Germany's enemies. Also, had he not restored Germany's territorial losses? Their faith in him held firm even in the face of the SA's excesses and the dissolute behaviour of many a Gauleiter. 'If only the Führer knew', they whispered as they watched. It took Stalingrad and the destruction of their homes to make them waver. By that time, of course, he had them in his grip. Wholesale terror helped him retain control of state and people in Germany and Occupied Europe. In 1943 the Gestapo was 45,000 strong. It was supported by their regular contacts with 60,000 agents and 100,000 informants.[3] In their repressive activities they could invoke the 'Kith and Kin system', by way of which, quite legally, they were able to arrest, torture and put to death members of any suspected person's family – and this system was used widely after the July 1944 bomb plot.

When developing this book I tried to discover what exactly it was like to live under the Nazi regime, the better to understand how this affected bishops, priests and religious. In June 2007, during a week-long visit to St Cuthbert's Seminary, Ushaw College, Durham, I was fortunate enough to meet and talk with a Dominican nun, Sister Walthera Brands OP. She had lived, as a child, under the occupation of the Nazis in Holland. I encouraged her to describe those times. She explained that the surveillance of the occupiers even permeated the games they played – they were forbidden to fly kites, for instance, for this might well be a way of sending messages to the Resistance. For the same reason, Holland's windmills could be operated only within stipulated hours. When squads of occupying troops marched by, often hurling insults at the Dutch people on the pavements, these people

3. J Taylor, and W Shaw, *Dictionary of the Third Reich*. London, 1997, pp. 107-8.

had to stand rigidly to attention until the troops had passed. To escape the humiliation some might retreat into nearby shops, but this was highly risky for the shops had little to sell and the shopkeeper might well be an informer.

I decided also to investigate what motivated people to become informers, remembering that informers had betrayed Blessed Bernard Lichtenberg, Father Max Metzger and the ten Boom family. There appeared to be many reasons: for ideological belief; for money; for food; for a lucrative job; to settle old scores with a neighbour; to establish a favourable Gestapo attitude to oneself and one's family, and so on. The block warden might be an informer, the helper with parish affairs might have been infiltrated as an informer, your own child might be an informer, as the parents of the girl discovered when they objected to her engagement to an SS man. We should bear in mind that bishops, priests and religious had to live out their vocations enmeshed within this web of watching. And now that the Catholic press had been suppressed, only the pulpit was left to them. Very many spoke their minds from the pulpit though aware that in its shadow, or at the back of the church, some informant or other was noting down whatever they uttered.

We know, of course, there are secularists and revisionists who advance the view that the response of the Catholic Church to the rise of the Nazis was generally spineless and even subservient. This has to be revealed as the gross calumny it is, for my three years' research into the issue has led me to precisely the opposite conclusion. My research supports the writer who, referring to the expression of Christian views that challenged the Third Reich, says this:

> Among German Catholic priests alone, the record is quite remarkable. In 1932, just prior to the Nazi rise to power, there were about twenty-one thousand Catholic priests in Germany. Of these more than a third (over eight thousand) clashed with the Reich, and several hundred have been documented as having perished at Nazi hands. No doubt many others, who will forever remain unknown, were eliminated as well.[4]

It is beyond dispute that 2,670 priests, from more than nineteen European countries, were imprisoned at Dachau, earning for it the

---

4. R Royal, *The Catholic Martyrs of the Twentieth Century*. New York, 2000, p. 132.

title of 'the priests' camp'. The largest group of these were the Poles, numbering 1,780 clergy. To these we would then need to add the clergy imprisoned in other camps throughout Europe. As to deaths, almost 600 died in Dachau alone and another 325 during the 'transport of invalids' to other locations: more Nazi euphemism, this time for secret execution. Two bishops also perished in Dachau, Michael Kozal of Poland, who was brutally tortured for his only 'crime' i.e. for *seeming* to be a potential anti-Nazi leader, and Gabriel Piguet of Clermont-Ferrand, who had sent priests to hear the confessions of Resistance fighters. Finally, we must not forget to add the numbers who died on the way to the camps to our total. Sadly, these numbers will never be accurately known but from time to time some clues emerge: out of a contingent of 483 sent to Dachau, only 130 were alive at the time of liberation.[5] A question clearly emerges: how can any of these facts ever be made to sound like complicity?

A few years ago, when I was moved beyond words to see the Mass vessels and vestments made clandestinely from scraps of metal and bits of cloth during my visit to the site of the Dachau camp, I asked myself what manner of men would risk their lives to perform their priestly duties . . . would sacrifice themselves for the sacrifice of the Mass? What manner of starving men would give their morsel of bread to another prisoner in the hope that he might live? And, thinking of far-away Auschwitz, what manner of man would volunteer for execution so as to save another man's life? Perhaps the epithet once applied to the miracles at Lourdes is fitting here too: 'to those who do not believe in God no explanation will suffice; to those who do believe in God no explanation is necessary.'

This book was nearing completion in the summer of 2008. I visited the sites of other concentration camps in my quest to discover more about life in the Nazi era. I believed this would help me to review more objectively what I had already written. At the site of Bergen-Belsen, where the silence is oppressive, two images stood out from the mass of information now presented in the large Memorial Hall. One was a photograph – of Barbara Cierlinka, a beautiful girl in her early twenties. She had been a resistance fighter in the Warsaw uprising and

5. Ibid., p. 134.

had been murdered, perhaps not far from where I stood. She seemed to represent all the beauty, in every context, that Hitler had destroyed. The second image arose from the thoughts of former prisoner Joseph Podemski. After his release he had written: 'The fact was nobody wanted us. Nobody came to embrace us or offer us love.' Instantly, I thought that had Pius XII or Bishop von Galen known of his plight he would never have wanted for love.

In Sachsenhausen, I read the words of former inmate Andrzej Szezypiorski: 'And I know one thing more – that the Europe of the future cannot exist without commemorating all those, regardless of their nationality, who were killed at that time with complete contempt and hate, who were tortured to death, starved, gassed, incinerated and hanged.' It saddened me so much to realise how fast we humans are at forgetting. The sadness intensified when I visited Zgody Square, the central square of the Jewish ghetto created in Cracow by the Nazis. A green building was pointed out to me as the location of resistance during the clearing of the ghetto. It had now become the premises of a business for the ordering of pizzas by telephone. On either side of the memorial to the resistance fighters were advertisements depicting the range of pizzas available.

With a Catholic friend, I walked the entire perimeter of the Birkenau camp. Its vastness was terrifying. This site alone could well have become the killing ground for all Hitler's victims. At the Auschwitz site we had hoped to be able to say the Rosary in Cell 18 of Block 11, the starvation bunker where Saint Maximilian Kolbe and his friends had been murdered. Such were the enormous crowds of people filing reverently past the Cell we were kept continuously on the move. This gave us only the merest glimpse of the Cell itself, a spray of flowers and the candle left there by Pope John Paul II. Yet there was an uplifting aspect even to the disappointment: if, still, so many came on pilgrimage to this place, perhaps Europe, cradled in Christianity, would never be robbed of that faith no matter what the humanists and the secular liberals tried to do to it.

By the time I had reached the final chapter of this book I think I understood much more of how Hitler came to power in Germany and what it must have been like to have lived under a regime so ferociously neo-pagan. The system by which ecclesiastical properties were seized, faith schools were closed, bishops, priests and religious were imprisoned, tortured and murdered, reached its nadir for me when, following 'The Night of the Long Knives', the head of Hitler's bodyguard burst into the Berlin office of Erich Klausener, general secretary of Catholic Action, refused him a priest and shot him dead as he begged for the Sacraments. Yet after the death came the glory for, as we saw in Chapter Four, the Bishop of Berlin refuted Nazi claims that Klausener had committed suicide, interred his ashes with a solemn requiem and ordered every church in the diocese to read out his obituary.[6]

I am neither historian nor theologian, merely an ordinary Catholic layman hoping to have made some small contribution to truth and justice. No doubt the cognoscenti will point to the shortcomings of this book, to which I can only respond that I have tried at all times to provide evidence for what I have written. This has not always been a distinguishing characteristic of the Church's detractors. At the end of the task my reward has been a significant strengthening of my personal faith, because far from being defensive about the Church's record in those despotic and capricious times, I find it a great strain not to be triumphalist.

As well as those whose stories have been written here we should also remember the countless thousands who stood firm in their faith in the face of threats, brutality and worse, who packed the streets in support of the 'Lion of Münster', who ensured the churches were full throughout the War. They express, for me, the difference between cafeteria Catholics and committed Catholics. Here in Britain today we need their example as we witness the closure of schools and adoption agencies, the gradual accommodation to embryonic stem-cell research, euthanasia and the continued broad-scale slaughter of the unborn. Naturally, these things are being achieved with the appropriate euphemisms: 'freedom', 'choice', 'reason', 'progress' and 'community cohesion'. Does all of this sound familiar?

---

6. M Burleigh, *Sacred Causes*. London, 2006, p. 177.

BIBLIOGRAPHY

Alex, Ben, *Dietrich Bonhoeffer*. Copenhagen, 1996.

Aranjo, Robert John SJ and Lucal, John A, *Papal Diplomacy and the Quest for Peace*. Naples, Florida, 2004.

Austrian Society of Mauthausen Concentration Camp, *Mauthausen*. Vienna, 1995.

Baigent, M and Leigh, R, *Secret Germany*. London, 1994.

Bethge, Eberhard, *Dietrich Bonhoeffer*. London, 1970.

——— *Dietrich Bonhoeffer: Letters and Papers from Prison*. London, 1971.

Blet, Pierre SJ, *Pius XII and the Second World War*. Leominster, 2003.

Bowden, John (ed.), *Christianity The Complete Guide*. London, 2005.

Bull, G, *Inside the Vatican*. London, 1982.

Bullock, Alan, *Hitler – A Study in Tyranny*. London, 1973 edn.

Burleigh, Michael, *The Third Reich: A New History*. London, 2000.

——— *Sacred Causes*. London, 2006.

Burns Oates, *The Persecution of the Catholic Church in the Third Reich – Facts and Documents*. London, 1940.

Burns, Paul, *Butler's Lives of the Saints*. London, 2003.

Butler, Rupert, *The Gestapo – A History of Hitler's Secret Police 1933-45*. Barnsley, 2004.

Carr, William, *A History of Germany 1815-1990*. London, 1991 4th edn.

Chadwick, Owen, *Britain and the Vatican during the Second World War*. Cambridge, 1988.

Chandler, Andrew (ed.), *The terrible alternative – Christian Martyrdom in the Twentieth Century*. London, 1998.

Cianfarra, Camille M, *The War and the Vatican*. London, 1945.

Coady, Mary Frances, *With Bound Hands: A Jesuit in Nazi Germany*. Chicago, 2003.

Cole, Mary, *Fr Franz Reinisch – Martyr of Conscience*. Manchester, 2007.

Cox, Caroline (Baroness) and Butcher, Catherine, *Modern Saints and Martyrs*. London, 2006.

Craig, Mary, Kent, Bruce, Couve de Mourville, M N L, Riesterer, Paul SJ, *Victims of the Nazis*. London, 1997.

Crampton, R J, *Eastern Europe in the Twentieth Century and After*. London, 1994.

Dalin, Rabbi David G, *The Myth of Hitler's Pope*. Washington DC, 2005.

Distel, Barbara and Jakusch, Ruth, *Concentration Camp Dachau – 1933-1945*. Munich, 1978.

Dowley, Tim, *The Christians – An Illustrated History*. Oxford, 2007.

Duffy, Eamon, *Faith of Our Fathers*. London, 2004.

——— *Saints and Sinners*. London, 2006.

Dumbach, Annette, Newborn, Jud, *Sophie Scholl & The White Rose*. Oxford, 2006.

Evans, Richard, J, *The Coming of the Third Reich*. London, 2003.

——— *The Third Reich in Power*. London, 2005.

——— *The Third Reich at War*. London, 2008.

Fischer, Klaus P, *Nazi Germany – A New History* London, 1995.

——— *The History of an Obsession – German Judeophobia and the Holocaust*. London, 1998.

Fulbrook, M, *A Concise History of Germany*. Cambridge, 2002.

Geyl, P, *History of the Low Countries*. London, 1964.

Gilbert, M, *The Righteous: The Unsung Heroes of the Holocaust*. London, 2002.

——— *Kristallnacht: Prelude to Destruction*. London, 2006.

Goldmann, Gereon OFM, *The Shadow of His Wings*. San Francisco, 2000.

Gollancz, Victor, *The Yellow Spot – Facts and Documents concerning the persecution of the Jews in Germany*. London, 1936.

Gollwitzer, Hellmut et al. (eds), *Dying We Live – letters written by prisoners in Germany on the eve of execution*. Glasgow, 1974.

Goodrick-Clarke, Nicholas, *The Occult Roots of Nazism*. London, 2004.

Gray, J and Acciano, R, *The Netherlands*. London, 2004.

Gumley, Frances and Redhead, Brian, *Protestors for Paradise*. London, 1993.

Gwynn, D, *Pius XI.* London, 1932.

Hankey, D, *Bernhard Lichtenberg Priester, Bekenner, Martyrer.* Berlin, 1994.

Harrington, J F, *A Cloud of Witnesses – Readings in the History of Western Christianity.* Boston, 2001.

Hart, David B, *The Story of Christianity.* London, 2007.

Helmreich, E C, *The German Churches under Hitler – Background, Struggle and Epilogue.* Detroit, 1979.

Heiden, Konrad, *The Fuehrer.* London, 1999.

Hitler, Adolf, *Mein Kampf.* London, 1969 edn.

Holmes, J Derek and Bickers, Bernard W, *A Short History of The Catholic Church.* London, 1992.

Hughes, P, *Pope Pius the Eleventh.* London, 1937.

Johnson, Eric, *The Nazi Terror: Gestapo, Jews and Ordinary Germans.* London, 1999.

Johnson, Paul, *The Papacy.* London, 1997.

Kelly, J N D and Walsh, M, *The Oxford Dictionary Of the Popes.* Oxford, 2005 edn.

Kershaw, Ian, *The 'Hitler Myth' Image and Reality in the Third Reich.* Oxford, 1987.

——— *Hitler 1889-1936: Hubris.* London, 1998.

Klemperer, Victor, *The Klemperer Diaries (2 vols).* London, 2006 edn.

Knopp, Guido, *Hitler's Holocaust.* Stroud, 2004.

Knowles, Leo, *Modern Heroes of the Church.* Huntington, Ind., 2003.

Knox, Ronald, *Nazi and Nazarene (Macmillan War Pamphlets, No 5).* London, 1940.

Koerbling, Anton SJ, *Father Rupert Mayer.* Cork, 1950.

Krieg, Robert A, *Catholic Theologians in Nazi Germany.* London, 2004.

Lapide, Pinchas E, *The Last Three Popes And The Jews.* London, 1967.

LeBor, Adam and Boyes, Roger, *Seduced by Hitler – The Choices of a Nation and the Ethics of Survival.* Naperville, Ill., 2004.

Legrande, Jacques, *Chronicle of the Second World War.* London, 1990.

Lewis, Keith D, *The Catholic Church in History – Legend and Reality.* New York, 2006.

Lynch, Michael, *Nazi Germany.* London, 2004.

McDonough, Frank, *Hitler and Nazi Germany.* Cambridge, 1999.

McInerny, Ralph, *The Defamation of Pius XII*. South Bend, Ind., 2001.

McManners, J, *The Oxford Illustrated History of Christianity*. Oxford, 2001.

MacIntyre, Alasdair, *Edith Stein: A Philosophical Prologue*. London, 2006.

Madrid, Patrick, *Pope Fiction*. San Diego, Calif., 2005.

Marchione, Margherita, *Pope Pius XII: Architect for Peace*. Mahwah, N. J., 2000.

——— *Consensus and Controversy: Defending Pope Pius XII*. Mahwah, N. J., 2002.

——— *Crusade of Charity*. Mahwah, N. J., 2006.

Matheson, P (ed.), *The Third Reich And The Christian Churches*. Edinburgh. 1981.

Micklem, N, *National Socialism And The Roman Catholic Church*. London, 1939.

Matthew, Monk, Couve de Murville, M L N and Clark, Hugh, *Edith Stein, Marcel Callo, Titus Brandsma*. London, 1997.

Mooney, B, *Shaping History – 100 Great Leaders*. London, 2006.

Moynahan, B, *The Faith – A History of Christianity*. London, 2002.

Norman, Andrew, *Adolf Hitler: The Final Analysis*. Staplehurst, Kent, 2005.

O'Carroll, Michael CSSp, *Pius XII: Greatness Dishonoured – A documented study*. Dublin, 1980.

Ottaway, Susan, *Hitler's Traitors: German Resistance to the Nazis*. Barnsley, 2003.

Owen, James, *Nuremberg: Evil on Trial*. London, 2006.

Portmann, Rev Heinrich, *Cardinal von Galen*. London, 1957.

Ratzinger, J (Pope Benedict XVI), *Milestones: Memoirs 1927-1977*. San Francisco, 1998.

Royal, Robert, *The Catholic Martyrs of the Twentieth Century*. New York, 2000.

Rhodes, Anthony, *The Vatican In The Age of The Dictators*. London, 1973.

Rosenbaum, Ron, *Explaining Hitler – The Search For The Origins Of His Evil*. London & New York, 1998.

Schmidt, Ulf, *Karl Brandt: The Nazi Doctor*. London, 2007.

Scholder, Klaus, *The Churches and the Third Reich (2 vols)*. London, Vol

I 1987, Vol II 1988.
Service, Robert, *A History of Twentieth Century Russia.* London, 1997.
Shirer, William L, *The Rise and Fall of the Third Reich (4 vols).* London, 1995 edn.
Smolén, Kazimierz and Swiebocka, Teresa, *Auschwitz – Crime Against Humanity.* Warsaw, 1990.
Stephenson, Jill, *Hitler's Home Front: Württemberg under the Nazis.* London, 2006.
Stone, Norman, *Hitler.* Sevenoaks, 1980.
Taylor, James, Shaw, Warren, *Dictionary of The Third Reich.* London, 1997.
ten Boom, Corrie, *The Hiding Place.* London, 2004.
Tolansky, Ethel and Scott, Helena, *Johann Gruber & Jacques Bunel.* London, 1999.
——— *Pius XII.* London, 2003.
Tolédano, Marc, *The Franciscan of Bourges.* London, 1970.
Walker, Reginald CSSp, *Pius of Peace.* Dublin, 1945.
Woodruff, D Smith, *The Ideological Origins of Nazi Imperialism.* New York, 1986.

http://www.spartacus.schoolnet.co.uk/GERniemoller.htm (4 August 2009)
http://www.dbonhoeffer.org/node/27 (4 August 2009)
http://www.dbonhoeffer.org/node/3 (4 August 2009)
http://jerome2007.tripod.com/restituta_kafka.htm (4 August 2009)
http://www.companysj.com/v211/delpajesuit.htm (4 August 2009)
http://www.ushmm.org/museum/exhibit/online/jacques/ (4 August 2009)
http://www.gusen.org/pers/bunel01x.htm (4 August 2009)
http://www.hartford-hwp.com/archives/61/197.html (4 August 2009)
http://www.savior.org/saints/gross.htm (4 August 2009)
http://87.106.6.16/beftp/glauben/ng/bioengl.htm (4 August 2009)
http://www.savior.org/saints/callo.htm (4 August 2009)
http://www.nizkor.org/hweb/camps/gusen/pers/callo01x.htm (4 August 2009)
http://www.columbia.edu/cu/augustine/arch/heroes.htm (4 August 2009)
http://www.ignatiusinsight.com/features2006/frakreuser_intervw_oct06.asp (4 August 2009)
http://www.newadvent.org/cathen/08629c.htm (4 August 2009)

INDEX